Voluntary Export Restraints in WTO and EU Law

Studies in Global Economic Law
Studien zum globalen Wirtschaftsrecht
Études en droit économique mondial

edited by Thomas Cottier

Volume 13

PETER LANG
Bern · Berlin · Bruxelles · Frankfurt am Main · New York · Oxford · Wien

Sabina Nüesch

Voluntary Export Restraints in WTO and EU Law

Consumers, Trade Regulation and Competition Policy

PETER LANG
Bern · Berlin · Bruxelles · Frankfurt am Main · New York · Oxford · Wien

Bibliographic information published by Die Deutsche Nationalbibliothek
Die Deutsche Nationalbibliothek lists this publication in the Deutsche Nationalbibliografie; detailed bibliographic data is available on the Internet at ‹http://dnb.d-nb.de›.

British Library and Library of Congress Cataloguing-in-Publication Data:
A catalogue record for this book is available from *The British Library*, Great Britain.

Library of Congress Cataloging-in-Publication Data

Nüesch, Sabina, 1971-
Voluntary export restraints in WTO and EU law : consumers, trade regulation, and competition policy / Sabina Nüesch.
p. cm. - (Studies in global economic law, ISSN 1423-9531 ; v. 13)
Includes bibliographical references.
ISBN 978-3-03911-767-3
1. Export controls–European Union countries. 2. Trade regulation–European Union countries. 3. Consumer protection–Law and legislation–European Union countries. 4. Foreign trade regulation–European Union countries. 5. General Agreement on Tariffs and Trade (Organization) 6. Competition–European Union countries. 7. International trade. I. Title.
KJE6794.N84 2010
382'.64094–dc22

2010031588

Inauguraldissertation zur Erlangung der Würde eines Doctor iuris der Rechtswissenschaftlichen Fakultät der Universität Bern. Die Fakultät hat diese Arbeit am 7. September 2006 auf Antrag der beiden Gutachter, Prof. Dr. Thomas Cottier [Erstgutachter] sowie Prof. Dr. Andreas R. Ziegler [Zweitgutachter], als Dissertation angenommen, ohne damit zu den darin ausgesprochenen Auffassungen Stellung nehmen zu wollen.

ISSN 1423-9531
ISBN 978-3-03911-767-3

Hochfeldstrasse 32, CH-3012 Bern, Switzerland
info@peterlang.com, www.peterlang.com, www.peterlang.net

Printed in Switzerland

Acknowledgements

First and foremost, I wish to thank my parents and my sisters, Corinna and Ursina, for their continued support. They have demonstrated enthusiasm for all my "projects" throughout, which has been a great source of encouragement.

I am particularly indebted to my supervisor, Prof. Dr. Thomas Cottier, who always had the greatest understanding for the time constraints that were placed on writing first the PhD and then the book by my full-time practical work. The same applies to my co-supervisor, Prof. Dr. Andreas R. Ziegler. Specifically, I wish to thank them for their benevolent interest in the topic and acknowledge their constructive comments and informative advice in transforming this text from a thesis into a book.

I have been very fortunate to find myself surrounded by so many friends who have been constantly helpful and encouraging in the long process of completing this "project" – I cannot begin to name them all. Special thanks must nevertheless go to Sten E.D. Rasmussen for reading parts of the thesis prior to completion, to Richard Whittle for acting as "sounding board", and to all those who provided me with love and such supportive friendship – very happy memories all together.

Table of Contents

CHAPTER V
Summing Up the "Non-Complaint" Situation
of Voluntary Export Restraints

Preface

International trade regulation is based upon a general ban of quantitative import and export restrictions. These measures amount to the most restrictive instruments of trade policy, having a strong impact on competition – much more than tariffs. They are admitted only in exceptional and legally defined constellations. Notwithstanding this principle, governments and private operators ingenuously have developed surrogate measures deploying similar effects over the years, circumventing WTO disciplines. So called voluntary export restraints (VERs) or orderly Marketing Arrangements or Agreements (OMAs) were frequently used, in particular by the EU and the US, prior to negotiations of appropriate disciplines during the Uruguay Round of the GATT (1986–1999) within the Agreement on Safeguards. Art. 11 of this Agreement today prohibits recourse to such governmental measures, and bars governments from inducing and encouraging similar measures by private operators. While these provisions subsequently reduced recourse to VERs and OMAs, the law is far from being efficient and settled. This is partly due to lack of transparency. Little is known about practices undertaken unless light is shed upon them by bringing a complaint which, if at all, has been very rare. Partly it is due to lack of effective legal protection of consumers and competitors who are inversely affected by such measures. Today, VERs often take the form of export cartels operated by private companies, and competition law generally does not protect consumers abroad against such practices. The relationship of trade regulation and competition law remains unclear.

The present doctoral thesis submitted to, and approved by, the Faculty of Law of the University of Bern, was elaborated over a number of years by Dr. Sabina Nüesch while practicing law in the EU Commission and in private practice. It researches the law and practice of VERs in WTO law and in EU law and is a remarkable achievement. The book ably explains the background, legal nature and the loopholes in addressing such measures in substantive and procedural terms. It does so in relation to EU law and WTO law, focusing on the interaction of the two legal systems in this field. The main hypothesis consists in a finding that legal protection is inadequate and results in a "non-complaint" situation in the field. The thesis undertakes to corroborate this point view. It offers a most valuable foundation for developing new disciplines in the field and prepares the ground to take matters up in the context of future multilateral disciplines on competition policy – within or without the World Trade Organization.

Prof. Thomas Cottier

Abbreviations

AB	Appellate Body
ACP	African, Caribbean and Pacific (states)
AJIL	American Journal of International Law
AJWH	Asian Journal of WTO & International Health Law and Policy
Am. U. Int'l L. Rev.	American University International Law Review
ATC	Agreement on Textiles and Clothing
BDI	Bundesverband der Deutschen Industrie e.V.
BISD	GATT – Basic Instruments and Selected Documents
Bull.	Bulletin of the European Union
CADE	Cahiers de Droit Européen
CBD	Convention on Biological Diversity
cdedse	Center for Development Economics, Delhi School of Economics
cf.	refer to (*confer*)
CFI	Court of First Instance
CIEL	Center for International Environmental Law, Geneva
CJCE	Court de justice de la Communauté européenne
CLEER	Centre for the Law of EU External Relations, T.M.C. Asser Instituut, The Hague (NL)
CLP	Committee on Competition Law and Policy (OECD)
CMLRev.	Common Market Law Review
CORE	Center for operations research and econometrics, Université Catholique de Louvain (B)
CSGR	Centre for the Study of Globalisation and Regionalisation, University of Warwick (UK)
D.D.C.	Federal District Court for the District of Columbia
Diss.	Dissertation
DoC	U.S. Department of Commerce
DoJ	U.S. Department of Justice
DSB	Dispute Settlement Body
DSU	Dispute Settlement Understanding
E.C.R.	European Court Reports
EA	Europa-Archiv
EC	European Community

ECJ	European Court of Justice
ECSC	European Coal and Steel Community
Ed./eds.	Editor(s)
EEC	European Economic Community
EERev.	European Economic Review
EFLR	European Food Law Review
EG	Europäische Gemeinschaft
EIoP	European Integration online Papers
EJIL	European Journal of International Law
ELRev.	European Law Review
et al.	and others (*et alii*)
et seq.	and following (*et sequentes*)
EU	European Union
EuGH	Europäischer Gerichtshof
EUI	European University Institute, Florence
EuR	Europa-Recht
EuZW	Europäische Zeitschrift für Wirtschaftsrecht
EWG	Europäische Wirtschaftsgemeinschaft
F.Supp.	Federal Supplement (Federal District Court opinions)
Fordham Int'l L.J.	Fordham International Law Journal
FTC	(U.S.) Federal Trade Commission
GATS	General Agreement on Trade in Services
GATT	General Agreement on Tariffs and Trade
Harv. Int'l L.J.	Harvard International Law Journal
HWWA	Hamburgisches Weltwirtschaftsarchiv
i.e.	that is (*id est*)
ibid.	in the same place (*ibidem*)
IIE	Institute for International Economics, Washington D.C.
ILS	International Legal Studies, Law School at University of California, Berkeley (CA)
ISNIE	International Society for New Institutional Economics, Washington University, St. Louis (MO)
JCMS	Journal of Common Market Studies
J. Competition L. & Econ.	Journal of Competition Law & Economics
JIEL	Journal of International Economic Law
J. Publ. Aff.	Journal of Public Affairs
JWT	Journal of World Trade
JWTL	Journal of World Trade Law (1967–1987 (vols. 1–21), as of 1988 continued as JWT)

LIEI	Legal Issues of Economic Integration
LTA	Long-Term Arrangement Regarding International Trade in Cotton and Textiles (BISD 11S/25)
METI	(Japanese) Ministry of Economy, Trade and Industry, cf. MITI
MFA	Multifibre Arrangement
MFN	Most-favoured nation
MITI	(Japanese) Ministry of International Trade and Industry, since 2001 reorganised as METI
MTO	Multilateral Trade Organisation
N°	Number
NBER	National Bureau of Economic Research, Cambridge (MA)
NILR	Netherlands International Law Review
NJW	Neue Juristische Wochenschrift
Nw. J. Int'l L. & Bus.	Northwestern Journal of International Law and Business
OECD	Organisation for Economic Co-operation and Development
OJ	Official Journal of the European Communities
OMA	Orderly Marketing Agreement
OMC	Organisation mondiale du commerce
p./pp.	Page(s)
PPR	Policy, Planning and Research (World Bank)
PRE	Policy, Research and External Affairs (World Bank)
Pub. L.	Public laws
RabelsZ	Rabels Zeitschrift für ausländisches und internationales Privatrecht
RDUE	Révue du Droit de l'Union Européenne
Reg.	Regulation
RIW	Recht der Internationalen Wirtschaft
RMUE	Revue du Marché Unique Européen
RTDE	Revue Trimestrielle de Droit Européen
SASPR	South Asia Poverty Reduction and Economic Management Unit (World Bank)
Sec.	Section
SPS	Sanitary and Phytosanitary Measures
STA	Short-Term Arrangement Regarding International Trade in Cotton and Textiles (BISD 10S/18)
Stat.	Statute
SZIER	Schweizerische Zeitschrift für internationales und europäisches Recht
TEU	Treaty on European Union
TFEU	Treaty on the Functioning of the European Union

TRIPS	Agreement on Trade-Related Aspects of Intellectual Property Rights
U.N.	United Nations
U.S.	United States (of America)
U.S.C.	United States Code (official version)
UK	United Kingdom
USITC	United States International Trade Commission
VCR	Video Cassette Recorder
VER	Voluntary Export Restraint
VIE	Voluntary Import Expansion
Vol.	Volume
VRA	Voluntary Restraint Agreement
W. Comp.	World Competition
WTO	World Trade Organisation
WuW	Wirtschaft und Wettbewerb
ZaöRV	Zeitschrift für ausländisches öffentliches Recht und Völkerrecht

Treaty of Lisbon: A Note on Terminology

This brief note is to highlight that, throughout this book, reference to the "European Community" (EC) shall be synonymous to "European Union" (EU) since – prior to the entry into force of the Treaty of Lisbon on 1 December 2009 – the competence in external trade matters, namely the Common Commercial Policy, only extended to the so-called first pillar of the EU, *i.e.* the EC. Accordingly, the term EC Treaty relates to the "Treaty establishing the European Community", as amended by Article 8 (ex Article G) of the Treaty on European Union (TEU). Article 8 TEU was in force up until 1 December 2009 whereupon it was repealed by the Treaty of Lisbon. When referring to Treaty articles, please also note that the case-law examined in this book predates the entry into force of the Treaty of Lisbon.

This book further mostly makes reference to the "Community of Fifteen", *i.e.* the EC prior to the enlargement of 1 May 2004 when Cyprus, Czech Republic, Estonia, Hungary, Latvia, Lithuania, Malta, Poland, Slovakia and Slovenia, and of 1 January 2007 when Romania and Bulgaria joined the European Union.

On 1 December 2009, the EC was replaced by the EU which succeeds it and takes over all its rights and obligations, and the EC Treaty became the "Treaty on the Functioning of the European Union" (TFEU). The following are changes in terminology that were introduced by the Treaty of Lisbon (but that are not used in this book for the abovementioned reasons):

- All references to "European Community" (or "Communities") are replaced by "European Union" ("EU law" instead of "EC Law").
- The term "common market" is formally replaced by the "internal market".
- The European Court of Justice (ECJ) is renamed the "Court of Justice" and the Court of First Instance (CFI) is renamed the "General Court".

In addition, the changes that are effected by the Treaty of Lisbon to the articles of the EC Treaty that are covered in this book are listed below. The table is not exhaustive and shows amendments to the EC Treaty, renamed the Treaty on the Functioning of the European Union (TFEU) and the Treaty on European Union (TEU).

Table of Equivalences

EC Treaty (old numbering)	**Summary of the provision**	**TEU or TFEU (new numbering)**	**Amendment**
Article 3(1)(g)	The activities of the Community include 'a system ensuring that competition in the internal market is not distorted'	Article 3(1)(b) TFEU	The Union shall have exclusive competence in *"the establishing of the competition rules necessary for the functioning of the internal market"*.
Article 10	Member States must ensure fulfilment of the obligations arising out of the Treaty	Repealed and replaced by new Article 3a TEU	No significant amendment.
Article 28	Prohibition of quantitative restrictions and measures having equivalent effect	Article 34 TFEU	--
Article 30	Derogation: free movement of goods	Article 36 TFEU	--
Article 81	Competition rules: prohibition of restrictive arrangements between undertakings	Article 101 TFEU	--
Article 226	Action for enforcement of Treaty obligations against a Member State brought by the Commission	Article 258 TFEU	--

EC Treaty (old numbering)	**Summary of the provision**	**TEU or TFEU (new numbering)**	**Amendment**
Article 227	Action for enforcement of Treaty obligations against a Member State brought by other Member States	Article 259 TFEU	--
Article 230	Action for annulment of Community acts *"Any legal or natural person may [...] institute proceedings against a decision addressed to that person or against a decision which, although in the form of a regulation or a decision addressed to another person, is of direct and individual concern to the former".*	Article 263 TFEU	Amended: *"Any natural or legal person may institute proceedings [...] against an act addressed to that person or which is of direct and individual concern to him or her, and against a regulatory act which is of direct concern to him or her and does not entail implementing measures."*
Article 234	Preliminary rulings	Article 267 TFEU	Added: jurisdiction of the Court of Justice to give preliminary rulings on the validity or interpretation of the acts of the institutions, bodies, offices or agencies of the Union.

EC Treaty (old numbering)	**Summary of the provision**	**TEU or TFEU (new numbering)**	**Amendment**
Article 241	Plea of illegality	Article 277 TFEU	Added: plea may be brought against an act of general application adopted by an institution, body, office or agency of the Union.
Article 249	Definition of regulations, directives and decisions	Article 288 TFEU	--
Article 288	Community liability	Article 340 TFEU	--

Comprehensive tables of equivalences can be found in the Official Journal of the European Union (OJ 2010 C 83/361).

Bibliography

Unless indicated otherwise, authors are cited by name and page reference. Contributions by authors published in journals/periodicals are cited by name and journal/periodical reference.

AHN Dukgeun, Restructuring the WTO Safeguard System, in: The WTO Trade Remedy System: East Asian Perspective, Matsushita M./Ahn D./Chen T.-J. (eds.), London 2006, pp. 11–31.

AIZCORBE Ana, Japanese exchange rates, export restraints, and auto prices in the 1980s, in: Monthly Labor Review, February 2007, pp. 17–22.

ALEMANNO Alberto, Recent Development: Judicial Enforcement of the WTO "Hormones" Ruling Within the European Community: Toward EC Liability for the Non-Implementation of WTO Dispute Settlement Decisions?, in: Harv. Int'l L.J., vol. 45(2), 2004, pp. 547–561.

ALEMANNO Alberto, Private parties and WTO Dispute Settlement System – Who bears the costs of non-compliance and why private parties should not bear them, in: Essays on the Future of the World Trade Organization, Chaisse J./Balmelli T. (eds.), Geneva 2008, pp. 245–282.

AMATO Filippo, International antitrust: what future?, in: W. Comp., vol. 24, (2001), pp. 451–473.

ARCURI Alessandra/POLI Sara, What Price for the Community Enforcement of WTO Law?, EUI Working Paper LAW 2010/01.

BAGCHI Sanjoy, The Integration of the Textile Trade into GATT, in: JWT, vol. 28(6), 1994, pp. 31–42.

BAGWELL Kyle/STAIGER Robert W., Domestic Policies, National Sovereignty and International Economic Institutions, NBER Working Paper N° 7293, 1999.

BALASSA Bela, The "New Protectionism" and the International Economy, in: JWTL, vol. 12, 1978, pp. 409–436.

BARFIELD Claude E., (Mis)managed Trade, in: Freedom to Trade: Refuting the New Protectionism, Cato Institute, 1997, pp. 39–48.

BECKER Florian, The Case of Export Cartel Exemptions: Between Competition and Protectionism, in: J. Competition L. & Econ., vol. 3, 2007, pp. 97–126.

BEEKMANN Harri, The 1994 Revised Commercial Policy Instrument of the European Union, in: W. Comp., vol. 19(1), 1995, pp. 53–75.

BEISE Marc/OPPERMANN Thomas/SANDER Gerald G., Grauzonen im Welthandel, Baden-Baden 1998.

BENEYTO José Maria, The EU and the WTO. Direct Effect of the Dispute Settlement System?, in: EuZW, vol. 7(10), 1996, pp. 295–299.

BERGSTEN C. Fred *et al.*, Auction Quotas and United States Trade Policy, Institute for International Economics, London 1987.

BERRY Steven/LEVINSOHN James/PAKES Ariel, Voluntary Export Restraints on Automobiles: Evaluating a Strategic Trade Policy, NBER Working Paper N° 5235, 1995.

BHAGWATI Jagdish, Afterword: The Question of Linkage, in: AJIL, vol. 96, 2002, pp. 126–134.

BHATTACHARJEA Aditya, Export Cartels – A Developing Country Perspective, cdedse Working Paper No. 120, 2004, and in: JWT, vol. 38(2), 2004, pp. 331–359.

BHATTACHARJEA Aditya, A Response to John Magnus on Joint Export Trade, in: JWT, vol. 39(1), 2005, pp. 185–186.

BIERNAT Ewa, The *Locus Standi* of Private Applicants under article 230(4) EC and the Principle of Judicial Protection in the European Community, Jean Monnet Working Paper 12/03, New York 2003.

BILAL Sanoussi, Political Economy Considerations on the Supply of Trade Protection in Regional Integration Agreements, in: JCMS, vol. 36(1), 1998, pp. 1–31.

BLOKKER Niels/DEELSTRA Jan, Towards a Termination of the Multi-Fibre Arrangement?, in: JWT, vol. 28(5), 1994, pp. 97–118.

BOCCARD Nicolas/WAUTHY Xavier, Export Restraints and Horizontal Product Differentiation, CORE Discussion Paper N° 9782, 1997.

BOSCHECK Ralf, The Governance of Global Market Relations: The Case of Substituting Antitrust for Antidumping, in: W. Comp., vol. 24(1), 2001, pp. 41–64.

BOURGEOIS Jacques H.J., Les relations extérieures de la Communauté européenne et la règle de droit: quelques réflexions, in: Du droit international au droit d'intégration: Liber Amicorum Pierre Pescatore, Capotorti Francesco/Ehlermann Claus-Dieter *et al.* (eds.), Baden-Baden 1987, pp. 59–78.

BOURGEOIS Jacques H.J., External Relations Powers of the European Community, in: Fordham Int'l L.J., vol. 22 (special issue – 0), 1999, pp. 149–173.

BOURGEOIS Jacques H.J., La clause de sauvegarde dans le commerce international de merchandises, in: RDUE, N° 1, 2000, pp. 101–115.

BOURGEOIS Jacques H.J./LAURENT P., Le "nouvel instrument de politique commerciale": un pas en avant vers l'élimination des obstacles aux échanges internationaux, in: RTDE, 1985, pp. 41–63.

BRAND Ronald A., Direct Effect of International Economic Law in the United States and the European Union, in: Nw. J. Int'l L. & Bus., vol. 19(2–3), 1996–1997, pp. 556–608.

BREWSTER Rachel, Rule-Based Dispute Resolution in International Trade Law, in: Virginia Law Review, vol. 92, 2006, pp. 251–288.

BRONCKERS Marco C.E.J., A legal analysis of protectionist measures affecting Japanese imports into the European Community – Revisited, in: Protectionism and the European Community, Völker E.L.M. (ed.), Second Edition, Deventer 1987, pp. 57–120 (cited: Bronckers (1987)).

BRONCKERS Marco C.E.J., Voluntary Export Restraints and the New GATT Safeguards Agreement, in: The Uruguay Round Results: A European Lawyer's Perspective, Bourgeois J.H.J/Berrod F./Gippini-Fournier E. (eds.), Brussels 1995, pp. 273–279 (cited: Bronckers (1995)).

BRONCKERS Marco C.E.J., Private Participation in the Enforcement of WTO law: The new EC Trade Barriers Regulation, in: CMLRev., vol. 33(2), 1996, pp. 299–318.

BRONCKERS Marco C.E.J., From 'Direct Effect' or 'Muted Dialogue' – Recent Developments in the European Courts' Case Law on the WTO and Beyond, in: JIEL, vol. 11(4), 2008, pp. 885–898.

BRONCKERS Marco C.E.J./MCNELIS Natalie, The EU Trade Barriers Regulation Comes of Age, in: JWT, vol. 35(4), 2001, pp. 427–482.

BROWN Christopher/MORIJN John, Case Review: Case C-263/02 P, *Commission v. Jégo-Quéré & Cie SA*, in: CMLRev., vol. 41(4), 2004, pp. 1639–1659.

CADOT Olivier/GRETHER Jean-Marie/DE MELO Jaime, Trade and Competition Policy – Where do we Stand?, in: JWT, vol. 34(3), 2000, pp. 1–20.

CALZOLARI Giacomo/LAMBERTINI Luca, Export Restraints in a Model of Trade with Capital Accumulation, Università degli Studi di Bologna, Economia, Working Paper 420, 2002 (also in: Proceedings of the X International Symposium on Dynamic Games and Applications, Petrosjan L.A./Zenkevich N.A. (eds.), International Society of Dynamic Games and St. Petersburg State University, vol. I, 2002, pp. 158–171).

CANDELA SORIANO Mercedes, Le traité CE et la fixation des prix dans le secteur du livre, in: RMUE, 1999, pp. 361–393.

CARLTON Dennis W./PERLOFF Jeffrey M., Modern Industrial Organization, Third Edition, Reading (MA) 1999.

CASTILLO DE LA TORRE Fernando, The Status of GATT in EC Law, Revisited – The consequences of the Judgment on the Bananas Import Regime for the Enforcement of the Uruguay Round Agreements, in: JWT, vol. 29(1), 1995, pp. 53–68.

CHARNOVITZ Steve, The WTO and the Rights of the Individual, in: Intereconomics, vol. 36 (2), 2001, pp. 98–108.

CHEYNE Ilona, International Agreements and the European Community Legal System, in: ELRev., vol. 19, 1994, pp. 581–598.

CHO Sungjoon, GATT Non-Violation Issues in the WTO Framework: Are They the Achilles' Heel of the Dispute Settlement Process?, Harvard Jean Monnet Working Paper 9/98, Cambridge (MA) 1998.

CHUA Adrian T.L., Reasonable Expectation and Non-Violation Complaints in GATT/WTO Jurisprudence, in: JWT, vol. 32(5), 1998, pp. 27–50.

COHEN Stephen D., The Route to Japan's Voluntary Export Restraints on Automobiles: An Analysis of the U.S. Government's Decision-Making Process in 1981, National Security Archive of The George Washington University, Working Paper N° 20.

COLEMAN John J./YOFFIE David B., Institutional Incentives for Protection: The American Use of Voluntary Export Restraints, in: Proceedings of the Academy of Political Science, vol. 37(4), 1990, pp. 137–150.

COTTIER Thomas, Die Durchsetzung der Prinzipien und Beschlüsse der WTO: Das Streitbeilegungsverfahren und seine Auswirkungen, in: Die Bedeutung der WTO für die europäische Wirtschaft, Köln 1997, pp. 121–137.

COTTIER Thomas, Dispute Settlement in the World Trade Organization: Characteristics and Structural Implications for the European Union, in: CMLRev., vol. 35(2), 1998, pp. 325–378.

COTTIER Thomas, A Theory of Direct Effect in Global Law, in: European Integration and International Co-ordination – Studies in Transnational Law in Honour of Claus-Dieter Ehlermann, von Bogdandy Armin/Mavroidis Petros C./Mény Yves (eds.), The Hague/London/New York 2002, pp. 99–124 (cited: Cottier (2002)).

COTTIER Thomas/NADAKAVUKAREN SCHEFER Krista, The Relationship between World Trade Organization Law, National and Regional Law, in: JIEL, vol. 1(1), 1998, pp. 83–122.

COTTIER Thomas/OESCH Matthias, Die unmittelbare Anwendbarkeit von GATT/WTO-Recht in der Schweiz, in: SZIER, vol. 14(2), 2004, pp. 121–154.

DANI Marco, Remedying European legal pluralism – The FIAMM and Fedon litigation and the judicial protection of international trade bystanders, Jean Monnet Working Paper 06/09, New York 2009.

DAVEY William J., Implementation in WTO Dispute Settlement: An Introduction to the Problems and Possible Solutions, Illinois Public Law and Legal Theory Research Papers Series, 2005, Research Paper No. 05-16.

DAS Bhagirath L., The GATT Multifibre Arrangement, in JWTL, vol. 17, 1983, pp. 95–105.

DAS Bhagirath L., Dismantling the Multifibre Arrangement?, in: JWTL, vol. 19, 1985, pp. 67–80.

DE BÚRCA Gráinne , Fundamental Rights and Citizenship, in: Ten reflections on the Constitutional Treaty for Europe, de Witte Bruno (ed.), Robert Schuman Centre for advanced studies, European University Institute, Florence 2003, pp. 11–44.

DE LEÓN Ignacio, The Dilemma of Regulating International Competition under the WTO System, in: ECLR, vol. 18(3), 1997, pp. 162–177.

DE LEÓN Ignacio, Should We Promote Antitrust in International Trade?, in: W. Comp., vol. 21(2), 1997, pp. 35–63.

DE MELO Jaime/MESSERLIN Partick A., Effects of European VERs on Japanese Autos, PPR Working Paper Series N° 21, World Bank, Washington D.C. 1988.

DE MELO Jaime/WINTERS L. Alan, Do Exporters Gain from VERs?, in: EERev., vol. 37(7), 1993, pp. 1331–1349.

DE SANTIS Roberto A., Why Exporting Countries Agree to Voluntary Export Restraints: The Oligopolistic Power of the Foreign Supplier, in: Scottish Journal of Political Economy, vol. 50(3), 2003, pp. 247–263.

DEAN Judith M./GANGOPADHYAY Shubhashis, Market Equilibrium under the 'Threat' of a VER, in: Journal of International Economics, vol. 20, 1991, pp. 137–152.

DELBRÜCK Jost, Structural Changes in the International System and its Legal Order: International Law in the Era of Globalization, in: SZIER, vol. 11(1), 2001, pp. 1–36.

DENTON Ross, The New Commercial Policy Instrument and AKZO v. DuPont, in: ELRev., vol. 13, 1988, pp. 3–27.

DESMEDT Axel, European Court of Justice on the Effect of WTO Agreements in the EC Legal Order, in: LIEI, vol. 27(1), 2000, 93–101.

DESTLER I.M., American Trade Politics, Second Edition, Washington D.C., Institute for International Economics and Twentieth Century Fund, 1992.

DIDIER Pierre, Les principaux accords de l'OMC et leur transposition dans la Communauté européenne, vol. 1, Bruxelles 1997.

DINOPOULOS Elias/KREININ Mordechai E., Import Quotas and VERs: A Comparative Analysis in a Three-Country Framework, in: Journal of International Economics, vol. 26, 1989, pp. 169–178.

DURAND Benoît/FONT GALARZA Andrés/MEHTA Kirtikumar, The Interface Between Competition Policy and International Trade Liberalisation. Looking into the Future: Applying a New Virtual Anti-Trust Standard, in: W. Comp., vol. 27(1), 2004, pp. 3–12.

EECKHOUT Piet, The Domestic Legal Status of the WTO Agreement: Interconnecting Legal Systems, in: CMLRev., vol. 34(1), 1997, pp. 11–58.

EECKHOUT Piet, Judicial Enforcement of WTO Law in the European Union – Some Further Reflections, in: JIEL, vol. 5(1), 2002, pp. 91–110.

EHLE Dirk, State Regulation under the U.S. Antitrust State Action Doctrine and Under E.C. Competition Law: A Comparative Analysis, in: ECLR, vol. 19(6), 1998, pp. 380–396.

EHLERMANN Claus-Dieter, Die innergemeinschaftliche Anwendung der Regeln des GATT in der Praxis der EG, in: EuR, N° 1, 1985, pp. 91–95.

EINHORN Talia, The Impact of the WTO Agreement on TRIPS (Trade-Related Aspects of Intellectual Property Rights) on EC Law: A Challenge to Regionalism, in: CMLRev., vol. 35(5), 1998, pp. 1069–1099.

ENGELBERGER Lukas, Die unmittelbare Anwendbarkeit des WTO-Rechts in der Schweiz, Diss., Bern 2004.

EPINEY Astrid/KADDOUS Christine/RIDORÉ Carl-Alex, La Communauté européenne et l'OMC – A propos du statut des règles du GATT/OMC dans l'ordre juridique communautaire, in: EFLR, vol. 8(3), 1998, pp. 291–316.

EVENETT Simon J./LEVENSTEIN Margaret C./SUSLOW Valerie Y., International Cartel Enforcement: Lessons from the 1990s, World Bank, Working Paper N° 2680, 2001.

EVERLING Ulrich, Das Recht in den internationalen Wirtschaftsbeziehungen der EG, in: EuR, N° 1, 1985, pp. 75–77.

FEENSTRA Robert C., Voluntary Export Restraint in U.S. Autos, 1980-81: Quality, Employment, and Welfare Effects, in: The Structure and Evolution of Recent U.S. Trade Policy, Baldwin Robert E./Krueger Anne O. (eds.), University of Chicago Press 1984, pp. 35–66.

FEENSTRA Robert C., Quality Change under Trade Restraints: Theory and Evidence from Japanese Autos, in: Quarterly Journal of Economics, 1988, pp. 131–161.

FIKENTSCHER Wolfgang/HEINEMANN Andreas, Der "Draft International Antitrust Code" – Initiative für ein Weltkartellrecht im Rahmen des GATT, in: WuW, vol. 44(2), 1994, pp. 97–107.

FINGER Michael J., GATT Experience with Safeguards: Making Economic and Political Sense of the Possibilities That the GATT Allows to Restrict Imports, World Bank, Policy Research Working Paper N° 2000, 1998.

FINGER Michael J./NG Francis/WANGCHUK Sonam, Antidumping as Safeguard Policy, World Bank, Working Paper N° 2730, 2001.

FINGER Michael J./ZLATE Andrei, WTO Rules that Allow New Trade Restrictions: The Public Interest is a Bastard Child, Paper prepared for the U.N. Millennium Project Task Force on Trade, 16 April 2003.

FLORY Thiébaut/MARTIN Frédéric-Paul, Remarques à propos des avis 1/94 et 2/92 de la Cour de justice des Communautés européennes au regard de l'évolution de la notion de Politique Commerciale Commune, in: CADE, no. 3–4, 1996, pp. 379–400.

FOX Eleanor M., The WTO's First Antitrust Case – Mexican Telecom: A Sleeping Victory for Trade and Competition, in: JIEL, vol. 9(2), 2006, pp. 271–292.

FRANÇOIS Joseph F./GLISMANN Hans H./SPINANGER Dean, The Cost of EU Trade Protection in Textiles and Clothing, Kiel Institute of World Economics, Working Paper N° 997, 2000.

FURSE Mark, Competition Law and the WTO Report "Japan – Measures Affecting Consumer Photographic Film and Paper", in: ECLR, vol. 20(1), 1999, pp. 9–13.

GAGLIARDI Andrea Filippo, The right of individuals to invoke the provisions of mixed agreements before the national courts: a new message from Luxembourg?, in: ELRev., vol. 24, 1999, pp. 276–292.

GAO Shumei/SONG Jihe, Quota Use under VERs: A theoretical framework and some evidence on MFA quota use, Heriot-Watt University, Discussion Paper Series in Economics, DP2004-E03, Edinburgh 2004.

GARCÍA-CASTRILLÓN Carmen Otero, Private Parties under the Present WTO (Bilateralist) Competition Regime, in: JWT, vol. 35(1), 2001, pp. 99–122.

GASPARON Philipp, The Transposition of the Principle of Member State Liability into the Context of External Relations, in: EJIL, vol. 10(3), 1999, pp. 605–624.

GREENAWAY David/HINDLEY Brian, What Britain Pays for Voluntary Export Restraints, Trade Policy Research Center, London 1985.

GRENNES Thomas, The Collision Course on Textile Quotas, Cato Policy Analysis N° 140, 1990.

GRILLER Stefan, Judicial enforceability of WTO law in the European Union. Annotation to Case C-149/96, *Portugal v. Council*, in: JIEL, vol. 3(3), 2000, pp. 441–472.

GYSELEN Luc, State action and the effectiveness of the EEC treaty's competition provisions, in: CMLRev., vol. 26, 1989, pp. 33–60.

HANF Dominik, Facilitating Private Applicants' Access to the European Courts? On the Possible Impact of the CFI's Ruling in *Jégo-Quéré*, in: German Law Journal, vol. 3(7), 2002, pp. 1–8.

HANF Dominik, Kicking the ball into the Member States' field: the Court's response to *Jégo-Quéré*, in: German Law Journal, vol. 3(8), 2002, pp. 1–3.

HERNÁNDEZ-LÓPEZ Ernesto, Recent Trends and Perspectives for Non-State Actor Participation in World Trade Organization Disputes, in: JWT, vol. 35(3), 2001, pp. 469–498.

HILF Meinhard, EG-Aussenkompetenzen in Grenzen, Das Gutachten des EuGH zur Welthandelsorganisation, in: EuZW, vol. 6(1), 1995, pp. 7–8.

HILF Meinhard, The ECJ's Opinion 1/94 on the WTO – No Surprise, but Wise?, in: EJIL, vol. 6(2), 1995, pp. 245–259.

HINDLEY Brian, European Venture: VCRs from Japan, in: What Britain Pays for Voluntary Export Restraints, Greenaway David/Hindley Brian, Trade Policy Research Center, London 1985, pp. 29–63.

HINDLEY Brian, Motor Cars from Japan, in: What Britain Pays for Voluntary Export Restraints, Greenaway David/Hindley Brian, Trade Policy Research Center, London 1985, pp. 64–99.

HINTON Eric F., Strengthening the Effectiveness of Community Law: Direct Effect, Article 5 EC, and the European Court of Justice, in: JILP, vol. 31, 1999, pp. 307–348.

HOEKMAN Bernard M./MAVROIDIS Petros C., Competition, Competition Policy, and the GATT, World Bank, Policy Research Working Paper N° 1228, 1993 (cited: Hoekman/Mavroidis (1993)).

HOEKMAN Bernard M./MAVROIDIS Petros C., Dumping, Antidumping and Antitrust, in: JWT, vol. 30(1), 1996, pp. 27–52.

HOEKMAN Bernard M./MAVROIDIS Petros C., Economic Development, Competition Policy and the WTO, World Bank, Policy Research Working Paper N° 2917, 2002 (cited: Hoekman/Mavroidis (2002)).

HOEKMAN Bernard M./SAGGI Kamal, Trading Market Access for Competition Policy Enforcement, World Bank, Working Paper N° 3188, 2004.

HOFFMANN A. B., Anti-competitive state legislation condemned under Articles 5, 85 and 86 of the EEC treaty: How far should the Court go after Van Eycke, in: ECLR, vol. 11, 1990, pp. 11–27.

HOFMANN Herwig C.H., Private Interest Representation in Trade Policy Instruments – A Different View, in: LIEI, vol. 31(2), 2004, pp. 115–141.

HUDEC Robert E., GATT/WTO Constraints on National Regulation: Requiem for an "Aim and Effects" Test, in: International Lawyer, vol. 32, 1998, pp. 619–649.

HUDEC Robert E., "Like Product": The Differences in Meaning in GATT Articles I and III, in: Regulatory Barriers and the Principle of Non-Discrimination in World Trade Law, Cottier Thomas /Mavroidis Petros C. (eds.), The University of Michigan Press, 2000, pp. 101–123.

IACOBUCCI Edward, The Interdependence of Trade and Competition Policies, in: W. Comp., vol. 21(2), 1997, pp. 5–33.

IMMENGA Ulrich, Export Cartels and Voluntary Export Restraints between Trade and Competition Policy, in: Pacific Rim Law & Policy Journal, vol. 4(1), 1995, pp. 93–151.

IMMENGA Ulrich, Entwicklung einer internationalen Wettbewerbsordnung – ein Instrument der Handelspolitik?, in: Die Bedeutung der WTO für die europäische Wirtschaft, Köln 1997, pp. 107–120.

INAMA Stefano/VERMULST Edwin, Customs and Trade Laws of the European Community, Kluwer Law International, The Hague 1999.

IPSEN Knut/HALTERN Ulrich R., Rule of Law in den internationalen Wirtschaftsbeziehungen: Die Welthandelsorganisation, in: RIW, vol. 40(9), 1994, pp. 717–723.

ITOH Motoshige/NAGAOKA Sadao, VERs, VIEs, and Global Competition, in: Global Competition Policy, Richardson David J./Graham Edward M. (eds.), Institute for International Economics, Washington D.C. 1997, pp. 475–499, online version available at http://www.iie.com/publications/chapters_preview/56/15ie1664.pdf (site last visited on 28 July 2010).

JACKSON John H., Status of Treaties in Domestic Legal Systems: A Policy Analysis, in: AJIL, vol. 86(2), 1992, pp. 310–340.

JACKSON John H., The World Trading System – Law and Policy of International Economic Relations, Second Edition, Cambridge (MA) 1998.

JACKSON John H./DAVEY William J./SYKES Alan O., Legal Problems of International Economic Relations, 4th edition, St. Paul (MN) 2002.

JONES Kent Albert , Voluntary Export Restraint: Political Economy, History and the Role of the GATT, in: JWT, vol. 23(3), 1989, pp. 125–140.

JONES Kent Albert, Export Restraint and the New Protectionism: The Political Economy of Discriminatory Trade Restrictions, The University of Michigan Press, 1994.

JUNG Youngjin, Modelling a WTO Dispute Settlement Mechanism in an International Antitrust Agreement – An Impossible Dream?, in: JWT, vol. 34(1), 2000, pp. 89–110.

KESSIE Edwini, Enhancing Security and Predictability for Private Business Operators under the Dispute Settlement System of the WTO, in: JWT, vol. 34(6), 2000, pp. 1–17.

KHANNA Ram, Market Sharing under the Multifibre Arrangement: conesquences of non-tariff barriers in the textiles trade, in: JWT, vol. 24(1), 1990, pp. 71–104.

KIM Yong/HORLICK Gary N., Private Remedies for Private Anti-Competitive Barriers to Trade: The Kodak–Fuji Example, in: Empirica, vol. 24, 1997, pp. 75–81.

KOJIMA Takaaki, International Conflicts over the Extraterritorial Application of Competition Law in a Borderless Economy, Weatherhead Center for International Affairs, Harvard University, Fellow Paper 2001–2002.

KOLEV Dobrin R./PRUSA Thomas J., Dumping and Double Crossing: The (In)Effectiveness of Cost-Based Trade Policy Under Incomplete Information, NBER Working Paper N° 6986, 1999.

KOMURO Norio, Kodak-Fuji Film Dispute and the WTO Panel Ruling; in: JWT, vol. 35(5), 1998, pp. 161–217.

KOOPMANN Georg, Wettbewerbspolitische Instrumente der Welthandelsorganisation, HWWA-Diskussionspapier N° 64, 1998.

KOSTECKI Michel M., Marketing Strategies and Voluntary Export Restraints, in: JWT, vol. 25(4), 1991, pp. 87–100.

KRENZLER Horst Günter/DA FONSECA-WOLLHEIM Hermann, Die Reichweite der gemeinsamen Handelspolitik nach dem Vertrag von Amsterdam – eine Debatte ohne Ende?, in: EuR, N° 3, 1998, pp. 223–241.

KRISHNA Kala, Trade Restrictions as Facilitating Practices, NBER Working Paper N° 1546, Cambridge (MA) 1985 (cited: Krishna (1985)).

KRISHNA Kala, What do Voluntary Export Restraints Do?, NBER Working Paper N° 2612, Cambridge (MA) 1988 (cited: Krisha (1988)).

KUIJPER Pieter J., The Conclusion and Implementation of the Uruguay Round Results by the European Community, in: EJIL, vol. 6(2), 1995, pp. 222–244.

KUIJPER Pieter J., The Court and the Tribunal of the EC and the Vienna Convention on the Law of Treaties 1969, in: LIEI, vol. 25(1), 1998, pp. 1–22.

KYVIK NORDÅS Hildegunn, The Global Textile and Clothing Industry post the Agreement on Textiles and Clothing, WTO Discussion Paper N° 5, Geneva 2004.

LAROUER Christophe, WTO Non-Violation Complaints: A Misunderstood Remedy in the WTO Dispute Settlement System, in: NILR, 2006, pp. 97–126.

LEAL-ARCAS Rafael, Exclusive or Shared Competence in the Common Commercial Policy: From Amsterdam to Nice, in: LIEI, vol. 30(1), 2003, pp. 3–14.

LEE Philip/KENNEDY Brian, The Potential Direct Effect of GATT 1994 in European Community Law, in: JWT, vol. 30(1), 1996, pp. 67–89.

LEE Yong-Shik, Critical Issues in the Application of the WTO Rules on Safeguards – In the Light of the Recent Panel Reports and the Appellate Body Decisions, in: JWT, vol. 34(2), 2000, pp. 131–147.

LEE Yong-Shik, Destabilization of the Discipline on Safeguards? Inherent Problems with the Continuing Application of Article XIX after the Settlement of the Agreement on Safeguards, in: JWT, vol. 35(6), 2001, pp. 1235–1246.

LEE Yong-Shik, Revival of Grey Area Measures? The US-Canada Softwood Lumber Agreement: Conflict with the WTO Agreement on Safeguards, in: JWT, vol. 36(1), 2002, pp. 155–165.

LEE Yong-Shik, Continuing Controversy on "Unforeseen Developments" – Reviewer's Note, in: JWT, vol. 37(6), 2003, pp. 1153–1157.

LEVENSTEIN Margaret C./SUSLOW Valerie Y., The Changing International Status of Export Cartel Exemptions, Ross School of Business Working Paper Series, Working Paper N° 897, November 2004, and in: Am. U. Int'l L. Rev., vol. 20, 2005, pp. 785–828.

LINDSEY Brink/GRISWOLD Daniel T./LUKAS Aaron, The Steel "Crisis" and the Costs of Protectionism, Cato Institute, Trade Briefing Paper, 1999.

MAGNUS John R., Joint Export Trade Provisions in Antitrust Laws: A Supporter's Perspective, in: JWT, vol. 39(1), 2005, pp. 181–184.

MAHNKEN Volker, Handelsbeschränkungsabkommen und –vereinbarungen der EG, in: Europäisches Aussenwirtschaftsrecht, Grabitz Eberhard/von Bogdandy Armin/Nettesheim Martin (eds.), München 1994, pp. 291–340.

MANIN Philippe, A propos de l'accord instituant l'organisation mondiale du commerce et de l'accord sur les marchés publics: la question de l'invocabilité des accords internationaux conclus par la Communauté européenne, in: RTDE, vol. 33(3), 1997, pp. 399–428.

MARSDEN Philip B., Dealing with International Exclusion – The Right Focus for the WTO Working Group on Trade and Competition Policy, in: W. Comp., vol. 21(2), 1997, pp. 91–110.

MARSDEN Philip B., WTO Decides First Competition Case – with Disappointing Results, in: Competition Law Insight, 2006, May edition, pp. 3–9.

MATSUSHITA Mitsuno, International Cooperation in the Enforcement of Competition Policy, in: Washington University Global Studies Law Review, vol. 1, 2002, pp. 462–475.

MAVROIDIS Petros C., Remedies in the WTO Legal System: Between a Rock and a Hard Place, in: EJIL, vol. 11(4), 2000, pp. 763–813.

MCCLENAHAN William, The Growth of Voluntary Export Restraints and American Foreign Economic Policy, 1956–1969, in: Business and Economic History, Hausman William J. (ed.), Second Series, Vol. 20, 1991, pp. 180–190.

MCRAE Donald M., The WTO in International Law: Tradition Continued or New Frontier?, in: JIEL, vol. 3(1), 2000, pp. 27–41.

MCRAE Donald M., Measuring the Effectiveness of the WTO Dispute Settlement System, in: AJWH, vol. 3(1), 2008, pp. 1–20.

MENGOZZI Paolo, La Cour de justice et l'applicabilité des règles de l'OMC en droit communautaire à la lumière de l'affaire *Portugal c. Conseil*, in: RDUE, N° 3, 2000, pp. 509–522.

MESSERLIN Patrick A., Antidumping Regulations or Procartel Law?, PRE Working Paper Series N° 397, World Bank, Washington D.C. 1990.

MONTAÑÀ I MORA Miquel, Equilibrium, A Rediscovered Basis for the Court of Justice of the European Communities to Refuse Direct Effect to the Uruguay Round Agreements?, in: JWT, vol. 30(5), 1996, pp. 43–59.

MONTI Giorgio, Article 81 EC and Public Policy, in: CMLRev., vol. 39(5), 2002, pp. 1057–1099.

MOORE Michael O., VERs and Price Undertakings under the WTO, in: Review of International Economics, vol. 13(2), 2005, pp. 298–310.

MUELLER Felix, Is the General Agreement on Tariffs and Trade Article XIX "Unforeseen Developments Clause" Still Effective Under the Agreement on Safeguards?, in: JWT, vol. 37(6), 2003, 1119–1151.

NAGAOKA Sadao, International Trade Aspects of Competition Policy, NBER Working Paper N° 6720, 1998.

NAKAGAWA Junji, Lessons from the Japan-China "Welsh Onion War", in: JWT, vol. 36(6), 2002, 1019–1036.

NELSON Douglas R., The Political-Economy of U.S. Automobile Protection, NBER Working Paper N° 4746, 1994.

NEUWAHL Nanette A., Shared Powers Or Combined Incompetence? More on Mixity, in: CMLRev., vol. 33(4), 1996, pp. 667–687.

NEUWAHL Nanette A., Individuals and the GATT: Direct Effect and Indirect Effects of the General Agreement on Tariffs and Trade in Community Law, in: The European Union and World Trade Law – After the GATT Uruguay Round, Emiliou Nicholas/O'Keeffe David (eds.), Chichester 1996, pp. 313–328.

NEVEN Damien J./MAVROIDIS Petros C., El mess in TELMEX – A comment on Mexico – measures affecting telecommunications services, in: World Trade Review, vol. 5(2), 2006, pp. 271–296.

NOLAND Marcus, Japan and the International Economic Institutions, Paper prepared for the Centre for Japanese Economic Studies, Macquarie University, Fifth Biennial Conference, Sydney 2000, pp. 1–18, online available at http://www.piie.com/publications/papers/paper.cfm?ResearchID=380 (site last visited on 28 July 2010).

NOWAK Carsten, Der Rechtsschutz von Beschwerdeführern im EG-Wettbewerbs- und EG-Aussenhandelsrecht, in: EuZW, vol. 11(15), 2000, pp. 453–458.

OHASHI Hiroshi, Anticipatory Effects of Voluntary Export Restraints: A Study of Home Video Cassette Recorders Market, 1978–86, Faculty of Commerce, University of British Columbia, Vancouver 2001.

O'NEILL Maria, On the Boundary Clash between EC Commercial Law and WTO Law, in: LIEI, vol. 32(1), 2005, pp. 65–86.

OSTERHOUDT BERKEY Judson, The European Court of Justice and Direct Effect for the GATT: A Question Worth Revisiting, in: EJIL, vol. 9, 1998, pp. 626–657.

PAPAKRIVOPOULOS Dimosthenis, The Role of Competition Law as an International Trade Remedy in the Context of the World Trade Organization, in: W. Comp., vol. 22(3), 1999, pp. 45–64.

PAUWELYN Joost, The Nature of WTO Obligations, Jean Monnet Working Paper 1/02, New York 2002.

PAUWELYN Joost, How to Win a World Trade Organization Dispute Based on Non-World Trade Organization Law? – Questions of Jurisdiction and Merits, in: JWT, vol. 37(6), 2003, pp. 997–1030.

PAUWELYN Joost, The Puzzle of WTO Safeguards and Regional Trade Agreements, in: JIEL, vol. 7(1), 2004, pp. 109–142.

PAUWELYN Joost, Adding Sweeteners to Softwood Lumber: The WTO-NAFTA 'Spaghetti Bowl' Is Cooking, in: JIEL, vol. 9(1), 2006, pp. 1–10.

PETERSMANN Ernst-Ulrich, Die EWG als GATT-Mitglied – Rechtskonflikte zwischen GATT-Recht und Europäischem Gemeinschaftsrecht, in: GATT und Europäische Gemeinschaft, Hilf Meinhard/Petersmann Ernst-Ulrich (eds.), Baden-Baden 1985, pp. 119–173.

PETERSMANN Ernst-Ulrich, Grey Area Trade Policy and the Rule of Law, in: JWT, vol. 22(2), 1988, pp. 23–44.

PETERSMANN Ernst-Ulrich, International Competition Rules for GATT – MTO World Trade and Legal System, in: JWT, vol. 27(6), 1993, pp. 35–86.

PETERSMANN Ernst-Ulrich, Darf die EG das Völkerrecht ignorieren?, in: EuZW, vol. 8(11), 1997, pp. 325–331.

POMFRET Richard, World Steel Trade at Crossroads, in: JWT., vol. 22(3), 1988, pp. 81–89.

PORGES Amelia/TRACHTMAN Joel P., Robert Hudec and Domestic Regulation: The Resurrection of Aim and Effects, in: JWT, vol. 37(4), 2003, pp. 783–799.

POWELL Jim, Protectionist Paradise?, in: Freedom to Trade: Refuting the New Protectionism, Cato Institute, 1997, pp. 57–68.

PREUSSE Heinz Gert, Voluntary Export Restraints – An Effective Means Against a Spread of Neo-Protectionism, in: JWT, vol. 25(2), 1991, pp. 5–17.

REGAN Donald H., Regulatory Purpose and "Like Products" in Article III:4 of the GATT (With Additional Remarks on Article III:2), in: JWT, vol. 36(3), 2002, pp. 443–478.

REUTER Alexander, Aussenwirtschafts- und Exportkontrollrecht, Deutschland/Europäische Union, München 1995.

RICHMAN Sheldon L., The Reagan Record on Trade: Rhetoric vs. Reality, Cato Institute, Policy Analysis N° 107, 1988.

ROBERTSON David, GATT Rules for Emergency Protection, Trade Policy Research Center, London 1992.

ROESSLER Frieder, Should Principles of Competition Policy be Incorporated into WTO Law Through Non-Violation Complaints?, in: JIEL, vol. 2(3), 1999, pp. 413–421.

ROESSLER Frieder, Beyond the Ostensible – A Tribute to Professor Robert Hudec's Insights on the Determination of the Likeness of Products Under the National Treatment Provisions of the General Agreement on Tariffs and Trade, in: JWT, vol. 37(4), 2003, pp. 771–781.

ROSAS Allan, Implementation and Enforcement of WTO Dispute Settlement Findings: an EU Perspective, in: JIEL, vol. 4(1), 2001, pp. 131–144.

RYDELSKI Michael Sànchez/ZONNEKEYN Geert A., The EC Trade Barriers Regulation, The EC's Move Towards a More Aggressive Market Access Strategy, in: JWT, vol. 31(5), 1997, pp. 147–166.

SACK Jörn, The European Community's Membership of International Organizations, in: CMLRev., vol. 32(5), 1995, pp. 1227–1256.

SCHEPEL Harm, Delegation of Regulatory Powers to Private Parties under EC Competition Law: Towards a Procedural Public Interest Test, in: CMLRev., vol. 39(1), 2002, pp. 31–51.

SCHLAGENHOF Markus, Grey-Area Trade Policy after the Uruguay Round – The Particular Case of Trade in Textiles and Clothing, in: W. Comp., vol. 19(2), 1995, pp. 106–117.

SCHMID Christoph, Immer wieder Bananen: Der Status des GATT/ WTO-Systems im Gemeinschaftsrecht, in: NJW, N° 4, 1998, pp. 190–197.

SCHUKNECHT Ludger, Trade Protection in the European Community, Harwood academic publishers, Reading 1992.

SNYDER Francis, The Gatekeepers: The European Courts and WTO Law, in: CMLRev., vol. 40(2), 2003, pp. 313–367.

SOKOL Daniel D., What Do We Really Know about Export Cartels and What is the Appropriate Solution?, in J. Competition L. & Econ., vol. 4, 2008, pp. 967–982.

SPINANGER Dean, Textiles Beyond the MFA Phase-Out, CSGR Working Paper N° 13, 1998.

SPITZER Florian, The Non-Violation Complaint in the WTO Law, Diss., Universität des Saarlandes, Berlin 2004.

STEINBERG Richard H., Judicial Law-Making, Internal Transparency, and External Transparency: Recent Institutional Developments at the WTO, ILS Working Paper Series, Volume 2003.

STEVENSON Cliff, Are World Trade Organization Members Correctly Applying World Trade Organization Rules in Safeguard Determinations?, in: JWT, vol. 38(2), 2004, 307–329.

STEWART Terence P./BRILLIANT Myron A., Safeguards, in: The GATT Uruguay Round – A Negotiating History (1986–1992), Stewart Terence P. (ed.), Deventer 1993, pp. 1711–1820.

STOLL Peter-Tobias, Freihandel und Verfassung. Einzelstaatliche Gewährleistung und die konstitutionelle Funktion der Welthandelsordnung (GATT/WTO), in: ZaöRV, vol. 57(1), 1997, pp. 83–146.

SUARDI Massimo, The Effects of Voluntary Export Restraints on the Quality of Imports, European Interuniversity Press and College of Europe, 1994.

SUNDBERG Drew/VERMULST Edwin, The EC Trade Barriers Regulation – An Obstacle to Trade?, in: JWT, vol. 35(5), 2001, pp. 989–1013.

SWEENEY Brendan J., Export Cartels: Is there a Need for Global Rules?, in: JIEL, vol. 10(1), 2007, pp. 87–115.

SYKES Alan O., The Safeguards Mess: A Critique of WTO Jurisprudence, U Chicago Law & Economics, Olin Working Paper N° 187, 2003.

SYKES Alan O., The Persistent Puzzles Of Safeguards: Lessons From The Steel Dispute, in: JIEL, vol. 7(3), 2004, pp. 523–564.

TANCREDI Antonello, EC Practice in the WTO: How Wide is the 'Scope for Manoeuvre'?, in: EJIL, vol. 15(5), 2004, pp. 933–961.

TANG Xiaobing, Textiles and the Uruguay round of multilateral trade negotiations, in: JWT, vol. 23(3), 1989, pp. 51–68.

TAYLOR Christopher T., The Economic Effects of Withdrawn Antidumping Investigations: Is There Evidence of Collusive Settlements, FTC Bureau of Economics Working Paper N° 240, 2001.

THIES Anne, *Biret* and beyond: The status of WTO rulings in EC law, in: CMLRev., vol. 41(4), 2004, pp. 1661–1682.

TIETJE Christian, Die Meistbegünstigungspflicht im Gemeinschaftsrecht, in: EuR, N° 4, 1995, pp. 398–415.

TOMUSCHAT Christian, Völkerrechtliche Grundlagen der Drittstaatsbeziehungen der EG, in: Hilf Meinhard/Tomuschat Christian (eds.), EG und Drittstaatsbeziehungen nach 1992, Baden-Baden 1991, pp. 139–161.

TOMZ Michael/GOLDSTEIN Judith/RIVERS Douglas, Membership Has its Privileges: Understanding the Effects of GATT and the WTO on World Trade, ISNIE Paper 2004.

TRACHTMAN Joel P., Trade and … Problems, Cost-Benefit Analysis and Subsidiarity, in: EJIL, vol. 9(1), 1998, pp. 32–85.

TRACHTMAN Joel P., Bananas, Direct Effect and Compliance, in: EJIL, vol. 10(4), 1999, pp. 655–678.

TRACHTMAN Joel P., The Domain of WTO Dispute Resolution, in: Harv. Int'l L.J., vol. 40, 1999, pp. 333–377.

TREBILCOCK Michael J., Competition Policy and Trade Policy, Mediating the Interface, in: JWT, vol. 30(4), 1996, pp. 71–106.

TREBILCOCK Michael J./HOWSE Robert, The Regulation of International Trade, Second edition, London 1999.

TRIDIMAS Takis/POLI Sara, *Locus standi* of individuals under Article 230(4): the return of Euridice?, in: Making Community Law: The Legacy of Advocate General Jacobs at the European Court of Justice, Moser Philip/Sawyer Katrine (eds.), Cheltenham 2008, pp. 77–99.

TUMLIR Jan, Protectionism: Trade Policy in Democratic Societies, American Enterprise Institution for Public Policy Research, 1985.

TURNER Philip/TUVERI Jean-Pierre, Some Effects of Export Restraints on Japanese Trading Behaviour, in: OECD Economic Studies N° 2, Paris 1984, pp. 93–107.

VAN DARTEL R.J.P.M., The EEC's Commercial Policy Concerning Textiles in: Protectionism and the European Community, Völker E.L.M. (ed.), Second Edition, Deventer 1987, pp. 121–158.

VAN DE GEVEL Ad J.W., From Confrontation to Coopetition in the Globalized Semiconductor Industry, Research Memorandum N° 792, Tilburg University, Faculty of Economics and Business Administration, 2000.

VAN DEN BROEK Naboth, Legal persuasion, political realism, and legitimacy: the European Court's recent treatment of the effect of WTO agreements in the EC legal order, in: JIEL, vol. 4(2), 2001, pp. 411–440.

VAN ROSSEM Jan Willem, Interaction between EU law and international law in the light of Intertanko and Kadi: The dilemma of norms binding the Member States but not the Community, CLEER Working Papers 2009/4.

VERDIER Thierry, Invisible Protection, Costly Information, and Results-Oriented versus Rules-Oriented Trade Policies, DELTA Paris and CEPR London 2001.

VERMULST Edwin A., A European Practitioner's View of the GATT System – Should Competition Law Violations Distorting International Trade Be Subject to GATT Panels?, in: JWT, vol. 27(2), 1993, pp. 55–76.

VERMULST Edwin/PERNAUTE Marta/LUCENTI Krista, Recent European Community Safeguards Policy: "Kill Them All and Let God Sort Them Out"?, in: JWT, vol. 38(6), 2004, 955–984.

VINING Aidan R./SHAPIRO Daniel M./BORGE Bernhard, Building the firm's political (lobbying) strategy, in: J. Publ. Aff., vol. 5, 2005, pp. 150–175.

WAELBROECK Michel, Les rapports entre les règles sur la libre circulation des marchandises et les règles de concurrence applicables aux entreprises dans la CEE, in: Du droit international au droit de l'intégration, Liber amicorum P. Pescatore, Baden-Baden 1987, pp. 781–803.

WAUTHY Xavier, A Note on Research and Development and Voluntary Export Restrictions, in: Economics Bulletin, vol. 6(1), 2002, pp. 1–6.

WEBER Daniel, Prozessuale Aspekte der Streitbeilegung im institutionellen Rahmen der Welthandelsorganisation (WTO): Amicus Curiae, Professionalisierung der Panelebene, fehlende Rückverweisungskompetenz des Appellate Body und die Abfolgeproblematik der Art. 21, 22 DSU, Witten 2007.

WEINRICHTER Norbert, Perspectives on the changing spirit of GATT, in: EIoP, vol. 3(10), 1999, pp. 1–12.

WIERS Jochem, One Day, You're Gonna Pay: The European Court of Justice in *Biret*, in: LIEI, vol. 31(2), 2004, pp. 143–151.

WILLE Serena B., Recapturing a Lost Opportunity: Article III:2 GATT 1994, Japan – Taxes on Alcoholic Beverages 1996, in: EJIL, 1998, vol. 9(1), pp. 1–22 (as of p. 182 of the online version).

WINTERS L. Alan, VERs and Expectations: Extensions and Evidence, in: The Economic Journal, vol. 104, 1994, pp. 113–123.

WOUTERS Jan/VAN EECKHOUTTE Dries, Giving Effect to Customary International Law through European Community Law, Katholieke Universiteit Leuven, Institute for International Law, Working Paper N° 25, 2002.

YAMADA Akinori, Recent Development of Competition Law and Policy in Japan, Speech held at the Fordham Corporate Law Institute Conference on International Antitrust Law and Policy, 16–17 October 1997.

ZAMPINI Florence, Les limites de la compétence externe de la Communauté européenne selon la CJCE et les limites de l'intervention judiciaire, in: Bourgeois Jacques H.J./Devost Jean-Louis/Gaiffe Marie-Ange (eds.), La Communauté européenne et les accords mixtes – Quelles perspectives?, Bruxelles 1997, pp. 27–48.

ZLEPTNIG Stefan, The Standard of Review in WTO Law: An Analysis of Law, Legitimacy and the Distribution of Legal and Political Authority, in: EIoP, vol. 6(17), 2002, pp. 1–33.

ZONNEKEYN Geert A., The Legal Status of WTO Panel Reports in the EC Legal Order: Some Reflections on the Opinion of Advocate General Mischo in the Atlanta Case, in: JIEL, vol. 2(4), 1999, pp. 713–722.

ZONNEKEYN Geert A., The Status of Adopted Panel and Appellate Body Reports in the European Court of Justice and the European Court of First Instance – The Banana Experience, in: JWT, vol. 34(2), 2000, pp. 93–108.

ZONNEKEYN Geert A., The status of WTO law in the Community legal order: some comments in the light of the Portuguese Textiles case, in: ELRev., vol. 25, 2000, pp. 293–302.

ZONNEKEYN Geert A., The Status of WTO Law in the EC Legal Order – The Final Curtain?, in: JWT, 34(3), 2000, pp. 111–125.

ZONNEKEYN Geert A., The Latest on Indirect Effect of WTO Law in the EC Legal Order: The *Nakajima* Case Law Misjudged?, in: JIEL, vol. 4(3), 2001, pp. 597–608.

ZONNEKEYN Geert A., EC Liability for the Non-Implementation of WTO Dispute Settlement Decisions–Advocate General Alber Proposes a 'Copernican Innovation' in the Case Law of the ECJ, in: JIEL, vol. 6(3), 2003, pp. 761–769.

ZONNEKEYN Geert A., The ECJ's *Petrotub* Judgment: towards a Revival of the "*Nakajima* Doctrine"?, in: LIEI, vol. 30(3), 2003, pp. 249–266.

Publications of International Organisations

GATT	Trade Policies For a Better Future ("Leutwiler Report"), Geneva 1985.
OECD	Competition and Trade Policies – Their Interaction, Paris 1984.
OECD	Obstacles to Trade and Competition, Paris 1993.
OECD	Trade and Competition Policies, Joint Report by the Committee on Competition Law and Policy and the Trade Committee, OECD/GD(94)36, 1994.
OECD	Antitrust and Market Access: The Scope and Coverage of Competition Laws and Implications for Trade, Paris 1996.

OECD	OECD Council, Recommendation concerning Effective Action against Hard Core Cartels, C(98)35/FINAL, 1998.
OECD	CLP Report on Positive Comity (DAFFE/CLP(99)19), Paris 1999.
OECD	Hard Core Cartels, Paris 2000 (also in: OECD Journal of Competition Law and Policy, vol. 2(2), 2000, pp. 1–56).
OECD	Issues for Trade and Competition in the Global Context, in: OECD Journal of Competition Law and Policy, vol. 5(3), 2003.
WTO	Report (1998) of the Working Group on the Interaction between Trade and Competition Policy to the General Council, WT/WGTCP/2.
WTO	Report (1999) of the Working Group on the Interaction between Trade and Competition Policy to the General Council, WT/WGTCP/3.
WTO	Report (2000) of the Working Group on the Interaction between Trade and Competition Policy to the General Council, WT/WGTCP/4.
WTO	Report (2001) of the Working Group on the Interaction between Trade and Competition Policy to the General Council, WT/WGTCP/5.
WTO	Report (2002) of the Working Group on the Interaction between Trade and Competition Policy to the General Council, WT/WGTCP/6.
WTO	Report (2003) of the Working Group on the Interaction between Trade and Competition Policy to the General Council, WT/WGTCP/7.

Other

U.S. Department of Commerce, Bureau of Industry and Security, Section 232 Investigations Program Guide – The Effect of Imports on the National Security, September 2004.

Judgments and Opinions of the ECJ

Case 14/61	*Koninklijke Nederlandsche Hoogovens en Staalfabrieken N.V. v. High Authority of the ECSC (Hoogovens)*, [1962] E.C.R. 253.
Case 25/62	*Plaumann & Co. v. Commission (Plaumann)*, [1963] E.C.R. 95.
Case 26/62	*NV Algemene Transport- en Expeditie Onderneming van Gend & Loos v. Netherlands Inland Revenue Administration (van Gend en Loos)*, [1963] E.C.R. 1.
Case 6/64	*Flaminio Costa v. E.N.E.L (Costa/ENEL)*, [1964] E.C.R. 1251.
Case 4/69	*Alfons Lütticke GmbH v. Commission (Lütticke)*, [1971] E.C.R. 325.
Case 22/70	*Commission v. Council (European Agreement on Road Transport – AETR)*, [1971] E.C.R. 263.
Case 5/71	*Aktien-Zuckerfabrik Schöppenstedt v. Council (Schöppenstedt)*, [1971] E.C.R. 975.
Case 22/71	*Béguelin Import Co. v. G.L. Import Export SA (Béguelin)*, [1971] E.C.R. 949.
Joined Cases 21–24/72	*International Fruit Company NV and others v. Produktschap voor Groenten en Fruit (International Fruit Company)*, [1972] E.C.R. 1219.
Case 9/73	*Carl Schlüter v. Hauptzollamt Lörrach (Schlüter)*, [1973] E.C.R. 1135.
Joined cases 40–48, 50, 54–56, 111, 113 and 114/73	*Coöperatieve Vereniging "Suiker Unie" UA and others v. Commission (Suiker Unie et al.)*, [1975] E.C.R. 1663.
Case 181/73	*R. & V. Haegeman v. Belgium (Haegeman)*, [1974] E.C.R. 449.
Case 2/74	*Jean Reyners v. Belgium (Reyners)*, [1974] E.C.R. 631.
Case 41/74	*Yvonne van Duyn v. Home Office (van Duyn)*, [1974] E.C.R. 1337.
Case 71/74	*Nederlandse Vereniging voor de fruit- en groentenimporthandel, Nederlandse Bond van grossiers in zuidvruchten en ander geimporteerd fruit "Frubo" v. Commission and Vereniging de Fruitunie (Frubo)*, [1975] E.C.R. 563.

Case 38/75	*Douaneagent der NV Nederlandse Spoorwegen v. Inspecteur der invoerrechten en accijnzen (Nederlandse Spoorwegen)*, [1975] E.C.R. 1439.
Cases 51/75, 86/75, 96/75	*EMI Records Ltd. V. CBS United Kingdom Ltd. (EMI/CBS)*, [1976] E.C.R. 811.
Case 87/75	*Conceria Daniele Bresciani v. Amministrazione Italiana delle Finanze (Bresciani)*, [1976] E.C.R. 129.
Case 41/76	*Donckerwolcke v. Procureur de la République (Donckerwolcke)*, [1976] E.C.R. 1921.
Case 13/77	*G.B.-Inno-B.M. v. Association des détaillants en tabac (Inno/Atab)*, [1977] E.C.R. 2115.
Joined cases 209–215 and 218/78	*van Landewyck et al. v. Commission (Fedetab)*, [1980] E.C.R. 3125.
Case 225/78	*Procureur de la République Besançon v. Bouhelier et al. (Bouhelier)*, [1979] E.C.R. 3151.
Case 112/80	*Dürbeck v. Hauptzollamt Frankfurt a.M.-Flughafen (Dürbeck)*, [1981] E.C.R. 1095.
Case 270/80	*Polydor Ltd. And RSO Records Inc. v. Harlequin Records Shops Ltd. And Simons Records Ltd. (Polydor)*, [1982] E.C.R. 329.
Case 17/81	*Pabst & Richarz KG v. Hauptzollamt Oldenburg (Pabst)*, [1982] E.C.R. 1331.
Case 104/81	*Hauptzollamt Mainz v. C.A. Kupferberg & Cie KG a.A. (Kupferberg)*, [1982] E.C.R. 3641.
Case 266/81	*Società Italiana per l'Oleodotto Transalpino (SIOT) v. Ministero delle finanze, Ministero della marina mercantile, Circoscrizione doganale di Trieste and Ente autonomo del porto di Trieste (SIOT)*, [1983] E.C.R. 731.
Cases 267–269/81	*Amministrazione delle Finanze dello Stato v. Società Petrolifera Italiana SpA (SPI) and SpA Michelin Italiana (SAMI) (SPI and SAMI)*, [1983] E.C.R. 801.
Joined cases 43 and 63/82	*Vereniging ter Bevordering van het Vlaamse Boekwezen, VBVB, and Vereniging ter Bevordering van de Belangen des Boekhandels, VBBB, v. Commission (VBBB-VBVB)*, [1984] E.C.R. 19.
Joined cases 240–242, 261, 262, 268 and 269/82	*Stichting Sigarettenindustrie (SSI) et al. V. Commission (SSI)*, [1985] E.C.R. 3831.

Case 123/83	*Bureau national interprofessionnel du cognac v. Guy Clair (BNIC v. Clair)*, [1985] E.C.R. 391.
Case 229/83	*Association des Centres distributeurs Édouard Leclerc et al. V. Au Blé Vert SARL (Au Blé Vert)*, [1985] E.C.R. 1.
Case 294/83	*Parti écologiste "Les Verts" v. European Parliament (Les Verts)*, [1986] E.C.R. 1339.
Case 1/84R	*Ilford v. Commission (Ilford)*, [1985] E.C.R. 423.
Joined Cases 142/84 and 156/84	*British-American Tobacco Company Ltd. And R. J. Reynolds Industries Inc. v. Commission (BAT and Reynolds)*, [1987] E.C.R. 4487.
Case 169/84	*Compagnie française de l'azote (Cofaz) SA et al. V. Commission (Cofaz)*, [1986] E.C.R. 391.
Case 174/84	*Bulk Oil v. Sun Oil*, [1986] E.C.R. 559.
Joined cases 209–213/84	*Criminal proceedings against Lucas Asjes et al. (Nouvelles Frontières)*, [1986] E.C.R. 1425.
Cases 133–136/85	*Walter Rau Lebensmittelwerke v. Bundesanstalt für Landwirtschaftliche Marktordnung*, [1987] E.C.R. 2289.
Case 311/85	*ASBL Vereniging van Vlaamse Reisbureaus v. ASBL Sociale Dienst van de Plaatselijke en Gewestelijke Overheidsdiensten (Vlaamse Reisbureaus)*, [1987] E.C.R. 3801.
Case 314/85	*Foto-Frost v. Hauptzollamt Lübeck-Ost (Foto-Frost)*, [1987] E.C.R. 4199.
Case 12/86	*Demirel v. Stadt Schwäbisch Gmünd (Demirel)*, [1987] E.C.R. 3719.
Case 66/86	*Ahmed Saeed Flugreisen and Silver Line Reisebüro v. Zentrale zur Bekämpfung unlauteren Wettbewerbs (Ahmed Saeed)*, [1989] E.C.R. 803.
Case 136/86	*Bureau national interprofessionnel du cognac v. Yves Aubert (BNIC v. Aubert)*, [1987] E.C.R. 4789.
Case 267/86	*Van Eycke v. ASPA (Van Eycke)*, [1988] E.C.R. 4769.
Case 70/87	*Fédération de l'industrie de l'huilerie de la CEE (Fediol) v. Commission (Fediol IV)*, [1989] E.C.R. 1781.
Case C-174/87	*Ricoh & Co. Ltd v. Council (Ricoh)*, [1992] E.C.R. I-1335.
Case C-179/87	*Sharp Corporation v. Council*, [1992] E.C.R. I-1635.
Case 30/88	*Greece v. Commission*, [1989] E.C.R. 3711.
Case 69/89	*Nakajima All Precision v. Council (Nakajima)*, [1991] E.C.R. I-2069.

Case C-106/89	*Marleasing v. La Comercial Internacional de Alimentacion (Marleasing)*, [1990] E.C.R. I-4135.
Case C-192/89	*Sevince v. Staatssecretaris van Justitie (Sevince)*, [1990] E.C.R. I-3461.
Case C-309/89	*Codorniú SA v. Council (Codorniú)*, [1994] E.C.R. I-1853.
Case C-358/89	*Extramet Industrie SA v. Council (Extramet)*, [1991] E.C.R. I-2501.
Case C-9/90	*Francovich et al. v. Italy (Francovich)*, [1991] E.C.R. I-5357.
Case C-18/90	*Office national de l'emploi v. Bahia Kziber (Kziber)*, [1991] E.C.R. I-199.
Case C-163/90	*Administration des Douanes et Droits Indirects v. Léopold Legros et al. (Legros)*, [1992] E.C.R. I-04625.
Case C-269/90	*Technische Universität München v. Hauptzollamt München-Mitte*, [1991] E.C.R. I-5469.
Case C-2/91	*Criminal proceedings against Wolf W. Meng (Meng)*, [1993] E.C.R. I-5751.
Case C-185/91	*Bundesanstalt für den Güterfernverkehr v. Gebrüder Reiff GmbH & Co. KG (Reiff)*, [1993] E.C.R. I-5801.
Case C-188/91	*Deutsche Shell AG v. Hauptzollamt Hamburg-Harburg (Deutsche Shell)*, [1993] E.C.R. 363.
Case C-225/91	*Matra v. Commission*, [1993] E.C.R. I-3203.
Case C-237/91	*Kazim Kus v. Landeshauptstadt Wiesbaden (Kus)*, [1992] E.C.R. I-6781.
Case C-245/91	*Criminal proceedings against Ohra Schadeverzekeringen NV (Ohra)*, [1993] E.C.R. I-5851.
Case C-312/91	*Procedural issue relating to a seizure of goods belonging to Metalsa Srl (Metalsa)*, [1993] E.C.R. I-3751.
Case C-432/92	*The Queen v. Minister of Agriculture, Fisheries and Food, ex parte S. P. Anastasiou (Pissouri) Ltd and others (Anastasiou et al.)*, [1994] E.C.R. I-3087.
Joined Cases C-46/93 and C-48/93	*Brasserie du Pêcheur SA v. Bundesrepublik Deutschland and The Queen v. Secretary of State for Transport, ex parte: Factortame Ltd and others (Brasserie du Pêcheur and Factortame)*, [1996] E.C.R. I-1029.
Case C-153/93	*Germany v. Delta*, [1994] E.C.R. I-2517.
Case C-188/93	*TWD Textilwerke Deggendorf GmbH v. Germany*, [1994] E.C.R. I-833.

Case C-280/93	*Germany v. Council (Bananas)*, [1994] E.C.R. 4973.
Case C-469/93	*Amministrazione delle Finanze dello Stato v. Chiquita Italia SpA (Chiquita Italia)*, [1995] E.C.R. I-4533.
Case C-5/94	*The Queen v. Ministry of Agriculture, Fisheries and Food, ex parte: Hedley Lomas (Ireland) Ltd. (Hedley Lomas)*, [1996] E.C.R. I-2553.
Case C-61/94	*Commission v. Germany*, [1996] E.C.R. I-3989.
Case C-70/94	*Fritz Werner Industrie-Ausrüstungen GmbH v. Germany (Werner)*, [1995] E.C.R. I-3189.
Case C-83/94	*Criminal proceedings against Peter Leifer et al. (Leifer et al.)*, [1995] E.C.R. I-3231.
Case C-96/94	*Spediporto v. SMG*, [1995] E.C.R. I-2883.
Case C-103/94	*Zoulika Krid v. Caisse nationale d'assurance vieillesse des travailleurs salariés (CNAVTS) (Krid v. CNAVTS)*, [1995] E.C.R. I-719.
Case C-190/94	*Dillenkofer et al. v. Germany (Dillenkofer et al.)*, [1996] E.C.R. I-4845.
Case C-122/95	*Germany v. Council (Bananas II)*, [1998] E.C.R. I-973.
Joined cases C-359/95 P and C-379/95 P	*Commission and Fance v. Ladbroke Racing Ltd. (Ladbroke)*, [1997] E.C.R. I-6265.
Case C-53/96	*Hermès v. FHT*, [1998] E.C.R. I-3603.
Case C-149/96	*Portugal v. Council*, [1999] E.C.R. I-8395.
Case C-162/96	*Racke GmbH & Co. v. Hauptzollamt Mainz (Racke)*, [1998] E.C.R. I-3655.
Case C-352/96	*Italy v. Council*, [1998] E.C.R. I-6937.
Case C-401/96	*Somaco v. Commission*, [1998] E.C.R. I-02587.
Case C-104/97 P	*Atlanta AG v. Council and Commission (Atlanta)*, [1999] E.C.R. I-6983.
Joined Cases C-300/98 and C-392/98	*Parfums Christian Dior SA v. TUK Consultancy BV and Assco Gerüste GmbH and Rob van Dijk v. Wilhelm Layher GmbH & Co. KG and Layher BV (Dior et al.)*, [2000] E.C.R. I-11307.
Case C-352/98	*Laboratoires pharmaceutiques Bergaderm SA and Jean-Jacques Goupil v. Commission (Bergaderm)*, [2000] E.C.R. I-5291.
Case C-377/98	*Netherlands v. Parliament and Council*, [2001] E.C.R. I-7079.
Case C-9/99	*Echirolles Distribution SA v. Association du Dauphiné et al.*, [2000] E.C.R. I-8207.

Case C-63/99	*The Queen v. Secretary of State for the Home Department, ex parte Gloszczuk (Gloszczuk)*, [2001] E.C.R. I-06369.
Case C-307/99	*OGT Fruchthandelsgesellschaft mbH v. Hauptzollamt Hamburg-St. Annen (OGT Fruchthandelsgesellschaft)*, [2001] E.C.R. I-3159.
Case C-50/00	*Unión de Pequeños Agricultores v. Council (UPA)*, [2002] E.C.R. I-6677.
Case C-76/00 P	*Petrotub and Republica v. Council*, [2003] E.C.R. I-79.
Joined Cases C-27/00 and C-122/00	*The Queen v. Secretary of State for the Environment, Transport and the Regions, ex parte Omega Air Ltd. Et al. (Omega Air et al.)*, [2002] E.C.R. I-2569.
Case C-198/01	*Consorzio Industrie Fiammiferi (CIF) v. Autorità Garante della Concorrenza e del Mercato (CIF)*, [2003] E.C.R. I-08055.
Case C-93/02 P	*Biret International v. Council (Biret)*, [2003] E.C.R. I-10497.
Case C-94/02 P	*Biret et Cie v. Council*, [2003] E.C.R. I-10565.
Case C-263/02 P	*Commission v. Jégo-Quéré (Jégo-Quéré)*, [2004] E.C.R. I-3425.
Case C-377/02	*Léon Van Parys NV v. Belgisch Interventie- en Restitutiebureau (BIRB) (Van Parys)*, [2005] E.C.R. I-1465.
Case C-351/04	*Ikea Wholesale Ltd. v. Commissioners of Customs & Excise (Ikea)*, [2007] E.C.R. I-7723.
Joined Cases C-120/06P and C-121/06P	*Fabbrica italiana accumulatori motocarri Montecchio SpA (FIAMM) and Others v. Council and Commission (FIAMM & Fedon)*, [2008] E.C.R. I-6513.
Case C-308/06	*The Queen, on the application of International Association of Independent Tanker Owners and Others v. Secretary of State for Transport (Intertanko)*, [2008] E.C.R. I-4057.
Opinion 1/75	Understanding on a Local Cost Standard, [1975] E.C.R. 1355.
Opinion 1/91	EEA, [1991] E.C.R. I-6079.
Opinion 2/91	ILO Convention 170, [1993] E.C.R. I-1061.
Opinion 2/92	OECD, [1995] E.C.R. I-521.
Opinion 1/94	Agreement Establishing the WTO, [1994] E.C.R. I-5267.
Opinion 3/94	GATT-WTO Bananas, [1995] E.C.R. I-4577.
Ruling 1/78	Article 103, Euratom, [1978] E.C.R. 2151.

Judgments of the CFI

Case T-44/90	*La Cinq v. Commission*, [1992] E.C.R. II-1.
Case T-7/92	*Asia Motor France et al. v. Commission (Asia Motor France II)*, [1993] E.C.R. II-669.
Case T-37/92	*Bureau Européen des Unions des Consommateurs and National Consumer Council v. Commission (BEUC and NCC)*, [1994] E.C.R. II-285.
Case T-513/93	*Consiglio nazionale degli spedizionieri doganali v. Commission (CNSD)*, [2001] E.C.R. II-1807.
Case T-387/94	*Asia Motor France et al. v. Commission (Asia Motor France III)*, [1996] E.C.R. II-961.
Case T-2/95	*Industrie des poudres sphériques v. Council*, [1998] E.C.R. II-3939.
Case T-228/97	*Irish Sugar v. Commission*, [1999] E.C.R. II-2969.
Joined cases T-33/98 and T-34/98	*Petrotub SA and Republica SA v. Council*, [1999] E.C.R. II-3837.
Joined cases T-191/98, T-212/98 to T-214/98	*Atlantic Container Line v. Commission*, [2003] E.C.R. II-3275.
Case T-18/99	*Cordis Obst und Gemüse Grosshandel GmbH v. Commission*, [2001] E.C.R. II-913.
Case T-30/99	*Bocchi Food Trade International GmbH v. Commission*, [2001] E.C.R. II-943.
Case T-52/99	*T. Port GmbH & Co. KG v. Commission*, [2001] E.C.R. II-981.
Case T-69/00	*Fabbrica italiana accumulatori motocarri Montecchio Spa and Others v. Council and Commission (FIAMM)*, [2005] ECR II-5393.
Case T-174/00	*Biret International v. Council*, [2002] E.C.R. II-17.
Case T-132/01	*Euroalliages and Others v. Commission*, [2003] E.C.R. II-2359.
Case T-135/01	*Giorgio Fedon & Figli Spa and Others v. Council and Commission (Fedon)*, [2005] ECR II-29.
Case T-177/01	*Jégo-Quéré & Cie v. Commission*, [2002] E.C.R. II-2365.

Case T-317/02 *Fédération des industries condimentaires de France (FICF) et al. v. Commission,* [2004] E.C.R. II-04325.

Case T-45/06 *Reliance Industries Ltd v. Council and Commission,* [2008] E.C.R. II-2399.

Commission Decisions

Commission Decision 72/1600 of 2 January 1973 relating to proceedings under Articles 85 and 86 of the EEC Treaty (IV/26.918 – *European Sugar Industry*), OJ 1973 L 140/17.

Commission Decision 74/634 of 29 November 1974 relating to proceedings under Article 85 of the Treaty establishing the EEC (IV/27.095 – *Franco-Japanese ball-bearings agreement*), OJ 1974 L 343/19.

Commission Decision 75/77 of 8 January 1975 relating to a proceeding under Article 85 of the EEC Treaty (IV/27.039 – *Preserved Mushrooms*), OJ 1975 L 29/26.

Commission Decision 78/670 of 20 July 1978 relating to a proceeding under Article 85 of the EEC Treaty (IV/28.852 – *GB-Inno-BM v. Fedetab*; IV/29.127 – *Mestdagh-Huyghebaert v. Fedetab* and IV/29.149 – *Fedetab Recommendation*), OJ 1978 L 224/29.

Commission Decision 80/47 of 20 December 1979 on surveillance and protective measures which Member States may be authorized to take in respect of imports of certain products originating in third countries and put into free circulation in another Member State, OJ 1980 L 16/14.

Commission Decision 82/506 of 15 July 1982 relating to a proceeding under Article 85 of the EEC Treaty (IV/29.525 and IV/30.000 – *SSI*), OJ 1982 L 232/1.

Commission Decision 83/126 of 30 March 1983 terminating the anti-dumping proceeding concerning imports of television image and sound recorders or reproducers originating in Japan, OJ 1983 L 86/23.

Commission Decision 84/405 of 6 August 1984 relating to a proceeding under Article 85 of the EEC Treaty (IV/30.350 – *Zinc Producer Group*), OJ 1984 L 220/27.

Commission Decision 85/206 of 19 December 1984 relating to a proceeding under Article 85 of the EEC Treaty (IV/26.870 – *Aluminium Imports from Eastern Europe*), OJ 1985 L 92/1.

Commission Decision of 20 October 2004 relating to a proceeding under Article 81(1) of the EC Treaty (Case COMP/C.38.238/B.2 – *Raw Tobacco Spain*), not yet published in the OJ.

GATT 1947 – Panel Reports

L/1923 adopted on 16 November 1962, 11S/95	Uruguayan Recourse to Article XXIII.
L/4687 adopted on 18 October 1978, 25S/68	EEC – Programme of Minimum Import Prices.
L/5047 adopted on 10 November 1980, 27S/98	EEC – Restrictions on Imports of Apples from Chile.
L/5504 adopted on 7 February 1984, 30S/140	Canada – Administration of the Foreign Investment Review Act.
L/6216 adopted on 10 November 1987, 34S/83	Japan – Customs Duties, Taxes and Labelling Practices on Imported Wines and Alcoholic Beverages.
L/6253 adopted on 2 February 1988, 35S/163	Japan – Restrictions on Imports of Certain Agricultural Products.
L/6309 adopted on 4 May 1988, 35S/116	Japan – Trade in Semi-Conductors.
L/6491 adopted on 22 June 1989, 36S/93	EEC – Restrictions on Imports of Dessert Apples – Complaint by Chile.
DS23/R adopted on 19 June 1992, 39S/206	United States – Measures Affecting Alcoholic and Malt Beverages.

WTO – Panel Reports and Appellate Body Reports

WT/DS8/R, WT/DS10/R, WT/DS11/R 11 July 1996	Japan – Taxes on Alcoholic Beverages ("Japan – Alcoholic Beverages II"), Panel Report.
WT/DS22/R 20 March 1997	Brazil – Measures Affecting Desiccated Coconut ("Brazil – Desiccated Coconut"), Panel Report.
WT/DS44/R 31 March 1998	Japan – Measures Affecting Consumer Photographic Film and Paper ("Japan – Film"), Panel Report.
WT/DS75/R, WT/DS84/R 17 September 1998	Korea – Taxes on Alcoholic Beverages ("Korea – Alcoholic Beverages"), Panel Report.

WT/DS87/R, WT/DS110/R 15 June 1999	Chile – Taxes on Alcoholic Beverages ("Chile – Alcoholic Beverages"), Panel Report.
WT/DS98/R 21 June 1999	Korea – Definitive Safeguard Measures on Imports of Certain Dairy Products ("Korea – Dairy"), Panel Report.
WT/DS121/R 25 June 1999	Argentina – Safeguard Measures on Imports of Footwear ("Argentina – Footwear"), Panel Report.
WT/DS155/R 19 December 2000	Argentina – Measures Affecting the Export of Bovine Hides and the Import of Finished Leather ("Argentina – Hides and Leather"), Panel Report.
WT/DS152/R 22 December 1999	United States – Sections 301–310 of the Trade Act of 1974 ("US – Section 301"), Panel Report.
WT/DS177/R, WT/DS178/R 21 December 2000	United States – Safeguard Measures on Imports of Fresh, Chilled or Frozen Lamb Meat from New Zealand and Australia ("US – Lamb"), Panel Report.
WT/DS194/R 29 June 2001	United States – Measures treating Exports Restraints as Subsidies ("US – Export Restraints"), Panel Report.
WT/DS236/R 27 September 2002	United States – Preliminary Determinations with Respect to Certain Softwood Lumber from Canada ("US – Softwood Lumber III"), Panel Report.
WT/DS238/R 14 February 2003	Argentina – Definitive Safeguard Measure on Imports of Preserved Peaches ("Argentina – Preserved Peaches"), Panel Report.
WT/DS204/R 2 April 2004	Mexico – Measures Affecting Telecommunication Services, Panel Report.
WT/DS247, G/ADP/D40/2, G/L/522/Add.1, WT/DS247/2 16 November 2006	United States – Provisional Anti-Dumping Measure on Imports of Certain Softwood Lumber from Canada, Notification of Mutually Agreed Solution
WT/DS248/R, WT/DS249/R, WT/DS251/R, WT/DS252/R, WT/DS253/R, WT/DS254/R, WT/DS258/R, WT/DS259/R 11 July 2003	United States – Definitive Safeguard Measures on Imports of Certain Steel Products ("US – Certain Steel Products"), Panel Report.

WT/DS257 29 August 2003	United States – Final Countervailing Duty Determination with Respect to Certain Softwood Lumber from Canada ("US – Softwood Lumber IV"), Panel Report.
WT/DS264/R 13 April 2004	United States – Final Dumping Determination on Softwood Lumber from Canada ("US – Softwood Lumber V"), Panel Report.
WT/DS277/R 22 March 2004	United States – Investigation of the International Trade Commission in Softwood Lumber from Canada ("US – Softwood Lumber VI"), Panel Report.
WT/DS311, G/L/679/Add.1, G/SCM/D60/2, WT/DS311/2 16 November 2006	United States – Reviews of Countervailing Duty on Softwood Lumber from Canada, Notification of Mutually Agreed Solution
AB-1996-2 4 October 1996, WT/DS8/AB/R, WT/DS10/AB/R, WT/DS11/AB/R	Japan – Taxes on Alcoholic Beverages ("Japan – Alcoholic Beverages II"), Appellate Body Report.
AB-1997-3 9 September 1997, WT/DS27/AB/R	European Communities – Regime for the Importation, Sale and Distribution of Bananas ("EC – Bananas III"), Appellate Body Report.
AB-1997-4 13 February 1998, WT/DS26/AB/R, WT/DS48/AB/R	European Communities – Measures Concerning Meat and Meat Products (Hormones) ("EC – Meat (Hormones)"), Appellate Body Report.
AB-1998-7 18 January 1999, WT/DS75/AB/R, WT/DS84/AB/R	Korea – Taxes on Alcoholic Beverages ("Korea – Alcoholic Beverages"), Appellate Body Report.
AB 1999-7 14 December 1999, WT/DS121/AB/R	Argentina – Safeguard Measures on Imports of Footwear ("Argentina – Footwear"), Appellate Body Report.
AB-1999-8 14 December 1999, WT/DS98/AB/R	Korea – Definitive Safeguard Measures on Imports of Certain Dairy Products ("Korea – Dairy"), Appellate Body Report.
AB-1999-5 22 October 1999, WT/DS34/AB/R	Turkey – Restrictions on Imports of Textile and Clothing Products ("Turkey – Textiles"), Appellate Body Report.

AB-2000-10 22 December 2000, WT/DS166/AB/R	United States – Definitive Safeguard Measures on Imports of Wheat Gluten from the EC ("US – Wheat Gluten"), Appellate Body Report.
AB-2001-1 1 May 2001, WT/DS177/AB/R, WT/DS178/AB/R	United States – Safeguard Measures on Imports of Fresh, Chilled or Frozen Lamb Meat from New Zealand and Australia ("US – Lamb"), Appellate Body Report
AB-2003-3 10 November 2003, WT/DS248/AB/R, WT/DS249/AB/R, WT/DS251/AB/R, WT/DS252/AB/R, WT/DS253/AB/R, WT/DS254/AB/R, WT/DS258/AB/R, WT/DS259/AB/R	United States – Definitive Safeguard Measures on Imports of Certain Steel Products ("US – Certain Steel Products"), Appellate Body Report.
AB-2004-2 11 August 2004 WT/DS264/AB/R	United States – Final Dumping Determination on Softwood Lumber from Canada ("US – Softwood Lumber V"), Appellate Body Report.

CHAPTER I

Voluntary Export Restraints

1 Introduction

There is something irresistible about colourful phrases such as free and fair competition and free and fair trade. One should, however, not succumb to the temptation of embracing these concepts uncritically. For one thing, freedom and fairness are multifaceted concepts, and for another, there is no guarantee that freedom and fairness are compatible: the liberty of some regularly depends on the restraint of others.

Although economists support international trade – and the liberalisation thereof – with abundant reasons including the theory of comparative advantage and efficiency in specialisation, the history of trade liberalisation suggests that public perception of national and political interests rarely coincide with the economists' judgment, and that lawyers and legislators try to catch up with ever-growing, more sophisticated devices of protectionism.

It appears to be common practice of countries to seek protection of domestic industries from international competition. Crisis conditions and disorderly international markets create particularly strong feelings for protectionism. Significant shifts in the competitive structure of the world economy generate political pressure for trade restrictions as specific sectors or industries seek to protect their declining performance through reduced import competition. Whereas the use of traditional protective devices for a government to restrict imports, such as tariffs and quotas on imports, have been successfully diminished or even been abolished by the GATT 1947 and its successor the WTO/GATT[1], countries persistently try to invent new forms of protectionism.

One of the most significant innovations in world trade policy for a protective device turned out to be Voluntary Export Restraints (VERs) since it was not foreseen by the architects of the GATT, and thus emerged to change the traditional view of protectionism.

Unlike classical protective devices, a VER is – simply put – a voluntary reduction by one country of its exports to another country. The specificity of a VER lays in the fact that the exporting country administers and controls the limitation on trade. In this sense, the export restraint is voluntary.[2]

The term appears, on the surface, ironic. In reality, export restraints are typically implemented upon the insistence of the importing country which seeks protection from a surge of imports from the exporting country. Often, such export restraints root in the threatened application and enforcement of unfair trade laws by the importing country, such as anti-dumping[3] or countervailing duties,[4] or the mere announcement of competition law investigations.[5] VERs are then "of-

1 For the purposes of this book, and for convenience and unless otherwise stated, the acronym "GATT" means not only GATT 1947 but also refers to its successor organisation, the WTO Agreement, more particularly (one of) its Annexes being GATT 1994.

2 It is interesting to note that economics literature explores the validity of the term "voluntary" export restraint by using another standard: If the foreign producer's profit increases by restraining exports to the domestic market, VERs are considered "voluntary". If the foreign producer's profit decreases by restraining export to the domestic market, VERs are considered "involuntary".

3 Interestingly, in economics literature it has also been discussed whether the withdrawal of an anti-dumping petition, without there being a known settlement, such as a suspension agreement or a voluntary export restraint, may further be a signal that foreign and domestic firms have reached a collusive settlement; Taylor, 19. If such was the case, the collusive behaviour could take the form of a privately negotiated VER, probably amounting to some sort of (export) cartel on supply and/or price allocation.

4 An illustrative example of how the imposition of anti-dumping and countervailing duties triggered the acceptance of VERs is the steel industry, cf. POMFRET, (1988) 22 JWT 81 *et seq.* See also Chapter I, 2.2.1.

5 The rationale behind anti-dumping and countervailing duty laws is not so different to the aim pursued by VERs, *i.e.* the protection of domestic producers.

fered" by the exporting country to appease the importing country and to avoid the effects of possible trade frictions between them. As a result, the VER has enabled the country seeking protection for one of its industries to attain the equivalent outcome without implementing tariffs or quotas, and/or without having to invest in lengthy investigation proceedings.

Nevertheless, a VER has several features which differentiate it from tariffs and import quotas. Firstly, it is a policy designed to protect producers in the importing country which is administered by the exporting country. Secondly, it is "source-specific" in the sense that it applies to a limited number of specified exporters (possibly only one) unlike tariffs and import quotas which usually apply to imports from most (or all) of a country's suppliers. An interesting implication of this property is that exporters which are not covered by a particular VER may increase their exports to the importing country when the VER is imposed. These "non-restrained exporters" tend to be primarily countries which are too small to warrant the costs of negotiating an agreement. Thirdly, VERs are typically implemented for a specified period in contrast to other types of trade barrier which are imposed for an indefinite period (although this may make little difference in practice). Summing up, VERs tend to be sector-specific, bilateral, quantitative, temporary and discriminatory.

1.1 A Word on the Concepts and the Notion of VERs

The concepts of VERs are as multi-facetted as is the inconsistent use of terminology[6].

Unlike competition law which is designed to protect consumer interests, the function of anti-dumping and countervailing duty laws is to only protect consumers theoretically in the long run by preventing a foreign company from driving domestic firms out of the market. In fact, domestic consumers face higher prices and fewer choices of product, *i.e.* the economic benefits of the remedies accrue to producers, and the economic costs accrue to consumers.

6 Just like the variety and different use of terms used in English literature, such as export restraint agreement (ERA), voluntary export restraint (VER), voluntary restraint agreement (VRA) or orderly marketing agreement (OMA) (JACKSON, 203),

In its most visible form, a VER occurs as a negotiated bilateral agreement, in which the government of an exporting country agrees to limit its exports of a particular product to an importing country to predetermined levels.[7] Since a restriction on the volume of exports is likely to raise the prices of the good in the market of the importing country, a VER may additionally be negotiated in terms of resale price maintenance.[8] Surprisingly, any such action is also called "voluntary restraint agreement" (VRA) despite the fact that the announcement of the restraint policy is promulgated by the exporting country alone, thus allowing the importing country to pretend it was not involved in the decision-making process and consequently, that there is no official agreement.[9] Another frequently used term for formally agreed export restraints is orderly market agreements (OMAs).[10]

True, the unilateral imposition of a formal export restraint by the exporting country, also known as "auto-limitation", does not require an agreement with the importing country. It may, however, still be the result of protectionist pressures in the importing country or serve to maximise profits in the exporting country.[11] In the latter case, the initiation of the export restraint is not necessarily of governmental nature but may be undertaken by the suppliers, *i.e.* the exporters themselves.

Export restraints may thus also be of informal nature – whether there is government involvement or not – and take the form of, for example, export forecasts, import surveillance, price monitoring, bi-

the German contributions add little to clarify the subtle differences by naming them, for example, "Selbstbeschränkungsabkommen", "Ausfuhrbeschränkungsvereinbarung" or "Marktordnungsabkommen" (MAHNKEN, 293; REUTER, 216).

7 JACKSON, 203; SCHUKNECHT, 101.

8 ROBERTSON, 76 *et seq.*

9 At odds with the majority of authors that underline the overlap of the various terms used as well as the lack of definition, BEISE/OPPERMANN/SANDER, 78, qualify VRAs as agreements in which the importing country explicitly accepts responsibility, thus making a modification of the restraint agreement dependant on their consent. According to SCHUKNECHT, 101, VRAs and OMAs differ from VERs in the sense that the former are modified and enforced by both parties.

10 The terminological confusion is hereby further enhanced as, in the U.S., OMAs are basically formalised VERs in the sense that they have to undergo the procedures laid down in Section 201–203 of the Trade Act of 1974.

11 JONES, 3.

lateral consultations or industry-to-industry arrangements. They then provide for an instrument to monitor the supplies towards a specific market, the importing country, in order to avoid the imposition of mandatory export restrictions.

The variations of contacts or agreements can thus be divided into three categories:[12]

- government-to-government;
- importing government to exporting industry; and
- industry-to-industry (domestic industry in the importing country to competing industry in the exporting country).

It has also been argued that the *legal features* of VERs are that they result from bilateral arrangements between importing and exporting countries, involve the use of private and/or public export restraints, and are deliberately used as a means to circumvent the basic principles of international and domestic trade and competition laws.[13] From this perspective, the above categories are, for the most part, of form and motivation, rather than effect.

The underlying motivation of a VER and the method in which it is implemented has, however, important implications for the status and the legality of VERs under trade and competition laws.

For the purposes of this thesis, it is thus important to clarify that

- in terms of *effect*, a VER is considered to be any restriction on exports that is administered unilaterally by the exporters or their government, and that is induced, whether directly through negotiation or indirectly by means of alternative pressure and intimidation, by the importers or their government; but that
- from a *legal perspective*, the decisive criterion on the notion of VER is whether, at any stage of giving effect to the VER, it can be qualified as governmental or non-governmental in nature.

12 JACKSON, 203.

13 PETERSMANN, (1988) 22 JWT 28 *et seq.*

1.2 Some Factual and Legal Observations

Observers of trade relations have accounted for hundreds of VERs in place in the late 1980s,[14] and it was claimed that over 10% of world trade in the mid-1990s was regulated by VERs.[15]

The significance of VERs as protectionist trade device – and not at last their doubtful success – has lead, however, to the negotiation of their outright ban in the Uruguay Round, when VERs were finally outlawed by the Agreement on Safeguards.[16]

Article 11:1(b) Agreement on Safeguards provides, *inter alia*, that

> […] a Member shall not seek, take or maintain any voluntary export restraints, orderly marketing arrangements or any other similar measure on the export or the import side. These include actions taken by a single Member as well as actions under agreements, arrangements and understandings entered into by two or more Members. […]

According to its original footnote 4, examples of similar measures include export moderation, export-price or import-price monitoring systems, export or import surveillance, compulsory import cartels and

14 For instance, *The Economist* claims the existence of nearly 300 VERs (see "Jousting for Advantage", in: *The Economist*, 22 September 1990, 5).

15 As do GAO/SONG at the opening of their discussion paper (with further annotations).

16 In the course of the negotiation of the Agreement on Safeguards, the GATT Secretariat (hereinafter "Secretariat") was also mandated to compile an inventory of GATT Article XIX actions and "*other measures which appear to serve the same purpose*" which included voluntary export restraints, orderly marketing arrangements, export forecasts, basic price systems, industry-to-industry arrangements etc. In the Secretariat's Background Note, more precisely in Annex B(i) thereof, (MTN.GNG/NG9/W/2/Rev.1, dated 17 August 1987, p. 7 *et seq.*), 96 export restraint arrangements were listed. The Secretariat not only pointed out that the list merely contained those arrangements of which it had knowledge but also that the information in the list is not definitive and subject to further comments. It appears thus fair to say that the list is more than likely non-exhaustive either. Moreover, the overall amount of listed arrangements had decreased by seven, down from 103 arrangements identified in a previous Draft Note by the Secretariat (MTN.GNG/NG9/W/2, dated 12 May 1987) in merely three months. The decrease occurred after the delegations of the Contracting Parties have been invited to verify, correct or complete the information.

discretionary export or import licensing schemes, any of which afford protection.

Moreover, Article 11:3 Agreement on Safeguards specifies that

> [M]embers shall not encourage or support the adoption or maintenance by public and private enterprises of non-governmental measures equivalent to those referred to in paragraph 1.

Following the Uruguay Round, pre-existing public or government-sponsored VERs and similar safeguard measures were to be phased out, and the last *visible* relic deriving from VERs vanished on 1 January 2005 when the Agreement on Textiles and Clothing (ATC) – a transitory regime following the Multifibre Arrangement (MFA) – ended, finally integrating textiles and clothing into the multilateral trading system.

Arguably, this represents the final end of VERs and leaves little room for legal discussion, and one may ask why and to what extent VERs are still worth revisiting. If one considers, however, that

- despite the reported popularity of VERs as a protective device, the lack of judicial cases relating to VERs is simply surprising. Only *few* attempts of challenging VERs have surfaced in the Western Hemisphere before the Agreement on Safeguards entered into force: most notably, (i) the European Community's[17] (EC's) challenge of the U.S.-Japan arrangement on semiconductors[18], and (ii) the U.S. Consumers Union's challenge of the VERs on steel[19];

17 Throughout this book, reference to the EC shall be synonymous to "European Union" (EU), please see in this context "Treaty of Lisbon: A Note on Terminology", p. XIX. On 1 December 2009 the EC was replaced by the EU which succeeds it and takes over all its rights and obligations, and the EC Treaty became the "Treaty on the Functioning of the European Union" (TFEU). Please note that this book also mostly makes reference to the "Community of Fifteen", *i.e.* the EC prior to the enlargement of 1 May 2004 when Cyprus, Czech Republic, Estonia, Hungary, Latvia, Lithuania, Malta, Poland, Slovakia and Slovenia, and of 1 January 2007 when Romania and Bulgaria joined the EU.

18 Panel Report on *Japan – Trade in Semi-Conductors*, L/6309.

19 *Consumers Union of U.S. Inc. v. William P. Rogers, Secretary of State, et al.*, 352 F. Supp. 1319 (D.D.C. 1973).

- Article 11:2 Agreement on Safeguards provided for *one exception per importing country* to maintain a restriction until the end of 1999, and only *one* of all the VERs in place in the mid-1990s, namely the EC's VER on automobiles from Japan, was officially phased out and registered in the Annex of the Agreement on Safeguards accordingly; and
- so far, *not a single* case invoking the sole infringement of Article 11 Agreement on Safeguards has been brought before the Dispute Settlement Body (DSB).

In light of these circumstances, it is hard to believe that all VERs shall appear to have ceased. For instance, it was suggested that the U.S.–Canada Softwood Lumber Agreement which was finalised in May 1996 fitted the legal features of a VER[20], by reducing the quantity of Canadian softwood lumber exports to the U.S., by lifting their prices with charges and supporting the softwood lumber price in the U.S. market,[21] but its illegality under the Agreement on Safeguards was not tested.[22] Also, in December 2000, it was reported that the Clinton Ad-

20 According to PETERSMANN, the legal features of VERs are that they result from bilateral arrangements between importing and exporting countries (usually in the form of price undertakings, quantitative restrictions, surveillance systems or export forecasts), involve the use of private and/or public export restraints, and are deliberately used as a means to circumvent the basic principles of international and domestic trade and competition laws, such as transparent trade policy-making on the import side, nondiscrimination, undistorted competition, and use of safeguard measures subject to substantive and procedural due process (PETERSMANN, (1988) 22 JWT 28 *et seq.*).

21 LEE, (2002) 36 JWT 161.

22 Instead, and almost immediately after the Softwood Lumber Agreement's expiration in 2001, the U.S. lumber industry petitioned the U.S. Department of Commerce (DoC) to impose countervailing duties and brought an anti-dumping claim arguing Canadian lumber companies were engaged in unfair price discrimination. The determination of anti-dumping duties by the DoC was brought before the DSB by Canada (Panel Report on *US – Softwood Lumber V*, WT/DS264) and subsequently appealed (Appellate Body Report on *US- Softwood Lumber V,* WT/DS264/AB/R). On 12 October 2006, the U.S. and Canada informed the DSB, however, that they had reached a mutually agreed solution in all disputes on trade of softwood lumber (WT/DS236/R, WT/DS247/R, WT/DS257/R, WT/DS264/R, WT/DS277/R and WT/DS311/R), and that such

ministration approached Ukrainian officials concerning the possibility of a negotiated restraint agreement on steel exports,[23] and in late 2001, China declined an offer from Japan that the two governments agree on a VER concerning certain vegetables.[24] Admittedly, there are few reports on VERs but one suggestion for their "disappearance" may be that government-sponsored VERs have been replaced by private industry-to-industry arrangements.[25]

Another explanation may be that the attraction of employing VERs, irrespective of whether they are government-sponsored or privately induced, is their lack of transparency, for many of the arrangements are clandestine. The phenomenon of VERs is therefore more likely to lie in their invisibility which, not at last, derives from their close relation to cartel-like agreements.[26] Attempting to remove the immediate threat of international competition by negotiating export restraints with foreign firms amounts, strictly speaking, to some sort

solution was in the form of a comprehensive agreement (a new Softwood Lumber Agreement), dated 12 September 2006 (G/ADP/D42/2, G/L/566/Add.1, WT/DS264/29 as amended on 12 October 2006 by G/ADP/D42/2/Add.1, G/L/566/Add.2, WT/DS264/29/Add.1).

23 *Inside U.S. Trade*, vol. 1, 5 January 2001, p. 12.

24 NAKAGAWA, (2002) 36 JWT 1025 (with further references).

25 As early as 1984, the OECD pointed out that where VERs are essentially private, they closely resemble international cartels and are generally subject to competition laws prohibiting cartels or other forms of collusive behaviour (*Competition and Trade Policies – Their Interaction*, OECD, 1984, paragraph 115).

26 Closely linked therewith is the "infant industry" argument which asserts that a new industry having a potential comparative advantage may not get started unless it is given a temporary protection against foreign competition. Whereas it is broadly accepted that (horizontal) co-operation between firms (who are potential competitors) does not restrict competition if it is the only commercially viable possibility to enter a new market, to launch a new product or service, or to carry out a specific project, most of the modern competition laws rigorously condemn a number of *per se* violations, such as the allocation of markets or customers, price-fixing and limitation of output (see *Hard Core Cartels*, OECD, 2000, 6). Most interestingly, the history of the negotiation of the Agreement on Safeguards reveals that it was considered that safeguard clauses, in order to be "adequate", must take account of the situations they are intended to cover. Such situation categories were proposed to include "infant industries" (cf., for instance, Submission by Switzerland of 18 July 1988, MTN.GNG/NG9/W/20, p. 7).

of market-sharing agreement. Consequently, such agreements are likely to restrict competition, as the supplying firms are required to form – *de facto* – an export cartel.[27]

Such agreements would have then both trade and competition policy implications. Article 11:3 Agreement on Safeguards not only forbids WTO Members to take part in any form in the conclusion or the functioning of such measures, but also to support or encourage measures (equivalent to VERs) of private nature.

1.3 Outline of the Thesis

In the main part of this introduction (Chapter I), an overview of the political economy of VERs as well as their historical background is given so as to illustrate their functioning and to understand the VERs' great appeal to the parties involved in such arrangements. Whilst, for the purposes of this thesis, emphasis is put on VERs in the external relations of the European Community (EC), it is pertinent to expand the discussion to other judicial decisions on VERs outside the EC, or rather the rarity of such decisions in the first place.

The following chapters are designated to detect the reasons for the absence on judicial cases on VERs, and are guided by the following considerations (which, however, will not all be dealt with extensively but rather in a selective, illustrative manner):

Who would actually make a formal complaint against a VER anyway? Country A that establishes (or encourages or supports) the VER is unlikely to complain against its own actions. The importing country B (or the industry in B) that signalled the need for restraint would hardly complain either, since the action is precisely what it had hoped for. Considering moreover that, within the WTO dispute settlement system, no *ex officio* cases are initiated, the only possible complainants would be

- an importing country C (or the industry in C), provided that it suffers greater competitive pressure due to an increase in the

27 KRISHNA (1988), 3; STOLL, (1997) 57 ZaöRV 103 *et seq.*

exports of A that have been diverted from B to the domestic market of C as a result of the VER between country A and B; or
- consumers.

If the VER was government-sponsored (*i.e.* either from government-to-government or from importing government to exporting industry), the following exemplary scenarios may be distinguished:

a) In order to be successful, Country C would have to demonstrate a violation of the Agreement on Safeguards in order to claim nullification or impairment pursuant to GATT Article XXIII.[28]
b) Individuals have no standing in the WTO. Succesfully challenging a VER would thus be dependent on *locus standi* before domestic courts and the effect of WTO/GATT provisions in the domestic legal order.
c) Alternatively, if the VER was attacked for infringing competition law, the following obstacles would have to be overcome. Most countries (i) do not apply their competition laws to (domestic) export cartels, unless these agreements produce effects on the domestic market, and/or (ii) allow for the "state compulsion defence" under which undertakings are not liable where the State by measures of public authority requires them to engage in anti-competitive behaviour.

If the VER was a pure industry-to-industry arrangement (resulting in an export cartel maintained by the exporting industry of Country A), possible scenarios include the following:

a) If neither governmental "encouragement" nor "support" of the private VER as stated in Article 11:3 Agreement on Safeguards can be demonstrated by Country C, it would be faced with the difficulty of raising a *prima facie* case of nullification

28 According to Article 14 Agreement on Safeguards, the provisions of, *inter alia*, GATT Article XXIII as elaborated and applied by the Dispute Settlement Understanding apply to consultations and the settlement of disputes arising under the Agreement on Safeguards.

or impairment under GATT Article XXIII by demonstrating the grounds and reasons for its invocation.

b) Individuals would most likely be devoid of remedies under trade law as there is no government involvement.
c) Again, from a competition law point of view, the difficulty in challenging a VER would lie in the fact that (domestic) export cartels are mostly considered not to affect the domestic market, leaving a possible complainant to seek an action in the importing country (Country B) where the effect is produced.

Chapter II addresses the difficulty of relying on WTO provisions before the European Courts (direct effect of WTO provisions in the EC legal order), reviewing firstly the relationship of WTO and EC law. This discussion is followed by the important, but often misunderstood, issue of what can be termed "invocability", a concept which is similar to "standing". It will thus be determined *who* is entitled to invoke a directly effective provision.

The thesis proceeds in Chapters III and IV in which the boundaries of challenging VERs are demonstrated. It becomes clear from the scenarios above that a successful complaint is not only cumbersome but bears a potential conflict between the trade policy of one country and the competition law of its trading partner. Again, the discussion places its focus on VERs in the external relations of the European Community.

Under this reservation, Chapter III discusses the boundaries of challenging VERs under EU jurisdiction. Within the EU legal order, the emphasis is put on three possibilities of individuals to challenge VERs that are, as a hypothesis, government-sponsored:[29]

- first, the reliance on provisions of the Agreement on Safeguards before the European courts to challenge the validity of a VER;

29 The limitation of the discussion to this hypothesis is motivated by the consideration that VERs of purely private nature most likely contravene competition law (in terms of market-sharing and limitation of output) – a discussion which will only be marginally touched upon in this thesis.

- second, the procedure provided for under the Trade Barriers Regulation (TBR)[30]; and
- third, a possible complaint under EU competition law.

Chapter IV is dedicated to the boundaries of challenging VERs within the WTO legal system. The successfulness of a complaint under GATT Article XXIII shall be determined by reviewing the nature and degree of government involvement necessary under Articles 11:1(b) and 11:3 Agreement on Safeguards on the one hand, and of "governmental measures" under a non-violation complaint pursuant to GATT Article XXIII:1(b) on the other. In particular, it is examined whether a WTO Member's omission to act, *i.e.* by tolerating private undertakings which have the same effect as the measures envisaged in Article 11:1(b) Agreement on Safeguards or by not applying domestic competition laws to private VERs, violates the "good faith" requirement in treaty observation and removes the substance of the Agreement on Safeguards.

Considering that the WTO legal system is primarily directed at measures of governmental (and not of private) nature, the aim of the discussion is to find alternative solutions that allow bringing private VERs within the scope of WTO dispute settlement, and may serve as inspiration for an alternative interpretation of Article 11 Agreement on Safeguards.

Chapter V contains the findings and concluding remarks on – what I term – the "non-complaint" situation of VERs, a sort of safe-harbour in which VERs (continue to) flourish despite their illegality, and describe how this should (and could) be overcome.

30 Council Regulation (EC) No. 3286/94 laying down Community procedures in the field of the common commercial policy in order to ensure the exercise of the Community's rights under international trade rules, in particular those established under the auspices of the World Trade Organization (WTO) (OJ 1994 L 349/71), as amended by Council Regulation (EC) No. 356/95 of 20 February 1995 (OJ 1995 L 41/3) and by Council Regulation (EC) No. 125/2008 of 12 February 2008 (OJ 2008 L40/1).

2 The Political Economy of Voluntary Export Restraints

The volume of economic and political literature dedicated to the effects of VERs is considerable and has grown in proportion to the global significance of VERs as trade instruments – mainly due to their non-transparent nature. Economists, research institutes and political scientists began to examine the phenomenon of VERs in the early 1980s – the "golden era" of grey area measures – and continue to resume the subject.

Interestingly, most theoretical economic analyses of VERs invariably conclude that they are harmful for the welfare of the importing country, and the traditional wisdom is that VERs may be beneficial for the exporting country, *i.e.* the country that restricts its exports. This conclusion would support the usage of the term "voluntary", representing the main characteristic of these export restrictions.

Historical experience reveals, however, that such export restrictions are usually not only induced – whether directly through negotiation or indirectly by means of alternative pressure and intimidation – by the importers or their trade authorities but that the successful negotiation of a VER is also the result of the obvious use of political and economic power.[31] Accordingly, a preference of large countries or trading blocs for such discriminatory practices may be detected,[32] again rendering the term "voluntary" somewhat inadequate. Especially in times of either domestic or international economic instability, large trading countries, such as the United States of America (U.S.), or important trading blocs like the European Community (EC) have sought to obtain temporary relief for certain of their industries by inducing trade restrictions on their (usually smaller) trading partners. The Back-

31 It is maintained that, while VERs violated GATT legalisms, they accorded well with the "reality of power politics" (FINGER, 6) which results from the VERs' ethic of reciprocity (FINGER/NG/WANGCHUK, 3 *et seq.*).

32 It has been argued, on a more general note, that regional integration agreements (and customs unions), such as the EC, may lead to an increase in the responsiveness of trade authorities to protectionist demands. This may be particularly the case if the regional integration agreement sets up an institutional framework which is open to (or even stimulates) lobbying activities; BILAL, (1998) 36 JCMS 20 *et seq.*

ground Note by the Secretariat on the "Inventory of Article XIX Actions and other Measures which Appear to Serve the Same Purpose"[33] reveals that the EC was involved in 50% of all the export restraint arrangements known to the GATT Secretariat. The U.S. hold second place in this doubtful hit list with 36%.[34] Naturally, the bilateralism of such actions contains advantages as certain trading partners can be singled out, and the extent of potential retaliation is hence minimised.

The reasons for the popularity of VERs have thus also to be addressed in the political sphere. Before the approach of political science is evaluated, the economic background of VERs is to be outlined. Since economic literature is usually highly technical, employing a variety of economic models, graphs, and mathematical equations, the following discussion mainly limits itself to the theoretical findings concerning the effects and consequences of VERs, thus summarising the achievements on the issue of a number of representative scholars and experts of economics.

2.1 The Economy of Voluntary Export Restraints

From an economic viewpoint, the main feature distinguishing VERs from tariffs and quotas is their inherently discriminatory nature, and the fact that they are administered by the exporting country. In their function as quantitative restrictions, VERs reduce supply in the importing country and cause an artificial increase in prices which is the source of quota rents. In the case of a quota, the rent accrues to the importing country. The same is true in respect to the levy of a tariff: the importing country imposes a tax and collects revenue. VERs, in contrast, are administered by the exporting country (or the export in-

33 MTN.GNG/NG9/W/2/Rev.1.

34 Own calculations based on Annex B(i) of the Background Note by the Secretariat on the "Inventory of Article XIX Actions and other Measures which Appear to Serve the Same Purpose", dated 17 August 1987 (*ibid.*). COLEMAN/ YOFFIE report that the U.S. and the EC accounted for more than 80% of all VERs in the late 1980s, (1990) 37 Proceedings of the Academy of Political Science 140. ITOH/NAGAOKA, 476, find, based on their research, a figure of 50% for the EC and 26% for the U.S.

dustry) which benefits from the rent collection.[35] Whilst this characteristic eases the bargaining process between the importing and the exporting country it may have negative effects on market competition in the exporting country.

2.2.1 The Impact of VERs on Price Levels

There are a number of alternatives of how an exporting producer would react in order to compensate for the reduced level of sales created by the VER: it could contemplate raising the prices to accommodate the restraint. Or it could reduce the quality and thus the demand for the restricted product. A reduction in quality will, however, only be desirable for the exporting producer, if lower production costs and the quantitatively limited sales exceed the profits accruing by means of a price increase. This implies that a VER is more likely to induce an exporting producer to increase the quality and hence the price of the restricted product.[36]

Typically, a VER affects a number of exporting producers which are usually in competition with each other. The initial studies of the economic effects of VERs focus on a two-country analysis, comparing the welfare of the importing country in the presence and the absence of the VER. *Feenstra*[37] documents the impact of the VER between Japan and the United States regarding the export of Japanese automobiles into the U.S. market on the list prices of Japanese cars by a collection of data on a variety of Japanese car models over the calendar years 1980 to 1985. He demonstrates that an *ad valorem* tariff will not affect the quality level chosen by the producers but that, in the presence of a VER on imports, the quality content, such as horsepower or vehicle size, will be increased. His calculation of changes in the national welfare recognises that the increase in Japanese import prices following the VER is partly due to such quality improvements.[38] In

35 COLEMAN/YOFFIE, (1990) 37 Proceedings of the Academy of Political Science 139.

36 GREENAWAY/HINDLEY, 5.

37 FEENSTRA, [1988] Quarterly Journal of Economics, 131 *et seq.*

38 Also referred to as quality upgrading (for a theoretical treatment of upgrading, cf. SUARDI, 20 *et seq.*); TURNER/TUVERI support this conclusion and suggest that the quality differences in cars exported reflect a deliberate upgrading of the

order to estimate the welfare loss resulting from the price rise induced by the VER (but uncompensated for by the increased quality), hedonic regressions are used to explain the variation in automobile prices on the basis of car model characteristics like length, weight, horsepower, gas mileage or air-conditioning. Therefrom, a general inflationary effect not related to the VER is subtracted in order to get the increase in import prices directly caused by the VER. After then deducing the result of quality improvement as a further indicator of the price increase, he reaches a *de facto* price increase for which the U.S. consumer is not compensated by a change in quality.

Simply put, the relationship between price increases and product differentiation[39] in the presence of an export restraint may be explained as follows: A VER acts similar to a capacity constraint on the foreign producer. This quantitative constraint generates not only an incentive for the exporting producer to increase prices and improve the quality of the products, but also for the domestic producer to increase prices in order to create rationing at the foreign producer and benefit from those rationed consumers who turn back to the domestic producer. In other words, VERs allow the domestic producer to act as monopolist along the residual demand. The level of this demand is dependent on the extent to which the rationed consumers are willing to buy the domestic product instead of refraining from consumption. It may therefore be alleged that capturing the rationed consumers will be crucial to boost residual demand (and prices), whereby product differentiation may be predestined to achieve this.[40]

product mix presented by Japanese producers anxious to maximise profits given the import volume ceilings imposed by the VER; TURNER/TUVERI, 100 *et seq.*

39 There have also been models which suggest that, where firms commit to strategic variables such as products' characteristics, VERs decrease Research and Development (R&D) expenses by the domestic producers. This proposal was, however, subsequently qualified to the end that no general finding may be made regarding innovation and R&D; see WAUTHY, (2002) 6 Economics Bulletin 6.

40 BOCCARD/WAUTHY, 3 *et seq.*

The economic finding that VERs are likely to cause price increases[41] is also supported by factual events. For instance, the Japanese VER on cars has led to fairly dramatic price increases: Japanese prices increased by approximately USD 800 in the first year in which the VER was put in place, and even more in the subsequent years. In 1987, the VER raised Japanese prices by a sales-weighted average of about USD 1775.[42] Another example is the U.S. machine tool industry, namely the National Machine Tool Builders Association, which submitted a petition to the Secretary of Commerce requesting import quotas based on the view that imports of machine tools threatened the national security.[43] After a review by the administration, President Ronald Reagan issued a statement that he intended to seek VERs with Taiwan, West Germany, Japan and Switzerland.[44] Most interestingly, the machine tool industry petitioned, *inter alia*, that the quotas inherent in the VER were to be expressed "*in terms of value, instead of units*" to prevent foreign producers from concentrating their exports to the U.S. in the "*highest priced models*".[45] The industry thus appears to have learned from other industries' experiences.

41 It was even suggested that, based on the example of the EC – Japan VER on Video Cassette Recorders, a VER already affects the pricing behaviour of the exporters concerned in its pre-implementing stage, see OHASHI, 3 *et seq.*

42 BERRY/LEVINSOHN/PAKES, 25. Other economic studies calculated that the VER added about USD 2'000 to the price of a midsize American car (BARFIELD, 41).

43 According to the "Section 232 Investigations Program Guide" compiled by the Bureau of Industry and Security (Office of Strategic Industries and Economic Security, Strategic Analysis Division) in September 2004, no other investigation conducted under the Trade Expansion Act of 1962 led to the initiation or negotiation of VERs (13 *et seq.*).

44 Presidential Statement on the Machine Tool Industry, 20 May 1986 (Ronald Reagan Presidential Library). Product lines to be targeted by the VER included machining centers, computer-controlled and non-computer-controlled lathes, computer-controlled and non-computer-controlled punching and shearing machines, as well as milling machines.

45 COLEMAN/YOFFIE, (1990) 37 Proceedings of the Academy of Political Science 146 (with further annotations).

2.1.2 The Creation of Rent-Seeking Activities

Given that a VER brings about higher prices of the restrained products, producers in the exporting country would want to increase their supplies to the more profitable markets, whereas the VER requires that the aggregate supply is lower. In order to achieve a reduced aggregate level of exports, the competing exporting producers must in some way be co-ordinated. This may be accomplished either by governmental intervention or through private arrangements. For instance, the allocation of export rights obliges a government to allow, if not even to favour, the creation of an export cartel. Whereas an auction system is rarely used in order to avoid the birth of an export monopoly, with the most efficient producer buying all disposable quotas, it is likely that intra-industry arrangements are used for the allocation of export rights. The effect of either means to achieve the export restraint is the creation of valuable export rights. If a government auctions the export rights for their full price, then the government receives the quota rents, thus making the quota rent an equivalent measure to a specific export tax. If the government gives away the export rights, or is not involved at all, then the quota rent would typically accrue to the exporting producers.[46] In effect, exporting producers (or their government) are given the tariff revenue that would be received by the importing country were a tariff used instead of a VER.[47]

Thus, established exporting producers not only capture quota rents but also obtain a strategic advantage with respect to new market entrants. A VER helps to create barriers to entry which act both among competitors in the exporting country and among different exporting countries when the VER involves several countries. At an international level, collusive behaviour may further be nourished with exporters sharing the benefits of rent transfers with the importing producers. VERs are thus a suitable device for market sharing.[48]

46 This rent transfer assumes a competitive market structure on both the exporting and the importing side. If the importing market is monopolised, the quota rents would accrue to the monopoly importer. See BERGSTEN *et al.*, 22.

47 JONES, 26.

48 Cf. Chapter I, 2.2.2.

2.1.3 The Effect of VERs on Different Import Sources

Since VERs are usually negotiated on a bilateral basis, different sources of imports can be treated differently, *i.e.* discriminatory. Domestic producers in the importing country are better off with a VER than without one, because the quantitative limitation of foreign supplies and the increase in prices gives them a competitive advantage. This is particularly true if the domestic producers are competitive vis-à-vis non-restricted suppliers. As far as these third-country suppliers are concerned, they end up with a highly improved situation: the strongest competitors are limited by the VER and the market price is higher so that the countries excluded from the VER can expand their exports or simply benefit from the rent created by the VER.[49]

Drawing on *Feenstra* to compute the price change of Japanese cars that was not compensated for by better car characteristics, *i.e.* quality, and attributing the remaining price increase to the VER, *Dinopoulos* and *Kreinin*[50] introduced a new framework that advances the traditional two-country general-equilibrium model in studying VERs. They claim that the traditional model fails to capture an essential distinction between an import quota and a VER. While an import quota is often levied on imports from all sources of supply, a VER is inherently discriminatory to one country. This is the case because a VER is usually negotiated with one supplying country at a time (in their study, the U.S. and Japan), leaving other suppliers (European suppliers) free of restrictions. According to their estimate, the U.S. welfare loss to Europe exceeds its loss to Japan, thereby demonstrating the significance of third-country suppliers. They conclude that (i) the welfare of the U.S. is higher under a quota than under an equivalent VER, (ii) the welfare of Europe (the EC as third country) is higher under a VER than a quota, and (iii) Japan's welfare is indeterminate because of the substitution from third-country sources.

49 However, when the producers in the third country appear to be much more efficient than domestic producers, the same political pressures which led to the creation of the VER will call for its extension to them. An example for such "snowball effect" is the conclusion of the Multifibre Arrangement (MFA).

50 DINOPOULOS/KREININ, (1989) 26 Journal of International Economics, 170 *et seq.*

Clearly, if a VER simply causes the replacement of imports from one foreign source by imports from another foreign source, the aim of effectively protecting the domestic industry is not advanced.[51] This is particularly true for cases of trade diversion, whereby the sales lost by a low-cost supplier due to a VER are replaced by higher-cost exporters, who are not restrained by a VER, rather than by domestic producers.[52]

Moreover, *de Melo* and *Winters*[53] claim that a fairly general theoretical model of a competitive industry subject to a VER shows that a VER is likely to lead to both industry contraction and spill-over to unrestricted export markets. By using the example of the Taiwanese leather footwear industry which was subject to a VER between July 1977 and June 1981 under an Orderly Marketing Program (or orderly marketing agreement, OMA) with the U.S., they demonstrate that a VER leads to rising private profits in the exporting country due to the rent transfer from abroad, and to a lower wage for the factors employed in the industry. It follows that the VER has strongly negative distributional implications for exporting countries as profits rise, and wages and employment fall. The possible loss at the industry level may thus reduce the welfare of the exporting country.

In particular, the effect of industry concentration is best understood if one considers that a VER also acts like an entry barrier in the market for exports. Firms in the exporting country which sell in the domestic market only are most likely to be subjected to a contraction of their size, whereas fellow firms that also export are likely to expand. Thus, the voluntary acceptance of export restraints may not only change the oligopoly structure in the market for exports, but also modify the degree of competition in the foreign supplier's domestic market. This implies that incumbent firms with, for instance, a license to

51 DE MELO/MESSERLIN demonstrate that in the event of the European VER on Japanese automobiles, the VERs did not arrest import penetration by third countries because the French consumers simply started buying Italian and German cars when the Japanese imports were restricted. In other words, market share was captured by countries not affected by the VER (DE MELO/MESSERLIN, 14 *et seq.*).

52 GREENAWAY/HINDLEY, 8.

53 DE MELO/WINTERS, (1993) 37 European Economic Review, 1331 *et seq.*

export have interest in renewing VERs in order also to protect their oligopolistic power in the domestic market.[54]

2.1.4 The Impact of VERs on Domestic Output

The output of a domestic industry protected by a VER is likely to rise when that industry is perfectly competitive. Provided that there are anti-competitive elements in the market structure of the industry, the impact of a VER on the domestic output is, however, questionable. Since the quantity of imports is restricted by the VER, a domestic producer is not constrained in his pricing and output policy by the availability of imported substitutes at a price he cannot affect. Contrary to the situation where he would be confronted with import inflows in case he raises his price above the import price, the domestic producer is now in the position to shape an individual pricing policy and output volume. Whereas the domestic producer was one among a number of competitors in the international market prior to the VER, he is now a monopolist with regard to the domestic market.

Provided that a VER covers all foreign producers, the domestic importer is protected to the extent that he can increase his prices and reduce the output in proportion to the shrinking overall market. The VER prevents the substitution of imported output for domestic output. The protection provided by the VER may thus reduce domestic output if a single producer dominates the domestic industry.[55] The effects of VERs on domestic output are therefore dependant on the market structure of the domestic industry.

In a perfectly competitive market, a VER is likely to increase the domestic output whereas in a monopolistic market it may have the opposite effect. Moreover, in oligopolistic markets where few firms

54 De Santis, (2003) Scottish Journal of Political Economy, 247 *et seq.* It was also suggested that the observation of VERs corresponds to their use as either coordinating or quasi-collusive devices in markets in which firms have increasing reaction functions, such as price competition with substitutes or quantity competition with complements; see Calzolari/Lambertini, 18.

55 Whether it is profitable for a single domestic producer to expand output appears to be linear to the severity of the VER, *i.e.* the tighter the restriction on imports the greater the incentive to increase output.

are protected by a VER, it is conceivable that those firms have an incentive to act like a single firm.[56] In a domestic monopoly or oligopoly, VERs also facilitate price-making power since the quantitative limits reduce competition in the importing country.[57] In this respect, a VER contributes to collusive behaviour and anti-competitive market structures.

2.1.5 Summary

It may thus be summarised that the main effect of the VER would be that both the higher-cost domestic producers and also the low-cost importers raise their prices above the level that would otherwise prevail. As a result, the total size of the market is restricted, the level of imports is restrained and consumers experience higher prices than they would in an unrestricted market. The latter can be explained by the fact that, without protection, the additional price competition that would have resulted would have put pressure on other manufacturers, both domestic and foreign, to lower their prices. Whether domestic producers have a higher rate of output and employment cannot be answered conclusively as it is dependent on the domestic market structure.

As regards the impact on market structure and competition, VERs clearly inhibit competition between the different exporters, since their relative market shares are essentially frozen at the time a VER is introduced. Moreover, VERs contribute to collusive behaviour, such as market sharing and price fixing. In terms of trade effects, it is likely that the existence of VERs tend to attract imports from other sources that are not subject to trade restrictions. This import substitution effect may mitigate the anti-competitive effects of the VERs.

These distinguishing economic characteristics offer useful guidance as to the question why VERs are perceived advantageous over tariffs and quotas as protectionist devices, and help to understand the political interests involved.

56 GREENAWAY/HINDLEY, 10.

57 For an economic analysis of the effects of VERs on output and price in monopolistic and oligopolistic import markets, cf. JONES, 29 *et seq*.

2.2 The Politics of Voluntary Export Restraints

Although professional economists repeatedly demonstrated that VERs are an undesirable protective device because of the large costs that reside on the consumers, it appears that these findings – probably often presented in too sophisticated models and based on ambiguous empirical evidence – have done little to dampen the enthusiasm for employing VERs and have lead more to confusion than to enlightenment of the general public. The popularity of VERs among trade politicians and protectionist interest groups (importing and exporting competitors) resides mainly in the fact that their price increases, trade diversion and surreptitious redistributive effects, such as protection rents, elude effective legal disciplines and judicial control. This creates a "no-fault" insurance protection for the actors that tempt a VER. In sum, VERs appear to be a convenient tool for governments and industries to "resolve" trade problems without being subjected to the scrutiny of domestic or international proceedings.

2.2.1 The Political Advantages of VERs for the Government and the Competitors of the Importing Country

Prior to the entry into force of the WTO Agreement, and with it the Agreement on Safeguards, the principal advantage of a VER stemmed from its ability to achieve protectionist ends at low political cost. Since a VER restricts trade on the exporting side, it allows governments under protectionist pressures to circumvent GATT provisions concerning quantitative and discriminatory trade barriers as well as domestic competition laws. Therefore, VERs could be implemented bilaterally and selectively. It usually sufficed to commit few countries and individual producers to restrain themselves in order to attain the desired effect. VERs had thus the international benefit that, unlike measures taken directly against imports, they were not subject to the GATT *proviso* allowing other nations to impose equivalent trade restrictions.[58] In other words, such arrangements do not involve an obligation on the part of the importing country to provide "compensation"

58 The danger of retaliatory measures is minimal since free trade interests are weakened and foreign producers receive compensation in form of rent income.

to the exporting country, as would be the case if the importing country unilaterally imposed equivalent restraints on imports.

Although this benefit eroded the GATT principle of non-discrimination (and of GATT Article XI), it still appealed to the trade authorities of the importing country. The political advantage thus lay in the discriminatory aspect of VERs.[59]

An interesting demonstration of this perception is found in the action brought against the U.S. State Department and foreign and domestic steel producers by the Consumers Union of U.S. Inc., in which efforts by the Executive Branch to bring about reduction in steel imports by means of self-imposed limitations on foreign steel producers were challenged. The factual background of the case was summarised as follows by the U.S. Court of Appeals (District Court of Colombia Circuit):[60]

After steel imports into the U.S. increased more than tenfold in the period between 1958 and 1968, with the great bulk of imports coming from Japan and the EC, the Executive Branch

> [...] regarded the problem created by steel imports as temporary in nature and thus amenable to a short-term solution. It concluded, moreover, that *unilaterally imposed mandatory quotas would pose a danger of retaliation under the GATT, prove inflexible and difficult to terminate*, and have a seriously adverse impact on the foreign relations of the United States. Import limiting agreements negotiated with other governments were likewise rejected on the State Department's advice that negotiated official restrictions, if achievable, would have political consequences for the foreign governments that would also affect our external affairs adversely. Accordingly, the Executive Branch concluded [in 1968] that *voluntary import restraint undertakings by foreign producers offered the best hope* of alleviating the domestic industry's temporary problems *at the least cost to United States foreign, economic and trade policies.* (emphasis added)

In addition, the fact that VERs are directly negotiated between governments or industries and covertly implemented, suggests that secrecy and non-transparency are seen as political advantages.[61] In particular the non-transparency surrounding VERs allows the governments to ap-

59 JONES, 27; PREUSSE, (1991) 25 JWT 8.

60 *Consumers Union of U.S. Inc. v. Henry A. Kissinger, Secretary of State, et al.*, 506 F.2d 136 (1974), 138.

61 BEISE/OPPERMANN/SANDER, 80.

pease domestic interest groups under various headings. Not only may a possible violation of international commitments be "covered", but the government is given a variety of grounds on how to justify the VER. As *Jan Tumlir*[62] has put it already in 1985:

> The current methods of conducting trade policy conflict with most other national objectives. [...] The game itself is of the negative-sum kind: it is about the distribution of losses, not gains. When market shares are negotiated bilaterally with some fifty supplying countries, as in textiles and clothing, or with some fifteen supplying countries, as in steel, it is impossible to satisfy all of them. [...] It is difficult to believe that the method of protection by export restraint was deliberately chosen at the politically responsible levels of governments in full knowledge of what it entails.

Assuming that the government of an importing country is a rational actor maximising a set of interests, it should nevertheless be conceived as an institution with "mixed motives".[63] That is, a government may have preferences for free trade and improving consumer welfare, but these preferences are often constrained by domestic political pressure for trade barriers. In particular in democratic countries, trade authorities may be confronted with the dilemma of maximising the national welfare through free trade and to secure the domestic industries' support by providing some form of trade protection.

It therefore comes as no surprise that domestic industries that persuade their governments to protect them from foreign competition have become very innovative in presenting their cases to the public as well as to the authorities. They have learned not to purely argue in terms of their own private gain but to assert that protection benefits the public interest. Often they appeal to the patriotism and nationalistic attitude of fellow citizens and thus, bring back a national tendency

62 TUMLIR, 54.

63 Acknowledging the VERs' appeal to the policymakers with mixed motives, *The Economist* wrote: "*[T]hese days politicians all over the world declare themselves in favour of free trade. When it comes to voting for it, they are not so sure. The reason is not just the pressure of special-interest politics, but the convenience that the VERs bring to the political decision-making process*" (cf. "The Economics of Free Trade", in: *The Economist*, 22 September 1990, 12).

towards mercantilism enhanced by the belief that national wealth is automatically improved by reducing imports.[64]

From the viewpoint of the government under protectionist pressure, the political appeal of VERs in such line of reasoning lies in the perception that a country dependent on foreign sources of supply is vulnerable. A strong and economically healthy country would thus be considered right in compelling foreign countries to reduce exports to its domestic market not only in order to redress a probable trade deficit but for the sake of national security.

The non-transparency of VERs may even satisfy the needs of a protectionist government that wishes to seem to be promoting trade liberalism. This is well illustrated by the VER on steel between the U.S. and the EC[65] , where policymakers sought to appear as free traders while actually acting as protectionists:

In July 1984, the USITC found by a three-to-two vote that imports had been a substantial cause of serious injury in five of the nine major steel import categories. Trade Representative William E. Brock announced that President Ronald Reagan was rejecting the USITC recommendation:[66]

64 Such arguments usually centre around "keeping the money at home" and are based on the view that when domestic residents buy imported goods, the country gets the goods and the foreigners get the money. On the other hand, when the residents buy domestic goods, the country keeps both the goods and the money. Hence the country gets richer by preventing imports. The utter fallacy of this argument is rooted in the crude mercantilistic theory which maintained that money is wealth itself. Similarly, arguments claiming that the domestic producers have a right to the domestic market and thus, by eliminating foreign imports, employment can be maintained or even increased, disregard that any shifts from imports to domestic production are offset by a contraction of exports. The importing industry can increase its output only by attracting more resources from the export industry. In fact, this argument amounts to saying that the country should not specialise in the commodities in which it has a comparative advantage.

65 In 1982, the U.S. and the EC negotiated a steel VER. In the "1984 Voluntary Restraint Agreement Program", twenty enforceable agreements were negotiated to limit steel imports for five years. These VERs were extended through March 1992.

66 DESTLER, 159.

> The President has clearly determined that protectionism is not in the national interest. It costs jobs, raises prices and undermines our ability to compete here and abroad.

But having advocated free trade, Brock further noted that American steel firms and workers faced an "unprecedented and unacceptable" surge of imported steel due to "massive unfair trade practices" and "diversion of steel imports into the U.S. markets due to quotas and import restraints in other nations". To eliminate such practices, the government would "vigorously enforce U.S. fair trade laws". Brock added:[67]

> The President's decision assumes the continuation of the US / European Community's arrangement on steel as well as voluntary agreements announced earlier by Mexico and South Africa [...] in some instances the US Trade Representative could be instructed to negotiate voluntary restraint agreements with [other] countries.

The promotion of VERs as "fair trade" measures (rather than protection) was a convenient manoeuvre for the Reagan Administration: After U.S. producers previously persuaded the government to conclude VERs with Japan and Western Europe in the period from 1969 to 1974 in the face of rising steel imports and falling prices, the Carter Administration convinced the firms that it would be better to implement a system of minimum import prices whereby imports below that price would trigger expedited anti-dumping investigations (so-called Trigger Price Mechanism) than negotiating VERs. Dissatisfied with the mechanism due to the surge of anti-dumping and countervailing duty suits, the U.S. Administration under Ronald Reagan promptly adopted a policy of dropping anti-dumping (and countervailing duty) cases in return for VERs, portraying the VERs as "fair trade" measures since the extent of the individual VERs would depend upon the expected size of countervailing duties.[68] This clearly illustrates the political paradox of appearing to support free trade while employing

67 *Ibid.*, 160.

68 POMFRET, (1988) 22 JWT 85.

protection.[69] Moreover, the aspect of negotiation, *i.e.* bilateral "co-operation", certainly appeals to the policymakers.

Interestingly, after VERs became prohibited by the Agreement on Safeguards, the U.S. returned to deploying the threat of anti-dumping investigations in those industries that had been the prime user of VERs (such as steel) to arrive at so-called "suspension agreements". In effect, the "agreement" is to suspend an anti-dumping investigation if the foreign firm agrees to raise its prices so that either the dumping margin is eliminated or any injurious effect on domestic firms is halted.[70]

The combined effects of the discriminatory aspect, non-transparency and the negotiation aspect of VERs contribute to another political advantage: namely the ease of VER implementation. While the implementation of tariffs and quotas is subject to legislative procedures – or as in the case of the EC to highly visible administrative procedures – a VER can be negotiated unhindered by open political processes and public scrutiny.[71] Consequently, VERs can be concluded in a short period of time. In addition, as a rule, VERs are restricted in time and subject to renegotiation, making them short-term trade policy instruments (while tariffs and quotas are regarded as long-term instruments).[72] The expeditious settlement of protectionist dis-

69 For an impressive overview of how an importing country politically preserves its free trade ideology whilst widely using protectionist actions, cf. RICHMAN, according to which protectionist actions employed by the U.S. included, *inter alia*, restraints on Japanese auto exports, setting total Japanese auto exports at 1.68 million vehicles in 1981–82, 8% below 1980 exports; negotiations to increase the restrictiveness of the Multi-Fibre Arrangement and extended restrictions to previously unrestricted textiles; "voluntary restraint agreements" to reduce steel imports from 18 countries, such as Brazil, Spain, South Korea, Japan, Mexico, South Africa, Finland, and Australia as well as the EC, guaranteeing domestic producers a share of the American market; or export restraints of machine tools from Taiwan, West Germany, Japan, and Switzerland, with some market shares rolled back to 1981 levels.

70 MOORE, (2005) 13 Review of International Economics 299 et seq.

71 Under the EC's old Common Import Regime, Council Regulation (EEC) No. 288/82 on common rules of import (OJ 1982 L 35/1), relatively few safeguard measures, including tariff quotas and quantitative restrictions, have been adopted. For an overview cf. INAMA/VERMULST, 22.

72 Quite to the contrary, *The Economist* portrayed VERs as the "new wave" of protectionism that may be here to stay for a long time. It claimed that nearly 300

putes is of particular importance to trade authorities or governments since the more quickly protectionist demands are satisfied the less potential political opposition has to be faced.[73]

Furthermore, whenever Member States imposed (or intended to impose) trade barriers by disregarding the Common Commercial Policy, the Commission has been quick in fulfilling the national protectionist requests on the EC level. When France closed its videocassette recorder market by channelling all Japanese imports through Poitiers, the Commission also negotiated a VER. French and Southern European Car producers lobbied extensively for an EC-wide VER with Japan, which some countries resisted and the Commission then negotiated.[74]

For import-competing producers, VERs offer a number of protectionist benefits, such as the ability to raise prices and expand output. In addition, VERs set quantitative limits on trade which is particularly perceived as an advantage if domestic producers are legging behind efficiency standards in foreign countries. Import-competing producers may thus try to fight import competition by identifying specific exporters as source of the market disruption and thereby heighten protectionist sentiments among policymakers.[75] VERs are also instigated by industries that believe they can extract more protection out of quanti-

VERs have been counted in the late 1980s, and the increasing number suggested, "*[i]f the recent revival of protectionism accelerates, the economic losses could eventually put all three oil shocks to shame*" (cf. "Jousting for Advantage", in: *The Economist*, 22 September 1990, 5). *The Economist* also feared that "*Japanese cars [will] remain overpriced for a long time to come, at least until the year 2000*" (cf. "Car Prices Driven Up", in: *The Economist*, 8 February 1992, 59).

73 The *New York Times* noted: "*Voluntary restraint agreements grow like weeds: they now cover autos, semi-conductors, machine tools, textiles, clothing and sugar, as well as steel. And no wonder: trade officials think of them as the no-fuss alternative to messy court fights and hostile questioning by Congress. But they typically cost consumers far more than formal remedies.*" (Cf. PASSELL Peter, "That Disturbing Deal on Steel", in: *New York Times*, 14 December 1988, D2).

74 Cf. Chapters I, 3.2.2 and 3.2.1 respectively.

75 Firms (or industries) that have the most influence on arranging a VER are usually large and well established, cf. KOSTECKI, (1991) 25 JWT 91 *et seq.* The size of certain industries suggests that its welfare indirectly but significantly affects the domestic perception of the trade protection. For example, the U.S. auto industry is said to be "so tied up in the American self-image" that it wins support from domestic policymakers (and consumers), cf. NELSON, 28.

tative limits than from the price increases associated with tariffs. It appears that trade authorities willingly comply with the demands of these interest groups the more politically powerful they are.[76] For instance, it is evidenced that only very politically influential industries can induce the EC to negotiate VERs. Whereas the agricultural[77], vehicle, steel, consumer electronics, textile and clothing, and machinery industries were amongst the strongest lobbyists and thus the most successful in receiving protection through VERs, the footwear industry usually had to instigate safeguard proceedings or to negotiate industry-to-industry arrangements.[78]

2.2.2 The Political Advantages for the Government and the Competitors in the Exporting Country

The government in the exporting country benefits from VERs by avoiding the political heat that it might otherwise suffer from pressures to take practical and/or legal actions against allegations from the importing country.[79] In considering a VER, trade authorities in the ex-

76 For instance, it is alleged that the campaign for steel protectionism in the U.S. highlights a classic problem of political economy, *i.e.* the problem of concentrated benefits and dispersed costs. The benefits of restrictions on foreign steel are concentrated in a relatively small steel-producing sector, while the costs are dispersed throughout the whole economy. Steel producers therefore have a clear and powerful incentive to lobby for protectionism; cf. LINDSEY/GRISWOLD/LUKAS, 13.

77 For instance, in *EEC – Restrictions on Imports of Apples from Chile* (L/5047), and *EEC – Restrictions on Imports of Dessert Apples – Complaint by Chile* (L/6491) it was freely admitted that the EC had negotiated VERs on apples with several Southern hemisphere countries (Argentina, Australia, New Zealand and South Africa). Neither of the cases dealt, however, with the legality of the VERs but with import restrictions that were placed on Chile which refused to accept a VER.

78 SCHUKNECHT, 116 *et seq.*, "Table on Voluntary Export Restraints and Similar Restraints, Arrangements in the EC, as of Mid-1999". Safeguard actions concerning footwear under the old Common Import Regime, *i.e.* under Council Regulation (EEC) No. 288/82 on common rules of import (OJ 1982 L 35/1), were taken in 1987 for imports from Korea and Taiwan into Italy and France, in 1988 for imports from Korea and Taiwan into the EC, and in 1992 for footwear imports from China into the EC; see also INAMA/VERMULST, 22.

79 For example, in 1985, the US semi-conductor industry filed an unfair trade petition against Japan (under Section 301 of the Trade Expansion Act of 1974), claiming discriminatory access to the Japanese market. Subsequently, three

porting country thus make a judgment as to the probability of more severe protectionist measures, along with the economic and political costs associated with such alternatives. In order to minimise the expected cost of a trade restraint, the negotiation of a VER – in which both trading partners have a hand in determining the extent of the restriction – may thus be preferred to a unilateral imposition of trade restrictions by the importing country.[80]

The political advantages of a VER for export-competing producers derive from the quantitative limitation it places on the export supply. In order to implement the VER, the government often forms or allows the formation of an export cartel.[81] In the case of the VERs on steel, for example, foreign steel industries were virtually forced to form export cartels since effective export restraints required the exporting country's industry association (or government) to assign quotas or market shares to each exporting steel producer.[82]

Once the cartel organisation is established (or promoted) by the VER, the collusive nature of VERs may be extended into the structure of world markets. Thereby, the anti-competitive impact is exacerbated by the exclusion (or restriction) of any new competitor entering the market. VERs thus ultimately provide the possibility to share markets and to build up barriers to market entry.

This not only applies to the exporting producers but also import-competing producers: By allocating a minimum level of projected domestic demand to the import-competing producers, the exporting producers are left with a market share that is subject to future demand fluctuations. Due to this risk carried by the exporters, they may chose

American companies and then the Department of Commerce filed anti-dumping suits. In the ensuing negotiations, Japan sought to reduce the pain of dumping duties (which would have been as high as 108% against some companies) by offering a VER on the most sensitive products known as dynamic random access memories (DRAMs). Recognizing the potentially dangerous effects of VERs, America's Semiconductor Industry Association rejected out of hand any Japanese offer of a VER. Cf. COLEMAN/YOFFIE, (1990) 37 Proceedings of the Academy of Political Science 147.

80 BEISE/OPPERMANN/SANDER, 81; JONES, 31.

81 PETERSMANN, 156. Cf. also *Competition and Trade Policies – Their Interaction*, OECD, 1984, paragraph 53.

82 JONES, 126; RICHMAN, 9.

to influence their market shares by additional pricing and distribution strategies.[83] Alternatively, a maximum level of exports is fixed, thus leaving the rest of the market to the import-competing producers who then bear the risk of demand fluctuations. Or else, exporters and import-competing producers may choose to share the risk of demand fluctuation by opting for a constant market share approach, thereby dropping the issue of future demand in the negotiation process of the VER.[84]

VERs may thus be used to turn competitors into co-operative partners. This may not only be achieved through paying off the exporters in the form of quota rents resulting from the restriction, but by interacting in a collusive direction with an outcome in terms of prices and profits that the exporters and import-competing producers would not be able to achieve otherwise.[85] Threats of administered protection also induce trading partners to collude under the terms of a VER, thus hoping to appease the domestic cries for protection.[86]

However, where VERs are essentially arranged between private parties, *i.e.* competitors in the importing and the exporting country, the VERs will generally be subject to competition laws prohibiting cartels or other forms of collusive anti-competitive behaviour. On the other hand, where privately negotiated and administered VERs are backed up by the governments' consent, they are considered trade measures and as such usually not subject to competition laws. For example, the EC regards measures that fall into the framework of a trade agreement between the EC and third countries as well as agreements imposed on firms of third countries by the authorities of those countries as measures of external trade policy which are not covered by Article 101 TFEU[87] (*ex* Article 81 EC Treaty).[88]

83 This may further lead to the inclusion of minimum price requirements or distribution strategies, such as the timing of supplies, into the VER agreement.

84 KOSTECKI, (1991) 25 JWT 89.

85 KRISHNA (1988), 3; KRISHNA (1985), 1.

86 For the inter-relation between anti-dumping protection and the proliferation of VERs, cf. KOLEV/PRUSA.

87 Consolidated version of the Treaty on the Functioning of the European Union, OJ 2010 C 83/47.

88 Competition and Trade Policies – Their Interaction, OECD, 1984, paragraph 113.

3 The History of Voluntary Export Restraints

The history of export restraints as trade policy instrument dates back to the 1930s, when Belgium and France assigned exporters the right to issue licences on goods subject to bilaterally negotiated quotas. In the turmoil of the worldwide crisis, such policies lifted the international industry-to-industry arrangements popular at this time to a formal level, with the expectation to establish order in the market. Similarly, in order to stem the surge of Japanese cotton textile imports which had risen by almost 600% between 1929 and 1936, American textile producers negotiated with their Japanese counterparts to limit their cotton goods deliveries to the U.S. market to a yearly quota and enjoyed thereby – apparently – the assent of both governments.[89] Trade policy during the depression in the 1930s was generally characterised by the imposition of non-tariff barriers, such as formal and informal ("voluntary") quota allocations, the rationalisation of production and the establishment of international cartels.[90]

Although economic growth emerged in the dawn of World War II the greater success story lay in the realm of economic performance in the post-war period. The speed and the scale of economic resurgence after 1947 were unprecedented in European history, and unmatched in any part of the world except Japan.[91] Growth clearly owed much to the start provided by Marshall Aid, to continuing interplay with the U.S., and to the climate of liberal democracy, which greatly favoured unfettered enterprise. Marshall Aid was essential in that it supplied the cash to sustain European trade and industry after the initial post-war upsurge faltered. The most prominent testimony of the dynamics of those years is the foundation of the GATT[92] in 1947 which was driven

89 JONES, 4 *et seq.*

90 BALASSA, 428.

91 For an overview of Japan's trade policy during the last century, cf. NOLAND, 2 *et seq.*

92 In 1994, the agreements signed in Marrakesh (Final Act Embodying the Results of the Uruguay Round of Multilateral Negotiations, April 15, 1994) expanded and substantially strengthened the rules of the GATT and created the WTO to administer those rules. Article II:4 of the WTO Agreement states that the GATT 1994 is "legally distinct" from GATT 1947. In order to prevent parallel applica-

by the idea of continuing trade liberalisation based on non-discrimination and the provision of a stable and predictable trading environment.[93]

Trade without discrimination[94] ensured by the GATT included both a most-favoured-nation[95] (MFN) status which concerns non-discrimination between the trading partners, as well as national treatment[96] requiring the contracting parties to accord treatment to imports from GATT members no less favourable than the treatment accorded to domestic products. During the 1950s, tariff reductions in the framework of GATT were negotiated bilaterally on an item-by-item basis. The benefits of these agreements also accrued to the contracting parties that did not actively participate in trade negotiations due to the unconditional application of the MFN clause: all are on an equal basis, and all share the benefits of any lowering of trade barriers.

Although the thought of trade liberalisation appeared to have been accepted broadly in the years following World War II, it was in the mid-1950s when the recourse to sectoral protectionism returned: In response to the growing international competition from Japan in the textile sector, the U.S. successfully negotiated a VER to limit cotton textile exports into the U.S. market in 1957.[97] Other developed countries followed the example of the U.S. and an entire network of bilat-

tion, the EC has made a declaration to no longer apply GATT 1947; cf. FOCUS (GATT Newsletter) N° 107 (Special Issue), p. 12.

93 According to the Preamble to GATT 1947, the contracting parties agreed to the formation of "reciprocal and mutually advantageous arrangements directed to the substantial reduction of tariffs and other barriers to trade and to the elimination of discriminatory treatment in international commerce". Increasing incomes, ensuring full employment, fostering the full use of resources and increasing the production and the exchange of goods were the primary objectives.

94 Further specific obligations relating to non-discrimination are, *e.g.* GATT Article XVII:1 (commercial activities of State enterprises) and GATT Article XIII:1 (non-discriminatory administration of quantitative restrictions).

95 GATT Article I requires each contracting party, to treat each other contracting party at least as favourably as it treats its most favoured trading partner (even non-GATT members) – though without primarily conferring a title to claim privileges. Cf. also TIETJE, [1995] EuR 399.

96 GATT Article III.

97 GRENNES, 2; ITOH/NAGAOKA, 476.

erally negotiated export restraints was built. Soon it was felt that those agreements should be incorporated in discussions on multilateral rules for trade in cotton products. Cotton importing and exporting countries hence adopted the Short-Term Arrangement Regarding International Trade in Cotton Textiles (STA) in 1961, allowing for quantitative import restrictions and thus legalising the existing VERs. Merely a year later, the STA was replaced by a Long-Term Arrangement (LTA) which became the predecessor of the famous Multifibre Arrangement (MFA)[98] of 1973.[99] Primarily devised as a temporary departure from the GATT rules, the initial VERs on cotton textiles have emerged to the most prominent orderly marketing agreement of world trade.[100]

The MFA was renegotiated four times, the last time in 1991, and it finally expired in 1994. It was followed by the Agreement on Textiles and Clothing (ATC) which came into force with the establishment of the WTO in 1995. It provided for the dismantling of the MFA by 1 January 2005, thus integrating the sector in the liberal scheme of GATT.[101]

Cotton and textiles were, however, not the only products targeted by VERs. The preparatory stage of the Tokyo Round[102] revealed that

98 In contrast to its predecessors, the MFA was negotiated under the auspices of GATT in order to gain closer international surveillance and discipline, for more details cf. the Note by the Secretariat on "Work already undertaken in the GATT on safeguards" (MTN.GNG/NG9/W/1), paragraph 9 *et seq.*

99 SCHLAGENHOF, (1995) 19 W. Comp. 110.

100 For an analysis of the EC's commercial policy with regard to textiles cf. VAN DARTEL, 121 *et seq.*

101 The literature dedicated to the MFA is abundant, to name but a few worth consulting: BAGCHI, (1994) 28 JWT 31 *et seq.*; BLOKKER/DEELSTRA, (1994) 28 JWT 97 *et seq.*; DAS, (1983) 17 JWTL 95 *et seq.* and (1985) 19 JWTL 67 *et seq.*; FRANÇOIS/GLISMANN/SPINANGER, 8 *et seq.*; KHANNA, (1990) 24 JWT 71 *et seq.*; SPINANGER 8 *et seq.*; TANG, (1989) 23 JWT 51 *et seq.* For a most recent discussion of the impact of liberalisation in the clothing and textile sector under the ATC, cf. KYVIK NORDÅS, 3 *et seq.*

102 The Tokyo Round took place from 1973–1979 and took a broader look at the trade rules than its predecessor, the Kennedy Round. The tariff negotiations led to further substantial reductions in customs duties but the talks failed with regard to fundamental reforms in agricultural trade, and did not manage to provide a new agreement on "safeguards" (emergency import measures). The first steps in that direction happened in the next round, the Uruguay Round.

several developed countries saw problems emerging in their markets from exports deriving from certain developing countries and especially Japan which led to an increasing number of VERs or orderly marketing arrangements with regard to products like leather, footwear, cutlery and other manufactured goods.[103] Why and how VERs proliferated in world trade despite the liberalisation brought about by the GATT will be demonstrated by the example of the trade relations of the EC.

3.1 The Emergence of VERs in the Trade Relations of the EC – The Example of Japan

For several decades, trade relations between the EC and Japan were characterised by various frictions which stem, at least partly, from the substitution of the Member States by the EC within the GATT and the incoherent (singular and common) commercial policy towards Japan.

Most of the EC Member States acceded GATT at an early stage.[104] Japan's request in 1951 to attend GATT meetings as an observer provoked opposition from several countries, amongst others, the Benelux countries, France and the UK. They feared that Japan's participation in the trade negotiations within GATT would seriously affect certain sectors – sectors in which Japan had a comparative advantage and thus increased competition for its Western European counterparts. This was particularly the case for textiles and clothing.[105] In the following decades, Japan repeatedly was (and still is) subject to allegations that it

103 MTN.GNG/NG9/W/1, paragraph 14.

104 The Benelux countries (Belgium, the Netherlands and Luxembourg), France and the United Kingdom (UK) were original signatories to GATT 1947. Denmark, Finland, Germany, Greece and Sweden joined in 1950, Austria and Italy in 1951, Portugal in 1962, Spain in 1963 and Ireland in 1967. For the sake of completeness it is noted that – for obvious historical reasons – only few of the Member States that joined the European Union on 1 May 2004, and 1 January 2007 ("Community of 27") were early signatories to GATT 1947, namely Cyprus (1963), Malta (1964), Poland (1967) and Hungary (1973). The Czech Republic and Slovakia only acceded to GATT 1947 in 1993, followed by Slovenia in 1994, Romania in 1995 and Bulgaria in late 1996.
Having gained their independence from Russia, the three Baltic States Estonia, Latvia and Lithuania eventually joined the WTO/GATT in 1999 and 2001 respectively.

105 BRONCKERS (1987), 59.

pressurises industries that play an important role in the EC, such as steel or automobiles, and industries that would have had the potential to become important if Japanese imports did not sweep competition from domestic industries, as in the case of consumer electronics.

3.1.1 Japan's Accession to the GATT

The initial opposition to grant Japan observer status in GATT did not last for long, and merely a year later Japan formally applied for accession. By then, the European countries had, however, not yet overcome their discomfort with Japan's integration into the GATT framework and wished to retain their right to apply safeguard measures to protect their domestic markets from imports emanating from Japan. Particularly, it was felt that GATT Article XIX, the most prominent safeguard clause, did not provide for discriminatory application, *i.e.* measures directed against a product from just one specific country, in this case Japan, because of the MFN clause. Recourse to GATT Article XIX would thus have led to a general rise of barriers to world trade. In order to avoid this, it was argued that an additional safeguard clause was required. Alternatively, it was suggested that contracting parties could invoke GATT XXIII:2 under which the application of safeguard actions on a discriminatory basis could be authorised. However, either solution was controversial, and no agreement could be reached.[106]

Meanwhile, the Ad Hoc Committee on Agenda and Intersessional Business was instructed to study the problems arising from Japan's accession to the GATT. In its "Report on the Accession of Japan",[107] the Ad Hoc Committee noted that in cases where remedial action consistent with the GATT leads to a general raising of tariff levels and other barriers to world trade, a situation impeding the attainment of the objectives of the GATT would be created, and would thus fall under GATT Article XXIII:1(c)[108]. Furthermore, it was considered

106 GATT Analytical Index, 534.

107 L/76, 13 February 1953.

108 GATT Article XXIII:1(c) on nullification or impairment states that "[I]f any contracting party should consider that any benefit accruing to it directly or indirectly under this Agreement is being nullified or impaired or that the attainment

that contracting parties whose interests were seriously affected should first seek consultations under GATT Article XXII, and only if those are unsuccessful, apply for the authorisation of a discriminatory safeguard measure under GATT Article XXIII:2.[109] In the course of the same year – Japan had been admitted to take part in the meetings of the GATT in the meantime – a number of contracting parties issued a Declaration[110] in which they stated that they were prepared to apply the GATT rules to Japan in anticipation of its accession and that they did not regard the approval of an interpretation of Article XXIII on the lines of that contained in the Report of the Ad Hoc Committee as necessary or desirable. Other contracting parties disagreed, among them France and the UK, which both refused to sign the Declaration.

Whereas Japan finally acceded to the GATT in September 1955 without the introduction of any new general safeguard clause, the majority of contracting parties invoked GATT Article XXXV[111], thus making the GATT rules inapplicable to their trade relations with Japan.[112]

of any objective of the Agreement is being impeded as the result of the existence of any other situation, the contracting party may, with a view to the satisfactory adjustment of the matter, make written representations or proposals to the other contracting party or parties which it considers to be concerned. [...]."

109 L/76, 13 February 1953, paragraph 8.

110 Declaration on Commercial Relations between Certain Contracting Parties and Japan, 24 October 1953, 2S/31.

111 GATT Article XXXV reads:
"1. This Agreement, or alternatively Article II of this Agreement, shall not apply as between any contracting party and any other contracting party if:
a) the two contracting parties have not entered into tariff negotiations with each other, and
b) either of the contracting parties, at the time either becomes a contracting party, does not consent to such application.
2. The contracting parties may review the operation of this Article in particular cases at the request of any contracting party and make appropriate recommendations."

112 According to observations of TOMZ/GOLDSTEIN/RIVERS, 7 *et seq.*, Japan holds the unwelcome distinction of being targeted more often and for longer periods than any other member of GATT.

3.1.2 Recourse to GATT Article XXXV

Some (at the time future) Member States of the EC, in particular Austria[113], the Benelux countries, France and the UK, sought to limit the consequences of Japan's accession by invoking GATT Article XXXV.[114] Other countries[115] did not invoke Article XXXV but continued nevertheless to discriminate against Japan, as was particularly the case for Italy.[116] It appeared that Japan was not so much concerned about the discriminatory practices upheld by those countries that did not rely on GATT Article XXXV but rather with its credibility as a valid trade partner as such. The refusal of developed countries to apply GATT rules to imports originating from Japan was a far more imminent obstacle and would prove to become Japan's biggest hindrance in actively taking part and advantage of the GATT system.

Subsequent to the adoption of the Treaties of Rome in 1957, the then "Community of Six", as a customs union[117], opened negotiations under GATT Article XXIV:6 to adjust the tariff concessions previously undertaken by the individual Member States, *i.e.* the Benelux

113 It is noteworthy that Austria relied on Article XXXV longer than any of the other future Member States of the EC, namely until 1976 when it finally withdrew the application of Article XXXV (L/4428 (October 1976)).

114 L/405 (1955).

115 Denmark, Finland, Germany, Greece and Sweden.

116 Cf. the factual study on market disruption compiled by the GATT Secretariat, L/1164, 33.

117 As an exception to the MFN clause, GATT permits the granting of regional preferences as long as specified criteria are fulfilled: Firstly, common tariffs and other measures resulting from the formation of the customs union, which are applicable to the trade of the constituent countries and third countries, must be set at a level that is on the whole not higher or more restrictive than what was imposed previously. Secondly, duties and other restrictions must be eliminated with respect to "substantially all trade". This prohibits agreements covering selected products and selective reductions of border measures. Thirdly, customs unions or free trade areas have to be fully pledged agreements within a reasonable length of time.
GATT Article XXIV:4 thus stipulates that "[t]he purpose of a customs union or of a free trade area should be to facilitate trade between the constituent territories and not to raise barriers to the trade of other contracting parties with such territories."

countries, France, Germany and Italy. On this occasion, Japan expressed its disapproval of the invocation of GATT Article XXXV by requesting an investigation into the implications of the Community concessions which implied that four out of the six tariff concessions previously negotiated with Japan would not be governed by GATT rules.[118]

During the same period, several contracting parties noted with concern that the sharp increase of imports of certain commodities could have various detrimental effects on the market of the importing country. For that reason the Secretariat was mandated to investigate the issue. It found that a variety of products, predominantly from the textiles and clothing sector, were subject to import restrictions applied by a number of contracting parties in response to the market disruption.[119] Following the establishment of a Working Party on "Avoidance of Market Disruption" in 1960, a Decision was adopted[120] recognising that

> (a) [I]n a number of countries situations occur or threaten to occur which have been described as 'market disruption'.
>
> (b) These situations generally contain the following elements in combination:
> (i) a sharp and substantial increase or potential increase of imports of particular products from particular sources;
> (ii) these products are offered at prices which are substantially below those prevailing for similar goods of comparable quality in the market of the importing country;
> (iii) there is serious damage to domestic producers or threat thereof;
> (iv) the price differentials referred to in paragraph (ii) above do not arise from governmental intervention in the fixing or formation of prices or from dumping practices. [...]
>
> (c) These situations have often led governments to take a variety of exceptional measures. In some cases importing countries have taken or maintained discriminatory measures either outside the framework of the General Agreement, or contrary to the provisions of the General Agreement. In some other cases exporting countries have tried to correct the situation

118 L/1245 (1959).
119 L/1164.
120 GATT Analytical Index, 534 *et seq.*

by taking measures to limit or control the export of the products giving rise to the situation.

(d) Such measures, taken unilaterally or through bilateral arrangement, may in some cases tend to cause difficulties in other markets and create problems for other contracting parties.[121]

Whereas those findings have not been further developed towards a solution, they nevertheless contributed indirectly to the multilateral negotiation of a special safeguard measure affecting a single industrial sector – cotton textiles.[122]

To further guide the divergent interests of the contracting parties in trade flows of sensitive products towards a mutually acceptable solution, a Working Party examined the context of recourses to GATT Article XXXV in respect to Japan and reached the conclusion that most of the contracting parties that invoked the provision, including the Benelux countries and France, did grant Japan MFN status regarding tariff concessions but reserved the right to impose discriminatory import restrictions on Japanese products.[123] During the Dillon Round (1960/61), the then "Community of Six" negotiated tariff concessions with Japan, thus apparently overcoming their dispute over the invocation of GATT Article XXXV.[124] A formal withdrawal[125] proved,

121 L/1374, Report of the Working Party on "Avoidance of Market Disruption – Establishment of Committee", adopted on 19 November 1960, 9S/108.

122 As aforementioned the LTA replaced the STA as of 1 October 1962 – though not under the auspices of GATT. As far as the (unofficial) position of GATT in respect of the LTA is concerned, cf. the Note by the Secretariat on "Work already undertaken in the GATT on safeguards" (MTN.GNG/NG9/W/1, paragraph 10 *et seq.*) and the GATT Analytical Index, 520 (with further annotations).

123 L/1531.

124 Most interestingly, in 1965, a Note by the Director-General on "The Application of Article XXXV in Relation to the Present Trade Negotiations" provided: "*[...] two contracting parties which are not applying the GATT to each other by virtue of an earlier invocation of Article XXXV by one of them, the procedure in the past has been that the latter, unless it intended to withdraw its invocation of the Article, would not submit offers to the other. The ruling and the procedure [...] are based on the earlier technique of tariff negotiation under which offers are made by each participant to other individual participants*". Cf. GATT Analytical Index, p. 1032.

125 The Benelux countries withdrew in October 1964 (L/2308) and France in January 1964 (L/2129).

however, to be dependent on further commitments of Japan towards the EC Member States which were set out in bilateral agreements containing potentially discriminatory safeguard clauses with the Benelux countries and France, respectively.[126]

Whereas the trade relations between Japan and the UK, Spain and Portugal respectively had been sorted out by means of bilateral arrangements – and that well before they acceded to the EC[127] – more complications arose from Ireland's accession to the GATT in 1967 when it also invoked GATT Article XXXV.[128] Although the Council had authorised the Commission already in 1970 to negotiate a trade agreement with Japan[129] and despite the failure of these negotiations mainly due to the EC's request for a bilateral safeguard clause for the entire Community[130], the Commission hoped to persuade Japan to accept a selective safeguard clause for the "Community of Nine" in the course of the negotiations on the abandonment of Ireland's recourse to GATT Article XXXV in 1974. As this hope appeared to be false, in 1975, the Council decided to withdraw on Ireland's behalf the recourse to GATT Article XXXV with regard to Japan.[131]

This course of events not only reflects the ambiguous feelings of certain Member States towards free trade with Japan, but also how the EC gradually contained the powers of individual Member States in external trade relations within the GATT.

126 BRONCKERS (1987), 62.

127 The UK which was to become a Member of the EC only in 1973 relinquished the recourse to Article XXXV gradually – first, in April 1963 (L/1992) for UK customs territories only, in March 1964 (L/2208), in November 1967 (L/2896) and finally, for UK overseas territories in May1970 (L/3396).
Spain and Portugal, which both joined the EC in 1986, ceased to invoke GATT Article XXXV in the early 1970s: Withdrawal by Spain in 1971 (L/3646) and withdrawal by Portugal in 1972 (L/3690).

128 L/2954.

129 *Fourth General Report* of the EC Commission, 1970, paragraph 448.

130 *Fifth General Report* of the EC Commission, 1971, paragraph 460; *Sixth General Report* of the EC Commission, 1972, paragraph 437.

131 L/4215.

3.1.3 The Replacement of the EC Member State Representations by the Community within the GATT

As demonstrated on the example of the Council's withdrawal of Ireland's recourse to GATT Article XXXV, the EC operates as a separate entity from its Member States. Its organs possess the capacity to take legally effective decisions. On the international scene, the recognition of the EC's international legal personality by third countries and international organisations allows it to act as a subject of international law.[132] Consequently, the EC is subject to relevant international customary law and has the possibility to acquire rights and obligations with other subjects by means of agreements.[133] The EC hence became a member of the WTO in its own right in 1995. Moreover, international agreements originally ratified by the Member States and which subsequently fall within the shared or exclusive competence of the Community, such as the GATT[134], are accepted as binding equally on the EC institutions and the Member States despite the fact that they do not fall strictly under Article 300 EC Treaty (now Article 218 TFEU). As to the exact extent of the powers of the Court of Justice to control the exercise of external affairs led by the executive institutions, the EC Treaty is silent.[135] It remains to be seen whether the Court will define its own powers in this respect under the TFEU.

Although the Community has been substituted for its Member States regarding their commitments under the GATT 1947 since July 1968[136], following the introduction of the Common Customs Tariff, the continuing membership of the Member States in the WTO was never an issue.[137] This is the case even despite the Commission's

132 Case 22/70, *AETR*, [1971] E.C.R. 263.

133 EVERLING, [1985] EuR 75.

134 Joined Cases 21–24/72, *International Fruit Company*, [1972] E.C.R. 1219, paragraph 18; Case 38/75, *Nederlandse Spoorwegen*, [1975] E.C.R. 1439; Cases 267–269/81, *SPI and SAMI*, [1983] E.C.R. 801; Case 266/81, *SIOT*, [1983] E.C.R. 731.

135 CHEYNE, (1994) 19 ELRev. 584.

136 The EC was able to exercise *de facto* membership of the GATT in place of the Member States without much friction because it fell in the area of the Common Commercial Policy which is in the exclusive competence of the EC. Cf. TOMUSCHAT, 156.

137 BRONCKERS (1987), 64.

claim of exclusive competence for the whole Uruguay Round negotiations and its results,[138] in particular the legalisation of the original GATT[139] brought about by the WTO Agreement[140]. Furthermore, the Court ruled in 1994[141] that the WTO Agreements relating to trade in goods fell within the Community's exclusive competence (Article 133 EC Treaty, Common Commercial Policy) while in the fields of services and intellectual property the competence was mixed,[142] and that the agreements therefore were to be concluded jointly by the EC and its Member States.[143]

Consequently, the decision concerning the conclusion by the EC of the WTO Agreement provides in Article 1:3[144]:

> The President of the Council is hereby authorized to designate the person empowered to take the measure provided for in Article XIV of the Agreement establishing the World Trade Organization in order to bind the European Community with regard to that portion of the Agreement falling within its competence.

Accordingly, Article XI:1 of the WTO Agreement states that the EC along with the contracting parties of the GATT 1947 (and among them the EC's Member States) shall become original members of the WTO. The EC therefore has all the rights and obligations stemming

138 SACK, (1995) 32 CMLRev. 1233.

139 GATT 1947 was *ad hoc* and provisional. The GATT has been amended and incorporated into the new WTO Agreements and exists now alongside the General Agreement on Trade in Services (GATS) and the Agreement on Trade-Related Aspects of Intellectual Property Rights (TRIPs).

140 For an introduction on the status and the structure of the WTO see, *e.g.*, IPSEN/HALTERN, [1994] RIW 719 *et seq.*

141 *Opinion 1/94,* Agreement Establishing the World Trade Organization, [1994] E.C.R. I-5267.

142 HILF, (1995) 6 EuZW 8. For a critical appraisal of Opinion 1/94 and the implied external powers doctrine see BOURGEOIS, (1999) 22 Fordham Int'l L.J. 159 *et seq.* and 167 *et seq.*

143 For critical remarks – especially concerning the obligation of co-operation of the EC and its Member States within the WTO – see, *e.g.*, FLORY/MARTIN, [1996] CaDE 392 *et seq.*

144 Council Decision 94/800 concerning the conclusion on behalf of the European Community, as regards matters within its competence, of the agreements reached in the Uruguay Round multilateral negotiations (1986–1994), OJ 1994 L 336/1.

from such membership. Except for the voting procedure[145], all details concerning the exercise of the respective competences between the EC and its members within the WTO are left open, thus allowing flexible internal rules to be established.

3.2 Common Commercial Policy versus National Measures

How difficult it proved to be to develop internal rules that allow for the creation of a truly "common" commercial policy may be illustrated by the EC's trade relations with Japan in two instances: motor cars and video cassette recorders. Although the EC's powers in external trade policy are incontestable, it is the protective measures taken by individual Member States against Japanese imports that reflect the paradox of the EC's commitment to liberal trade and the maintenance of discriminatory trade practices.

3.2.1 The Japanese VERs on Motor Cars

According to the *Donckerwolcke*[146] judgment, the full responsibility in the matter of commercial policy was transferred to the Community by means of Article 133(1) EC Treaty [*ex* Article 113 EEC Treaty, now Article 207 TFEU], and all measures of commercial policy of national character are only permissible (after the end of the transitional period) by virtue of specific authorisation by the Community.[147] Despite this requirement, some Member States have repeatedly resorted to actions reducing Japanese imports, such as the negotiation of VERs on Japanese cars by officials of the Belgian government (allegedly on behalf of the Benelux countries) and by Germany in 1981.[148] Italy appeared

145 Article IX:1 WTO Agreement.

146 Case 41/76, *Donckerwolcke*, [1976] E.C.R. 1921.

147 *Ibid.*, paragraph 32; subsequently upheld in Case 174/84, *Bulk Oil v. Sun Oil*, (1986) E.C.R. 559, paragraph 31.

148 Although these VERs were never published, it appears that Japan maintained its car exports to the Benelux countries at the 1980 level, and that car exports to Germany were not allowed to exceed an increase of 10% compared to the export volume of the previous year (cf. BRONCKERS (1987), 66). However, in the case of Germany it appears that the export volume of Japanese cars increased by 15% until 1989, sug-

to rely on the bilateral agreement entered into with Japan in the 1960s which limited car exports in either direction to 2'200 units per annum, and the French government voiced in 1977 its refusal to allow the Japanese share of the French market to exceed 3%.[149] In the UK, there have been informal arrangements between the British Society of Motor Manufacturers and the Japanese Automobile Manufacturers Association, limiting the share of the UK car market of Japanese cars to between 10% and 11%.[150]

Another aspect of how the import of goods originating in third countries may be restricted was contained in Article 134 EC Treaty. Under this provision, Member States were allowed, subsequent to specific authorisation by the Commission, to maintain national measures of commercial policy on condition that the national measures of national policy existed previously or were allowed to exist by virtue of Community legislation.[151] Such measures must apply not only to direct imports of third countries but also to indirect imports via other Member States. The ECJ, still in the *Donckerwolcke* judgment, explicitly stated that Article 134 EC Treaty [*ex* Article 115 EEC Treaty] is designed for measures "*particularly in the form of derogation from the principle of free circulation within the Community or products which originated in third countries and which were put into free circulation in one of the Member States.*"[152]

As far as Italy is concerned, it appears that the Commission had repeatedly permitted Italy by virtue of Article 134 EC Treaty to impose intra-Community restrictions in order to cordon off Italy's quota on direct Japanese car imports.[153] A similar authorisation was issued to Spain in order to prevent indirect imports of Japanese cars.[154]

gesting that the VER between Germany and Japan was less rigidly enforced or not regarded as absolutely binding (cf. *Handelsblatt*, 23 August 1990, p. 6).

149 Cf. HINDLEY, 64 *et seq.*

150 For instance, the *Financial Times* referred to a "gentleman's agreement" between the British and the Japanese car industry (cf. "Japan car sales in UK agree with forecast", in: *Financial Times*, 28 May 1982, p. 7).

151 Case 1/84R, *Ilford*, [1985] E.C.R. 423.

152 Case 41/76, *Donckerwolcke*, [1976] E.C.R. 1921, paragraph 28.

153 See, for example, OJ 1986 C 91/3.

154 OJ 1986 C 161/3.

Whilst the Commission asserted that those Member States that had negotiated bilateral safeguard agreements with Japan[155] are no longer allowed to take independent action against Japanese imports, it nevertheless omitted to take any steps against the VERs on car exports. Instead, and in fact shortly before Belgium and Germany concluded their VERs, the Council approved the Commission's intention to start negotiations with Japan on the unilateral restriction of car exports to the Community.[156]

When Japan, in February 1983, agreed for the first time to restrain exports of several products to the Community as a whole, it appeared, however, that the Commission did not act with the authorisation of the Council as laid down in Article 133(3) EC Treaty.[157] The VER negotiated between the Commission and the Japanese government not only covered cars but also video recorders, colour TV tubes, motorcycles, machine tools, light commercial vehicles, quartz watches, forklift trucks, colour TV sets and hi-fi equipment.[158] As to the details of the VERs, there is little information that was made publicly available.[159]

155 Mostly, the authorisation of safeguard clauses were periodical and extended the validity of the trade agreements concluded by certain Member States. For example, the safeguard clauses of the Benelux countries and France were authorised by Council Decision 86/456/EEC (OJ 1986 L266/32), or the "exchange of notes on voluntary export control" between the UK and Japan by Council Decision 86/19/EEC (OJ 1986 L29/26). The possibility of extension was established by Council Decision 69/494/EEC on the progressive standardisation of agreements concerning commercial relations between Member States and third countries and on the negotiation of Community agreements (OJ 1969 L326/39).

156 Bull. of the EC, 1981, N° 5, sec. 1.3.8.

157 BRONCKERS (1987), 69.

158 Bull. of the EC, 1983, N° 2, sec. 8 *et seq.*

159 Not only is there hardly any official publication of the EC covering the issue of VERs, the lack of transparency is also reflected in the little information provided to the GATT Secretariat. As of 1 January 1995, the only notified actions of the EC under GATT Article XIX were, with the exclusion of agricultural products (cf. GATT Analytical Index, 539 *et seq.*):

- import licences limited to a certain quantity of tape recorders originating in Japan and Korea. The action was taken by the EC but applied to Italy between 1 April 1973 and 31 December 1973;

Instead, the Commission proclaimed the conclusion of these VERs as a leap forward for the resolution of trade frictions on Community level. It regarded the successful negotiation of the VERs as a further step in the recognition of the exclusive powers in commercial policy not only by the Member States but also by third countries.[160]

Then again, after the termination of the VERs of 1983 at the end of 1985, it appeared that the Commission was still struggling to overcome the arbitrariness of certain Member States towards Japanese car imports in the early 1990s. In exchange for the existing restrictions on Japanese car imports to France, Italy, the UK and Spain, the Commission intended to offer Japan a transition period (starting 1 January 1993) during which a surveillance system would monitor the total exports of Japanese cars into the Community and whereby the existing national measures should be gradually reduced and finally abolished.[161] Again, the Commission did not seek authorisation for the initiation of the negotiations from the Council since – and as it was openly admitted – the compatibility of the formal negotiation of a VER with the GATT was not beyond doubt.[162] The agreement reached on 1 July 1991 was thus of informal nature and the public was merely informed about certain elements of the agreement.[163]

- annual quotas for portable TV sets applying to imports from Korea, Japan and Singapore into the UK for the period of 22 July 1977 to 22 June 1979. As from 22 June 1979, a VER came into effect;
- a global quota of tableware and other articles of stoneware emanating from Korea. The measure was introduced on 1 January 1983 and terminated on 16 April 1983 when it was replaced by a VER, whereby Korea undertook to make exports of these products to France and UK subject to export licences and set quantitative limits for the calendar years 1983–1985 (cf. Commission Reg. No. 873/83, OJ 1983 L 96/8); and
- global quotas of certain electronic quartz watches with digital display originating from Hong Kong, Japan, Korea, Macao and Taiwan for the period of 20 April 1984 and 31 December 1986 (cf. Commission Reg. No. 1087/84, OJ 1984 L 106/31).

160 See, for example, "Brussels jubilant on Japan deal", *Financial Times*, 15 February 1983, p. 4.

161 OPPERMANN/BEISE/SANDER, 94.

162 *Financial Times*, 20 July 1990, p. 1.

163 See, for instance, European Political Cooperation (EPC), Press Release P. 66/91, 18 July 1991; or *Frankfurter Allgemeine Zeitung*, Nr. 173, 29 July 1991, p. 9.

In the transition period between 1993 and 2000, restrictions on Japanese car imports were to be continued. During this period, the suppliers of Japanese cars were allowed to double their car exports to the EC from 1.2 million to 2.4 million units. For the evaluation of its share of the EC car market, Japan was further obliged to take into consideration the production in European transplants. At the end of the transition period, around half of the Japanese market share was to emanate from direct imports and the other half from European production. For direct imports, export ceilings were established.[164] The surveillance of the market developments of Japanese producers in the EC were surveyed by those Member States which previously restricted market entry by means of individual measures.

At first sight, this VER appeared to represent a compromise at Community level between protectionist Member States that hoped to adjust their domestic production to global competition within the transition period and those Member States that proclaimed liberal trade. In early 1992, however, it was reported that France sought to "improve" its situation by means of an agreement with two Japanese car producers which undertook to restrict their supplies from British transplants towards the French market. In addition, the supply of components, emanating from France, to the Japanese producers located in the UK was to be increased.[165] With hindsight the Commission was probably too optimistic because the VER did not appear to have brought about a Community policy towards Japan. In terms of a "ricochet" effect, the VER on Japanese cars represents a clear illustration of how the EC – whether intentionally or not – contributed to the emergence of restrictive trade practices.

Moreover, the VER proved to be of particular significance since it actually endured until 31 December 1999. Although the Agreement on Safeguards, which entered into force on 1 January 1995, imposes severe prohibitions on the use of any safeguard measures, or the use of VERs, other than permitted under the Agreement, a phasing-out pe-

164 For the end of the transition period, the Commission envisaged an import quota of 190'000 for the UK, 150'000 for France, 138'000 for Italy, 79'000 for Spain and 23'000 for Portugal.

165 BDI-Pressemitteilung 12/92, 3 February 1992. It remains unclear, however, who exactly was party to the agreement.

riod of four years as of the entry into force of the WTO Agreement and its Annexes for existing measures was permitted. Provision was made for one exception per importing country to maintain a restriction until the end of 1999.[166] The EC has been the only member to the WTO which has seized the opportunity to notify an existing measure under this provision, namely the above VER on cars from Japan.[167] The Annex of the Agreement on Safeguards thus specifies as products covered by this exception: passenger cars, off road vehicles, light commercial vehicles, light trucks (up to 5 tonnes), and the same vehicles in wholly knocked-down form.

166 Article 11:2 Agreement on Safeguards.

167 In this context it is interesting to note that the EC was not the only one "threatened" by the motor car exports from Japan: Across the Atlantic, the U.S. likewise negotiated a formal VER with the Japanese government in 1981, reducing the Japanese automobile exports by 7.7% (equalling a reduction from the 1980 level of 1.82 million units to 1.68 million units) for the period of one year. Not surprisingly, it was the Japanese Ministry of International Trade and Industry (MITI) that announced the VER on 2 May 1981. In addition to the export reduction for the period from 1 April 1981 to 31 March 1982, MITI indicated that a decision on a second year of restraints would be made after observing the 1981 market performance of the U.S. industry. On 29 March 1982, partly as a response to protectionist pressures on Capitol Hill, Japan renewed the VER for the period April 1982 to March 1983 at the 1.68 million units' ceiling. On 3 February 1983, again in response to congressional pressure, Japan renewed the VER for a third year at the current ceiling levels. On 1 November 1983, the Japanese government announced that it would raise its VER limit from 1.68 million to 1.85 million units during the period April 1984 to March 1985. In October 1984, Ford, Chrysler, American Motors, and the United Auto Workers urged the Reagan Administration to extend the Japanese VER for a fifth year, from April 1985 to March 1986. General Motors and the American International Automobile Dealers Association, however, came out against a continuation of the VER. In March 1985, President Reagan decided not to ask Japan to continue the VER for a fifth year. Following this decision, Japan announced that it would hold auto exports to the U.S. to 2.3 million units in 1985 which began the unilateral automobile VER between Japan and the United States. Whilst in early 1992, the export ceiling stood still at 1.65 million units, the VER was abandoned subsequent to the entry into force of the WTO Agreement and its Annexes. See also COHEN, 1 *et seq.*

3.2.2 The EC – Japan VER on Video Cassette Recorders (VCRs)

As in the case of the VER on Japanese cars, the VER controlling Japanese imports on video cassette recorders was characterised by a lack of transparency as well as a complex inter-relation of national measures that led to the negotiation of a Community-wide VER. Despite the scarcity of the information available, certain aspects of the agreement are clear: in February 1983, representatives of the Commission and MITI concluded a VER on VCRs which included a system of minimum prices and the possibility to vary the agreed level of exports depending on the sales of producers in the EC.[168] Whatever the details of Japan's commitment, the most interesting aspect of the VER on Japanese VCRs is the political background that led to its negotiation.

Although the Commission had been preoccupied with the question of how it could effectively gain a grip on the Common Commercial Policy, it saw itself constrained by the various national measures undertaken against Japanese imports. It appeared to be clear that if it did not satisfy the aspirations of the most protective Member States, their governments would continue to negotiate their own bilateral agreements in order to master domestic market disruptions. On the other hand, by opting for a protectionist stance the Commission had to face serious opposition from more liberal Member States. The political background of the VER on VCRs goes, however, beyond the general contest between the Commission and the Member States over the "control" of external trade policy.

The European VCR system that was protected by the VER was 'Video 2000', a product developed by Philips and manufactured solely by Philips and Grundig. In 1982, the market share of 'Video 2000' within the EC totalled around 15%. The remaining 85% of the EC market for VCRs was held by two Japanese systems, notably VHS, developed by JVC, and Betamax, a Sony product.[169] In December 1982, the Commission received a complaint lodged by the "Association of Firms with Common Interest in Video 2000" alleging that the Japanese producers were dumping VCRs with the intention of eliminating 'Video 2000' from the market. On the basis of evidence brought

168 Cf. GREENAWAY/HINDLEY, 3.
169 HINDLEY, 30.

about mainly by Philips and Grundig, the Commission announced the initiation of an anti-dumping proceeding concerning imports of VCRs originating in Japan.[170] Whilst, undoubtedly, the uncertainties accompanying an anti-dumping investigation made the negotiation of a VER for the Japanese more attractive, there was an additional source of pressure on the Japanese VCR industry and government to negotiate a VER that preceded the anti-dumping complaint.

As from October 1982, the French government required all imports of VCRs into France to obtain customs clearance at a small post located in Poitiers. Prompted by the French concern about sharply rising VCR imports from Japan, all VCR imports henceforth were channelled through this customs bureau, staffed with only two inspectors. On 21 December 1982, Japan requested consultations with the EC, *i.e.* the Commission, under GATT Article XXIII for nullification and impairment of the French import restrictive measure on VCRs.[171] The Commission was thus confronted with the prospect of facing a GATT investigation of a measure which offered little room of defence and for which it was not responsible. At the same time, the Commission issued a reasoned opinion to the French government pursuant to Article 226(1) EC Treaty (now Article 258 TFEU), alleging that the change in customs clearance procedures constituted a measure having equivalent effect as a quantitative restriction.[172] With reference to Article 28 EC Treaty (now Article 34 TFEU), the Commission addressed, however, only a restriction of intra-Community trade for imports of VCRs manufactured in the EC and did not touch upon the French restriction to the extent that it affected Japanese VCR imports. The reluctance to challenge the measure in regard to the Japanese imports became particularly apparent in January 1993, when the requirement for customs clearance ceased to apply for VCRs made in the EC. It continued, however, to apply to Japanese VCRs, including those that had first been imported through another Member State.[173]

170 Cf. OJ 1982 C 338/27.
171 L/5427.
172 Bull. of the EC, 1982, N° 12, 3.3.2.
173 BRONCKERS (1987), 76.

Pursuant to Articles 28 and 29 TFEU (*ex* Articles 23 and 24 EC Treaty), the determinant of European trade policy is the customs union, which shall be attained by principal mechanisms, such as the free circulation of goods originating in the Member States. Accordingly, a Common Customs Tariff and a Common Commercial Policy shall be adopted towards third countries and consequently, goods originating from third countries, after they have cleared customs, shall also benefit from free circulation within the internal market. These principles clearly demonstrate that it is important to distinguish between the internal and the external dimension of the customs union. As far as goods from third countries are concerned, the internal dimension implies that such products circulate freely between the Member States once they have been legally "put into free circulation". In other words, subject to some qualifications (*e.g.* adherence to import rules), third country goods benefit from the same treatment as goods originating from Member States. The external dimension defines the treatment accorded to products originating from third countries due to a Common Commercial Policy and its related legal instruments.[174]

The application of Article 34 TFEU (*ex* Article 28 EC Treaty) to third country goods was already addressed by the ECJ in *Donckerwolcke*[175] when it held that

> [i]t appears from Article 9 *(now Article 28 TFEU)* that, as regards free circulation of goods within the Community, products entitled to "free circulation" are definitively and wholly assimilated to products originating in Member States. The result of this assimilation is that the provisions of Article 30 *(now Article 34*

174 INAMA/VERMULST, 5 *et seq.*
Common rules for imports are laid down in Council Regulation No. 3285/94 (OJ 1994 L 349/53, as modified by Regulation No. 139/96 (OJ 1996 L 21/7)). Article 1(2) of the Regulation provides as a general rule that the products covered by it "*[s]hall be freely imported into the Community and accordingly, [...] shall not be subject to any quantitative restrictions.*"
Until the completion of the internal market, the Common Import Regime on quantitative restrictions for goods originating in third countries was laid down in Council Regulation No. 288/82 (OJ 1982 L 35/1), which was repealed by Council Regulation No. 518/94 (OJ 1994 L 67/77), both containing similar clauses. Council Regulation No. 3285/94 further incorporated the WTO Agreement on Safeguards and replaced Council Regulation No. 518/94.

175 Case 41/76, *Donckerwolcke*, [1976] E.C.R. 1921.

> *TFEU)* concerning the elimination of quantitative restrictions and all measures having equivalent effect are applicable without distinction to products originating in the Community and to those which were put into free circulation in any one of the Member States, irrespective of the actual origin of these products. Measures having an effect equivalent to quantitative restrictions prohibited by the Treaty include all trading rules enacted by Member States which are capable of hindering, directly or indirectly, actually or potentially, intra-Community trade[176] *(parenthesis added)*.

This general statement may be interpreted in the sense that imported goods also enjoy the benefit of the mutual recognition principle once they have been lawfully marketed. The ECJ, however, qualified its statement by holding that the assimilation to products originating in Member States only shows full effect if these goods are subject to the same conditions of importation. Irrespective of the Member State in which the goods were put in free circulation, these import conditions were considered decisive in two respects, regarding customs as well as commercial considerations.[177] Moreover, the ECJ had repeatedly rejected challenges to national measures having equivalent effect by holding that the provisions of the EC Treaty, *i.e.* Article 28 (now Article 34 TFEU), cannot as such be transposed to relations with non-Member countries.[178]

It is in this context that the negotiation of the VER on Japanese VCRs has to be placed. Ultimately, it was the Commission's slackness in effectively challenging the French measure, which continued to channel at least all Japanese VCR imports through Poitier – whether direct or indirect imports – that led Japan to the acceptance of the VER. The VER was negotiated with the Commission in February 1983. Subsequently, France returned to the usual customs clearance

176 *Ibid.*, paragraphs 17–19.

177 *Ibid.*, paragraph 25. It may be questioned, however, what the Court's reference to import criteria with regard to "commercial considerations" entails.

178 This is the case even if there is a directly effective bilateral agreement between the EC and the third country containing a similar provision. Cf. Case 225/78, *Bouhelier*, [1979] E.C.R. 3151, paragraph 6; Case 270/80, *Polydor*, [1982] E.C.R. 329, paragraph 19.
Previously, in Cases 51/75, 86/75, 96/75, *EMI/CBS*, [1976] E.C.R. 811, paragraph 20, the Court also made explicit that the common import regime only relates to quantitative restrictions to the exclusion of measures having equivalent effect.

procedures of VCR imports and abolished its operation in Poitier, and the Commission did not pursue its infringement action pursuant to Article 226 EC Treaty (now Article 258 TFEU) against France. Furthermore, on 18 March 1983, the Commission was informed that Philips and Grundig, the main members of the "Association of Firms with Common Interest in Video 2000" were withdrawing the anti-dumping complaint. The Commission communicated in its Decision[179] that the withdrawal followed "*the implementation of the unilateral decision taken by the Japanese authorities to moderate in 1983 and 1984 the exports of VCRs from Japan to the EC and to set up an export floor-price system.*" The Commission terminated the anti-dumping procedure, considering that "*under these circumstances, [...] protective measures are at present unnecessary.*"

Apparently, after the termination of the VER in December 1985, the Japanese authorities continued to voice their intention to moderate exports and to supervise the export of sensitive products to the EC.[180]

3.2.3 The EC's Controversial Perception of VERs

In the case of Japanese VCRs, and in most other cases, the Commission has characterised VERs as unilateral measures taken by the exporting country rather than "trade agreements" that result from negotiations with or on the initiation of the importing country. This approach appears to be at odds with the "Commission Decision on surveillance and protective measures which Member States may be authorised to take in respect of imports of certain products originating in third countries and put into free circulation in another Member State".[181] According to Article 1 of this Decision, its scope extends to third country imports that are likely to be the subject of protective

179 Commission Decision 83/126 of 30 March 1983 terminating the anti-dumping proceeding concerning imports of television image and sound recorders or reproducers originating in Japan (OJ 1983 L 86/23).

180 Answer of the Commission to Parliamentary Question No. 2011/85 (OJ 1986 C 150/7).

181 Commission Decision 80/47 of 20 December 1979 on surveillance and protective measures which Member States may be authorised to take in respect of imports of certain products originating in third countries and put into free circulation in another Member State (OJ 1980 L 16/14).

measures under Article 134 EC Treaty, and applies, *inter alia*, in cases in which these imports are subject to voluntary export restraint measures applied by the third country *by virtue of a trade agreement*. Arguably, this means that the Commission's possible authorisation of national restrictions on intra-Community trade complementary to the VER could be considered as some sort of involvement of the EC in the completion of the VER, and the VER would hence to be qualified as a trade "agreement" for the purposes of the Decision.

The ambiguous stance of the Commission is heightened by the fact that it considers VERs a lesser evil than unilateral restrictions imposed by the EC. In *Unwrought Aluminium*,[182] the Commission considered that a *negotiated solution* to the problem of imports of unwrought aluminium into the Community would help to ensure problem-free growth in trade in unwrought aluminium between the Community and the countries concerned in this investigation in the future and would, therefore, serve the Community interest. The Commission further noted that it was *forced* to conclude that such a solution is not within reach at present because the non-member countries concerned lack the means to implement it effectively.[183]

Interestingly, the Commission's view appears to have been endorsed by the ECJ in the (first) *Dürbeck*[184] case, when it held that

> [t]he Commission's attempt to secure the agreement of the exporting countries to a voluntary restriction of their exports to the Community before it decided on the temporary suspension of imports from Chile cannot [...] be regarded as unacceptable under Community law since that attempt reflects the Community's endeavour not to adopt except as a last resort coercive measures such as those in issue [...].

This is hardly persuasive since it encouraged the use of VERs to the detriment of unilateral trade restrictions which are – contrary to VERs – subject to domestic (and international) scrutiny.

182 Commission Regulation No. 2227/93 imposing quantitative restrictions on imports of unwrought aluminium originating in Armenia, Azerbaijan, Belarus, Georgia, Kazakhstan, Kyrgyzstan, Moldova, Russia, Tajikistan, Turkmenistan, Ukraine, Uzbekistan, Estonia, Latvia and Lithuania (OJ 1993 L 198/21).

183 *Ibid.*, at 24.

184 Case 112/80, *Dürbeck*, [1981] E.C.R. 1095, paragraph 39.

At odds with the Commission's usual approach towards VERs, the Commission decided, most surprisingly, merely a year after, in *Tableware and Stoneware,*[185] to reject the indication of South Korea, the main supplier of the products at issue, that its industry was prepared to negotiate a VER with the French and United Kingdom producers. Instead, the Commission considered that such action, *i.e.* the negotiation of a VER, would be tantamount to a deviation from the procedure conducted under Council Regulation (EEC) No. 288/82,[186] and that any defensive measures are matters which may be undertaken only by the Community authorities. Moreover, the Commission pointed out that any such protective measure must be compatible with the Community's international obligations and accordingly, the procedures of Regulation 288/82 should be applied.[187]

Whilst the public at large could only speculate on the objective and effects of VERs,[188] the Commission added further confusion to the discussion by stating that it is not prepared to make any cost-benefit analysis, showing, *inter alia*, the effects on consumers, concerning trade restrictions maintained with third countries (among others the VER on Japanese VCRs).[189] Thus, the Commission not only furthered the lack of transparency inherent in all VERs, it openly opposed a major recommendation of the *Leutwiler Report*,[190] namely that in each country the costs and benefits of trade policy actions – whether exis-

185 Commission Regulation No. 3528/82 of 23 December 1982 introducing protective measures in respect of imports into France and the United Kingdom of tableware and other articles of a kind commonly used for domestic or toilet purposes, of stoneware, and terminating the Community investigation procedure in respect of articles of common pottery (OJ 1982 L 369/27).

186 OJ 1982 L 35/1, the "old" Common Import Regime.

187 Commission Regulation No. 3528/82 of 23 December (OJ 1982 L 369/27), Recitals 33–35.

188 Although, in the Answer of the Commission to Parliamentary Question No. 214/85, an overview of the existing VERs concluded between the Community and third countries is given, it cannot afford to give the public a concrete understanding of the operation and effects of VERs (OJ 1985 C 341/5).

189 Cf. Answer of the Commission to Parliamentary Question No. 1289/94 (OJ 1985 C 113/4).

190 GATT, Trade Policies for a Better Future (commonly referred to as "Leutwiler Report"), 1985.

ting or prospective – should be analysed through a 'protection balance sheet'. Furthermore, the *Leutwiler Report* makes a point that has become apparent from the above examples:[191]

> major reason why things have gone wrong with the trading system is that trade policy actions have often escaped scrutiny and discussion at the national level. Clearer analysis and greater openness in the making of trade policy are badly needed [...].

Retrospectively, it may be alleged that the Commission has done little to dampen the enthusiasm surrounding the use of VERs as trade instruments – whether it negotiated the VERs itself, it authorised Member States to continue their application of import restrictions or whether it simply tolerated the various actions undertaken by governments or industries to protect their markets. It also omitted to conduct a more effective Common Commercial Policy by not bringing the bilateral export restrictions that some of the Member States occasionally negotiated independently with third countries before the Court on the ground that they had infringed Article 133 EC Treaty (now Article 207 TFEU). Furthermore, by refusing to, for example, conduct an in-depth economic analysis of the effects of VERs on consumers, the Commission undoubtedly contributed to the avoidance of any public debate, thus enhancing non-transparency.

All these aspects are well illustrated by the *BEUC and NCC*[192] case. The Bureau Européen des Unions des Consommateurs (BEUC), a non-profit-making consumer association at Community level, and the National Consumer Council (NCC), a body set up by the UK government to represent consumer interests, submitted a complaint to the Commission claiming that the agreement concluded between the British Society of Motor Manufacturers and Traders (SMMT) and the Japan Automobile Manufacturers Association (JAMA) restricting the export of Japanese cars to the UK to 11% of the total annual car sales in that country is contrary to the competition provisions of the EC Treaty (Articles 81 and 82 EC Treaty, now Articles 101 and 102 TFEU). In its reply, the Commission emphasised the "commercial

191 *Ibid.*, 35.

192 Case T-37/92, *BEUC and NCC*, [1994] E.C.R. II-285.

consensus" reached between the Community and Japan, whereby all bilateral agreements concerning quantitative restrictions on the importation of cars from Japan and restrictions on registration were to be replaced by a common Community policy by the end of 1992, and stated that in these circumstances there was not, in its view, a sufficient Community interest in opening a formal investigation procedure regarding the SMMT-JAMA arrangement for being anti-competitive.[193] The "commercial consensus" referred to by the Commission is, of course, the Japanese VERs on motor cars discussed above.[194]

In its pertinent parts, the Commission's reply to *BEUC and NCC* may be summarised as follows:[195]

> We have no reason, [due to the arrangement on motor vehicles agreed between the Commission, on behalf of the Community, and the Japanese authorities], to doubt that the arrangement between SMMT and JAMA will end by 1st January 1993.
>
> If we were to 'investigate and evaluate' the *effects in the past of the arrangements*, we would have to take into account the fact that while they were in operation the Community had no common policy on direct exports of cars from Japan. The Commission therefore did not object to Member States' measures restricting those imports. [...] Also, the Commission does not consider itself obliged to investigate *possible past* infringements of competition law if the main purpose of such an investigation would be to facilitate possible claims for compensation by private parties *(emphasis added)*.
>
> The fact that we do not propose to investigate the past *and present* SMMT-JAMA arrangements does not [...] constitute an expression of opinion as to the lawfulness of any possible aspect of the arrangements [...] *(emphasis added)*.
>
> We do not accept your argument [...] that commercial policy considerations should not be taken into account when deciding whether to carry out an investigation under EC competition rules into arrangements concerning direct exports to the Community from a third country [...]. *The situation would have been different if the SMMT-JAMA arrangements had not been known to, and permitted by, the UK authorities, or if they had primarily concerned trade between EC*

193 *Ibid.*, paragraphs 3 *et seq.*

194 For details, see Chapter I.3.2.1, *supra.*

195 Case T-37/92, *BEUC and NCC*, [1994] E.C.R. II-285, paragraph 11.

> *Member States, or if the arrangement was likely to continue after the Community policy comes into effect (emphasis added).*

BEUC and NCC subsequently brought an action for annulment of the Commission's refusal to initiate competition proceedings before the Court of First Instance, arguing that the Commission's reasons for this refusal were insufficient and unlawful. Pointing out that the "commercial consensus" between the Community and Japan was not recorded in writing and that it was not an official agreement but rather a political commitment, the CFI considered that such commitment would not necessarily put an end to the SMMT-JAMA arrangement.[196] It therefore concluded that the Commission was not entitled to infer from the "commercial consensus" that the privately arranged VER would surely come to an end.

In addition, the CFI found that the fact that the UK authorities permitted the SMMT-JAMA arrangement for reasons of commercial policy could not be used by the Commission to justify its decision not to open an investigation. It stressed that the arrangement is not a national measure of commercial policy, but is rather in the nature of a concerted practice between groupings of economic operators, which is liable to fall within the scope of Articles 81 and 82 EC Treaty (now Article 101 and 102 TFEU) if it has as its object or effect to restrict imports into a Member State.[197] Moreover, it reminded the Commission of the settled case-law that the fact that the conduct of undertakings was known, permitted or even encouraged by national authorities is, in any event, irrelevant to the question whether the competition provisions of the EC Treaty apply.[198]

As regards the Commission's speculation that trade between Member States was not affected by the SMMT-JAMA arrangement, and that there was therefore no Community interest to investigate, the CFI supported *BEUNC and NCC* and noted that such arrangements are, by their very nature, liable to impair the functioning of the common market. As measures restricting imports into the Community and affecting the entire territory of a Member State, they are liable to interfere with the

196 *Ibid.*, paragraph 59.

197 *Ibid.*, paragraphs 66 *et seq.*

198 *Ibid.*, paragraph 69 (with further case references).

natural movement of trade, thus affecting trade between Member States, and to reinforce the compartmentalisation of markets on a national basis, thereby holding up the economic interpenetration which the EC Treaty is intended to bring about. It concluded that the Commission's rejection of the initiation of the investigation could not be justified solely by reference to the fact that infringement did not primarily concern trade between Member States, and thus considered it to be insufficiently reasoned.[199]

Whereas the judgment in *BEUC and NCC* may but be welcomed, it does not alter the observation that the Commission's approach towards VERs was clearly biased. Also, there is no record that suggests that the matter had been pursued any further, hence leaving the public largely in the dark on both the operation of VERs as well as the potential illegality of private VERs under trade and competition law.

4 The Popularity of Voluntary Export Restraints and the Rarity of Case Law

4.1 Understanding the Functioning and Popularity of VERs

VERs are protective devices employed by the importing country to protect its injured and/or competitively inferior domestic industry from international competition. This implies that it is *in effect* the importing country that avails itself of the VER despite its voluntary nature, because the importing country or the import-competing industry reaches out for protection by initially asking for such "voluntary" restraint by the exporting country. Usually, the importing country threatens that the exporting country employ a VER so as not to be subjected to a more severe restriction directly employed by the importer.

Today, the welfare comparison between a quota and a VER seems academically exhausted as most economists agree that first, the welfare of an importing country is higher under a quota than a quota-equi-

199 *Ibid.*, paragraph 75.

valent VER; second, the welfare of an exporting country subject to a VER depends on the type of quota or VER and its export-price elasticity; and third, an unaffected exporter's welfare is higher under a VER than a quota. This is to say that VERs do not necessarily accrue benefits to the exporters concerned in absolute terms, but help avoiding a harsher unilateral import quota or a universally applied tariff that would have been imposed by the importing country.

It can be concluded that the only winners from a VER are producers in third countries. On the other hand, producers in a third country may also be confronted with the problem of redirected exports emanating from producers subject to the VER. The restricted exporters are likely to try to regain the lost export market by enlarging their presence in other countries. In response to this, pre-emptive anti-dumping measures (as those adopted by Germany and France at the beginning of the Japanese VER of cars to the U.S.) or the extension of the scope of managed trade are likely to be adopted.

VERs protect the domestic industry at a high cost to domestic consumers. By choosing a VER instead of a tariff consumers are adversely affected by carrying the burden of higher domestic prices (both of the imported and the domestically produced good) and in the form of forgone tariff revenues. The consumers of the importing country are hence not only those who finally pay the net social cost of VERs, but also the eventual benefits reaped by the other groups involved. Further it may be claimed that even the change in relative prices brought about by the upgrading of exports should be considered as a welfare reduction for consumers, because it is the consequence of a policy measure and not a change in tastes or production conditions.

Whatever the distribution of the associated rents of VERs, they are associated with deadweight losses on the consumption and on the production side. Here the classical argument of interest group theory on the relative cohesion and strength of winners (established producers in exporting and importing country) and losers (consumers and market entrants) from protectionism turns out to be crucial in explaining the diffusion of VERs: their lack of transparency contributes further to weakening the probability of a reaction on the part of consumers.

Given the overwhelming dissatisfaction[200] with the effects and consequences of the VERs, one would assume a unanimous rejection of VERs as part of future trade policy.[201] Already by the late 1980s, it was apparent how costly the VERs had been and how their benefits had not matched their large costs. For instance, it is estimated that the annual cost to consumers in the UK through the Japanese VER on video recorder exports accounted for GBP 80 million; the annual cost to British consumers by the VER on motor cars from Japan was around GBP 175 million, in the most optimistic scenario; the restriction on non-leather footwear imports from Taiwan and Korea is estimated to have cost consumers GBP 28 million, and the one on clothing imported from Hong Kong and other developing countries accounted for an estimated GBP 52 million.[202] A news report from *The Economist* alleges that "*[t]he victim is the consumer at a cost of USD 7 billion a year for Europeans buying Japanese cars in the late 1980s*".[203] Across the Atlantic, the situation does not appear to be any better: As a result of the VER between the U.S. and Japan on Japanese car imports, it is estimated that the U.S. consumers paid an extra USD

200 Even the media appeared to be critical of VERs by labelling them as "*among the most pernicious items in [America's] protectionist arsenal*". (WORK Clemens P./BLACK Robert F., "Uncle Sam as Unfair Trader", in: *U.S. News and World Report*, 12 June 1989, p. 42). The *New York Times* claims that "*[t]here is not any justice in these restrictions*". (POWELL James, "Steel Import Restraints Flood the Market With Choice", in: *New York Times*, 7 August 1988, Sec. 3, p. 2). And *The Economist* called the US-Japan automobile VER "*one of the worst errors in the recent history of American trade policy*" (cf. "Once and Future GATT", in: *The Economist*, 22 September 1990, p. 40).

201 The more it is surprising that, merely a few years ago, it was reported that the Clinton administration approached Ukrainian officials concerning the possibility of a negotiated restraint agreement on steel exports in December 2000 when both parties attended a meeting of the OECD's Steel Committee (cf. *Inside U.S. Trade*, vol. 1, 5 January 2001, p. 12). However, last-minute talks to negotiate the VER on steel in order to provide import relief to the U.S. steel companies failed since the Ukraine rejected as too restrictive the U.S. offer on quotas for a range of products, particularly out-to-length plate (cf. *Inside U.S. Trade*, vol. 19(3), 19 January 2001, p. 1 *et seq.*).

202 GREENAWAY/HINDLEY, 25.

203 Cf. "Protectionist Free Trade", in: *The Economist*, 9 October 1993, p. 59.

80 million.[204] According to another report, the costs for American consumers were USD 13.1 billion for the textile and apparel MFA, USD 6.9 billion for the Japanese automobile VER, and USD 2.3 billion for the steel VER in 1988. It is further estimated that total barriers including the VERs cost U.S. consumers more than USD 80 billion in 1988, mainly in higher prices of the restricted imported goods and the protected domestic goods.[205]

The most obvious answer to the question why VERs nevertheless proliferated over the past decades is that some actors, whether public or private, reap large enough (political) benefits from the VERs to induce them to overlook their negative consequences. The appeal of VERs as trade policy instruments may be explained by the fact that they are temporary (although most have been extended), do not induce retaliation, and appear less protective. In addition, VERs have almost infinite flexibility which provides "no-fault" insurance protection, for VER promoters are not expected to define their objectives in any but the vaguest of terms which means that there is little danger of being accused of failure. It may further be argued that trade protection removes the incentives for companies to make the difficult decisions needed to become cost competitive. In this sense, VERs create a "non-complaint" situation since both the exporters and the protected industry have an incentive to maintain protection at a cost to domestic con-

204 CARLTON/PERLOFF, 589.
Most interestingly, another study concerning the VER placed on exports of Japanese automobiles is at odds with much of the existing empirical literature on this issue. In particular, BERRY/LEVINSOHN/PAKES estimate that first, the VERs did not significantly raise prices when they were initiated, but that they were responsible for higher prices of Japanese cars in the late 1980s. Second, it is suggested that, summing over the years for which the VERs were binding, the VERs increased the profits of U.S. producers by about (1983) USD 9.5 billion. It is further found that U.S. producers responded to the VERs by selling more cars, but that they did not significantly raise prices as it was typically the price sensitive consumers which switched from Japanese to domestic cars. Thirdly, the study concludes that the VERs resulted in a small net welfare loss to the U.S.

205 Cf. WORK Clemens P./BLACK Robert F., "Uncle Sam as Unfair Trader", in: *U.S. News and World Report*, 12 June 1989, p. 42 *et seq.*, citing estimates of Gary Clyde Hufbauer (Georgetown University trade expert and Institute for International Economics Senior Fellow).

sumers, and neither is under pressure to adjust to competitive market conditions.[206]

Being a so-called "grey area measure", VERs bear – in addition to the economically adverse effects – significant *information costs* because of their non-transparency: the costs of the bargaining procedures and of the actual implementation are relatively high. In addition, the implementation occurs secretly and bypasses a number of principles incorporated in international and domestic trade and competition laws by lacking a specific legal basis, transparent discussion and procedural guarantees. The contravention of "due process guarantees" by a VER may even amount to a *violation of individual freedoms and property rights of the adversely affected consumers*.[207]

Moreover, the pure fact that VERs are asked for by domestic industries, or bargained upon by public bodies, constitutes in itself a harassment of the future behaviour of exporters, *i.e.* foreign competitors, on the domestic market.[208] This effect is created even in the absence of any material implementation of the VER.[209]

VERs are unique as protective measures inasmuch as they are designed in a way that the importing country is not blamed for a protectionist action (hence preserving its free-trade ideology) but gains the

206 BERGSTEN et al., 152: "VERs contain the seed of their own self-perpetuation."

207 Cf. PETERSMANN, (1988) 22 JWT 27.

208 JONES, (1989) 23 JWT 137.

209 For example, one of the empirical tests of strategic trade policy reveals that a mere expectation of a future VER has a substantial impact on the firms' current exports to a market. On the basis of data concerning VER-subjected Taiwanese leather footwear (1978–1984), Japanese export goods (1981–1987), and Korean video recorders (1986–1987), it is argued that exporters are more likely to reduce their exports in response to a threatened VER the more collusive they are and the more discriminatory and restrictive the threatened restriction. Cf. WINTERS, (1994) 104 The Economic Journal 113 *et seq.*
Another effect of an expected VER to restrain an exporter B, which is competing with exporter A already subjected to a VER, is that the mere expectation raises the domestic equilibrium price. It is demonstrated that the stronger the threat of a VER on exporter B, the higher the domestic equilibrium price, even if the VER is never imposed. Cf. DEAN/GANGOPADHYAY, (1991) 20 Journal of International Economics, 137 *et seq.*

benefits of protecting its injured and/or competitively inferior domestic industry from international competition.

Whereas it is now apparent why the protected domestic industry and trade politicians favour VERs to other trade policy instruments, it is still quite incomprehensible why the losers from VERs, *i.e.* domestic consumers are allowing VERs. Traditionally, free traders have perceived consumers as a natural constituency for international openness. The prolonged existence and persistent growth of the VERs stem, at least partially, from the lack of awareness by the majority of domestic consumers which is a direct result of the non-transparency inherent in most VERs.

4.2 The Rarity of Judicial Decisions on VERs

Many and probably most of the VERs are more than likely inconsistent with the obligations of GATT.[210] There has been abundant literature explaining as to how VERs violate the GATT,[211] in particular Article I (most-favoured-nation clause), Article III (national treatment), Article X (transparency), Article XI (prohibition of quantitative restrictions) and Article XIII (discriminatory administration of quantitative restrictions). Moreover, pursuant to the general principle of international public law spelled out in Article 41 of the 1969 Vienna Convention of the Law of Treaties[212], it was suggested that VERs cannot

210 JACKSON, 205.

211 Authoritative work has been undertaken, for example, by BRONCKERS (1987), 96 *et seq.*, JONES, 6 *et seq.*, MAHNKEN, 306 *et seq.*, OPPERMANN/BEISE/SANDER, 99 *et seq.*, PETERSMANN, 155 *et seq.*, PETERSMANN (1988) 22 JWT 30 *et seq.*, SCHLAGENHOF, (1995) 19 W. Comp. 108 *et seq.*

212 Article 41 of the 1969 Vienna Convention provides:
"*Two or more of the parties to a multilateral treaty may conclude an agreement to modify the treaty as between themselves alone if:*
the possibility of such a modification is provided for by the treaty; or
the modification in question is not prohibited by the treaty and
does not affect the enjoyment by the other parties of their rights under the treaty or the performance of their obligations;
does not relate to a provision, derogation from which is incompatible with the effective execution of object and purpose of the treaty as a whole."

be justified with respect to third countries, which are members to the GATT, but are not participating in the VER.

With regard to governmental measures that restrain exports, for instance, GATT Article XI:1 is clearly attracted, by stating, *inter alia*, that

> [n]o prohibitions or restrictions, other than duties, taxes or other charges, whether made effective through quotas, [...] export licenses or other measures, shall be instituted or maintained by any Contracting Party on the [...] exportation or sale for export of any product destined for the territory of any other Contracting Party.

Moreover, a Note by the Director-General of the GATT on safeguards comments that

> [e]xport restrictions are generally prohibited under Article XI unless covered by an exception. Measures limiting exports to certain contracting parties only are, in any case, contrary to the provisions of Article XIII (except in the exceptional situations laid down in Article XIV) which provides for the non-discriminatory application of such restrictions. It may be argued that this is a very legalistic way of looking at the matter and that 'voluntary export restraints' are not, in fact, export restrictions but import restrictions which are administered by the exporting country. They would, once again, only be in conformity with the General Agreement if they were justified under a particular exception to Article XI and administered in accordance with the provisions relating to the non-discriminatory administration of quantitative restrictions contained in Article XIII. *In fact 'voluntary' export restraints are clearly contrary to the present rules of the General Agreement and are only 'outside the General Agreement' in the sense that governments have not brought them formally to the GATT for examination* (emphasis added).[213]

The language of GATT Article XI:1 therefore seems to cover virtually any measure restraining exports undertaken by a governmental body. In addition, with the establishment of the WTO, the Agreement on Safeguards forbids WTO Members to seek, take or maintain any voluntary export restraints, orderly marketing arrangements or any other similar measure on the export or import side (Article 11:1(b) Agreement on Safeguards).[214]

213 86MDF/4, 6, paragraph 11, as cited in the GATT Analytical Index, 532.

214 According to a footnote inserted in this paragraph, examples of similar measures include export moderation, export-price or import-price monitoring systems, ex-

Given that VERs contravene the Agreement on Safeguards and are most likely incompatible with GATT, the question remains as to why VERs appear to be sheltered from judicial review. One loophole regarding challenging VERs in the WTO/GATT system may derive from the fact that it does not apply to the actions of private parties (or industries) unless there is some sort of government involvement. According to Article 11:3 Agreement on Safeguards WTO Members shall not encourage or support the adoption or maintenance non-governmental measures equivalent to VERs by public and private enterprises. In other words, if there is neither encouragement nor support, the WTO dispute settlement system is not attracted, and a possible action would have to be brought before domestic courts.

Moreover, the WTO is not, nor can it become, some kind of supranational body that imposes its predetermined values and standards on national governments by initiating *ex officio* cases. All WTO disputes are brought by WTO Member governments (private business operators do not have access to the WTO dispute settlement system of the WTO)[215], and the WTO dispute proceedings are thus conducted at inter-governmental level. The basis for the conclusions reached by panels in any such dispute is simply the rules that each sovereign government has itself chosen to abide by. The Appellate Body exists to review the legal basis of panel conclusions in accordance with the principles of international public law. Also, the retention of national regulatory differences, and the national policy objectives underlying them, is not questioned by the WTO system. Consequently, they are not *per se* the subject of dispute settlement scrutiny, but rather, whether the measures themselves are discriminatory, or in other ways breach the agreed multilateral trade rules.

But who would actually complain about a VER? The exporting country or the exporting industry usually establishes a VER in response to a request or a threat of the importing country, and is thus unlike-

port or import surveillance, compulsory import cartels and discretionary export or import licensing schemes, any of which afford protection.

215 The limited participation of private parties in WTO dispute settlement is discussed, for instance, by CHARNOWITZ, (2001) 36 Intereconomics 98 *et seq.*; HERNÁNDEZ-LÓPEZ, (2001) 35 JWT 469 et seq.; HOFMANN, (2004) 31 LIEI 118 *et seq.*; KESSIE, (2000) 34 JWT 10 *et seq.*

ly to complain against itself. The importing country (or the competing industry in the importing country), as being the most affected by the VER, is hardly to complain either since it induced the VER.

Despite these discouraging observations, two categories of probable complainants remain:

- third countries (or industries in third countries), and
- consumers.

Third countries (or industries in third countries) may find it difficult to complain because they may have the benefit of increasing their exports due to the fact that they are not covered by the VER. In such scenario, they would not have an incentive to go against the VER. Conversely, they could be confronted with the problem of redirected exports emanating from the country subject to the VER. In cases where the restricted exporting country is likely to try to regain the lost export market by enlarging their presence in other countries, the trade diversion may put greater competitive pressure on the third country market[216] which, in return, may trigger a complaint under WTO/GATT. In any event, third countries would then still have to prove that they have been harmed, claiming nullification or impairment pursuant to GATT Article XXIII[217] which is again a considerable obstacle to overcome in order for a complaint to be successful.

Consumers are faced with similar hurdles. Considering that the GATT/WTO dispute settlement system is not open to private litigation, challenging VERs – whether they are government-sponsored or purely private – depends on the standing of individuals and foremost,

216 Diversion of trade exports to unprotected markets is, along with the high social costs and the tendency to induce quality upgrading, one of the most important drawbacks of VERs as trade policy instrument; cf. JONES, 64.

217 The Panel Report on *Uruguayan Recourse to Article XXIII* (L/1923, paragraph 15) notes, *inter alia*:
"While it is not precluded that a prima facie case of nullification or impairment could arise even if there is no infringement of GATT provisions, it would be in such cases incumbent on the country invoking Article XXIII to demonstrate the grounds and reasons for its invocation. Detailed submissions on the part of that contracting party on these points were therefore essential for a judgement to be made under this Article".

on the effect GATT/WTO provisions are accorded in the domestic jurisdictions concerned.

Considering that some claimed that over 10% of world trade in the mid-1990s was regulated by VERs,[218] it is – despite the aforementioned adversities – miraculous why the Western Hemisphere has only seen very few cases in which VERs were challenged. The discussion of the most important ones, namely EC's challenge of the U.S.-Japan arrangement on semi-conductors and the U.S. Consumers Union's challenge of VERs on steel, may provide guidance as to why there is, such reluctance to test VERs in courts.

4.2.1 The EC's Challenge of the U.S.-Japan Arrangement on Semi-Conductors

In 1988, the EC lodged a complaint with the GATT against an "Arrangement concerning Trade in Semi-Conductor Products" (the "Arrangement") which was formally concluded between Japan and the U.S. in September 1986.[219] The historical background of the Arrangement lay in the fact that the U.S. used to be the largest producer of semiconductors in the 1970s, but started to face serious competition from Japan which became increasingly important as both producer and exporter of semi-conductor products in the early 1980s. As Japanese exports exceeded those of the U.S. for the first time in 1981, it was only a matter of time until the U.S. semi-conductor industry started to express concerns to the U.S. Government, alleging market access impediments to the Japanese market and possible unfair trade practices of Japanese companies in the U.S. market.[220]

These allegations were backed up by the United States Semi-conductor Industry Association filing a petition under Section 301 of the Trade Act of 1974 against the Japanese Government and complaints brought by several U.S. companies under the anti-dumping law in mid-1985. Not surprisingly, these events not only led to the negotiation of the Arrangement between the governments of Japan and the U.S. but also placed the conclusion of the Arrangement under the

218 As do GAO/SONG at the opening their discussion paper (with further annotations).

219 Panel Report on Japan – Trade in Semi-Conductors, L/6309.

220 *Ibid.*, paragraph 10.

condition to suspend the anti-dumping procedures initiated in the U.S. against imports of certain categories of Japanese semi-conductors[221] as well as the Section 301 proceedings on allegedly restricted market access for U.S. semi-conductor producers.[222]

The Arrangement essentially regulated three main issues: (i) market access whereby the Japanese Government undertook to impress upon the Japanese producers and users of semi-conductors the need to aggressively take advantage of increased market access opportunities in Japan for foreign based firms which wished to improve their actual sales performance and position,[223] (ii) prevention of dumping which was to be achieved by the Japanese Government monitoring cost and prices on a list of semi-conductor products exported to the U.S. as well as monitoring of third country markets, and (iii) general provisions on consultations, on the conditions of amending and terminating the Arrangement, and on the preservation of GATT rights and the interests of third countries.[224]

In its complaint, the EC alleged, *inter alia*, that the measures applied by the Japanese Government to exports of semi-conductors at prices below company-specific costs to certain third countries to implement the Arrangement it had concluded with the U.S. restricted exports of semi-conductors and therefore contravened GATT Article XI. It further considered that the Third Country Market Monitoring system, as established by the Japanese Government, lacked transparency and was thus inconsistent with Japan's obligations under GATT Article X.

Pursuing a twofold strategy, the EC argued that the application of measures, judged to be inconsistent with the GATT obligations of a

221 Namely, Erasable Programmable Read Only Memory (EPROM), and 256 Kilobits and above Dynamic Random Access Memory (DRAM).

222 Panel Report on *Japan – Trade in Semi-Conductors,* L/6309, paragraphs 11 and 12.

223 In particular, this was to be achieved by the Japanese Government's establishment of an organisation which was to provide sales assistance, quality assessment, research fellowship programmes, exhibitions, etc., for foreign semi–conductor producers, and through promotion of long-term relationship between Japanese buyers and foreign producers. Such promotion included joint product development programmes as well as full and equitable access for foreign companies to patents resulting from government-sponsored research and development.

224 Panel Report on *Japan – Trade in Semi-Conductors,* L/6309, paragraphs 13 *et seq.*

contracting party, constituted, in accordance with established GATT practices, a *prima facie* case of nullification or impairment, and that it was therefore not necessary for the Community to provide evidence of the actual damage to its trade caused by the measures undertaken by the Japanese authorities.[225] Alternatively, the EC submitted that, in the absence of a violation of specific GATT provisions, the application of the Third Country Market Monitoring system by Japan had still nullified or impaired the benefits accruing to the EC for the "*simple reason that it deprived the other contracting parties of the most basic benefit of free trade, which was the freedom to buy [...].*"[226] It was put forward that any measure which significantly impeded exports to any contracting party without its consent and which was not covered by one of the exceptions foreseen in the GATT, as well as intergovernmental agreements, such as the Arrangement between Japan and the U.S., necessarily involved nullification or impairment of the benefits to other contracting parties resulting from the GATT.[227]

Of most interest is, however, the resemblance of the Third Country Market Monitoring system put in place by Japan with a VER: in addition to the Arrangement's request not to export semi-conductors at prices below company-specific costs, a statutory requirement for Japanese exporters of semi-conductors to report data on export prices was established. This data collection was complemented by quarterly supply and demand forecasts by MITI which then communicated to manufacturers its concern about the need to accommodate their production levels to the forecasts. Moreover, the issuance of export licences for semi-conductors was closely linked to the information provided on costs and export prices.[228]

According to the information provided by the Japanese Government in the course of the panel, the objective of these forecasts were to provide a reference for Japanese manufacturers in their production schedules, impressing upon them the need to reflect real demand in

225 *Ibid.*, paragraphs 68 and 96.

226 Whilst the EC explicitly referred to the freedom to buy "*at prices at which companies were willing to sell*", it may be contemplated that the freedom to buy also included the *quantity* which companies are willing to sell.

227 Panel Report on *Japan – Trade in Semi-Conductors,* L/6309, paragraphs 69 and 97.

228 *Ibid.,* paragraphs 99 and 100.

their production. Individual companies were expected voluntarily to bring their production almost in line with the forecasts, taking into account the appropriate total production. The Japanese Government submitted that it did not allocate production volume to individual companies, and noted further that for manufacturers to conspire on production volume was against the anti-trust laws in Japan.[229] Although observers later labelled these measures by MITI as a "production cartel"[230], it is interesting to note that the semi-conductor industry was never subject to an antitrust investigation. Moreover, the indirect production control, coupled with the issuance of export licences, amounted to a *de facto* export cartel which is a typical feature of a VER.[231]

The consistency of the Third Country Market Monitoring system with GATT Article XI:1 may therefore give an indication on the legality of VERs under the GATT. In particular, it shall be elaborated whether Japan's contention that the measures to implement the Third Country Market Monitoring system were not legally binding governmental measures limiting the right of Japanese producers and exporters to export semi-conductors at any price they wished, and that the exports were limited by private enterprises in their own self-interest, represents a valid argument to place such allegedly private action outside the purview of GATT Article XI:1.

a) *The Meaning of "Measures" Covered by GATT Article XI*

Regarding GATT Article XI:1, the Panel noted that its wording was comprehensive in the sense that it referred to all measures instituted or maintained by a contracting party prohibiting or restricting the importation, exportation or sale for export of products other than measures that take the form of duties, taxes or other charges. Although the WTO system rejects *stare decisis*,[232] the Panel referred to a previous case

229 *Ibid.*, paragraphs 26 and 27.

230 VAN DE GEVEL, 46.

231 As has been pointed out previously, the implementation of a VER is likely to favour the formation of export cartel (cf., *e.g.*, PETERSMANN, 156).

232 JACKSON/DAVEY/SYKES, 349 *et seq.*; TRACHTMAN, (1999) 40 Harv. Int'l L.J. 337. The *stare decisis* principle is not followed formally by international tribunals, and in public international law, past decisions are not binding: the Appel-

where import regulations allowing the import of a product in principle, but not below a minimum price level, constituted a restriction on importation within the meaning of Article XI:1. The Panel therefore considered that the principle applied to restrictions on imports of goods below certain prices was equally applicable to restrictions on exports below certain prices.[233]

In response to the contention of the Japanese government that the measures undertaken in the framework of the Third Country Market Monitoring system were not restrictions within the meaning of GATT Article XI:1 since they were by their nature neither legally binding nor mandatory, the Panel pointed out that GATT Article XI:1 refers broadly to measures and not, like other GATT provisions, to laws or regulations. Hence, it concluded that the legal status of a measure instituted or maintained by a contracting party restricting the exportation or sale for export of products was not necessarily decisive in determining whether or not it fell under GATT Article XI:1.[234]

In order to support this finding, the Panel referred to an earlier panel report[235] in which Japan, the defendant, had argued that import restrictions on certain agricultural products were justified under GATT Article XI:2(c) because they were necessary to the enforcement of "governmental measures" restricting domestic supplies. Replying to

late Body is not supposed to make definitive interpretations since, according to Article IX:2 WTO Agreement, the exclusive authority to adopt interpretations of the WTO Agreement and the Multilateral Trade Agreements lies with the Ministerial Conference and General Council. Nevertheless, it is to be noted that, generally, previous decisions and doctrine in WTO jurisprudence are that persuasive and central to the discourse of dispute settlement, that a *de facto stare decisis* is observed (cf. STEINBERG, 43).

233 Panel Report on *Japan – Trade in Semi-Conductors,* L/6309, paragraphs 104 and 105. For instance, in a panel concerning a system of minimum import prices (and an associated additional security system) for tomato concentrates maintained by the EC, it was considered that these measures did not qualify for the exemptions provided by GATT Article XI:2, and therefore concluded that the system was inconsistent with the obligations of the EC under GATT Article XI (cf. *EEC – Programme of Minimum Import Prices* (L/4687), paragraph 4.14).

234 Panel Report on *Japan – Trade in Semi-Conductors,* L/6309, paragraph 106.

235 Panel Report on *Japan – Restrictions on Imports of Certain Agricultural Products*, L/6253.

the contention of the U.S., the complainant, that some of the measures which Japan had described as governmental measures, were in many cases non-legally binding administrative guidance and were "*only an appeal for private measures to be taken voluntarily by private parties*", and could therefore not justify the import restrictions,[236]

Japan submitted that "*to the extent that governmental measures were effective, it was irrelevant whether or not the measures were mandatory and statutory*". Japan further specified that the governmental measures "*were effectively enforced by detailed directives and instructions [to local governments and/or farmers' organizations]*", and that "*such centralised and mutually collaborative structure of policy implementation was the crux of government enforcement in Japan*".[237]

Interestingly, the Panel found that the practice of "administrative guidance" played an important role in the enforcement of the Japanese supply restrictions on certain agricultural products. Noting that administrative guidance is a "*traditional tool of Japanese government policy based on consensus and peer pressure*", the Panel consequently decided to base its judgements on the effectiveness of the measures[238], rather than its legal status.

Likewise, in *Japan – Trade in Semi-Conductors*, the Panel therefore considered that the Japanese Government's measures did not need to be legally binding to take effect because "*[t]here were reasonable grounds to believe that there were sufficient incentives or disincentives for Japanese producers and exporters to conform*".[239]

b) The Degree of Government Involvement Necessary to Be Caught under GATT Article XI

Aware of the implications of its first finding, the Panel stressed that not all governmental requests of non-mandatory nature could be regar-

236 *Ibid.*, paragraph 3.2.5.
237 *Ibid.*, paragraph 3.2.6.
238 *Ibid.*, paragraph 5.4.1.4. It is noteworthy that the Panel also stressed that, in view of the special characteristics of the Japanese society, the approach taken in this particular case should not be interpreted as a precedent in other cases where societies are not adapted to this form of enforcing government policies.
239 Panel Report on *Japan – Trade in Semi-Conductors,* L/6309, paragraph 111.

ded as falling within the scope of GATT Article XI:1. It pointed out that relations between governments and industries vary from country to country, from industry to industry, and from case to case, and that the spectrum of governmental involvement has a wide range.[240] Correctly, the Panel thus focused on what degree of government involvement is necessary as to constitute a contravention of GATT Article XI.

In order to determine whether the Japanese measures implementing the Third Country Market Monitoring system for semi-conductors violated GATT Article XI:1, the Panel developed a two-step test: First, it considered whether the measures undertaken by MITI would provide sufficient incentives or disincentives in order to be effective. Second, the Panel examined whether the operation of these measures were essentially dependent on government action or intervention. Provided that these two (cumulative) tests were met, the contested measures could be considered as operating in a manner equivalent to mandatory requirements, thus rendering the difference between the measures and mandatory requirements into one of form and not of substance for the purposes of GATT Article XI:1.[241]

Evaluating the effectiveness of the measures, the Panel considered that, in light of the commitments undertaken by the Japanese Government within the Arrangement, Japanese producers and exporters of semi-conductors must have been aware of their government's undertaking to the U.S. to ensure that certain sales of semi-conductors did no longer take place. The Panel deemed further that they would also have known that any sale contrary to their government's commitment would have adversely affected Japan due to non-performance. Moreover, it was submitted that the producers were conscious about the fact that their government, by means of the Third Country Market Monitoring system, had all the necessary information to identify any producers or exporters selling at prices below cost. Drawing on those circumstances, the Panel concluded that the administrative guidance performed by the Japanese authorities did not require to be legally binding, as *"there were reasonable grounds to believe"* that

240 *Ibid.*, paragraph 108.
241 *Ibid.*, paragraph 109.

there were sufficient incentives or disincentives for Japanese producers and exporters to conform.[242]

Although the Panel did not consider that these circumstances were, by themselves, sufficient to ensure compliance, it appears that the first test was satisfied with the substantiation of the effectiveness of the measures on the balance of probabilities since the Panel went on to consider the additional government measures, aimed at ensuring the compliance of producers and exporters with the Arrangement.

The second test applied by the Panel thus focused on the manner in which the measures operated. On the basis of the Japanese Government's own description of the measures, such as administrative guidance to achieve production cut-backs, actions aimed at reducing supplies and squeezing out grey market transactions, as well as measures relating to production and export administration that have the sole purpose and effect to avoid below cost sales of semi-conductors in third country markets, the Panel examined the structural elements of their implementation. Whilst the producers were required to submit detailed information on costs on a regular basis, the exporters were, under penalty in case of failure, subject to a statutory requirement to supply information on export prices. In addition, in cases where the exporter was not a producer, the origin of the transaction had to be declared and identified.

The Panel hence observed that this system of monitoring provided the Japanese government not only with comprehensive information in order to identify any source of below cost pricing, but also with a strategic tool that would lead any producer or exporter to the conjecture that their government was in a position to have this information.[243] In respect of the quarterly supply and demand forecasts compiled by MITI, the Panel judged that the Japanese Government had intervened to facilitate the reduction of the production levels of semi-conductors through the operation of these forecasts. In an *argumentum e contrario*, the Panel further considered that "*if Japanese producers and exporters were subject to any measure restricting the exportation or sale for export of semi-conductors, they would have to adjust their produc-*

242 *Ibid.*, paragraphs 110 and 111.
243 *Ibid.*, paragraph 113.

tion levels accordingly". Consequently, the operation of the supply-demand forecasts strengthened the effectiveness of the other measures adopted.[244]

Whilst, in the first test, the Panel contented itself with the substantiation of reasonable grounds that the measures provided sufficient incentives or disincentives for producers and exporters of semi-conductors to comply and thus to be effective despite their legally non-binding nature on the balance of probabilities, in the second test, it specifically addressed the strengthening of their effectiveness by means of government actions and interventions, thus demanding a concrete substantiation going beyond a mere description of the measure, and hence, beyond reasonable doubt.

c) Brief Analysis of the Conclusions of the Panel

Considering the combination of the above factors, the Panel concluded that the Japanese government had created an administrative structure, consisting of recurring direct requests by MITI, combined with the statutory requirement for exporters to submit information on export prices, the systematic monitoring of company and product-specific costs and export prices, and the institution of a supply and demand forecasts mechanism, which was designed to directly influence the behaviour of private companies, thus exerting maximum possible pressure on the private sector to cease exports at prices below company-specific costs as well as above forecast levels. Furthermore, the manner in which the measures were operated, led the Panel to the conclusion that they not only facilitated strong peer pressure to comply with the requests by MITI but also fostered a climate of uncertainty as to the circumstances under which exports of semi-conductors could take place. According to the Panel, the entirety of the measures involved bore all the characteristics essential to a formal system of export control, with the mere distinction that it lacked formal, legally binding obligations as regards the exportation or sale for export of semi-conductors. Holding, however, that this amounted to a difference in form rather than substance, the Panel concluded that the way in

244 *Ibid.*, paragraph 114.

which the measures were managed was equivalent to mandatory requirements and thus inconsistent with GATT Article XI:1.[245]

Since the Panel found the Japanese measures to be inconsistent with GATT Article XI:1, it did not consider it necessary to make a finding on whether or not their administration was contrary to the most-favoured-nation provision of GATT Article I, as it was alleged by the EC on the grounds that they only applied to Japanese exports to 16 countries, 14 of which were contracting parties. With reference to *Canada – Administration of the Foreign Investment Review Act*[246], the Panel thus stated "*[t]hat, once a measure had been found to be inconsistent with the General Agreement whether or not it was applied discriminatorily, the question of its non-discriminatory administration was no longer legally relevant.*"[247]

In a similar line of reasoning, the Panel also felt that the present case did not call for a decision on the EC's claim that the lack of information on the Third Country Market Monitoring system for export prices contravened the transparency requirement laid down in GATT Article X, since the Japanese measures had already been found to be inconsistent with GATT Article XI.[248]

The remaining question to be answered by the Panel was thus whether the Japanese measures put EC exporters of semi-conductors at a competitive disadvantage vis-à-vis those of the United States, thus nullifying or impairing benefits accruing to the EC under the GATT and impeding the attainment of objectives of the General Agreement within the meaning of Article XXIII. In respect of the EC's subsidiary claim of non-violation nullification and impairment, the Panel consid-

245 *Ibid.*, paragraph 117.

246 *Canada – Administration of the Foreign Investment Review Act*, L/5504, paragraph 5.16, in which the Panel did not consider it necessary to decide [in this particular case] whether the general reference to the principles of non-discriminatory treatment referred to in GATT Article XVII:1 also comprises the national treatment principle since it had already found the purchase undertakings at issue to be inconsistent with GATT Article III:4.

247 Report on *Japan – Trade in Semi-Conductors*, L/6309, paragraph 122.

248 *Ibid.*, paragraph 128. Thereby, the Panel added that at issue was thus the elimination of the measures or bringing them into conformity with GATT, not their publication.

ered, however, that the evidence submitted by the EC relating to access to the Japanese market were not as such as to find them inconsistent with the provisions of the General Agreement.[249] This finding implies that the Panel, at least in the present case, has put particular emphasis on the burden of proof, requiring the "detailed justification" submitted by the complaining party who brought the non-violation case to be tangible and concrete. In this context, it further appears that the Panel required substantiation of a causal link between the invoked measures and the nullified or impaired benefits.

Another interesting observation that deserves reiteration is that the administrative arrangements surrounding the export of semi-conductors "*[e]xhibited the rationale as well as the essential elements of a formal system of export control.*"[250] This statement qualifies the widely used justification for VERs, namely that they escape scrutiny under the GATT provisions (prior to the Agreement on Safeguards, of course) because they are either purely based on private measures or derive from (non-binding) government actions (or omissions) which merely provide an appeal for private parties to act accordingly. It therefore appears that the imposition of legally binding obligations is not necessary in order for private export restraining practices to be caught by the GATT provisions. However, the difficulty in bringing a VER, whether administered or negotiated between private parties (or industries) with governments, lies in establishing the degree of government involvement.

Corollary to the fact that the GATT/WTO system does not apply to the actions of private enterprises (or industries) is that private parties, which have been directly affected by a foreign country's export restraining policy, cannot seek any kind of remedy, including a non-violation remedy. Instead, the private enterprise or industry is subject to a tortuous political procedure, *i.e.* "championing", which requires the enterprise to persuade its government to file a complaint with the WTO on its behalf. Since the lobbying251 of relevant government

249 *Ibid.*, paragraph 131.

250 *Ibid.*, paragraph 117.

251 For a discussion of the critical elements of a political lobbying strategy, see VINING/SHAPIRO/BORGE, (2005) 5 J. Publ. Aff. 150 *et seq.*

officials may turn out to be a costly and time-consuming process, private parties may thus prefer to challenge the illegality of export restraints before domestic courts.

4.2.2 The U.S. Consumers Union's Challenge of the VERs on Steel

In 1972, the Consumers Union of the U.S. challenged the legality of VERs on steel which were mutually made between certain foreign steel companies as a result of negotiations initiated by the Secretary of State at the direction of the President. Under these arrangements, nine Japanese steel companies, British Steel Corp. and various Western European steel manufacturers belonging to the European Coal and Steel Community (ECSC) undertook by detailed agreements to reduce substantially the amounts of steel they would import into the U.S. for domestic sale. These arrangements which had been monitored and assisted by the Secretary, were consummated in May 1972, and continued through the calendar year 1974.

In a suit against the State Department as well as domestic and foreign steel producers, the Consumers Union of the U.S. contended before the District Court of Columbia[252] that the actions of the State Department officials in stimulating and implementing these arrangements are, in effect, *ultra vires*, and that no member of the Executive Department, including the President, had power under the Constitution and laws of the U.S. to enter into or to arrange the resulting restrictions on foreign commerce in steel. Moreover, it was initially alleged that the steel arrangements violate the Sherman Act.[253] This contention was, however, dismissed by the Consumers Union with prejudice[254] – although it continued to be made in support of the Consumers Union general position that any restraint offensive under the antitrust laws

252 Consumers Union of U.S. Inc. v. William P. Rogers, Secretary of State, et al., 352 F. Supp. 1319 (D.D.C. 1973).

253 Section 1 of the Sherman Act 1 prohibits "[e]very contract, combination in the form of trust or otherwise, or conspiracy, in restraint of trade or commerce among the several States, or with foreign nations [...]" (15 U.S.C. § 1).

254 This is to say that the contention was dismissed for good reason and the Consumers Union was barred from bringing an action on the same claim, *i.e.* the case became *res iudicata*.

cannot be negotiated by the President or his representatives in view of congressional pre-emption in this field.

In a memorandum of opinion, the District Court declared that first, the Executive has no authority under the Constitution or acts of Congress to exempt the VERs on steel from the antitrust laws and that such arrangements are not exempt; and second, that the Executive is not pre-empted and may enter into agreements or diplomatic arrangements with private foreign steel concerns as long as these undertakings do not violate legislation regulating foreign commerce, and that there is no requirement that all such undertakings be first processed under the Trade Expansion Act of 1962.

The District Court further stated that the foreign companies who were apparently persuaded by officials of the State Department to enter into the steel arrangements proceeded on the stated assumption that the mutual agreements achieved were legal under U.S. law, and thus presumably immune from scrutiny under the Sherman Act. Leaving open whether official assurances to this effect may or may not have been given, the District Court found that there is no doubt that the companies proceeded in the belief that the arrangements were legal under U.S. law and that the quiescence of all public authorities of the U.S. on this score had to be noted. Because the Consumers Union had dropped the question whether the Sherman Act had been violated or not, the District Court felt that it had not to decide on this point. Nevertheless it chose to state that it is apparent that very serious questions can and should be raised as to the legality of the arrangements under the Sherman Act, and that the undertakings of the foreign steel companies were made on a mistaken assumption which at least was encouraged, albeit in good faith, by the State Department. It further urged the parties to re-examine their positions and premises in the light of this memorandum and the declarations made.

a) The Affirmative Findings of the Court of Appeals

In the appeal filed by the State Department as well as the domestic and foreign steel producers, the U.S. Court of Appeals, District of Columbia Circuit, repeated that the original complaint by the Consumers Union contained two separate and distinct claims: first, that the VERs were continuing violations of Section 1 of the Sherman Act, and second, that the State Department violated U.S. law by facilitating, bringing about and negotiating the export limitations set forth in VERs without compliance with Section 301 or Section 352 of the Trade Expansion Act of 1962.[255]

In respect of the declaration made by the District Court on the Executive's lack of authority to exempt the VERs from the antitrust laws, the Court of Appeals found that there was nothing in the record that shows the Executive as purporting to grant such an exemption. With reference to a communication of the Department of Justice (DoJ) that no assurances of immunity from the antitrust laws had been given to any of the steel producers, stressing that the Executive did not and would not request any party to enter into an arrangement it believed to be unlawful, the Court of Appeals felt that declarations made by the District Court are without judicial force or effect. It continued to explain that the Sherman Act issue disappeared from the case when the Consumers Union stipulated its dismissal with prejudice. In view of the abandonment of the antitrust claim, the Court of Appeals thus concluded that it had no occasion to concern itself with the discussion of the precise scope of the Sherman Act.[256]

The Court of Appeals then turned to the District Court's declaration that the Executive is not pre-empted, and that there is no requirement that all such undertakings be first processed under the Trade Expansion Act of 1962. Reciting the principal purpose of this Act to, *inter alia*, stimulate the economic growth of the U.S. and to maintain and enlarge foreign markets for its products by means of trade agreements[257], it noted that the President was authorised to enter into such

255 Consumers Union of U.S. Inc. v. William P. Rogers, Secretary of State, et al., 352 F. Supp. 1319 (D.D.C. 1973), 139.

256 *Ibid.*, 140 and 141.

257 Section 1801 (19 U.S.C. § 1801) reads:
"The purposes of this chapter are, through trade agreements affording mutual trade benefits
(1) to stimulate the economic growth of the United States and maintain and enlarge foreign markets for the products of United States agriculture, industry, mining, and commerce;
(2) to strengthen economic relations with foreign countries through the development of open and non-discriminatory trading in the free world; and
(3) to prevent Communist economic penetration."

trade agreements whenever he determined that any existing duties or other import restrictions of any foreign country or the U.S. are unduly burdening and restricting the foreign trade of the U.S.[258] Moreover, he was given the legislative power to modify or continue any existing duty or other import restriction, to continue existing duty-free or excise treatment, or to impose additional import restrictions, as he determines to be necessary or appropriate to carry out the trade agreement.[259] In respect of these presidential powers, the U.S. Tariff Commission[260] fulfilled an advisory function which also included public hearings.[261]

Section 301 of the Trade Expansion of Act of 1962 provided that the Tariff Commission shall undertake investigations of injuries allegedly being done to domestic businesses by, for example, increased imports flowing from a trade agreement. It further provided that, subsequent to public hearings, the Tariff Commission should make a report to the President.[262] In cases where the report affirmatively found injury to domestic industries, the President was given the authority to increase or impose tariff duties or other import restrictions under Section 351 of the Trade Expansion Act of 1962,[263] or alternatively, to negotiate agreements with foreign governments limiting the export from those countries to the U.S. under Section 352 of the Trade Ex-

258 19 U.S.C. § 1821(a). According to sub-section 1, the President's authority to enter into a trade agreement was limited to a period of five years (1962–1967).

259 19 U.S.C. § 1821(a)(2).

260 The U.S. Tariff Commission has become the U.S. International Trade Commission (USITC) in 1975, cf. 19 U.S.C. § 2231(a) and (b).

261 19 U.S.C. §§ 1841 and 1843. Sections 1841–1846 were repealed in 1975 (Pub. L. 93–618, title VI, Sec. 602(d), Jan. 3, 1975, 88 Stat. 2072).

262 19 U.S.C. § 1901. Sections 1901 and 1902 were repealed in 1975 (Pub. L. 93–618, title VI, Sec. 602(d), (e), Jan. 3, 1975, 88 Stat. 2072). Cf. 19 U.S.C. §§ 2251 *et seq.*

263 19 U.S.C. § 1981(a)(1). Regarding the reference to § 1901, cf. note above, and 19 U.S.C. 2251 *et seq.* As aforementioned, the President's authority to negotiate trade agreements was limited in time. 19 U.S.C. § 1981(e) hence provides, *inter alia*, that "*[n]o trade agreement shall be entered into under section 1821(a) of this title unless such agreement permits action in conformity with the provisions of this section.*" Action in conformity with Section 1981 includes, for example, a report to the Congress and the adoption of a resolution of approval within specific time limits.

pansion Act of 1962.[264] Section 232 contains the national security clause providing, *inter alia*, that no action shall be taken pursuant to Section 1821(a) to decrease or eliminate the duty or other import restrictions on any product, if the President determines that such reduction or elimination would threaten to impair the national security.[265]

The Court of Appeals deduced from the set of those provisions that there was a purpose on the part of Congress to delegate legislative powers to the President, so as to give him the possibility to use them in certain defined circumstances or to further certain stated objectives. It found that, in the absence of such delegation of powers, the President would not be in the position to adjust tariffs or impose mandatory import restrictions. Since, as in the present case, the President did not pretend to possess such powers, the Court of Appeals concluded that the President was not required to conform to the procedures specified in the statutes conferring the powers, as would be the case if he had actually used them.[266]

Drawing upon this finding, the Court of Appeals continued to qualify the nature of the VERs on steel. It considered that they do not purport to be enforceable, either as contracts or as governmental measures with the force of law. It judged that they are merely a "statement of intent" on the part of the foreign producers. Acknowledging that the Executive's reception of these undertakings, coupled with its stated willingness to hold consultations on the mutual concerns about the steel import situation, contributed to the foreign producers' expectations that unilateral actions are taken in accordance with the Trade Expansion Act of 1962, the Court of Appeals nevertheless found that the President is not bound in any way to refrain from taking such steps if he deemed them to be in the national interest. Similarly, it held that

264 At that time embodied in 19 U.S.C. § 1981. The possibility to negotiate an orderly marketing agreement (OMA) is now contained in Section 201 (escape clause) of the Trade Act of 1974 (cf. in particular 19 U.S.C. § 2253(3)(e)) and in Section 406 of the Trade Act of 1974 (19 U.S.C. § 2436) for cases where import increases from non-market economy countries are the significant cause of material injury.

265 19 U.S.C. § 1982(a).

266 Consumers Union of U.S. Inc. v. Kissinger, Secretary of State et al., 352 F. Supp. 1319 (D.D.C. 1973), 142 and 143.

Congress is not inhibited from enacting the legislation it desires to regulate the import of steel.[267]

Accordingly, the Court of Appeals declared that communicating, through the Secretary of State, what levels of steel imports the President considers tolerable so as not to initiate legal steps to limit steel imports, merely enables foreign steel producers to conform their actions accordingly. Seemingly aware of the novel questions that were raised in this litigation, the Court of Appeals pragmatically held:

> Regardless of whether the producers run afoul of the antitrust laws in the manner of their response [to the Executive's communication of acceptable import levels], nothing in the process leading up to the voluntary undertakings or the process of consultation under them differentiates what the Executive has done here from what all Presidents, and to a lesser extent all high executive officers, do when they admonish an industry with the express or implicit warning that action, within either their existing powers or enlarged powers to be sought, will be taken if a desired course is not followed voluntarily.[268]

The conclusion of the Court of Appeals is therefore that the question of congressional pre-emption is simply not pertinent to executive action of this sort. Consequently, it ordered that the District Court's declaration with respect to antitrust exemption is vacated, and that the State Department is not precluded by any provision of the U.S. Code from following the course they did, *i.e.* the negotiation of VERs. The Court of Appeals thus affirmed the appealed order.[269]

b) The Dissenting Opinion of Circuit Judge Leventhal

It appears that the Court of Appeals avoided any decision that reached beyond the dispute presented, reflecting that the Court was not willing to take a role in the shifting emphasis between competing branches of government and leaving ultimate solutions as regards the negotiation of VERs to the democratic process. Whilst the majority of the Court of Appeals appeared to opt for a cautious approach, apparently aware of the political (and economic) implications deriving from a judgment that, under similar circumstances, would declare the negotiation of

267 *Ibid.*, 143.
268 *Ibid.*, 143.
269 *Ibid.*, 144.

VERs illegal, dissent was expressed by Circuit Judge Leventhal, in particular with respect to the nature of VERs.

In taking an approach emphasising the effect and enforceability of VERs, Circuit Judge Leventhal voiced reservations as to the Court's pronouncement that the congressional statutes are not pertinent to the present case because the arrangements, incorporated in letters from foreign steel producers which describe themselves as "voluntary restraint undertakings", did not contemplate the mandate of judicial enforceability. He considered that these VERs are bilateral and establish obligations.[270]

Turning first to the effect of the VERs, Circuit Judge Leventhal regarded them as having an economic effect that parallels that of import restrictions proclaimed by the President, since the presidential action – in communicating through the State Department the acceptable import levels of steel – goes far beyond a simple speech or announcement. In his view, this effect implies the nature of the arrangements as being far from mere expressions of desire or intent but rather solemn negotiated bilateral understandings. Circuit Judge Leventhal hence considered that the VERs are not unilateral announcements but the culmination of bilateral discussions that were not only participated in, but initiated by State Department officials. Dismantling the final letters that embody the specific steel limitations by "voluntary restraint undertakings" on the part of foreign steel producers as pure litany, he concluded that the circumstances are instinct with bilateral agreements.[271]

Suggesting that foreign steel producers which have marketed their products in the U.S. do not voluntarily withhold production unless some reciprocal aspect indicating that forbearance is to their advan-

270 *Ibid.*, 146, where he also sarcastically holds that "[t]heir [the VERs'] bite persists notwithstanding the majority's [the Court's majority] effort to coat them as bland vanilla."

271 *Ibid.*, 149. He further supported this finding by pointing out the specificity of the limitations imposed which indicates that they were the result of bilateral bargaining and agreement. In this respect, he also questioned the logic of the foreign steel producers' unilateral offer to "consult" with the U.S. government on levels of steel exports that they have already (unilaterally) fixed, *i.e.* to consult on a "fait accompli".

tage, Circuit Judge Leventhal alleged that this incentive was given by the U.S. Government, *i.e.* the Executive Branch, when it declared that it would not take or initiate other measures to limit steel imports, and that the undertakings would not violate U.S. law.[272] In his view, the inference of bilateral agreements is strengthened when the agreements are placed in a historical context. Export forbearance has historically been obtained by diplomatic exchange of notes[273] or negotiations between the U.S. and foreign governments. Consequently, he argued that international agreements are not limited to those embodied in formal documents but include, as in the present case, the specifying of an arrangement, together with mutual assurances and understandings as to how the parties will behave in response. To cast the steel restraints as unilateral actions rather than agreements is thus an exaltation of form over substance.

Secondly, Circuit Judge Leventhal dealt with the enforceability of the VERs. Putting forward that the very specificity of the limitations contained in the letters of intent makes violations easy to detect and thus the arrangements easy to enforce, he considered that it is by no means clear whether the Executive is without sanctions if the foreign producers fail to abide by the arrangements. He further contemplated that the threat of future unilateral steps taken by the U.S. to limit steel imports carries considerable weight, which is well illustrated by the fact that Japanese producers made compensatory adjustments when they, for example, exceeded their quota in 1969 established by the previous VERs.[274] In support of this consideration, Circuit Judge Leventhal maintained that principles of *promissory estoppel* may bind the foreign producers once the Executive has relied on their representation that they intend to abandon any right they may have had to exceed the limitations stated in the VERs – or as the Executive has relied in this case to take other steps to limit steel imports. Moreover, he

272 *Ibid.*, 150.

273 With reference to the limitation of Japanese textile exports to the U.S. in the 1930s, he stressed that the diplomatic notes themselves referred to an "agreement" or "gentlemen's agreement". Cf. Appendix of *Consumers Union of U.S. Inc. v. Kissinger, Secretary of State, et al.*, 352 F. Supp. 1319 (D.D.C. 1973), 158 *et seq.*

274 *Ibid.*, 150. The previous VERs started in 1969 and lasted for three years (cf. *ibid.*, 147).

contended that, even if the parties did not contemplate judicial enforcement, the arrangements still embody a trade restraint, and that a trade agreement may be "enforceable" only in the sense that it depends on "good faith" performance by the parties, which is particularly true for international agreements between countries. He thus found that the reliance on good faith does not make the VERs any less solemn agreements which are both intended to affect the conduct of the parties and likely to have that result.[275]

In light of the above arguments, Circuit Judge Leventhal concluded that the VERs on steel present an import restraint having a composite characteristic, in terms of their effect and nature, so as to be subject to the procedures and requirements set forth in the Trade Expansion Act of 1962, thus finding that the executive negotiation and acceptance of the undertakings are an activity in a field that has been pre-empted by Congress. Reiterating the legislation passed by Congress in respect of general import restrictions available to the President, such as a proclamation under the escape clause (Section 301 of the Trade Expansion Act of 1962) or orderly marketing agreements (Section 352(a) of the Trade Expansion Act of 1962), he stressed that these provisions retain procedural safeguards to ensure against Executive finalisation of restraints in secrecy.[276] Acknowledging the delicacy of the issue of pre-emption and demonstrating understanding for the Court of Appeals in deferring the matter to the President and Congress to clarify, he nevertheless maintained that he would have decided this case against the Executive.[277]

4.3 Preliminary Conclusion

Interestingly, both the Panel in *Japan – Trade in Semi-Conductors* and the approach of Judge Leventhal, dissenting the Court of Appeals' judgment in *Consumers Union of U.S. v. Kissinger*, rely on the nature of VERs and their effect. Despite the non-mandatory nature of such

275 *Ibid.*, 151.
276 *Ibid.*, 154 *et seq.*
277 *Ibid.*, 158.

agreements, they equally conclude that the complex of behaviours surrounding VERs amount to a system that is comparable to a legally binding measure and thus susceptible to judicial control.

The political sensitiveness is, however, well reflected in both cases: whilst the Panel as well as the Court of Appeals required a substantial degree of government involvement to be demonstrated, the Court of Appeals failed to recognise the "effects doctrine" developed by Judge Leventhal, thus leaving a clarification of the matter to the legislative and executive organs rather than stipulating its illegality. Similarly, the Panel, first, by elaborating a test designed to appreciate the substantiation of the VER's effectiveness and second, by merely stating that for the purposes of a non-violation case the evidence submitted by the EC relating to access to the Japanese market was not sufficient, *i.e.* not sufficiently "detailed", has provided a precedent which leaves as many questions open as it answered. Also, by not finding it necessary to pronounce itself neither in respect of a possible violation of the non-discrimination principle nor as regards the transparency clause contained in GATT Article X, the Panel failed to shed some light on two of the most prominent characteristics of VERs, their inherently discriminatory aspect and the non-transparency leading to their implementation.

Being, as to date, the only cases in which governmental involvement was challenged in respect of VERs under trade law (as opposed to competition law), they nevertheless bear a considerable importance as to the boundaries of their judiciability. Considering that various observers of trade relations have accounted hundreds of VERs in place in the 1980s, the lack of judicial cases is astonishing – but self-explanatory for the complexity of VERs as trade policy instruments. In particular, the classical argument of governments or import-competing producers that the VERs are unilateral measures and thus beyond their influential sphere further demonstrates the difficulty in bringing such a case before a court. This discouraging situation is heightened by the fact that the most obvious losers from VERs, *i.e.* consumers, are limited in successfully challenging VERs to the extent that the evidence alleging a governmental involvement submitted by them has to undergo extensive scrutiny, or alternatively, that they cannot rely on international provisions in a domestic (or European) court.

CHAPTER II

The Relationship of WTO Law and EU Law

Whereas it is recognised that international agreements may confer rights upon individuals which can be invoked in courts, in most jurisdictions limitations are placed on the derivation of such rights from international agreements. The issue is whether such agreements provide for legal rules capable of enforcement through litigation when private parties contend that their rights have been affected, or whether they simply contain rules applicable to sovereign states. In EC law, the possibility for an individual to invoke international provisions in a national context is determined by the question whether these rules are directly applicable or not. Before discussing the domestic legal status of the WTO Agreements, and in view of challenging VERs the Safeguards Agreement, it is thus necessary to examine the question of whether and how an international agreement becomes binding upon the Community (and its Member States), and of whether and when it becomes part of EC law.

1 The Status of International Agreements in the EU Legal Order

Once an international agreement has been concluded the question arises as to what extent it produces effect within the Community legal system.[278] Accordingly, four issues may be distinguished: (i) the provisions of an international agreement as an integral part of Community

278 Summaries are given, for instance, by ENGELBERGER, 154 *et seq.*; LEE/KENNEDY, (1996) 30 JWT 74 *et seq.*; WOUTERS/VAN EECKHOUTTE, 32 *et seq.*

law, (ii) their possible direct effect, (iii) their location within the hierarchy of norms, and (iv) their judicial application.

1.1 International Agreements as "Integral Part" of EU Law

The first inquiry must be whether international law is directly applicable within the Community legal system irrespective of internal implementation. In this context, the term direct applicability is thus not used as being synonymous to direct effect as it is done by the ECJ and some of the legal writers but refers to international agreements which do not need further implementing steps after their conclusion to become applicable in the law of the parties to the agreement.

The EC Treaty did not offer much guidance on the status and effect of international agreements in the EC legal system, except that, pursuant to Article 300(7) EC Treaty, agreements concluded under these conditions are "*binding on the institutions of the Community and on Member States*". Apart from that, the EC Treaty is silent on this matter, and the Treaty on the Functioning of the European Union, namely Article 218 TFEU, has fully removed a reference to bindingness, thus leaving it to the Community courts to provide some answers.

In *Haegeman*,[279] the ECJ referred for the first time to agreements "adopted by the Community", *in casu* the Association Agreement entered into with Greece by virtue of Article 300 EC Treaty, as – from the date it comes into force – an "*integral part of Community law*".[280] Expanding on this finding, the ECJ later explained in its judgment in *Kupferberg*[281] that an international agreement concluded by the Community institutions must be considered an integral part of the Community legal system because the Member States, in ensuring respect for the commitments arising from such agreement, fulfil an obligation not only in relation to the counter-party of the agreement but also and above all in relation to the Community which has assumed responsibility for the due performance of the agreement. According to the

279 Case 181/73, *Haegeman*, [1974] E.C.R. 449.
280 *Ibid.*, paragraph 5.
281 Case 104/81, *Kupferberg*, [1982] E.C.R. 3641.

Court it follows from the "*Community nature*" of such provisions that their effect in the Community may not be allowed to vary, and that is therefore for the Court to ensure their uniform application.[282]

In order for a provision to be directly applicable, it must be unconditional, sufficiently clear and precise to be judicially applied, and it must not require any further implementation by an institution with discretionary power in this matter.[283] The Court held that an international agreement will be directly applicable "*when, regard being had to its wording and the purpose and nature of the agreement itself, the provision contains a clear and precise obligation which is not subject, in its implementation or effects, to the adoption of any subsequent measure*".[284] International agreements are therefore part of the applicable law in the sense of Article 220 EC Treaty (now, in substance, Article 19 TEU).

1.2 The Doctrine of Direct Effect

The issue of direct applicability is often confused with the narrower question of direct effect, concerning whether an international provision can be invoked by an individual.

Ever since *van Gend en Loos*,[285] the Court of Justice has construed textually programmatic EC Treaty provisions as constituting individual rights that have direct effect. The ECJ's reasoning was that provisions will have direct effect when (i) they have a clear and binding aim, (ii) do not involve the exercise of broad discretionary powers, and (iii) are legally complete. Coupled with the doctrine of primacy (*Costa v. ENEL*)[286], EC law has been given predominance over national law in order to leverage Community law the utmost effective-

282 *Ibid.*, paragraphs 13 and 14.

283 For a summary of the criteria cf. Opinion of Advocate General Mayras delivered on 28 May 1974 in Case 2/74, *Reyners*, [1974] E.C.R. 631.

284 Case 17/81, *Pabst*, [1982] E.C.R. 1331, paragraph 27; Case 12/86, *Demirel*, [1987] E.C.R. 3719, paragraph 14; Case C-18/90, *Kziber*, [1991] E.C.R. I-199, paragraph 15.

285 Case 26/62, *van Gend en Loos*, [1963] E.C.R. 1.

286 Case 6/64, *Costa/ENEL*, [1964] E.C.R. 1251.

ness and to ensure uniform application. This is also known as the *effet utile* principle[287] which may best be described as a teleological argument designed to overcome the structural weakness of Community law compared with the full range of state powers. It is a means to give Community law the most far-reaching effect in any given case. Methodologically, it is more than a mere rule of interpretation but it is surely not apt to bring about an amendment of the TFEU. It may be termed as an unwritten instrument in the hands of the ECJ to develop Community law.[288]

Arguably, international agreements concluded with other states or international organisations may be seen as traditional international treaties binding only upon the signatories. The ECJ held, however, that international agreements can also, in certain circumstances, be directly effective. In particular, it considered that if the question was not settled in the agreement itself, the Court would decide on a case-by-case basis whether an individual could rely on the provisions of an international agreement.[289] Interestingly, the ECJ also utilised the *effet utile* principle in interpreting international agreements, in particular with regard to association and free trade agreements.

Regarding association agreements, the ECJ built up on *Haegeman* in its judgment in *Bresciani*[290] holding that the imbalance between the

287 Doctrine of useful effect of Community law (*effet utile*).

288 As a literate example for the application of the *effet utile* principle within the Community see Case 41/74, *van Duyn*, [1974] E.C.R. 1337, paragraph 12: "*Where the Community authorities have, by directive, imposed on Member States the obligation to pursue a particular course of conduct*, the useful effect of such an act would be weakened if individuals were prevented from relying on it before their national courts and if the latter were prevented from taking it into consideration as an element of Community law. *Article 177, which empowers national courts to refer to the Court questions concerning the validity and interpretation of all acts of the Community institutions, without distinction, implies furthermore that these acts may be invoked by individuals in the national courts. It is necessary to examine, in every case, whether the nature, general scheme and wording of the provisions in question are capable of having direct effects on the relations between Member States and individuals*" (emphasis added).

289 Case 104/81, *Kupferberg*, [1982] E.C.R. 3641, paragraph 17.

290 Case 87/75, *Bresciani*, [1976] E.C.R. 129 where the Yaounde Convention was examined.

obligations assumed by the Community towards the associated states does not prevent recognitions by the Community that some of its provisions have direct effect.[291] The Court also dealt in *Kupferberg*[292] with certain aspects of balance of obligations between the parties, more specifically with the question whether reciprocity or the absence thereof, has any bearing on direct effect. Under the reservation that there must be *bona fide* performance of every international agreement, the fact that one of the parties did not recognise direct effect is not in itself such as to constitute a lack of reciprocity in the implementation of the agreement.[293]

Having declared the imbalance of obligations in itself as insufficient to determine direct effect, the ECJ turned to examine the wording of the obligations. In its judgment in *Bresciani*, it found that by expressly referring – in a provision contained in the association agreement – to an article of the EC Treaty, the Community undertook precisely the same obligation towards the associated states as, in the EC Treaty, the Member States assumed towards each other. Since the obligation concerned was specific and not subject to any implied or express reservation on the part of the Community, it was considered capable of conferring on those subject to Community law the right to rely on it before the courts.[294]

In *Polydor*[295], however, the Court focused on the argument that the aims of the international agreement were different from those of the EC Treaty. It found that the similarity of terms is not a sufficient reason for transposing the provisions of the free trade agreement with Portugal to the above-mentioned case-law.[296] Moreover, it relied on the reciprocity argument that the Community would suffer by granting direct effect to agreements that may not be granted similar effect in the courts of the other parties to those agreements. It therefore considered that the scope of that case-law must be determined in the light of – or one may say limited to – the Community's objectives and ac-

291 *Ibid.*, paragraph 23.

292 Case 104/81, *Kupferberg*, [1982] E.C.R. 3641.

293 *Ibid.*, paragraph 18.

294 Case 87/75, *Bresciani*, [1976] E.C.R. 129, paragraph 25.

295 Case 270/80, *Polydor*, [1982] E.C.R. 329.

296 *Ibid.*, paragraph 15.

tivities as set forth by the EC Treaty which led the Court to emphasise the importance of ultimately uniting national markets into a single market having the characteristics of a domestic market.[297] In other words, the ECJ was of the opinion that the free trade agreement with Portugal was clearly not intended to achieve a comparable outcome which led it to limit granting direct effect merely based on the similarity of wording.

In its in judgment in *Legros*,[298] the ECJ confirmed the line of jurisprudence initiated in *Polydor* with respect to free trade agreements. La Réunion, a French overseas department, imposed a levy called "octroi de mer" which was based on customs valuation on all goods imported from outside the region. Asked whether this charge was compatible with the Community's free trade agreement with Sweden, the ECJ repeated that identity of words in the EC Treaty and in a free trade agreement does not necessarily imply identity of interpretation.[299] In this case, the ECJ considered that the free trade agreement's *effet utile* would be severely impaired if the provision in question were to be interpreted more restrictively than its EC counterparts,[300] and concluded that the "octroi de mer" contravened the free trade agreement.

This line of reasoning has since been spelled out on several occasions. The ECJ reiterated that

> [t]he extension of the interpretation of a provision in the [EC] Treaty to a comparably, similarly or even identically worded provision of an agreement concluded by the Community with a non-member country depends on, *inter alia*, the aim pursued by each provision in its own particular context. A comparison between the objectives and context of the agreement and those of the Treaty is of considerable importance in that regard.[301]

With regard to the association agreement with Poland, for instance, the ECJ clearly emphasised the difference in holding that the agreement "*[...] is designed simply to create an appropriate framework for*

297 *Ibid.*, paragraph 16.
298 Case C-163/90, *Legros*, [1992] E.C.R. I-04625.
299 *Ibid.*, paragraphs 23 to 25.
300 *Ibid.*, paragraph 26.
301 Case C-63/99, *Gloszczuk*, [2001] E.C.R. I-06369, paragraph 49; Case 312/91, *Metalsa*, [1993] E.C.R. I-3751, paragraph 11.

the Republic of Poland's gradual integration into the Community, [...], whereas the purpose of the Treaty is to create an internal market, establishment of which involves the abolition, as between Member States, of obstacles to the free movement of goods, persons, services and capital."[302] Based on this observation, the ECJ concluded that the provision concerned lacked direct effect, and that an individual could hence not rely on it before the Court.

Another consideration raised by the ECJ in connection with obligations deriving from an international agreement concerned possible dispute solving mechanisms, such as consultation procedures or understandings on interpretation. For instance, the free trade agreement with Portugal provided not only for a special institutional framework but also contained safeguard clauses enabling the parties to derogate from certain obligations. This lead the ECJ in its judgment in *Kupferberg*[303] to find that the mere fact of having established a special institutional framework for consultations and negotiations in relation to the implementation of the agreement is not in itself sufficient to exclude all judicial application of the agreement. It hence concluded that none of these criteria could prevent individuals from relying on the provisions of the Agreement before a court in the Community.[304] Therefore, neither the imbalance of obligations undertaken in an international agreement nor the differences in their application are considered to be at odds with the principle of reciprocity.

The ECJ expanded on this finding by applying similar standards for determining direct effect regarding provisions of decisions taken by an "institutional" body set up by the international agreement. In *Demirel*,[305] which dealt with the free movement of workers under the association agreement with Turkey, the Court had to examine the effect of decisions adopted by the Council of Association. The peculiarity of this case lay in the fact that, in structure and content, the asso-

302 Case C-63/99, *Gloszczuk*, [2001] E.C.R. I-06369, paragraph 50.

303 Case 104/81, *Kupferberg*, [1982] E.C.R. 3641.

304 *Ibid.*, paragraph 20. Similarly, in *Bresciani*, the ECJ found that the inclusion of a consultation mechanism in the Yaounde Convention regarding the conditions of application of the article concerned did not prevent it from having direct effect ([1976] E.C.R. 129, paragraphs 24 and 25).

305 Case 12/86, *Demirel*, [1987] E.C.R. 3719.

ciation agreement merely set out the aims of the association and laid down guidelines for the attainment of those aims, whereas in respect of certain specific matters only protocols annexed to the agreement provided for detailed rules. In addition, certain decision-making powers were conferred on the Council of Association in order to achieve the aims set out in the agreement.[306] Based on these circumstances, the ECJ was prepared to apply the criteria established in its previous case-law to the only decision which the Council of Association had adopted so far[307] – if it had concerned the matter at hand which was not the case.

Likewise, in confirming the approach taken in *Demirel*, the Court considered in a later judgment that due to the power of decision vested in the Association Council of the association agreement with Turkey, and the fact that the Association Council had placed by decision certain obligations within an institutional framework of the association, the decision in question forms, from its entry into force, an integral part of the Community legal system.[308] The implementation of that decision did hence not require the adoption of supplementary measures at Community level. In *Sevince*,[309] the Court also held that, like provisions of agreements concluded by the Community with non-member countries, provisions adopted by an Association Council created by an association agreement must be regarded as being directly applicable when, regard being had to their wording and their purpose and nature, as well as to those of the association agreement, they contain a clear and precise obligation which is not subject, in its implementation or effects, to the adoption of any subsequent measure. The ECJ further explicitly stated that "*[t]he same criteria apply in determining whe-*

306 *Ibid.*, paragraphs 16 and 17.

307 *Ibid.*, paragraph 14 and 22. The ECJ further found that neither the provisions of the association agreement nor of the protocols were directly applicable in a challenge of national measures because they were not sufficiently precise and unconditional (paragraph 23). In fact, it considered that the agreement as a whole lacked direct effect (like in Joined Cases 21–24/72, *International Fruit Company*, [1972] E.C.R. 1219).

308 Case 30/88, *Greece v. Commission*, [1989] E.C.R. 3711, paragraph 13.

309 Case C-192/89, *Sevince,* [1990] E.C.R. I-3461.

ther the provisions of a decision of the Council of Association can have direct effect".[310]

Reiterating that measures emanating from bodies which have been established by an international agreement, and which have been entrusted with responsibility for its implementation, are directly linked to the agreement which they implement, form part of the Community legal order,[311] the ECJ also considered that "recommendations" of a Joint Committee fall within this category of measures. As the term already suggests, however, such recommendations were considered not to confer upon individuals rights which they may enforce before national courts, but the ECJ declared at the same time that the national courts are nevertheless obliged to take them into consideration in order to resolve disputes submitted to them, especially when they are of relevance in interpreting the provisions of the international agreement.[312]

In addition to provisions in association[313] and free trade agreements, the Court of Justice has continued to find directly effective provisions in bilateral trade agreements as, for example, the national treatment, *i.e.* non-discrimination, provision of the co-operation agreement between the EC and Morocco.[314]

Provided that a provision is sufficiently clear and precise, and does not require the adoption of subsequent implementing measures, the additional elements examined by the ECJ when determining whether an international agreement is capable of having direct effect may thus be summarised as follows: (i) reciprocity in the initial balance of the obligations, (ii) reciprocity in the ability to enforce these obligations, (iii) the possibility of derogation, and (iv) the method of dispute settlement established by the agreement. None of these elements was, however, considered in itself sufficient to devoid a provision of being directly effective.

310 *Ibid.*, paragraph 15.

311 *Ibid.*, paragraph 10.

312 Case C-188/91, *Deutsche Shell*, [1993] E.C.R. 363, paragraphs 17 and 18.

313 See also Case C-432/92, *Anastasiou et al.*, [1994] E.C.R. I-3087 for the EC/Cyprus association agreement.

314 Case C-18/90, *Kziber*, [1991] E.C.R. I-199, paragraph 23.

1.3 The Classification of International Agreements in the Hierarchy of Norms

The EC Treaty (now the TFEU) does not explicitly address how the different forms of Community law relate to international law.[315] The effect of direct applicability within the Community legal order is that international agreements take priority over secondary legislation[316] and other Community acts. International agreements can therefore be used to challenge their validity,[317] though not the provisions of the Treaty itself.

The Court of Justice did not expressly rule on the relationship between primary Community law and international law. In its judgment in *Racke*[318], the ECJ held, however, that the Community must respect general international law in the exercise of its powers. It concluded therefore, that the Community is required to comply with the rules of customary international law, and that these rules are also binding on the institutions and form part of the Community legal order. Moreover, having regard to Article 218(11) TFEU (*ex* Article 300(6) EC Treaty) which states that opinions (of the ECJ) may be obtained as to whether a proposed agreement is compatible with the provisions of the Treaty, implies that international law is subordinate to primary Community law.[319]

315 The primacy of international agreements over national law is not questioned. The general acknowledgement of the supremacy of Community law over national law precludes that international agreements concluded by the Community prevail national law.

316 The ECJ accepts in its constant case-law that international agreements are supreme to all secondary Community law as, *e.g.*, Case C-103/94, *Krid v. CNAVTS*, [1995] E.C.R. I-719, paragraphs 21 *et seq.*, Joined Cases 21–24/72, *International Fruit Company*, [1972] E.C.R. 1219, paragraph 7.

317 *Ibid.* and Case 9/73, *Schlüter*, [1973] E.C.R. 1135, where the ECJ held that "[t]he validity of acts of the institutions, [...], cannot be tested against a rule of international law unless that rule is binding on the Community and capable of creating rights of which interested parties may avail themselves in a court of law" (paragraph 27).

318 Case 162/96, *Racke*, [1998] E.C.R. I-3655, paragraphs 45 and 46.

319 PETERSMANN, (1997) 8 EuZW 327.

The question whether the Court of Justice may use international law to review both secondary legislation and discretionary administrative acts of the other Community institutions, even though international law must be subordinate to the founding Treaties within the Community legal system,[320] is thus directly linked to the hierarchy of norms. The question of the hierarchy of norms does, however, not arise as a matter of EC law unless a provision of an international agreement is directly effective and invocable.

1.4 The Judicial Application of International Agreements

The case-law of the Court of Justice demonstrates that it has constantly sought to develop a comprehensive and uniform body of Community law. It is obvious that the ECJ has extended its jurisdiction beyond the competence of the Community, and also maximised the scope of judicial intervention in the light of Article 300(6) EC Treaty (now Article 218(11) TFEU).[321] The ECJ has not only accepted a broad interpretation of the notion of an agreement,[322] but has also been willing to deal with unclear formulations of questions put before it.[323] Moreover, it has stressed that an opinion on certain questions can be asked for, irrespective of the fact that these questions may be dealt with by means of other remedies, in particular by an action for annulment under Article 263 TFEU (*ex* Article 230 EC Treaty).[324] The result of the jurisprudence is that the ECJ will accept any question for judicial review which gives rise to the substantive or the formal validity of an international agreement with regard to its compatibility with the founding Treaties.[325]

320 EHLERMANN, (1985) 1 EuR 93.

321 ZAMPINI, 33 *et seq.*

322 *Opinion 2/92*, OECD, [1995] E.C.R. I-521, paragraph 8.

323 In particular questions which concern the division of powers between the Community and the Member States; cf. *ibid.*, paragraph 13 and *Opinion 1/94*, Agreement Establishing the WTO, [1994] E.C.R. I-5267, paragraph 9.

324 *Opinion 2/92*, [1995] E.C.R. I-521, paragraph 14.

325 *Ibid.* and *Opinion 1/75*, Understanding on a Local Cost Standard, [1975] E.C.R. 1355, on 1361, and, on 1360 where the Court highlights that the compatibility

From this it is evident that the ECJ's competence to express its opinion is preventive and that the effectiveness of its judicial intervention is limited. It would contradict the logic of Article 218(11) TFEU (*ex* Article 300(6) EC Treaty) if the Court ruled on the compatibility of an agreement that has already been concluded, since an adverse opinion requests a previous amendment of the Treaties before entry into force of the agreement.[326] As the Court itself pointed out, the purpose is to forestall complications which would result from legal disputes concerning the compatibility of international agreements binding upon the Community with the Treaty.[327] In any case, the Court affirmed that it is still possible to bring an action for annulment against the Council's decision to conclude the agreement.[328]

Judicial review concerns the extent to which the ECJ may use international law to examine the discretion of the other institutions in the creation and interpretation of international and Community law. In the light of the concepts of co-ordination and harmonisation the Court of Justice has successfully developed its role in resolving conflicts when the subject matter falls within the competence of the Community. Nevertheless, the ECJ has not accepted the review of legality of an international agreement itself but has taken account of the specific character of international agreements as a source of Community law.[329] Moreover, the Court's position reflects the fact that the Community legal order is based on the rule of law which means that neither the Member States nor the institutions can evade judicial scrutiny.[330]

In *Haegeman*,[331] the ECJ stated that the association agreement with Greece concluded under Articles 300 and 308 EC Treaty (*ex* Articles 228 and 235 EEC Treaty, now Articles 218 and 352 TFEU))

has to be assessed in regard to all the rules of the Treaty, those which determine the extent of the powers as well as the substantive rules.

326 *Opinion 3/94*, GATT-WTO Bananas, [1995] E.C.R. I-4577, paragraph 13.

327 *Opinion 1/75,* [1975] E.C.R. 1355, on 1360.

328 *Opinion 3/94,* [1995] E.C.R. I-4577, paragraph 22.

329 EPINEY/KADDOUS/RIDORE, (1998) 8 EFLR 303 *et seq.*

330 Explicitly stated in Article 263(1) TFEU (ex Article 230(1) EC Treaty): "The Court of Justice shall review the legality of acts [...] intended to produce legal effects [...]".

331 Case 181/73, *Haegeman*, [1974] E.C.R. 449.

was an act of a Community institution, the Council in this case. Since the provisions of the agreement were found to form an integral part of Community law, the Court, accordingly, had jurisdiction to deliver a preliminary ruling concerning their interpretation.[332] The ECJ did not distinguish between the provisions falling within the Community's competence and those falling within the competence of the Member States even though the association agreement was a mixed agreement.[333]

The ECJ, furthermore, held in *Kupferberg*[334] on the free trade agreement with Portugal, which was not a mixed agreement, that the Member States taking measures to implement some of its provisions fulfilled not only an obligation towards the non-member country but above all towards the Community.[335] In addition, it pointed out that the effect of such provisions may not vary according to whether their application is in practice within the responsibility of the Community institutions or of the Member States due to their Community nature. The Court concluded that it is therefore in its jurisdictional framework to interpret the provisions of the agreement in order to ensure their uniform application throughout the Community.[336]

The Court of Justice has never explicitly ruled that provisions of a mixed agreement falling within the competence of the Member States do not come under its jurisdiction – nor has it stated that Community law does not determine the domestic legal status of such provisions. As aforementioned, in *Demirel*,[337] the Court adopted a broad interpretation of the Community's competence to conclude association

332 *Ibid.*, paragraphs 2 to 6. In *Demirel*, the Court repeated that an international agreement is an act taken by a Community institution in the sense of Article 267(1)(b) TFEU (*ex* 234(1)(b) EC Treaty) and that it is, therefore, competent to interpret the agreement ([1987] E.C.R. 3719, paragraph 7).

333 The issue of the distinction of the competencies within mixed agreements was neither addressed in Case 87/75, *Bresciani*, [1976] E.C.R. 129, nor in Case 17/81, *Pabst*, [1982] E.C.R. 1331.

334 Case 104/81, *Kupferberg*, [1982] E.C.R. 3641.

335 *Ibid.*, paragraph 13.

336 *Ibid.*, paragraph 14.

337 Case 12/86, *Demirel*, [1987] E.C.R. 3719.

agreements, and in *Sevince*,[338] it considered decisions of the association council as being an integral part of Community law.

The notion of shared competence[339] in the Court's case-law[340] has to be seen as including not only the process of negotiation and conclusion of an agreement, but also the fulfilment of the obligations undertaken. This was made particularly clear in *Opinion 1/94*,[341] where the ECJ explicitly referred to the above if the subject matter of an agreement falls in part within the competence of the Community and in part within that of the Member States. It stressed the necessity of close co-operation between the Member States and the Community institutions[342] by concluding that unity in the international representation of the Community requires such commitment.[343]

338 Although the Court limited its jurisdiction in so far as the agreement was an act adopted by one of the Community institutions. Cf. Case C-192/89, *Sevince,* [1990] E.C.R. I-3461 and Case C-237/91, *Kus*, [1992] E.C.R. I-6781.

339 The concept of "shared power" or "joint competence" seems to be used interchangeably by the Court of Justice. In any event, it implies a duty of co-operation which, according to NEUWAHL, the ECJ offered as "*[t]he panacea for situations where the Community Court risked being debilitated by the presence of the individual Member States, or the Member States by the existence of the Community*" (NEUWAHL, (1996) 33 CMLRev. 668).

340 For a critical analysis of the Court's jurisdiction on mixed agreements: EECKHOUT, (1997) 34 CMLRev. 15 *et seq.*; GASPARON, (1999) 10 EJIL 609 *et seq.* The evolution of shared competence in the EC's Common Commercial Policy between the Amsterdam Treaty and the Nice Treaty are explored by LEAL-ARCAS, (2003) 30 LIEI 3 *et seq.*

341 *Opinion 1/94*, [1994] E.C.R. I-5267, paragraph 109.

342 The position seems to be that the duty of close co-operation does not amount to an obligation to reach a common position but only to an obligation to use best endeavours to do so. For practical problems that may arise and possible solutions cf. KRENZLER/DA FONSECA-WOLLHEIM, (1998) EuR 230 *et seq.*

343 See also *Ruling 1/78*, Article 103, Euratom, [1978] E.C.R. 2151, paragraphs 34 to 36, and *Opinion 2/91*, ILO Convention 170, [1993] E.C.R. I-1061, paragraph 36.

2 The Domestic Legal Status of the WTO/GATT

The case-law of the Court of Justice demonstrates that it is prepared to grant direct effect to provisions of international agreements as well as decisions of institutional bodies that have been set up and vested with decision-making powers by an international agreement, provided that such provision or decision is sufficiently clear and precise, and does not require the adoption of subsequent implementing measures. Somewhat proleptic, it is submitted that the standard applied to determine whether an individual may equally rely on a provision belonging to the GATT and/or WTO Agreements differs considerably which has caused an abundance of literature analysing the legal status of, in particular GATT 1947, within the EC legal order.[344]

As will be discussed hereinafter, elements like the lack of reciprocity in the initial balance of obligations or in the ability to enforce these obligations, the possibility of derogation from the agreement or the method of dispute settlement which the Court of Justice has found on various occasions of not being capable to devoid a provision of having direct effect, are valued quite differently with regard to WTO/GATT. Moreover, it appears that this "double standard" is shared by all EC institutions, not just the Court.

2.1 The Approach of the EC Institutions in the Case of the WTO/GATT

The Commission proposed[345] in its explanatory memorandum for the conclusion of the results of the Uruguay Round that it should not be possible for individuals to invoke the provisions of the WTO Agreements directly before national or Community courts because many of

344 To name but few: COTTIER (2002), 99 *et seq.*; COTTIER/NADAKAVUKAREN SCHEFER, (1998) 1 JIEL 83 *et seq.*; ENGELBERGER, 156 *et seq.*; EPINEY/KADDOUS/RIDORÉ, (1998) 8 EFLR 297 *et seq.*; MANIN, (1997) 33 RTDE 422 *et seq.*; NEUWAHL, 313 *et seq.*; WOUTTERS/VAN EECKHOUTTE, 35 *et seq.*

345 Doc. COM (94) 143 final.

the other WTO members would explicitly exclude such direct effect.[346] In the United States, GATT 1947 has, at times, been reviewed to determine its "self-execution" (the U.S. equivalent to direct effect)[347] and the Congress has now made clear, when implementing the results of the Uruguay Round,[348] that the WTO Agreements do not provide rules that are enforceable by private parties.[349] The Commission therefore could not accept that, for example, subsidiaries of U.S. companies would be able to enforce their rights directly through Community (and Member States') courts, whilst subsidiaries of EC companies in the United States would have to go through the Commission, a Member State or the procedure provided by Regulation 3286/94[350].

This political reasoning is contrary to the view of the Court of Justice as declared in *Kupferberg*[351] where it held in Paragraph 18:

346 KUIJPER, (1995) 6 EJIL 226.

347 For an introduction to the U.S. Doctrine of self-execution see JACKSON, (1992) 86 AJIL 320, and particularly with regard to GATT, cf. BRAND, (1996–1997) 19 *Northwestern Journal of international Law and Business* 560 *et seq.*

348 The rules of the GATT have by statute less than full legal effect: The Uruguay Round Agreement Act of 1994 (Pub. L. No. 103–465, 108 Stat. 4809) states in Section 102, *Relationship of the Agreements to United States Law and State Law*, that "*no provision of any of the Uruguay Round Agreements [...] that is inconsistent with any law of the United States shall have effect*". It also provides that only the U.S. government can bring an action to challenge the validity of a state law as incompatible with a Uruguay Round provision and furthermore, that no private party can challenge any legal measure of the federal government as inconsistent with the WTO Agreements.

349 BRAND, (1996–1997) 19 Northwestern Journal of international Law and Business 559.

350 Council Regulation No. 3286/94 of 22 December 1994 laying down Community procedures in the field of the common commercial policy in order to ensure the exercise of the Community's rights under international trade rules, in particular those established under the auspices of the World Trade Organization (OJ 1994 L 349/71), as amended by Council Regulation (EC) No. 356/95 of 20 February 1995 (OJ 1995 L 41/3). Regulation 3286/94 was further amended by Council Regulation (EC) No. 125/2008 of 12 February 2008 (OJ 2008 L 40/1) to include the right of enterprises to bring complaints on (alleged) obstacles to trade, which are solely the subject of a right of action established under international trade rules laid down in a *bilateral* trade agreement.

351 Case 104/81, *Kupferberg*, [1982] E.C.R. 3641.

> According to the general rules of international law there must be bona fide performance of every agreement. Although each contracting party is responsible for executing fully the commitments which it has undertaken it is nevertheless free to determine the legal means appropriate for attaining that end in its legal system unless the agreement, interpreted in the light of its subject-matter and purpose, itself specifies those means. Subject to that reservation *the fact that the courts of one of the parties consider that certain of the stipulations in the agreement are of direct application whereas the courts of the other party do not recognise such direct application is not in itself such as to constitute a lack of reciprocity in the implementation of the agreement (emphasis added)*.

Irrespective of this finding and following the Commission's proposal, the EC Council of Ministers, nevertheless, declared at the time it ratified the WTO Agreements:

> Whereas, by its nature, the Agreement establishing the World Trade Organization, including the Annexes thereto, is not susceptible to being directly invoked in Community or Member State courts.[352]

The acts of the Council, the Commission and the European Parliament which sought to exclude the fixed justiciability of the WTO Agreements have, however, no legal effect. According to Article XVI(5) of the WTO Agreement, reservations can only be made to the extent provided in the WTO Agreements, which do not foresee acts such as those issued by the institutions of the Community. Furthermore, such declarations have to be made at the time of the conclusion of the Agreements. Thus, unilateral and *ex-post* declarations cannot alter the legal character of the WTO/GATT obligations.[353]

352 Council Decision 94/800, OJ 1994 L 336/1, Recital 11.

353 In this context, Advocate General Saggio's view on the preamble of Council Decision 94/800 and its role in the debate on the status of the WTO agreements is noteworthy. Stating that it is for the Court to determine whether or not WTO agreements have direct effect, the Advocate General underlined that the principles of treaty interpretation do not allow to accord much importance to the will of a party expressed in a unilateral interpretation which does not form part of the treaty (Opinion of Advocate General Saggio of 25 Feburary 1999, Case C-149/96, *Portugal v. Council*, [1999] E.C.R. I-8395, paragraph 20). Therefore, in the Advocate General's view, the Council's statement on the effect of the WTO agreements is to be seen as a political statement that should not affect the judge's competence.

Due to the separation of powers, it is the Court of Justice that determines the effect of a law once it has been enacted by the legislator. It is therefore for the ECJ to decide whether provisions of the WTO Agreement and/or its Annexes enjoy direct effect.[354] Accordingly, it must conduct a substantive analysis of the legal status of the WTO/GATT provisions when called upon to do so.

2.2 The Reluctance of the Court of Justice to Grant Direct Effect to WTO Rules

The ECJ's case-law regarding the WTO/GATT presents a contrast to its doctrine of *effet utile* in the European context. Although various international agreements[355] have been found to have direct effect and have been applied by the Court of Justice, two main arguments have consistently been used to deny the direct effect of GATT provisions. First, it has been argued that the GATT was characterised by significant flexibility[356] and provided an instrument of negotiation rather than adjudication, especially with regard to the diplomatic nature of the dispute settlement mechanism. This also entailed that the provisions of GATT were not sufficiently precise (unconditional and clear). Second, the lack of reciprocity in the initial balance of the obligations undertaken as well as in the ability to enforce them was considered decisive for a provision not to have direct effect.

354 As the Court of Justice stated explicitly in the *Bananas-Case* (Case C-280/93, *Germany v. Council (Bananas)*, [1994] E.C.R. 4973) in paragraph 111, only the Court has the competence to determine the status of an agreement in the Community legal order. The same was, for instance, proclaimed by Advocate General Tesauro in *Hermès* (Opinion of Advocate General Tesauro of 13 November 1997, Case C-53/96, *Hermès v. FHT,* [1998] E.C.R. I-3603, paragraph 25).

355 See Chapter II, 2.1. A summary of the ECJ's doctrine on the legal status of international agreements is also given, *e.g.*, by LEE/KENNEDY, (1996) 30 JWT 74 *et seq.*

356 To illustrate that the GATT is characterised by considerable flexibility, in particular regarding the possibility of derogation, exceptional measures and the weak dispute settlement mechanism, the Court referred to GATT Articles XIX, XXII and XXIII.

2.2.1 Flexibility – An Argument for any Occasion?

In *International Fruit Company*,[357] the Court of Justice considered the question of direct effect concerning GATT for the first time. Therein, it was admitted that the GATT is an international agreement binding upon the Community, and therefore, a Community rule inconsistent with the GATT can in principle be declared invalid by the ECJ. At the same time, the ECJ stated that individuals could not rely on GATT provisions before court because the agreement lacked direct effect.[358]

The Court reached this conclusion based on a consideration of the "spirit, general scheme and the terms of the General Agreement".[359] It held that, because the GATT "*is based on principles of negotiations undertaken on the basis of reciprocal and mutually advantageous arrangements*", and is "*characterised by the great flexibility of its provisions, in particular those conferring the possibility of derogation, the measures to be taken when confronted with exceptional difficulties, and the settlement of conflicts between the contracting parties*", it did not provide individuals with rights which could be invoked in national courts.[360] Considering that the case was brought before it for a preliminary ruling pursuant to Article 234 EC Treaty (now Article 267 TFEU), the practical consequence is that the ECJ cannot declare invalid a Community rule which is incompatible with the GATT under this procedure.[361]

The doctrine developed in *International Fruit Company* has been confirmed and strengthened by the Court of Justice in the *Bananas-Case*[362] when it held that Member States could not enforce GATT provisions in actions before the Court under Article 230(1) EC Treaty (now Article 263(1) TFEU). The Court used the arguments put forward in *International Fruit Company* to conclude that

357 Joined Cases 21–24/72, *International Fruit Company*, [1972] E.C.R. 1219.

358 LEE/KENNEDY, (1996) 30 JWT 70 *et seq.*

359 Joined Cases 21–24/72, *International Fruit Company*, [1972] E.C.R. 1219, paragraph 20.

360 *Ibid.*, paragraph 21.

361 BENEYTO, (1996) 7 EuZW 298.

362 Case C-280/93, *Germany v. Council (Bananas)*, [1994] E.C.R. 4973.

> [t]hose features of GATT, from which the Court concluded that an individual within the Community cannot invoke it in a court to challenge the lawfulness of a Community act, also preclude the Court from taking provisions of GATT into consideration to assess the lawfulness of a regulation in an action brought by a Member State.[363]

Arguably, the reasoning in *International Fruit Company* is justified in order to impede national courts unilaterally declaring inapplicable a Community rule which is inconsistent with the GATT. The uniform interpretation and application of Community law requires, however, that the Court of Justice controls its validity. In *Foto-Frost*[364], this rationale was explicitly laid down by the ECJ where it held that national courts are obliged to refer any question on validity of Community legislation to the Court. Because judicial review is exclusive to the Court, the lack of direct effect of GATT should, therefore, not hinder the possibility of declaring invalid a Community rule incompatible with the GATT. Nevertheless, the Court consistently held that the nature and structure of the GATT precluded any of its provisions from having direct effect, also when a Member State and not only an individual directly contested the validity of Community legislation.

Although the Court of Justice traditionally denied direct effect to the GATT, it did allow some of the agreement's provisions to have legal significance within the Community. It held that GATT provisions could be used to interpret the meaning of Community legislation which expressly referred to those provisions (the so-called *Fediol* doctrine).

A Community industry, *Fediol*, lodged a complaint against Argentina's system of different export taxation pursuant to which higher taxes were levied on the raw materials (soya beans) than on the processed products (soya meal and oil) and quantitative restrictions on the exportation of soya beans were upheld.[365] The ECJ held that GATT Article III (national treatment, prohibition of discriminatory taxes) could be used to interpret the meaning of "illicit commercial practices" under the EC's New Commercial Policy Instrument Regula-

363 *Ibid.*, 5073.

364 Case 314/85, *Foto-Frost*, [1987] E.C.R. 4199.

365 Case 70/87, *Fediol IV*, [1989] E.C.R. 1781.

tion[366]. This was permitted as this regulation required the Community to comply with its international obligations. The ECJ distinguished its previous direct effect holdings by stating that "*[t]he GATT provisions have an independent meaning, which for the purposes of their application in specific cases, is to be determined by way of interpretation*".[367] In the end, the Court found, however, that the contested measures did not constitute an illicit commercial practice.

Another remarkable exception was made by the Court of Justice when it found that GATT provisions could be used to interpret Community legislation when that legislation implemented a specific GATT provision, hence granting direct effect to such provision (also known as the *Nakajima* doctrine). The cornerstone was laid in a case involving a Japanese company, *Nakajima*,[368] which sold matrix printers on the Community market. At the request of the Committee of European Printer Manufacturers, the Commission initiated anti-dumping procedures against *Nakajima* and the Council imposed a definitive anti-dumping duty of 12%.[369] *Nakajima* sought annulment of the regulation imposing the duty, raising a plea of inapplicability with regard to the Community's basic Anti-Dumping Regulation[370] because it allegedly conflicted with the GATT Anti-Dumping Code.

Recalling its earlier jurisprudence in *International Fruit Company*,[371] the ECJ considered that the GATT Anti-Dumping Code could be used as ground for reviewing the legality of the anti-dumping margin. In a manner similar to its decision in *Fediol IV,* the Court held that this was possible because the regulation "*was adopted in accor-*

366 Council Regulation (EEC) No. 2641/84 of 17 September 1984 on the strengthening of the common commercial policy with regard in particular to protection against illicit commercial practices (OJ 1984 L 252/1).

367 Case 70/87, *Fediol IV,* [1989] E.C.R. 1831.

368 Case 69/89, *Nakajima*, [1991] E.C.R. I-2069.

369 Council Regulation (EEC) No. 3651/88 of 23 November 1988 imposing a definitive anti-dumping duty on imports of serial-impact dot-matrix printers originating in Japan (OJ 1988 L 317/33).

370 *In casu*, Council Regulation 2176/84/EEC on Protection Against Dumped or Subsidised Imports from Countries not Members of the European Economic Community (OJ 1984 L 201/1) as substituted by Council Regulation 2423/88 (OJ 1988 L 209/1).

371 Joined Cases 21–24/72, *International Fruit Company*, [1972] E.C.R. 1219.

dance with existing international obligations, in particular those arising from Article VI of the General Agreement and from the Anti-Dumping Code".[372] In the view of the ECJ, this resulted from the second and third recitals in the preamble of the basic Anti-Dumping Regulation.[373] Again, the Court found, however, that the substantive provisions of the Anti-Dumping Code had not been infringed and therefore rejected the plea of illegality.

Strictly speaking, the approach taken in *Nakajima* may not be regarded as an exception to the absence of direct effect of GATT provisions. Addressing the question of direct effect appears superfluous if the EC intends to *implement* a particular obligation entered into within the framework of the GATT which was explicitly recognised by the ECJ when it held that *Nakajima* was not relying on the direct effect of the GATT Anti-dumping Code as the Council had argued.[374] In other words, by arguing that international obligations have been transposed into EC law, there is no need to rely on the international obligations directly.[375]

In the light of the rule of consistent interpretation[376] which provides that an ambiguously worded national (or regional) provision has to be construed in accordance with international obligations, it is nevertheless difficult to understand the Court's rationale to limit the application of the GATT to the two exceptions[377] established in the *Fediol* and the *Nakajima* doctrines described above.

Inspired by *Marleasing*,[378] the Court of Justice explicitly stated that the rule of consistent interpretation would apply to international

372 Case 69/89, *Nakajima*, [1991] E.C.R. I-2069, paragraph 30.

373 *Ibid.*, paragraphs 29 to 32.

374 *Ibid.*, paragraph 28.

375 EECKHOUT, (1997) 34 CMLRev. 45 *et seq.*; ZONNEKEYN, (2003) 30 LIEI 263.

376 COTTIER/NADAKAVUKAREN SCHEFER, (1998) 1 JIEL 88.

377 Both doctrines have been referred to as embodying the so-called "principle of implementation" since they both involve the implementation of GATT law in the EC legal order; cf. EECKHOUT, (1997) 34 CMLRev. 56. It is, however, also suggested to explicitly distinguish between the two exceptions and refer to them as the "clear reference exception" (*Fediol* doctrine) and the "implementation exception" (*Nakajima* doctrine); cf. SNYDER, (2003) 40 CMLRev. 342.

378 In Case C-106/89, *Marleasing*, [1990] E.C.R. I-4135, paragraph 48, the Court held: "It is settled law that where the wording of secondary Community law

agreements. After reiterating the general rules of interpretation, such as the requirement of *bona fide* performance similar to *Kupferberg*, the Court found that "*[t]he Community must interpret terms in such a way as to encourage the attainment of the objectives pursued*".[379] It then held that not only interpretation but also Community legislation is to be designed consistently with international obligations:

> Likewise, an implementing regulation must, if possible, be given the interpretation consistent with the basic regulation. [...] Similarly, the primacy of international agreements concluded by the Community over provisions of secondary Community legislation means that such provisions must, so far as possible, be interpreted in a manner that is consistent with those agreements.[380]

2.2.2 Reciprocity – The Imperfection of Mutual Commitments

As aforementioned, the Court of Justice examined the issue of reciprocity in various respects, in particular the reciprocity in the initial balance of obligations and reciprocity in the ability to enforce these obligations. In the case of GATT 1947, it was, foremost, the lack of absolute reciprocity in enforcing the GATT rules, that was used for denying direct effect.

Admittedly, international agreements, such as the Community's free trade or association agreements, are distinct from the GATT by their bilateral character[381] and because they intended to implement va-

[sic!] is open to more than one interpretation, preference should be given to the interpretation which renders the provision consistent with the Treaty rather than the interpretation which leads to its being incompatible with the Treaty" (emphasis added).

379 Case C-61/94, *Commission v. Germany*, [1996] E.C.R. I-3989, paragraphs 30 and 31 involving the interpretation of the GATT International Dairy Agreement (IDA).

380 *Ibid.*, paragraph 52.

381 It may be interesting to note that PAUWELYN argues that the nature of [WTO], *i.e.* also GATT obligations are bilateral rather than multilateral. He draws this conclusion based on the consideration that the distinction is linked to the question of standing. Whereas legal standing to invoke responsibility for breach of a bilateral obligation is limited to the state at the other end of the bilateral relationship, breach of a multilateral obligation, in contrast, can be invoked either (i) by each and every one of the other parties to the multilateral treaty, in case of multilateral obligations *erga omnes partes*, or (ii) by any state, in case of obligations *erga omnes*, that is, binding on all states of the international community; cf. PAU-

rious stages of economic integration between the Community and its treaty partners, whereas GATT was designed to create a mechanism for negotiating non-discriminatory and reciprocal tariff reductions among its contracting parties.

In *Kupferberg*,[382] for example, the ECJ dealt with the free trade agreement between the Community and Portugal which eliminated all tariffs and other barriers to trade between the two parties, and in *Pabst*[383] and *Sevince*[384], the Greek and Turkish association agreements, respectively, created customs unions between the parties. Also the Yaounde Convention considered by the ECJ in *Bresciani*[385] provided for non-reciprocal duty free entry into the Community of goods from the ACP countries. In short, all these agreements created some form of integration. When dealing with the GATT, in contrast, the Court always pointed out, by referring to the agreement's preamble, that the purpose was to enter into reciprocal and mutually advantageous arrangements directed to the substantial reduction of tariffs and other barriers to trade and to the elimination of discriminatory treatment in international commerce.[386]

Based on these considerations it may be argued that the Court of Justice rightly noted that the GATT does neither pursue economic integration nor anticipate the creation of a single market but rather allowed the contracting parties to preserve diverse markets provided that the principles of non-discrimination and most-favoured-nation treatment are adhered to. However, since the Court of Justice has granted direct effect to clear, precise and unconditional provisions of other multilateral treaties, in particular the Lomé Conventions[387] which also provide for a system of tariff preferences, this argument appears

WELYN, 10. According to DELBRÜCK, on the other hand, the WTO fundamental legal principles posess *erga omnes* effect (DELBRÜCK, (2001) 11 SZIER 18).

382 Case 104/81, *Kupferberg*, [1982] E.C.R. 3641.

383 Case 17/81, *Pabst*, [1982] E.C.R. 1331.

384 Case C-192/89, *Sevince*, [1990] E.C.R. I-3461.

385 Case 87/75, *Bresciani*, [1976] E.C.R. 129.

386 For instance, Joined Cases 21–24/72, *International Fruit Company*, [1972] E.C.R. 1219, paragraph 21; Case 9/73, *Schlüter*, [1973] E.C.R. 1135, paragraph 29; Case C-280/93, *Germany v. Council (Bananas)*, [1994] E.C.R. I-4973, paragraph 106.

387 Case C-469/93, *Chiquita Italia*, [1995] E.C.R. I-4533.

less convincing – despite the Court's recent application of the arguments used to deny direct effect to WTO provisions to the interpretation of the United Nations Convention on the Law of the Sea (UNCLOS), to which the EC is a party.[388]

It must be acknowledged that reciprocity in this context is much more a political argument than a legal one. However, non-reciprocity turns out to be a compelling argument when granting direct effect gives rise to a substantial imbalance of the rights and obligations of the contracting parties. Considering that the GATT establishes a system of well calculated and balanced package deals, the equilibrium of performance would be harmed.[389]

One has also to consider that both the United States[390] and Japan[391], both being large trading partners of the EC, have explicitly stated that the GATT will not have direct effect. This may indicate a common position of WTO/GATT members as regards the nature of the Agreements. Furthermore, the lack of reciprocity in the enforcement of the WTO/GATT rules may even help to resolve disputes because it allows the members to settle a dispute by means of negotiation prior to a formal judgment on the validity of a measure under the GATT.[392]

388 Case C-308/06, *Intertanko*, [2008] E.C.R. I-4057. For a critical review of the *Intertanko* case, see BRONCKERS, (2008) 11 JIEL 885 *et seq.*, and VAN ROSSEM, CLEER Working Papers 2009/4.

389 MONTAÑA I MORA, (1996) 30 JWT 55.

390 For an overview cf. BRAND, (1996–1997) 19 *Northwestern Journal of international Law and Business* 562 *et seq.* More correctly, U.S. law does not deny direct effect to GATT but only the federal government has standing to invoke it; cf. TRACHTMAN, (1999) 10 EJIL 657.

391 The Japanese Supreme Court has held that a measure found to be in contravention of a GATT provision is not void. Such a violation, however, permits other countries to open negotiations so as to rectify the violation. That is to say that a violation of the GATT has only political rather than directly legal implications. Cf. also JACKSON, (1992) 86 AJIL 334 *et seq.*

392 LEE/KENNEDY, (1996) 30 JWT 88.

2.2.3 Dispute Settlement – Negotiation rather than Adjudication?

The dispute settlement mechanism of the GATT 1947 was mainly criticised because it did not require rule based adjudication to reconcile disputes.[393] Article XXIII was designed in a diplomatic rather than a judicial manner. The ECJ's reasoning in denying direct effect seems justified if one bears in mind that one of the purposes of GATT 1947 was to establish a system of multilateral rounds of reciprocal trade negotiations. Thus, it effectively created a dynamic relationship between the contracting parties in order to launch the process of trade liberalisation and resolve disputes by means of cross-sector bargaining which could have been seriously undermined by the interference of individuals invoking a directly effective provision of the GATT 1947.

Admittedly, this feature is unique to GATT, rendering it substantially different to dispute settlement methods contained in other international agreements examined by the Court of Justice. These agreements usually provided for static systems that resulted from one-time negotiations over the rights and obligations of the parties (such as consultation committees or association councils).

The Dispute Settlement Understanding (DSU)[394] brought about by the Uruguay Round significantly strengthened the GATT 1947 dispute settlement mechanism. Despite the shift towards a more legalistic dispute resolution mechanism,[395] the extent to which the rules can now be applied by national courts, especially within the Member States of the EC, is not entirely clear. While the DSU is available to apply the WTO/GATT rules in disputes between states, few member states of the WTO[396] have demonstrated their willingness to give the WTO the

393 OSTERHOUDT BERKEY, (1998) 9 EJIL 636 (with further annotations).

394 Understanding on Rules and Procedures Governing the Settlement of Disputes, 15 April 1994, WTO Agreement, Annex 2.

395 It seems, nevertheless, that there is still enough space for political arrangements and that the panel is not completely judicial since the final say on the interpretation of the WTO and its multilateral Agreements rests with political and intergovernmental bodies (Article XI of the WTO Agreement). COTTIER, (1998) 35 CMLRev. 325 *et seq.*

396 During the middle stages of the Uruguay Round, Switzerland took the initiative attempting to ensure that either the domestic legal systems of the members should assure direct effect or self-executingness on a case-by-case basis, or that

kind of authority European Member States have relinquished to the European Court of Justice.

2.3 The Situation after the Entry into Force of the WTO Agreement and its Annexes

It remains thus to evaluate whether the European Court of Justice is prepared to open the door to direct effect of the WTO Agreement and its Annexes beyond the accepted exceptions where the EU intended to implement a particular obligation assumed in the context of the WTO, or where the EU measure refers expressly to the precise provisions of the WTO agreements. If the ECJ maintains its established practice that "the WTO agreements are not in principle among the rules in the light of which the Court is to review the legality of measures adopted by the Community institutions", the question of direct effect very much boils down to the question of justiciability, or rather injusticiability of WTO provisions, leaving – for instance – the prohibition of VERs under the Safeguards Agreement a dead letter.

2.3.1 Cases on the Effect of WTO Provisions

Whereas the Court of Justice continued to adhere to the "implementation principle", *i.e.* allowing WTO/GATT provisions exceptionally to have direct effect (either under the "implementation exception" as developed in the *Nakajima* or the "clear reference exception" under the *Fediol* doctrine)[397] in order to review the compatibility of a Commu-

the agreements themselves should stipulate which provisions are considered to be directly applicable. Switzerland accordingly considered that the direct effect of certain provisions should not *a priori* be excluded. For further details cf. ENGELBERGER, 83 *et seq.* For the current status of WTO provisions in the Swiss legal order see COTTIER/OESCH, (2004) 14 SZIER 121 *et seq.*

397 Again, in *Werner,* the ECJ did not hesitate to refer to GATT Article XI to confirm and support its findings on the interpretation of the EC Export Regulation (Case 70/94, *Werner,* [1995] E.C.R. I-3189, paragraph 23). See also Case 83/94, *Leifer et al.*, [1995] E.C.R. I-3231, paragraph 24.

nity act[398] with the text of the GATT,[399] it was not until November 1999 that it took the chance to state its view on the direct effect of the WTO Agreement and its annexed multilateral agreements in detail.

Portugal had challenged, pursuant to Article 230 EC Treaty (now Article 263 TFEU), Council Decision 96/386[400] which concluded two bilateral Memoranda of Understanding (MoU) between the EC, on the one hand, and Pakistan and India on the other.[401] These MoU related to the arrangements of access to textile markets and have evolved following the Uruguay Round where the ATC was introduced into the WTO package. Portugal alleged that the MoU, especially the regulations regarding imports of textiles[402], violated, *inter alia*, certain principles laid down in the WTO/GATT. The Portuguese government

398 In *Italy v. Council*, the ECJ examined the legality of certain articles of a Community regulation on tariff quotas for imports of rice that was adopted to implement agreements concluded between the EC, Australia and Thailand following negotiations undertaken in accordance with GATT Article XXIV:6 as a result of the accession of Austria, Finland and Sweden to the Community (Council Regulation (EC) No. 1522/96 of 24 July 1996 on the introduction and administration of certain tariff quotas for imports of rice and broken rice, OJ 1996 L 190/1). Considering that the preamble to the regulation explicitly referred to the negotiations conducted pursuant to GATT Article XXIV:6 and to the Council's recognition of its obligations under international agreements (recitals 1 and 8), the ECJ held that in cases where the Community intended to implement a particular obligation entered into within the framework of GATT, the Court must review the lawfulness of the Community act in question from the point of view of the GATT (Case C-352/96, *Italy v. Council*, [1998] E.C.R. I-6937, paragraphs 19 to 21).

399 Paradoxically, a Community act implementing a GATT rule can be subject to judicial review while subsequent acts that might be in contradiction with the GATT cannot be examined by the Court for the mere absence of an explicit reference to an international rule. CASTILLO DE LA TORRE, (1995) 29 JWT 61 *et seq.*

400 Council Decision 96/386/EC of 26 February 1996 concerning the conclusion of Memoranda of Understanding between the European Community and the Islamic Republic of Pakistan and between the European Community and the Republic of India on arrangements in the area of market access for textile products (OJ 1996 L 153/47).

401 Case C-149/96, *Portugal v. Council*, [1999] E.C.R. I-8395.

402 Council Regulation (EEC) No. 3030/93 of 12 October 1993 on common rules for imports of certain textile products from third countries (OJ 1993 L 275/1), as modified by Council Regulation No. 3289/94 (OJ 1994 L 349/85).

claimed that, referring to the Court's previous case-law,[403] the Court must review the legality of Community measures in light of GATT rules if either the adoption of the measures implementing obligations assumed within the context of GATT is at issue or a Community measure refers expressly to specific provisions of the GATT. It argued further that due to the changes brought about by the Uruguay Round, notably in the area of dispute settlement, agreements concluded within the framework of the WTO should be treated differently from GATT 1947.[404]

Although Portugal stressed that the case did not raise the question of direct effect but rather addressed the circumstances under which a Member State may rely on the WTO agreements before the Court for the purpose of reviewing the legality of a Community measure, the ECJ took this opportunity to pronounce its views on the direct effect of the WTO agreements, *i.e.* to determine the legality of an act of Community secondary legislation in the light of the WTO rules. Summing up, the ECJ made the following points:

- In conformity with the principles of public international law, it is for the courts of the contracting parties, *in casu* for the Court of Justice within the framework of its jurisdiction under the EC Treaty (now TFEU), to decide what effect the provisions of an international agreement are to have in the internal legal order of the contracting parties if that question has not been settled by the agreement.[405]
- According to international law there must be *bona fide* performance of every agreement and each contracting party must determine the legal means appropriate for attaining that end in its legal system, unless the agreement, interpreted in the light of its subject-matter and purpose, itself specifies those means.[406]

403 Case C-280/93, *Germany v. Council (Bananas)*, [1994] E.C.R. 4973, paragraph 111.

404 Case C-149/96, *Portugal v. Council*, [1999] E.C.R. I-8395, paragraph 31.

405 *Ibid.*, paragraph 34. This point was already made in Case 104/81, *Kupferberg*, [1982] E.C.R. 3641, paragraph 17.

406 *Ibid.*, paragraph 35. The same has already been pointed out in Case 104/81, *Kupferberg*, [1982] E.C.R. 3641, paragraph 18.

– The WTO agreements do not determine those means.[407] Admitting that the WTO agreements differ significantly from the provisions of GATT 1947, in particular by reason of the strengthening of the system of safeguards and the mechanism for resolving disputes,[408] the Court nevertheless found that they accord considerable importance to negotiation between the parties.[409] In order to illustrate the importance of negotiation, it pointed out that the DSU provides for interim compensation in cases where the immediate withdrawal of the inconsistent measure is impractical. The Court further specified that, according to Article 22(1) DSU,[410] compensation is only a temporary measure available in the event that the recommendations and rulings of the Dispute Settlement Body (DSB) provided for in Article 21(1) DSU[411] are not implemented within a reasonable period of time, thus reflecting the preference for full implementation of a recommendation.[412] Pursuant to Article 22(2) DSU,[413] however, the party that has failed to imple-

407 *Ibid.*, paragraph 41.

408 Drawing on Article 3(7) DSU, the ECJ admitted that the main purpose of the dispute settlement mechanism is in principle to secure the withdrawal of the measures that are found to be inconsistent with the WTO rules.

409 Case C-149/96, *Portugal v. Council*, [1999] E.C.R. I-8395, paragraph 36.

410 Article 22(1) DSU reads: "Compensation and the suspension of concessions or other obligations are temporary measures available in the event that the recommendations and rulings are not implemented within a reasonable period of time. However, neither compensation nor the suspension of concessions or other obligations is preferred to full implementation of a recommendation to bring a measure into conformity with the covered agreements. Compensation is voluntary and, if granted, shall be consistent with the covered agreements".

411 Article 21(1) DSU provides: "Prompt compliance with recommendations or rulings of the DSB is essential in order to ensure effective resolution of disputes to the benefit of all Members".

412 For an implementation record of the WTO members see the analysis undertaken by DAVEY, 7 *et seq.*

413 Article 22(2) DSU states that "[i]f the Member concerned fails to bring the measure found to be inconsistent with a covered agreement into compliance therewith or otherwise comply with the recommendations and rulings within the reasonable period of time determined pursuant to paragraph 3 of Article 21, such Member shall, if so requested, and no later than the expiry of the reasonable pe-

ment the recommendations and rulings within this reasonable period of time is, if requested, to enter into negotiations with any party having invoked the dispute settlement procedure with a view to finding mutually acceptable compensation.[414]

- Despite the further consolidation of international trade law, requiring judicial organs to refrain from applying domestic laws which are inconsistent with the WTO agreements would have the consequence of depriving the legislative of executive organs of the parties of the possibility of finding negotiated solutions even on a temporary basis, as it is afforded by Article 22 DSU.[415]
- The WTO agreements are still founded, like GATT 1947, on the principle of negotiations with a view to entering into reciprocal and mutually advantageous arrangements and are thus distinguished, from the viewpoint of the Community, from the agreements concluded between the Community and non-member countries which introduce a certain imbalance of obligations.[416]
- Furthermore, the most important commercial partners of the Community have concluded that the WTO agreements are not among the rules applicable when reviewing the legality of their rules of domestic law. The Community legal order must follow the same course because the lack of reciprocity in relation to the WTO agreements may lead to disuniform application of the WTO rules. It would in fact deprive the legislative or executive organs of the Community of the scope for ma-

riod of time, enter into negotiations with any party having invoked the dispute settlement procedures, with a view to developing mutually acceptable compensation. If no satisfactory compensation has been agreed within 20 days after the date of expiry of the reasonable period of time, any party having invoked the dispute settlement procedures may request authorisation from the DSB to suspend the application to the Member concerned of concessions or other obligations under the covered agreements".

414 Case C-149/96, *Portugal v. Council*, [1999] E.C.R. I-8395, paragraphs 37–39.

415 *Ibid.*, paragraphs 40 and 46.

416 *Ibid.*, paragraph 42.

noeuvre enjoyed by their counterparts in the Community's trading partners.[417]

In view of the Court it follows that, having regard to their nature and structure, the WTO agreements are not in principle among the rules in the light of which the Court is to review the legality of measures adopted by the Community institutions. The Court consequently confirmed the case-law that it has continuously repeated since *International Fruit Company*, and affirmed the two exceptions, under which the provision of the GATT may be invoked: first, where a Community act requires the EC to comply with its international obligations (clear reference); and second, where a Community act purports to implement a specific GATT provision.[418]

As is well known, the judgment in *Portugal v. Council* provoked a wide variety of responses and sometimes dissent among legal writers based on the consideration that the WTO rules should be considered as a criterion of the legality of Community measures.[419] This criticism did, however, not cause the ECJ to review its position: For instance, in *Netherlands v. Parliament and Council*,[420] the applicant government claimed that Directive 98/44/EC[421] created obligations for the Member States that were incompatible with those resulting from their international undertakings and in particular with the WTO Agreement and the Convention on Biological Diversity (CBD)[422].

417 *Ibid.*, paragraphs 43, 45 and 46. This argument has since been repeated, for instance, in Joined Cases C-27/00 and C-122/00, *Omega Air et al.*, [2002] E.C.R. I-2569, paragraph 92.

418 Case C-149/96, *Portugal v. Council*, [1999] E.C.R. I-8395, paragraphs 47 and 49. For an attempt to defend the Court's exclusion of full direct effect, see EECKHOUT, (2002) 5 JIEL 91 *et seq.*

419 For instance, DESMEDT, (2000) 27 LIEI 100; GRILLER, (2000) JIEL 441 *et seq.*; MENGOZZI, [2000] RDUE 509 *et seq.*; VAN DEN BROEK, (2001) 4 JIEL 411 *et seq.*; ZONNEKEYN, (2000) 25 ELRev. 293 *et seq.*

420 Case C-377/98, *Netherlands v. Parliament and Council*, [2001] E.C.R. I-7079.

421 Directive 98/44/EC of the European Parliament and of the Council of 6 July 1998 on the legal protection of biotechnological inventions (OJ 1998 L 213/13).

422 Convention on Biological Diversity signed on 5 June 1992 in Rio de Janeiro, approved by the European Community by Council Decision 93/626/EEC of 25 October 1993 (OJ 1993 L 309/1).

In its judgment, the ECJ found that the lawfulness of a Community instrument cannot in principle be assessed in the light of the WTO agreements having regard to their nature and structure. It added, however, that such exclusion cannot be applied to the CBD, which, unlike the WTO Agreement, is not strictly based on reciprocal and mutually advantageous arrangements. Even the fact that the CBD may contain provisions which do not have direct effect, does not preclude review by the courts of compliance with the obligations incumbent on the Community as a party to that agreement.[423]

Thus, according to the Court, provisions of agreements that are not based on reciprocal and mutually advantageous arrangements may be considered as a criterion of legality even if they do not create rights for individuals. Conversely, the provisions of agreements which, like the WTO agreements, are based on reciprocal and mutually advantageous arrangements, are not directly applicable nor can they, in principle, be considered as a criterion of the legality of Community measures.

And yet again, limiting its considerations to the bare minimum, the ECJ followed the same line in *OGT Fruchthandelsgesellschaft*.[424] Asked for a preliminary ruling on whether GATT Articles I and XIII were such as to create rights which individuals might rely on directly before a national court in order to oppose the application of the Community regime for the import of bananas that the DSB had found to be inconsistent with the WTO rules, the ECJ considered that the answer to that question could be clearly deduced from the judgment in *Portugal v. Council*. It therefore confined itself to issue a reasoned order, holding that there was no reason to deviate from that judgment, and that "*[t]he common organisation of the market in bananas, as introduced by Regulation No 404/93 and subsequently amended, is not designed to ensure the implementation in the Community legal order of a particular obligation assumed in the context of GATT, nor does it refer expressly to specific provisions of GATT.*"[425] The ECJ thus neglected to elaborate on whether the existence of a negative ruling of the

423 Case C-377/98, *Netherlands v. Parliament and Council*, [2001] E.C.R. I-7079, paragraphs 52–54. A similar finding was already made in Case C-162/96, *Racke*, [1998] E.C.R. I-3655, paragraphs 45, 47 and 51.

424 Case C-307/99, *OGT Fruchthandelsgesellschaft*, [2001] E.C.R. I-3159.

425 *Ibid.*, paragraph 28.

DSB was to be considered an exceptional situation comparable to the exceptions accepted in *Nakajima* and *Fediol IV* respectively.[426]

In its judgment in *Petrotub*,[427] the ECJ made clear, however, that it had not abandoned[428] the "implementation exception" developed in *Nakajima*. Setting aside the previous judgment of the Court of First Instance[429], the ECJ effectively annulled a Council Regulation[430] imposing definitive antidumping duties on imports of certain seamless pipes and tubes of iron or non-alloy steel originating in Hungary, Poland, Russia, the Czech Republic, Romania and the Slovak Republic, relating to the calculation method used for the anti-dumping margin and in so far as it concerned imports into the Community manufactured by *Petrotub* and *Republica*.

The ECJ pointed out that the preamble to the EC Anti-dumping Regulation, and more specifically the fifth recital therein, clearly shows that the purpose of that Regulation is, *inter alia*, to transpose into EC law as far as possible the new and detailed rules contained in the WTO Anti-dumping Agreement[431] which include, in particular, those relating to the calculation of dumping, so as to ensure a proper and transparent application of those rules.[432] According to the ECJ, it

426 Case 69/89, *Nakajima*, [1991] E.C.R. I-2069, paragraph 31, and Case 70/87, *Fediol IV*, [1989] E.C.R. 1781, paragraphs 19 to 22.

427 Case C-76/00 P, *Petrotub*, [2003] E.C.R. I-79.

428 In the meantime, the CFI had several occasions to pronounce its views on the "implementation exception" and had advocated a narrow interpretation of the *Nakajima* doctrine. It was even suggested that the narrow interpretation used by the CFI was intended to limit as much as possible the ability of individuals to rely on WTO law in proceedings before the European courts; see ZONNEKEYN, (2001) 4 JIEL 608. See Case T-18/99, *Cordis Obst und Gemüse Grosshandel GmbH v. Commission*, [2001] E.C.R. II-913; Case T-30/99, *Bocchi Food Trade International GmbH v. Commission*, [2001] E.C.R. II-943; Case T-52/99, *T. Port GmbH & Co. KG v. Commission*, [2001] E.C.R. II-981; and Case T-132/01, *Euroalliages and Others v. Commission*, [2003] E.C.R. II-2359. For an more detailed discussion of the CFI cases cf. O'NEILL, (2005) 32 LIEI 72 *et seq.*

429 Joined Cases T-33/98 and T-34/98, *Petrotub SA and Republica SA v. Council*, [1999] E.C.R. II-3837.

430 Council Regulation (EC) No. 2320/97 of 17 November 1997 (OJ 1997 L 322/1).

431 Agreement on Implementation of Article VI of the General Agreement on Tariffs and Trade 1994 (OJ 1994 L 336/103).

432 *Petrotub*, [2003] E.C.R. I-79, paragraph 55.

is therefore established that the EC adopted the Anti-dumping Regulation in order to satisfy its obligations arising from the WTO Anti-dumping Agreement and that it intended to implement the particular obligations laid down by the provision in question.[433] After concluding that it was therefore able to review the legality of the contested regulation in the light of the WTO Anti-dumping Agreement, the ECJ also recalled that EC law must, so far as possible, be interpreted in a manner that is consistent with international law, in particular where its provisions are intended specifically to give effect to an international agreement concluded by the EC.[434]

Moreover, it is noteworthy that it is allegedly recognised by the European Courts that, in cases where a proceeding consists of several administrative steps, the annulment of one of these steps does not annul the complete proceeding. The anti-dumping proceeding appears to be an example of such a multi-step proceeding. Consequently, the annulment of parts of the definitive anti-dumping regulation does not imply the annulment of the entire procedure prior to the adoption of the regulation in question, according to the Council. On the other hand, pursuant to Article 266 TFEU (*ex* Article 233 EC Treaty), the Community institutions are obliged to comply with the judgment of the Court of Justice. Accordingly, the Community institutions have the possibility to remedy the aspects of the contested regulation which led to its annulment, while leaving unchanged the uncontested parts which are not affected by the judgment.

Finally, it should be pointed out that the Court of Justice – in line with its previous case-law regarding GATT – opted in a judgment relating to interim measures in intellectual property (IP) disputes pursuant to Article 234 EC Treaty (now Article 267 TFEU) to refuse the direct effect of TRIPs.[435] In two separate cases, Dutch courts, which were asked to order interim measures pursuant to Dutch law, found that Article 50(6) TRIPs imposes limits on the duration of such measures and that those limits do not appear in the national legislation. It

433 *Ibid.*, paragraph 56.
434 *Ibid.*, paragraph 57.
435 Joined Cases C-300/98 and C-392/98, *Dior et al.*, [2000] E.C.R. I-11307.

was thus on the ECJ to ascertain whether the national courts are required to comply with the time limits imposed by Article 50(6) TRIPs.

Article 50(6) TRIPs provides for the timely application of provisional measures ordered by judicial authorities[436] so as to prevent an infringement of an IP right from occurring, and in particular, to prevent the entry into the channels of commerce in their jurisdiction of goods (Article 50(1)(a) TRIPs), to preserve relevant evidence in regard to the alleged infringement (Article 50(1)(b) TRIPs) or, *inaudita altera parte*, to contravene irreparable harm to the right holder caused by any delay (Article 50(2) TRIPs).

Council Decision 94/800[437] on the conclusion of the Uruguay Round Agreements states in Recital 11 that, by its nature, the WTO Agreement is not susceptible to being directly invoked in Community or Member State courts. However, the unilateral declaration of the Council cannot settle this issue since, according to Article 220 EC Treaty (now, in substance, Article 19(1) TEU), the ECJ is entrusted with the observation of the law in the interpretation and application of the Treaties.

Correctly, the ECJ had not only endorsed this task in *Portugal v. Council*[438] but also in the first important preliminary question in respect to Article 50 TRIPs, the *Hermès* case[439] which did, by the way, not address the question of direct effect.[440] Therein, the ECJ held that

436 Article 50(6) TRIPs reads: "[…], provisional measures taken on the basis of paragraphs 1 and 2 shall, upon request by the defendant, be revoked or otherwise cease to have effect, if proceedings leading to a decision on the merits of the case are not initiated within a reasonable period, to be determined by the judicial authority ordering the measures where a Member's law so permits or, in the absence of such a determination, not to exceed 20 working days or 31 calendar days, whichever is longer".

437 OJ 1994 L 336/1.

438 Case C-149/96, *Portugal v. Council*, [1999] E.C.R. I-8395.

439 Case C-53/96, *Hermès v. FHT*, [1998] E.C.R. I-3603.

440 The ECJ held that "[a]lthough the issue of the direct effect of Article 50 of the TRIPs Agreement has been argued, the Court is not required to give a ruling on that question, but only to answer the question of interpretation submitted to it by the national court so as to enable that court to interpret [the] procedural rules in the light of that article"; ibid., paragraph 35. It has been argued that Advocate

it has jurisdiction to interpret Article 50 TRIPs in order to meet the needs of national courts when they are called upon to apply national rules with a view to ordering provisional measures for the protection of rights arising under EC legislation and falling within the scope of TRIPs.[441] In cases where TRIPs can apply to situations falling both within the scope of national law and within that of EC law – as is the case with trademarks – the ECJ found itself competent to interpret it in order to forestall future interpretational discrepancies.[442] The ECJ further argued that the necessity of close co-operation between the Member States and the Community institutions is part of the fulfilment of their commitment undertaken by them under joint competence[443] – as is TRIPs.[444]

After recalling the approach taken in *Hermès*, the ECJ confirmed in *Dior*[445] that Article 50 TRIPs, as a procedural provision, should be applied in the same way in every situation wherever it is capable of applying both to situations covered by national and by EC law. For practical and legal reasons, it required the judicial authorities of Member States and of the EC to give it a uniform application. The ECJ thus considered that it would be in the best position to ensure this, and that it was not restricted to do so solely in the field of trademarks.[446] As in the case of GATT, the ECJ then found that the provisions of TRIPs had – based upon their purpose, context and wording – no direct effect, and are not such as to create rights upon which individuals may rely directly before the courts by virtue of EC law.

Acknowledging, however, that this finding does not fully resolve the problem raised by the Dutch courts, it continued that, in a field to which TRIPs applies and with respect to which the EC has already legislated, the judicial authorities of the Member States are required

General Tesauro tried to pull the ECJ in the direction of direct effect (WEINRICHTER, (1999) 3 EIoP 12), but obviously failed.

441 Case C-53/96, *Hermès v. FHT,* [1998] E.C.R. I-3603, paragraphs 28 and 29.

442 *Ibid.*, paragraphs 32 and 33.

443 *Opinion 1/94,* [1994] E.C.R. I-5267, paragraph 108.

444 On joint competences and the duty of co-operation in *Opinion 1/94*, cf. HILF, (1995) 6 EJIL 255.

445 Joined Cases C-300/98 and C-392/98, *Dior et al.*, [2000] E.C.R. I-11307.

446 *Ibid.*, paragraphs 37 and 38.

by virtue of EC law to act (when ordering interim measures based on national law) as far as possible in the light of the wording and the purpose of Article 50 TRIPs. On the other hand, in a field in which the EC has not yet legislated and which consequently falls within the competence of the Member States, the protection of IP rights, including interim measures, do not fall within the scope of EC law. Accordingly, EC law neither requires nor prohibits that the legal order of a Member State accords the right to rely on Article 50(6) TRIPs to individuals, or that it obliges the national courts to apply that provision of their own motion.[447]

The ECJ's reasoning in these two cases is obviously based on the principle of consistent interpretation, according to which the Court may interpret the national law of the Member States in the light of TRIPs, even if the TRIPs provision in question does not have direct effect. Considering that the ECJ has considered in *Hermès* that TRIPs has primacy over the national law of the Member States,[448] the approach taken by the ECJ appears to contravene this finding. In fact, it could be argued that the ECJ should have turned to the principle of consistent interpretation only after excluding the direct effect of Article 50 TRIPs,[449] since the ECJ's approach omits to take into account that direct effect and the principle of consistent interpretation produce different consequences on the primacy of the TRIPs over national law.

If a provision of a national law is incompatible with a directly effective provision of TRIPs, the national provision does no longer display effects. However, if a TRIPs provision does not have direct effect, the principle of consistent interpretation does not expunge the effects of a provision of national law incompatible with that TRIPs provision. Thus, granting direct effect would have been the better option than the principle of consistent interpretation if expressing primacy of TRIPs over national legislation was intended. The same is true for the achievement of uniform application of TRIPs within the Member

447 *Ibid.*, paragraphs 47 and 48.

448 Case C-53/96, *Hermès v. FHT,* [1998] E.C.R. I-3603, paragraph 28.

449 As it was suggested by Advocate General Tesauro (Opinion of Advocate General Tesauro delivered on 13 November 1997 in *Hermès v. FHT,* [1998] E.C.R. I-3603, paragraph 41).

States.[450] On the other hand, it has to be admitted that the TRIPs was concluded under joint (or shared) competence which leaves little room for the Court of Justice to impose single-handedly obligations on Member States in areas that are, in the end, within national sovereignty.[451] The decision to opt for consistent interpretation rather than addressing direct effect may therefore have been a diplomatic one.

2.3.2 Cases on the Effect of WTO Dispute Settlement Body Decisions

Having wrapped up the European courts' stance towards direct effect of WTO provisions as such, the question arises whether the same conclusion applies where a WTO Dispute Settlement Body (DSB) ruling or recommendation finds that certain Community measures are inconsistent with those provisions.[452] It might be easily inferred from the ECJ's previous reasoning that DSB decisions – negotiable by Contracting Parties, even if only temporarily – are for that reason not cogent[453] and do not create absolute or immediate obligations, *i.e.* neither confer rights on individuals, as was, in fact, expressly argued by Advocate General Mischo in the *Atlanta* case.[454]

450 GAGLIARDI, (1999) 24 ELRev. 290.

451 NEUWAHL, (1996) 33 CMLRev. 678.

452 For instance, COTTIER argued that in cases where adopted panel or Appellate Body reports are simply ignored, courts should no longer apply the rules or measures found inconsistent with WTO/GATT in those reports (COTTIER, 134). It was also suggested that rulings of the DSB that find an EC measure to be inconsistent with the WTO/GATT should be considered as "finally" establishing illegality, and and that the infringed rules should therefore be accorded a "limited" direct effect within the EC legal order so as to remedy the situation, see SCHMID, [1998] NJW 190 *et seq.*

453 It has been argued, however, that DSB decisions are binding for the EC and the compesation mechanism cannot prevent those decisions from being invoked in legal proceedings before the Community courts; ZONNEKEYN, (2000) 34 JWT 103.

454 Opinion of Advocate General Mischo delivered on 6 May 1999 in Case C-104/97 P, *Atlanta*, [1999] E.C.R. I-6983, paragraphs 27 to 30. For a comment on Advocate General Mischo's Opinion, see ZONNEKEYN, (1999) 2 JIEL 713 *et seq.*

This approach was subject to criticism because neither compensation nor retaliation[455] are methods of settling disputes, but merely temporary instruments whose aim is to put pressure on the defaulting party to comply and to ensure that any benefits accruing to the other WTO Members are not nullified or impaired as a consequence of the failure to comply immediately or within the reasonable period of time set in that particular case.[456] two later judgments[457] handed down by the Court of Justice have been awaited eagerly by European lawyers since Advocate-General Alber had concluded in his Opinion[458] that WTO law was to have direct effect when the DSB has decided on the incompatibility of a Community measure with WTO law, and if the Community had not acted to bring its measure into conformity within the reasonable period of time accorded to it.[459]

The facts of the *Biret* case(s) require little introduction as they address the intractable beef hormones dispute between the EC and the United States and Canada that has been going on ever since the 1980s.

455 The importance of (political rather than economic) retaliation with a view to enhance compliance is well illustrated by MCRAE, (2008) 3 AJWH 9.

456 ZONNEKEYEN, (2000) 34 JWT 123.

457 Case C-93/02 P, *Biret International v. Council*, [2003] E.C.R. I-10497 and Case C-94/02 P, *Biret et Cie v. Council*, [2003] E.C.R. I-10565. The two cases dealt with the same situation on which the Court ruled on the same day. For convenience and unless otherwise stated, observations will refer only to the judgment in Case C-93/02 P, *Biret International v. Council*.

458 For comments on the Opinion of Advocate General Alber, see O'NEILL, (2005) 32 LIEI 76 *et seq.*; ZONNEKEYN, (2003) 6 JIEL 761 *et seq.*

459 Advocate-General Alber has placed emphasis on the fact that DSB decisions are binding, at least in the sense that they cannot be circumvented by negotiation between the parties. Acknowledging that there may be cases where non-compliance with such decisions is a commercial policy option, he considers that non-compliance ultimately depends solely on the fact that such decisions are unenforceable because they pertain to international law which in principle does not admit coercive measures. The fact that DSB decisions are unenforceable is therefore not a valid reason for the Court not to comply with them. Since non-compliance "is not a lawful option", irrespective of whether it is viable from a commercial policy point of view, he suggested that the Court should support the principle of legality and recognise that DSB decisions are binding when the period allowed for complying with them expires, at the latest (Opinion of Advocate General Alber delivered on 15 May 2003 in *Biret*, *supra*, paragraphs 85 to 88).

The EC had prohibited the import of hormone-treated cattle and beef from non-EU Member States. Under the WTO regime, such ban may be justified under the provisions of the Agreement on the Application of Sanitary and Phytosanitary Measures (SPS Agreement) if valid scientific evidence is presented for the import ban being a health and safety measure. The U.S. and Canada opposed the ban, filing a complaint with the WTO Dispute Settlement Body which, ultimately, ruled[460] that the EC had infringed several provisions of the SPS Agreement. The EC was given fifteen months to rectify the illegal situation and meet its obligations under the DSB ruling, but it failed to meet the deadline.

Biret, a French meat and other foodstuffs trading company, and its majority shareholder filed actions for damages for losses sustained as a result of the EC's non-implementation of the DSB ruling with the Court of First Instance,[461] arguing that the EC's beef hormone legislation had been contravening the relevant WTO provisions (particularly those of the SPS Agreement) since the entry into force of the WTO, and that there had been persistent denial of the EC to lift the embargo despite its reported incompatibility with the SPS Agreement.

The CFI dismissed the actions on the ground that there was an "*[i]nescapable and direct link between the decision and the plea alleging infringement of the SPS Agreement, and the decision could therefore only be taken into consideration if the Court had found that Agreement to have direct effect in the context of a plea alleging the invalidity of the directives in question*".[462] The CFI concluded, with explicit reference to the precedents mentioned above, that it is clear from firmly established case-law[463] that the WTO agreements do not have direct effect, and that *Biret* could therefore not rely on an infringement of the SPS Agreement to hold the EC liable.

The appeal of *Biret* to the European Court of Justice proved to be equally unsuccessful because, ultimately, the ECJ dismissed the appeal in its entirety on the basis that *Biret* did not incur any damages

460 AB Report on *EC – Meat (Hormones)*, WT/DS26/AB/R, WT/DS48/AB/R.

461 Case T-174/00, *Biret International v. Council*, [2002] E.C.R. II-17; Case T-210/00, *Établissements Biret et Cie SA v. Council*, [2002] E.C.R. II-47.

462 Case T-174/00, *Biret International v. Council*, [2002] E.C.R. II-17, paragraph 67.

463 *Ibid.*, paragraph 61.

after the expiration of the time period to comply with the DSB ruling as it had gone out of business prior to that. Nevertheless, the ECJ appeared to show some inclination to recognise the possibility of Community law being curtailed by DSB findings and, hence, individuals recovering damages,[464] by leaving a loophole: The ECJ indirectly stated that it was not required to rule expressly on the question of the effect of DSB decisions due to temporary reasons, *i.e.* the period for the Community to comply with the DSB decision not having elapsed yet.[465] Although the ECJ ultimately followed its established practice that "the WTO agreements are not in principle among the rules in the light of which the Court is to review the legality of measures adopted by the Community institutions", it is significant that it criticised the Court of First Instance for not taking sufficient account of the DSB's adoption of the Appellate Body Report on *European Communities – Measures Concerning Meat and Meat Products,* dated 13 February 1998. The ECJ found that the CFI's self-imposed limitation to mechanically applying to the DSB decisions the principles laid down in the judgment in *Portugal v. Council* on the subject of the WTO rules did not suffice to deal with the plea concerning infringement of the SPS Agreement.[466] It therefore faulted the CFI for having reduced the issue of invocability of the DSB report to the one of direct effect of WTO rules.[467]

Drawing on these observations of the Court, it would appear that the ECJ is ready to accept a third exception allowing direct effect of WTO rules on Community law: Whereas it considered that the WTO rules cannot have any direct effect with regard to cases preceding the deadline for implementation of the award "without rendering ineffec-

464 ALEMANNO, [2004] 45 Harv. Int'l L.J. 557 *et seq.*

465 Since the Community had stated that it intended to comply with its WTO obligations but that it needed a reasonable time to do so (under Article 21(3) of the DSU it was granted a period of 15 months for that purpose, expiring on 13 May 1999), the ECJ found that, for the period prior to 13 May 1999, the Community Courts could in any event not carry out a review of the Community measures in question without rendering ineffective the grant of that period by the DSB (Case C-93/02 P, *Biret International v. Council*, [2003] E.C.R. I-10497, paragraph 62).

466 *Ibid.*, paragraph 57.

467 ALEMANNO, 264.

tive the grant of a reasonable period for compliance with the DSB recommendations or decisions, as provided for in the dispute settlement system put in place by the WTO agreements",[468] the ECJ does not seem to rule out the possibility of WTO provisions having direct effect in the period thereafter. This conclusion may, moreover, be confined to cases where the Community has indicated that it intended to comply with its WTO obligations as established in the award – the latter being a fact that has been noted by the ECJ.[469]

Whereas one could but welcome the ECJ's judgments in *Biret* because it appears to be prepared to waive the requirement of reciprocity, thereby increasing the pressure on the legislative and administrative organs of the EC in the future when it comes to implementing the DSB's decisions, it was soon made clear that direct effect of WTO provisions was subject to the same exceptional circumstances as defined in the case-law prior to *Biret.*

In the judgment in *Van Parys*,[470] the ECJ was called upon to pronounce its view on the validity of Regulation No 404/93[471] on the common organisation of the market in bananas which regulated, *inter*

468 Taking into account that *Biret* had been in liquidation years before the DSB decision and the expiration of the reasonable period of time, the ECJ's reasoning strongly suggests that bringing a damages claim before the reasonable period time for complying with the WTO ruling has elapsed, would not be useful because it held "*[i]n those circumstances and without it being necessary to consider what damage might be suffered by individuals as a result of the Community's failure to implement a DSB decision finding a Community measure incompatible with the WTO rules, the Court finds that in the present case [...] the Community cannot, on any view, have incurred liability*" (Case C-93/02 P, *Biret International v. Council*, [2003] E.C.R. I-10497, paragraph 64). See WIERS, (2004) 31 LIEI 147.

469 This potential third exception has been termed "exception of enforceability", and it has been argued that it was different from the exceptions under the "implementation principle" in so far as the latter contained a "subjective element", *i.e.* the Community's *intention* to implement or clearly refer to WTO provisions; see THIES, (2004) 41 CMLRev. 1671.

470 Case C-377/02, *Van Parys*, [2005] E.C.R. I-1465.

471 As laid down in Council Regulation (EEC) No 404/93 of 13 February 1993 on the common organisation of the market in bananas (OJ 1993 L 47/1) as amended by Council Regulation (EC) No 1637/98 of 20 July 1998 (OJ 1998 L 210/28) and its implementing measures.

alia, a system of trade with third states. The system traditionally distinguished between, on the one hand, traditional and non-traditional bananas originating in the African, Caribbean and Pacific States (ACP states), and third state bananas, on the other. Certain of these third states brought a complaint before the WTO which ended in a report by the Appellate Body, finding that certain features of the system of trade with third states set up under Regulation No 404/93 were incompatible with GATT 1994. Following the adoption of that report by the DSB,[472] the Council amended Regulation No 404/93 by Regulation No 1637/98, so as to comply "with the Community's international commitments under the World Trade Organisation (WTO)".[473]

The amended system for the imports of bananas, however, not only maintained the distinction under the former trade system but also provided for an import licence scheme monitored by the Member States. The new system was challenged again on the ground that it had not removed the infringement of GATT regarding trade with third states,[474] which led the Community to introduce another amendment.[475] During all these events, *Van Parys*, a company established in Belgium which had imported bananas into the EC for more than 20 years, applied to the relevant Belgian authority (Belgisch Interventie- en Restitutiebureau, BIRB) for several import licences in 1998 and 1999. BIRB refused, however, to issue it with import licences for the full quantity *Van Parys* applied for on the basis of the aforementioned Community regulations governing the import of bananas.[476]

Van Parys subsequently brought two actions before the Raad van State against the decisions of the BIRB, submitting that they were

472 AB Report on European Communities – Regime for the Importation, Sale and Distribution of Bananas, WT/DS27/AB/R.

473 So it is stated in the second recital to Regulation No 1637/98 (OJ 1998 L 210/28).

474 Cf. *European Communities – Regime for the Importation, Sale and Distribution of Bananas*, Request for Consultations by Honduras, Mexico, Guatemala, Panama and the United States, 25 January 1999 (WT/DS158/1, G/L/290, S/L/65, G/LIC/D/27); Requests to Join Consultations: Communication from Ecuador, 27 January 1999 (WT/DS158/2) and Communication from Belize, 10 February 1999 (WT/DS158/3).

475 Council Regulation (EC) No 216/2001 of 29 January 2001 amending Regulation No 404/93 (OJ 2001 L 31/2).

476 Case C-377/02, *Van Parys,* [2005] E.C.R. I-1465, paragraphs 31–34.

unlawful because of the unlawfulness, in the light of the WTO rules, of the regulations on which these decisions were based. In response to the questions from the Raad van State in that regard, the Court of Justice issued a preliminary ruling on whether the WTO agreements give Community nationals a right to rely on those agreements in legal proceedings challenging the validity of Community legislation where the DSB has held that both that legislation and subsequent legislation adopted by the Community in order, *inter alia*, to comply with the relevant WTO rules are incompatible with those rules.

The ECJ started by reiterating that it is settled case-law that, given their nature and structure, the WTO agreements are not in principle among the rules in the light of which the Court is to review the legality of measures adopted by the Community institutions.[477] Without further consideration, it continued that it is only for the Court to review the legality of Community measures in the light of the WTO rules, where the Community has intended to implement a particular obligation assumed in the context of the WTO, or where the Community measure refers expressly to the precise provisions of the WTO agreements.[478]

Somewhat apodictically, the ECJ stated that the Community's undertaking after the adoption of the DSB's decision to comply with the WTO rules was not intended to assume a particular obligation in the context of the WTO which was capable of justifying an exception to the impossibility of relying on WTO rules before the Community Courts. It was also not such as to enable the Community Courts to exercise judicial review of the Community provisions in the light of WTO rules.[479]

477 *Ibid.*, paragraph 39 (referring to Case C-149/96, *Portugal v. Council*, [1999] E.C.R. I-8395, paragraph 47; Case C-307/99, *OGT Fruchthandelsgesellschaft*, [2001] E.C.R. I-3159, paragraph 24; Joined Cases C-27/00 and C-122/00, *Omega Air et al.*, [2002] E.C.R. I-2569, paragraph 93; Case C-76/00 P, *Petrotub and Republica v. Council*, [2003] E.C.R. I-79, paragraph 53 and Case C-93/02 P, *Biret International v. Council*, [2003] E.C.R. I-10497, paragraph 52). Most recently the stance was once more "cemented" in Joined Cases C-120/06 P and 121/06 P, *FIAMM & Fedion*, [2008] E.C.R. I-6513, paragraph 111.

478 Case C-377/02, *Van Parys,* [2005] E.C.R. I-1465, paragraph 40.

479 *Ibid.*, paragraph 41.

Emphasising the "considerable importance of negotiation" in the WTO dispute settlement system by recalling the findings in *Portugal v. Council*,[480] the Court pointed out that a dispute remains on the agenda of the DSB according to Article 22(8) DSU until it is resolved, that is until the measure found to be inconsistent has been "removed" or the parties reach a "mutually satisfactory solution" (Article 21(6) DSU). In addition, where no agreement as to the compatibility of the remedies taken to comply with the DSB's recommendations and decisions can be reached, the dispute is further decided "through recourse to these dispute settlement procedures" (Article 21(5) DSU) which includes again negotiated solutions.[481]

In other words, and more specifically, the expiry of the time-limit accorded to the Community to comply with the DSB's decision does, in view of the ECJ, not imply that the Community had exhausted the possibilities under the WTO dispute settlement system of finding a solution to the dispute between it and the other parties. It therefore concluded that the possibility of the legislative or executive organs of the EC to reconcile its obligations under the WTO Agreement and its Annexes by means of negotiation could be compromised if the Community Courts were entitled to judicially review the lawfulness of the relevant Community measures in light of the WTO rules – irrespective of whether the time-limit has expired or not.[482]

Accordingly, a private party may not, in principle, rely in proceedings before a court of a Member State on the fact that Community legislation is incompatible with certain rules of the WTO even where the DSB has declared that legislation to be incompatible with such rules – unless that Community measure was intended to ensure the enforcement within the Community legal order of a particular obligation assumed in the context of the WTO or expressly refers to specific provisions of the WTO agreements. Neither of these exceptions was, however, accepted in the present case.[483]

480 *Ibid.*, paragraphs 42 to 45.
481 *Ibid.*, paragraphs 46 and 47.
482 *Ibid.*, paragraphs 48, 50 and 51.
483 *Ibid.*, paragraphs 52 and 53.

The impossibility to rely on DSB rulings has since explicitly been confirmed in the *FIAMM & Fedon*[484] cases, thereby clarifying two points that have been (and partly remain) subject to debate.

Firstly, the ECJ ruled expressly (and for the first time) that there is *no distinction* to draw between the direct effect of (substantive) WTO provisions and the direct effect of DSB decisions:[485]

> A recommendation or a ruling of the DSB finding that the substantive rules contained in the WTO agreements have not been complied with is, whatever the precise legal effect attaching to such a recommendation or ruling, *no more capable* than those rules of conferring upon individuals a right to rely thereon before the Community courts for the purpose of having the legality of the conduct of the Community institutions reviewed *(emphasis added)*.

Secondly, the ECJ eliminated the ambiguity left behind from *Biret* by clarifying that, even after the expiration of the deadline of the DSB recommendations, they cannot be relied upon by private parties to claim damages.[486]

3 Invocability of Directly Effective WTO Provisions

It is apparent from the discussion of the ECJ's case-law that WTO provisions may be granted direct effect within the limits of the exceptions allowed under the "implementation principle", and that they take priority over secondary legislation and other Community acts. However, this does not necessarily mean that they are "invocable". Invoca-

484 Joined Cases C-120/06P and C-121/06P, *FIAMM & Fedon*, [2008] E.C.R. I-6513.

485 *Ibid.*, paragraph 129.

486 *Ibid.*, paragraphs 130 and 133. ROSAS, (2001) 4 JIEL 140, adds another element when he argues that such claims are unlikely to be successful as a matter of principle since private traders do not have a subjective right to tariff concessions, meaning that the EC may not be held liable for any damage resulting from the suspension of concessions vis-à-vis the EC due to its failure to implement a DSB ruling.

bility of directly effective WTO provisions is determined by "standing" in the EC legal order. For example, WTO provisions can be directly effective in disputes between different units or levels of government (Community institutions), or between the government and private parties ("vertically"), but not between private citizens or companies ("horizontally").[487]

Under the TFEU, invocability (or standing) is only addressed in a "vertical" context. Directly effective WTO provisions may be used:

- by the Commission to challenge the validity of national measures under Article 258 (*ex* Article 226 EC Treaty) or of Community acts under Article 263 (*ex* Article 230 EC Treaty)[488];
- by the Member States to review the validity of measures of other Member States under Article 259 (*ex* Article 227 EC Treaty)[489] or of Community acts under Article 263 (*ex* Article 230 EC Treaty);
- by individuals to challenge the validity of Community acts under Articles 263(4) (*ex* Article 230(4) EC Treaty)[490], 277 (*ex*

487 JACKSON, (1992) 86 AJIL 317.

488 Article 263 TFEU reads, *inter alia*:
(1) The Court of Justice shall review the legality of acts adopted jointly by the European Parliament and the Council, of acts of the Council, of the Commission and of the ECB, other than recommendations and opinions, and of acts of the European Parliament intended to produce legal effects vis-à-vis third parties.
(2) It shall for this purpose have jurisdiction in actions brought by a Member State, the European Parliament, the Council or the Commission on grounds of lack of competence, infringement of an essential procedural requirement, infringement of this Treaty or of any rule of law relating to its application, or misuse of powers.

489 Article 259(1) TFEU provides: A Member State which considers that another Member State has failed to fulfil an obligation under this Treaty may bring the matter before the Court of Justice.

490 Any natural or legal person may, under the conditions laid down in [Article 263(1) and (2) TFEU], institute proceedings against an act addressed to that person or which is of direct and individual concern to them, and against a regulatory act which is of direct concern to them and does not entail implementing measures.

Article 241 EC Treaty)[491] or 267 (*ex* Article 234 EC Treaty) (preliminary ruling).

As explained below, invocability (or standing) is established in principle, disagreement remains as to whether an individual can invoke a provision of an international agreement under Article 263 or via a referral by a national court under Article 267 TFEU.

*3.1 Locus Standi under Article 263 TFEU (*ex *Article 230 EC Treaty)*

Although the ECJ has accepted, subject to the requirement that individual applicants can show that the challenged Community act is of direct and individual concern to them, that international agreements fall within the wording of Article 263 TFEU (*ex* Article 230 EC Treaty),[492] an individual's ability to access the courts has been a subject of concern in the EC for a long time.[493]

Article 263(4) TFEU allows any natural or legal person to institute proceedings, within a certain time limit, against Community measures if these are of direct and individual concern to them. The definition of individual access has first been elaborated in the *Plaumann* case,[494] where the ECJ held that persons other than the addressees of a decision can only claim to be "*individually concerned if that decision affects them by reason of certain attributes which are*

491 Article 277 TFEU (*ex* 241 EC Treaty) reads: Notwithstanding the expiry of the period laid down in Article 263, sixth paragraph, any party may, in proceedings in which an act of general application adopted by an institution, body, office or agency of the Union is at issue, plead the grounds specified in Article 263, second paragraph, in order to invoke before the Court of Justice the inapplicability of that act.

492 For instance, Joined Cases 21–24/72, *International Fruit Company*, [1972] E.C.R. 1219; Case 69/89, *Nakajima*, [1991] E.C.R. I-2069.

493 As DE BÚRCA has noted: "There are few questions on which the EU law academic world (not to mention the CFI and the Advocates General of the ECJ) is so united as that the right of individuals to seek judicial review by the ECJ under Article 230 is excessively restrictive, and that it undermines respect for the principle of access to justice in the EU" (DE BÚRCA, 26).

494 Case 25/62, *Plaumann*, [1963] E.C.R. 95.

peculiar to them or by reason of circumstances in which they are differentiated from all other persons and by virtue of these factors distinguishes them individually just as in the case of the person addressed".[495]

The ECJ has since been extremely rigid in its restrictive interpretation of this Article,[496] garnering the criticism of lawyers, academics and even Advocates General. Even the Court of First Instance had attempted to expand the notion of individual concern when it said that a restrictive interpretation was no longer in line with what a Community (that is based on the rule of law) needed, *i.e.* the need to have the legality of Community acts checked. In effect, a rigorous application of the *Plaumann* test meant that an affected private party (which was not the addressee of the act) had to first breach the Community act before getting access to court where it could then contest its legality.

Rather than relaxing its standards for demonstrating "direct" and "individual" concern, the Court of Justice chose to allow individuals (who do not meet these standards) the opportunity of challenging the directives at issue through the national courts via the preliminary reference mechanism.[497] The ECJ took the view "*[t]hat in the Articles [230] and 241, on the one hand, and in Article [234] on the other, the Treaty established a complete system of legal remedies and procedure designed to permit the Court of Justice to review the legality of measures adopted by the institutions*".[498]

Thus, according to the ECJ, individuals are protected against general measures which they cannot contest directly in the Community

495 *Ibid.*, at 107.

496 Although the ECJ has permitted derogations from the *Plaumann* doctrine in areas such as State aid and anti-dumping, it appears unwilling to reformulate the doctrine itself (see Case 169/84, *Cofaz*, [1986] E.C.R. 391; Case C-309/89, *Codorniú SA v. Council*, [1994] E.C.R. I-1853; Case C-358/89, *Extramet*, [1991] E.C.R. I-2501).

497 Cases 133–136/85, *Walter Rau Lebensmittelwerke v. Bundesanstalt für Landwirtschaftliche Marktordnung*, [1987] E.C.R. 2289. However, the ECJ did hold that if an individual would "without any doubt" have had standing under Article 230(4), he or she could not rely on the Article 234 preliminary reference mechanism to challenge a law. See also Case C-188/93, *TWD Textilwerke Deggendorf GmbH v. Germany*, [1994] E.C.R. I-833.

498 Case 294/83, *Les Verts*, [1986] E.C.R. 1339, paragraph 23.

Courts by a dual system of protection. Where a Community institution is responsible for the administrative implementation of such measures, individuals may bring a direct action before the Court against implementing measures addressed to them and plead the illegality of the underlying general measure under Articles 263 and 277 TFEU. Where implementation is a matter for national authorities, the individual can plead the invalidity of the general measure before the national court and encourage the latter to request the Court of Justice for a preliminary ruling. Even though the ECJ appeared to alleviate the problem by slightly expanding the scope of Article 267 TFEU, *lacunae* in the European legal system remained which was evidenced, once more, by two cases, *UPA*[499] and *Jégo-Quéré*[500].

Advocate General Jacobs (and the CFI in *Jégo-Quéré*) pointed out in the *UPA* case that the "complete system of remedies" provided by Articles 230, 234 and 241 EC Treaty (now Articles 263, 234 and 277 TFEU) may not always provide an "effective remedy". There may be circumstances where individuals, denied access to the Community Courts because of the restrictive standing rule in Article 263(4) TFEU, may not be able to gain access to a national court otherwise than by infringing the law in expectation that criminal or other enforcement proceedings will be brought against them when the national court may be persuaded to refer to the Court of Justice the issue of the validity of the measure. In Advocate General Jacobs' view, besides the various practical disadvantages which may attend the making of a reference in the context of criminal proceedings, such a procedural avenue exposes the individuals in question to an intolerable burden of risk.[501]

A similar line of reasoning was used by the Court of First Instance in *Jégo-Quéré* which preceded the *UPA* judgment of the ECJ. Although the CFI agreed with the Commission's position that the French fishing company was "directly" concerned but lacked "individual" concern,[502] as defined by the *Plaumann* test, it nevertheless

499 Case C-50/00, *UPA*, [2002] E.C.R. I-6677.

500 Case T-177/01, *Jégo-Quéré & Cie v. Commission*, [2002] E.C.R. II-2365.

501 Opinion of Advocate General Jacobs delivered on 21 March 2002 in *UPA*, [2002] E.C.R. I-6677, paragraphs 37 and 43.

502 *Jégo-Quéré* is a French fishing company operating fishing boats over 30 meters in length which use nets of a mesh of 80mm in the waters south of Ireland. A

agreed to look at the problem from the view of *Jégo-Quéré*'s access to courts and its right to an effective remedy (as a fundamental right enshrined in the common constitutional traditions of the Member States)[503]. In the CFI's view it was "*[n]ecessary to consider whether, in a case such as this, where an individual applicant is contesting the lawfulness of provisions of general application directly affecting his legal situation, the inadmissibility of the action for annulment would deprive the applicant of the right to an effective remedy*".[504] The CFI concluded that, in order to ensure effective judicial protection for individuals, a new understanding of "individual" concern was needed.[505] In particular, it stressed that there is no compelling reason to read into the notion of individual concern, within the meaning of Article 263(4) TFEU, a requirement that an individual applicant seeking to challenge a general measure must be differentiated from all others affected by it in the same way as an addressee.[506]

Despite the arguments put forward by the CFI in *Jégo-Quére* and by Advocate General Jacobs, the Court of Justice did not feel able to reinterpret the admissibility conditions in Article 263(4) TFEU (*ex* Article 230(4) EC Treaty) in *UPA*. In fact, the ECJ confirmed its "hard line" attitude towards individual access in the Commission's appeal in *Jégo-Quéré*[507], ultimately overturning the CFI's decision.[508] In both instances, it basically refused to use an individual's "right to

new EC regulation banned the use of such nets in boats over 30 meters in length. *Jégo-Quéré* sought to challenge this regulation.

503 Also Advocate General Jacobs pointed out the existence of a fundamental right to effective judicial protection, which is a recognised principle of Community law and inherent in the system of remedies established by the EC Treaty; Opinion of Advocate General Jacobs delivered on 21 March 2002 in *UPA*, [2002] E.C.R. I-6677, paragraph 23.

504 T-177/01, *Jégo-Quéré & Cie v. Commission*, [2002] E.C.R. II-2365, paragraph 43.

505 It was suggested that the CFI "deliberately" took the opportunity to review individual concern in an attempt to widen the possibilities for individuals to challenge Community measures in order to increase the legitimacy and credibility of Community law; see BIERNAT, 33.

506 *Ibid.*, paragraphs 49 and 50.

507 Case C-263/02 P, *Jégo-Quéré*, [2004] E.C.R. I-3425.

508 For a detailed discussion of the ECJ's judgment in *Jégo-Quéré*, see BROWN/MORIJN, (2004) 41 CMLRev. 1639 *et seq.*

an effective remedy" and a rationale for expanding its rules on standing. Rather than assessing the completeness of the jurisdictional system, and then assessing the need for individual access at the European level, the ECJ assumed the completeness of the system of remedies in order to achieve the division of jurisdictional competences.[509] In other words, the ECJ chose again to place the burden of effective remedies and access onto the national courts,[510] thus promoting the use of Article 267 TFEU by severely restricting all other ways for individuals to challenge Community acts. In addition, and critically, it determined that any future change in the system must be conducted politically through Treaty amendment by the Member States themselves.

In this context, it may be noteworthy that the wording of Article 263(4) TFEU (*ex* Article 230(4) EC Treaty) is a reminiscence of Article III-365(4) of the Treaty establishing a Constitution for Europe (Constitution for Europe)[511]:

> Any natural or legal person may, under the conditions laid down in paragraphs 1 and 2 *[of Article III-365]*, institute proceedings against an act addressed to that person or which is of direct and individual concern to him or her, and against a regulatory act which is of direct concern to him or her and does not entail implementing measures.

The changes introduced via Article III-365 of Constitution for Europe have clearly been motivated by the desire to draw Article 263(4) TFEU nearer to the principle of effective judicial protection but the wording suggests that the reluctance to abolish the standards of "individual concern" has not been overcome. However, the possibility to bring an action against a "regulatory act which is of direct concern to him or her and does not entail implementing measures" seems to

509 BIERNAT, 40.

510 HANF, (2002) 3 German Law Journal, Issue No. 8, paragraph 17.

511 OJ 1994 C 310/1. The Treaty establishing a Constitution for Europe was signed on 29 October 2004 by the (then) 25 Member States but failed to enter into force due to lacking ratification by all the signatory States (France and the Netherlands have rejected the Constitution for Europe in a referendum on 29 May 2005 and 1 June 2005, respectively). Instead, the European leaders reached a compromise and agreed to adopt, not a Constitution, but a reform treaty for the European Union, namely the Treaty of Lisbon (OJ 2007 C 306/1).

tackle the problem of "self-executing", *i.e.* directly effective acts, which – as we have seen – cannot be challenged under the current system, unless the individual first breaches the law in order to have access to the courts.[512]

The term "regulatory act" appears to mean any act other than a legislative act. Private applicants would therefore appear to be able to bring a direct action before the General Court (*ex* Court of First Instance) challenging administrative acts which curtail rights of, or place obligations on individuals but lack implementing measures, provided that the applicants can demonstrate a direct concern. With regard to legislative acts (current regulations and decisions) and administrative acts entailing implanting measures, the standing rule of "direct and individual concern" still apply. Consequently, the discussion of standing will most likely be redefined along the distinction between "legislative" and "non-legislative" (administrative) acts[513] – which is arguably unfortunate since, in the light of the fundamental right to judicial protection, *locus standi* should not depend on the nature of the contested measure but on whether it affects adversely the interests of the individual. Whether these considerations can be of persuasive use when interpreting *locus standi* under the Treaty of Lisbon[514] remains to be seen.

For the purposes of the dissertation, and at the risk of simplifying matters, there are strong indications to conclude that invoking directly effective WTO provisions will be as restricted in the future as it is under the EC's current legal system. From the point of view of the principle of effective judicial protection, however, at least one other reform brought about by the Constitution for Europe requires mentioning.

Article I-29 of the Constitution for Europe (which resembles Article 220 EC Treaty) has introduced an element of judicial subsidiarity, providing that "*[M]ember States shall provide remedies sufficient to ensure effective legal protection in the fields covered by Union law*"

512 BIERNAT, 51.

513 BROWN/MORIJN, (2004) 41 CMLRev. 1656.

514 The Treaty of Lisbon (OJ 2007 C 306/1) entered into force on 1 December 2009, amending the Treaty on the European Union (OJ 2010 C 83/13) and the Treaty establishing the European Community (OJ 2010 C 83/47).

(Article I-29(1), second indent), and the exact wording has been maintained by the Treaty of Lisbon.[515] Considering that WTO/GATT are recognised to constitute an "integral part of the Community legal system" (and therefore are arguably covered by Union law), it may prove easier to bring an action before national courts. Then again, it may be assumed that such recognition represents nothing more than the codification of existing case-law[516] – which will most likely end again in a reference to the Court of Justice for a preliminary ruling.[517]

*3.2 Reference for a Preliminary Ruling under Article 267 TFEU (*ex *Article 234 EC Treaty)*

It becomes apparent from the Court of Justice' case-law regarding Article 263(4) TFEU that it has, at the expense of possibilities for individuals to bring direct actions, expanded the scope of Article 267 TFEU. By requiring Member States to establish a system of legal remedies and procedures which ensure respect for the right to effective judicial protection, the ECJ is in the comfortable position to hold the Member States responsible for *lacunae* in such protection – instead of relaxing the standards of "direct and individual concern".

In this context, one has to remember that an Article 267 TFEU procedure for a preliminary ruling requires a national implementation measure and is, thus, not available in those cases in which an individual seeks to challenge a directly applicable EC act which does not require implementation measures. With regard to the invocability of directly effective WTO provision, this has serious implications. Although the ECJ has accepted to review the legality of Community acts in the light of international agreements regardless of whether direct effect was demonstrated,[518] the ECJ indicated in later judgments that direct effect is indispensable to the question as to whether it will re-

515 Article 19(1) of the consolidated versions of the Treaty on European Union and the Treaty on the functioning of the European Union (OJ 2008 C 115/13).

516 See Case 294/83, *Les Verts*, [1986] E.C.R. 1339, paragraph 23.

517 See Case 314/85, *Foto-Frost*, [1987] E.C.R. 4199.

518 As in Case 181/73, *Haegeman*, [1974] E.C.R. 449, paragraph 5, or Case 38/75, *Nederlandse Spoorwegen*, [1975] E.C.R. 1439, paragraphs 13 *et seq.*

view the legality of Community acts under the procedure of Article 267 TFEU (*ex* Article 234 EC Treaty).[519]

This implies that, in cases where the Community act does not require implementation (for instance, a regulation that intends to implement an obligation deriving from WTO obligations or containing a clear reference to such obligation), the interested individual has only the possibility to provoke an infringement against the directly applicable act which may then allow him to challenge the enforcement measure or sanction imposed either by the Community or by a Member State administration.

Another shortcoming for individuals seeking to challenge a directly effective WTO provision is that they are forced to pass through the national courts in order to have access to the European Courts, hence encompassing additional costs in terms of time and money. At last, but not at least, another hardly assessable factor for private applicants to access the European courts under Article 267 TFEU is the national courts' willingness to make use of a reference for a preliminary ruling.[520]

Given the above observations, it would appear that the chances of successfully invoking directly effective WTO provisions are considerably limited when challenging the validity of a Community act. As a final point, however, it should be mentioned that private parties (business operators) may not solely be interested in having such act declared null and void. It is conceivable that they are equally – if not predominantly – interested in claiming compensation for the damages that they have incurred due to the Community act that is incompatible with the terms of an international agreement, or are otherwise affected by the non-implementation of a DSB's rulings touching upon the markets in which they do business.

519 Case 266/81, *SIOT*, [1983] E.C.R. 731; Cases 267–269/81, *SPI and SAMI*, [1983] E.C.R. 801.

520 HANF, (2002) 3 German Law Journal, Issue No. 7, paragraphs 14 to 16.

3.3 A Short Comment on Liability

Within the European Community non-contractual, or tortuous, liability is dealt with under two regimes. Whereas the liability of Community institutions for breaches of Community law finds its source in Article 230(2) TFEU (*ex* Article 288(2) EC Treaty) and is applied by the European Court of Justice pursuant to Article 268 TFEU (*ex* Article 235 EC Treaty), the liability of Member States has its origin only in the case-law of the ECJ,[521] especially in the framework of preliminary rulings pursuant to Article 267 TFEU (*ex* Article 234 EC Treaty).

Ever since its judgment in *Brasserie du Pêcheur and Factortame*,[522] the Court of Justice has progressively brought its regime on State liability in line with the system of Community liability, culminating in the *Bergaderm* case,[523] where it recalled that, unless there is a particular justification, the conditions under which a Member State may incur liability for damage caused to individuals by a breach of Community law cannot differ from those governing the liability of the Community in like circumstances because the protection of the rights which individuals derive from Community law cannot vary depending on whether a national authority or a Community authority is responsible for the damage.[524]

Article 230(2) TFEU (*ex* Article 288(2) EC Treaty) provides that, in the case of non-contractual liability, the Community is, in accor-

521 Although the EC Treaty (now TFEU) does not mention any liability of Member States, the ECJ declared it in the famous *Francovich* and *Brasserie du Pêcheur and Factortame* judgments as "inherent in the system of the Treaty" (Cases C-6/90 and C-9/90, *Francovich*, [1991] E.C.R. I-5357, confirmed in Joined Cases C-46/93 and C-48/93, *Brasserie du Pêcheur and Factortame*, [1996] E.C.R. I-01029).

522 Joined Cases C-46/93 and C-48/93, *Brasserie du Pêcheur and Factortame*, [1996] E.C.R. I-01029.

523 Case C-352/98, *Bergaderm*, [2000] E.C.R. I-5291, in which the ECJ redefined the original criteria for Community liability as laid down in Case 4/69, *Lütticke*, [1971] E.C.R. 325, and Case 5/71, *Schöppenstedt*, [1971] E.C.R. 975. The "Schöppenstedt test" used to ascertain whether a sufficiently flagrant [or serious] violation of a superior rule of law for the protection of the individual has occurred.

524 Case C-352/98, *Bergaderm*, [2000] E.C.R. I-5291, paragraph 41, with reference to *Brasserie du Pêcheur and Factortame*, [1996] E.C.R. I-1029, paragraph 42.

dance with the general principles common to the laws of the Member States, to make good any damage caused by, *inter alia*, its institutions in the performance of their duties. Reiterating its previous case-law, the ECJ pointed out that the system of rules which the Court has worked out with regard to the said provision takes into account, *inter alia*, the following factors: (i) the complexity of the situations to be regulated, (ii) difficulties in the application or interpretation of the texts and, more particularly, (iii) the margin of discretion available to the author of the act in question.[525]

Although *Bergaderm* was about Community liability, the ECJ recalled its case-law regarding Member State liability for damages incurred to individuals, and stated that Community law confers a right to reparation where three conditions are met:[526]

- the rule of law infringed must be intended to confer rights on individuals;
- the breach must be sufficiently serious;
- there must be a direct causal link between the breach of the obligation and the damage sustained by the injured parties.

Whereas the ECJ did not expand on the first condition, it pointed out that different tests applied for finding a "sufficiently serious breach" of Community law. Whereas the "*mere infringement of Community law*" may be sufficient to establish the existence of a sufficiently serious breach in cases where the Member State or the Community institution has "*only considerably reduced, or even no, discretion*",[527] the decisive test for finding such breach is, in all other cases, whether the Member State or the Community institution concerned "*manifestly and gravely disregarded the limits on its discretion*".[528] In other

525 *Ibid.*, paragraph 40, with reference to *Brasserie du Pêcheur and Factortame*, *supra*, paragraph 43.

526 Case C-352/98, *Bergaderm*, [2000] E.C.R. I-5291, paragraph 42. See also Joined Cases C-120/06P and C-121/06P, *FIAMM & Fedon*, [2008] E.C.R. I-6513, paragraph 106.

527 *Ibid.*, paragraph 44, and Case C-5/94, *Hedley Lomas*, [1996] E.C.R. I-2553, paragraph 28.

528 *Ibid.*, paragraph 43, recalling the finding in C-190/94, *Dillenkofer et al.*, [1996] E.C.R. I-4845, paragraph 25.

words, the same tests apply for the purposes of non-contractual liability – whether it is the Community institutions or the Member States.

Considering that the Court of Justice already held in *Brasserie du Pêcheur and Factortame* that "*[t]he right of individuals to rely on the directly effective provisions of the Treaty before national courts is only a minimum guarantee and is not sufficient in itself to ensure the full and complete implementation of the Treaty*", and that "*[t]he full effectiveness of Community law would be impaired if individuals were unable to obtain redress when their rights were infringed by a breach of Community law*",[529] the explicit development of *ius commune* of State and EC liability in *Bergaderm* may have interesting implications for claiming damages for breach of WTO provisions or DSB decisions.

Such implications have since been clarified in the *FIAMM & Fedon*[530] cases – at least to some extent – when the ECJ did little more than repeating the familiar arguments to deny direct effect of WTO provisions or DSB decisions and affording the Community's political institutions an almost infinite scope for manoeuvre at any point of the WTO dispute settlement procedure, thereby ruling that the same reasons apply to the review of the legality of a Community measure as to the claim for damages.[531]

After the dismissal of the claims for liability for unlawful conduct due to lack of direct effect, the remedy of liability *for legal conduct*[532] was tested, primarily by the Court relying on an examination of the Member States' legal systems (ruling out the existence of a principle of Community liability in the case of a lawful act or omission of legislative nature)[533]:

529 Joined Cases C-46/93 and C-48/93, *Brasserie du Pêcheur and Factortame*, [1996] E.C.R. I-1029, paragraph 20.

530 Joined Cases C-120/06P and C-121/06P, *FIAMM & Fedon*, [2008] E.C.R. I-6513.

531 *Ibid.*, paragraph 111 and 124. In this context it was argued that this, as such, does not preclude an action in damages *after* the final settlement of the dispute before the DSB as the negotiation competences of the Community institutions concerned would then already have unfolded to their largest extent possible; see ARCURI/POLI, 17.

532 For a detailed analysis of this aspect see DANI, 14 *et seq.*

533 *Ibid.*, paragraphs 151, 152 and 175.

> [...] as Community law currently stands, no liability regime exists under which the Community can incur liability for conduct falling within the sphere of its legislative competence in a situation *where any failure of such conduct to comply with the WTO agreements cannot be relied upon before the Community courts (emphasis added).*[534]

The wording chosen by the ECJ suggests that, in the absence of direct effect, a possible claim for damages for lawful conduct is inadmissible. Uncertainty remains, however, as to whether the remedy for non-contractual liability for lawful conduct is not available *altogether* or whether it may (still) be available to private parties in the event of a directly effective provision.

Drawing upon *Bergaderm* on the one hand and *FIAMM & Fedon* on the other, a preliminary observation must be that a finding of direct effect of a provision does not in itself guarantee a successful claim for damages by an individual. Admittedly, the ECJ referred to the "ensurement of the full and complete implementation" of the EC Treaty but this should not preclude the ability of individuals to invoke non-contractual liability since there are also rules of Community law that do not have direct effect but are nevertheless intended to confer rights on individuals.[535] Ultimately, *FIAMM & Fedon* seem, however, to have ruled out a comparable approach with a view to WTO provisions (or DSB decisions) lacking direct effect. Considering the three criteria that should be decisive, the following comments are in place:

The WTO provision infringed must be *intended to confer rights on individuals*: Whether the infringed WTO provision is intended to confer rights on individuals will have to be assessed on a case-by-case basis and which, in any event, will be met if a WTO provision has been found to be directly effective. The "intention to confer rights on individuals" should, however, not be equated with direct effect as the two concepts are not identical. Specifically, direct effect implies the intention to confer rights but not every right conferred on individuals is necessarily laid down in a directly effective provision – an ambiguity remaining from *FIAMM & Fedon* when the ECJ failed to make

534 *Ibid.*, paragraph 179.

535 As has already been recognised, for instance, in Case C-9/90, *Francovich*, [1991] E.C.R. I-5357. See also WIERS, (2004) 31 LIEI 148.

clear whether the principle of Community liability in the event of a lawful act or omission of legislative nature cannot be invoked in a claim for damages by private parties altogether (in cases in which the damages are caused specifically by a Community infringement of WTO law) or only in the absence of direct effect.

There must be a *sufficiently serious breach*: In view of the supremacy of a WTO provision over national legislation and secondary Community law, it may be assumed that a breach exists if a DSB decision has found a Community act to contravene a WTO provision. However, whether that breach is considered sufficiently serious is not easily determined. Considering that the ECJ has ruled that the decisive test to establish "sufficiently serious breach" depends on the discretion of the Community institutions or the Member States concerned, two cases should be distinguished. In light of the flexibility argument used by the ECJ to deny direct effect of WTO provisions and DSB decisions, in particular the possibility for negotiated solutions within the WTO dispute settlement mechanism, it is conceivable that, if liability of Community institutions was claimed, the discretion of the Community institutions would be considered wide – almost infinite (as was made manifest in the *FIAMM & Fedon* cases). This would mean that an individual would have to demonstrate a "manifest and grave disregard of the limits on their discretion", which ideally – in the light of *FIAMM & Fedon* – should further be tested in a situation where the Community institutions have "exhausted" their negotiation competence, *i.e.* situations that are confined to the period after a final settlement of a dispute under the WTO regime. On the other hand, in cases where Member States' liability is at issue, and the Member States have no or very limited discretion, the mere infringement as established by the DSB decision may prove to be sufficient to demonstrate the existence of a sufficiently serious breach. For example, *Van Parys* may have been more successful if, instead of challenging the validity of the regulations on the common organisation of the market in bananas based upon which it was refused certain import licences,[536] it had considered instead claiming damages incurred to it by that refusal.

536 See Case C-377/02, *Van Parys*, [2005] E.C.R. I-1465.

There must be a *direct causal link between the breach of the obligation deriving from the WTO provision and the damage* sustained by the injured parties: Again, causality would have to be assessed in the individual case.

These observations demonstrate that compensation claims for Community acts that contravene WTO provisions or DSB decisions are, albeit ambitious in terms of burden of proof, still possible and may put pressure on the competent authorities (and courts) to review their position regarding the enforceability of WTO provisions. Admittedly, a fundamental change in the approach towards granting direct effect to WTO provisions is highly unlikely but a surge in liability claims may compel the Community to, at least, comply more swiftly with DSB recommendations and rulings.

4 Preliminary Conclusion

The Community case-law regarding reliance on provisions of international agreements is not uniform. To the contrary, the standard applied to determine whether an individual may rely on provisions of international agreements appear to differ depending on whether these provisions belong to the GATT and/or WTO agreements or to other international agreements.

Regarding multilateral trade rules, as established first by the GATT 1947 and then its successor the WTO Agreement and its Annexes, the ECJ has consistently relied on two main arguments in order to deny them direct effect: First, it has been argued that the GATT was characterised by significant flexibility, such as the possibility of derogation or exceptional measures, and provided an instrument of negotiation[537] rather than adjudication, especially with respect to the partly

537 A notable attempt to classify the different kinds of mutually agreed solutions in the dispute settlement process found in EC practice was undertaken by TANCREDI. He distinguishes four categories: a) agreements *infra ordinem*, *i.e.* expressly permitted by the DSU, insomuch as they represent the positive result of

diplomatic nature of the dispute settlement mechanism. This also entailed that the provisions of GATT were considered not to be sufficiently precise (unconditional and clear). Second, the granting of direct effect was refused due to the lack of reciprocity in the initial balance of the obligations undertaken as well as in the ability to enforce them.

Private parties as well as Member States were only allowed to rely on GATT provisions in order to challenge the validity of Community acts if the Community legislation concerned either expressly referred to them, or if the EC intended to implement an obligation entered into under GATT. It appears that the primary motivation behind the Court's reluctance to apply GATT law directly, was the fact that other GATT contracting parties did not accord it direct effect, and the ECJ considered that such unilateral approach might fetter the EC institutions in exercising their discretion in matters of foreign commercial policy. It must be acknowledged that reciprocity in this context is much more a mercantilist argument than a legal one, and that non-reciprocity turns out to be a compelling argument in cases where the granting of direct effect gives rise to a substantial imbalance of the rights and obligations of the contracting parties.[538] Considering that the WTO establishes a system of well calculated and balanced package deals, the equilibrium of performance would be harmed.

either the preliminary 'diplomatic' phase or of the consultations held during the panel procedure; b) agreements *infra ordinem* concluded under Articles 22(2) and 22(8) DSU; c) agreements *extra ordinem*, *i.e.* not provided for by the DSU text, and *praeter legem*, whose aim is to fill the lacunae in a treaty; d) agreements *extra ordinem* and *contra legem*. TANCREDI, (2004) 15 EJIL 948 *et seq.*

538 For example, Article 3:3 DSU calls for the "prompt" settlement of situations in which a Member considers that any benefits accruing to it directly or indirectly under the covered agreements are being impaired. Article 4 DSU requires consultation between the involved parties before the establishment of a panel, while Article 5 DSU offers the use of offices, conciliation and mediation. Negotiations may even take place on a parallel track to a panel procedure. Article 12:7 DSU provides that "*where the parties to the dispute have failed to develop a mutually satisfactory solution*, the panel shall submit its findings in a written report", which will be submitted for adoption to the Dispute Settlement Body (DSB) 20 days later (emphasis added).

It was often argued, however, that the WTO Agreement and its Annexes, such as the GATT or the TRIPs, possess the characteristics to be directly effective, *i.e.* that the provisions are clear, comprehensive and sufficiently precise, and that the strengthening of the dispute settlement to a legally binding mechanism brought about by the Uruguay Round is capable of overcoming the historical reluctance to accord it direct effect. This has clearly not been the case.

For instance, by holding that in a field to which TRIPs applies and with respect to which the EC has already legislated, the judicial authorities of the Member States are required "*by virtue of EC law*" to act (when ordering interim measures based on national law) as far as possible in the light of the wording and the purpose of Article 50 TRIPs, the ECJ merely satisfies the rules set in the *Nakajima* case. The preamble to Council Regulation 3288/94[539] which was enacted to implement the rules of TRIPs related to trademarks reads: "*In order to ensure that all relevant Community legislation is in full compliance with the TRIPs Agreement, the Community must take certain measures in relation to current Community acts on the protection of intellectual property rights [...].*"

However, the ECJ appears not even to reason in this line but rather contents itself with the application of an interpretation method that allows it to solve the problem via a backdoor, *i.e.* by requesting compliance "*by virtue of EC law*" rather than granting direct effect to Article 50(6) TRIPs at least in the field of trademarks. In that sense, the ECJ does not contribute much to the demarcation line between the competences of the Member States and the Community.

It can be assumed from the above that the ECJ also tries to mitigate the problem by an indirect approach as far as IP rights other than trademarks are concerned, *i.e.* by applying a rule of interpretation, according to which national legislation should be construed insofar as possible in accordance with the international commitments undertaken. It seems to be just one more step to adopt a rule of presumption, according to which national authorities are presumed to be obliged, absent dire conflicting public interests, to apply their discretion in a

539 OJ 1994 L 349/83.

manner that conforms to international obligations.[540] Such an approach may allow for a cautious step-by-step assessment, but does not offer easier solutions when private parties apply for interim measures in cases of IP violations, other than trademark violations, in different Member States and get different protection.

The members of the WTO/GATT have a primary obligation to remedy laws and practices held to be inconsistent with their obligations under the DSU and GATT Article XXIII. Measures and practices under national (or regional) law that are inconsistent with the WTO have thus to be brought into compliance with WTO obligations within a reasonable time.[541] However, the duration of this time period is unclear. A member may offer adequate compensation in diplomatic negotiations until a solution to the dispute can be found domestically. A much as there is no obligation to accept such an offer, there is no means to seek immediate removal of the measure. The member whose benefits were nullified and impaired may merely withdraw concessions, if necessary by means of cross-sanctions, provided that such nullification and impairment was decided under Article 22 DSU.

Moreover, there is no obligation to perform in non-violation cases, and remedies are limited to compensation[542] which may form part of a final settlement[543]. In addition, members of the WTO are obliged to enforce obligations internally only to the extent that they have the necessary constitutional powers.[544] Although this provision may not ensure that the enforcement of international rules can be entirely respected by sub-national levels, it can be argued that the political entities of the Community have the necessary competence to do so regarding WTO/GATT, especially in light of the exclusive Common

540 In this respect cf. EINHORN, (1998) 35 CMLRev. 1098.

541 Article 21(1) DSU. For a detailed analysis see WEBER, Prozessuale Aspekte der Streitbeilegung im institutionellen Rahmen der Welthandelsorganisation (WTO) – Amicus Curiae, Professionalisierung der Panelebene, fehlende Rückverweisungskompetenz des Appellate Body und die Abfolgeproblematik der Art. 21, 22 DSU, Witten 2007.

542 Article 26(1)(b) DSU.

543 Article 26(1)(d) DSU.

544 GATT Article XXIV(12), Understanding on the Interpretation of Article XXIV of the General Agreement on Tariffs and Trade, paragraphs 13–15.

Commercial Policy. Moreover, the provision clearly concerns the obligation to enforce WTO rules falling in the jurisdiction of the competent government.

Admittedly, granting direct effect may deprive the Community from its rights after the issuance of an adverse panel report. If the Court of Justice declared invalid a measure contrary to WTO rules, for instance before the panel had even decided whether the measure violated WTO rules, the Community would lose its choice of how to remedy the injury caused by the measure. By transposing, however, the same line of arguments to situations where DSB recommendations and decisions have found a Community measure to be incompatible with the WTO rules and the time-limit set by it to remedy the situation has expired, one could contend that the Court of Justice simply did not want to politically expose itself by granting direct effect for two main reasons. Firstly, the denial of direct effect may result from the desire to preserve the best legal position for the Community within the WTO/GATT system. Secondly, it can be seen as a reaction to the conduct of the Member States and the Community's political institutions. Their political support for the cause of free trade has not been matched by legal commitments. The Court of Justice appears to simply not want to facilitate such a contradictory approach or take such a politically sensitive decision itself.

As a consequence of this – apparently "settled" – case-law, individuals who are directly affected by a Community measure which is inconsistent with WTO rules are left (almost) empty handed. The avenue for a direct action under Article 263(4) TFEU (*ex* Article 230(4) EC Treaty) is severely restricted by the standing rule of "direct and individual concern". Moreover, unless the Community measure concerned was intended to ensure the enforcement within the Community legal order of a particular obligation assumed in the context of the WTO or expressly refers to specific provisions of the WTO agreements, an individual has in principle no chance of successfully challenging the validity of a Community measure contravening WTO provisions. Admittedly, the Court of Justice has somewhat extended the application of Article 267 TFEU (*ex* Article 234 EC Treaty) by requiring the Member States to provide for remedies sufficient to ensure effective legal protection, but this is unlikely to lead to a flood of successful cases since this procedure is not only costly in terms of time and money but also depends on whether a national court is prepared to refer the case for a preliminary ruling.

As relying on direct effect does not constitute a viable route, some advancement regarding individuals' rights may result from liability claims. The main argument there would be that the Community should be held responsible for damages stemming from conduct that is not compliant with WTO law, including the failure to implement rulings and recommendations of the DSB. Whilst the Court of Justice has ruled out claims for damages unlawful as much as lawful conduct in the absence of direct effect, uncertainty remains as to whether the remedy for non-contractual liability for lawful conduct is not available altogether or whether it may (still) be available to private parties in the event of a directly effective provision. Until this has been clarified, it may still be hoped that a surge in liability claims is capable of putting pressure on the Community to enhance compliance with, and therefore implementation of, DSB recommendations and rulings.

CHAPTER III

The Boundaries of Challenging Voluntary Export Restraints within the EU Legal Order

The boundaries of challenging VERs within the EC legal order shall be predominantly discussed under the assumption that private parties, such as undertakings that are adversely affected by a VER and consumers, are most likely to complain about VERs that are hypothetically government-sponsored.[545] Thereby, the emphasis is put on three possibilities: first, the reliance on provisions of the Agreement on Safeguards before the European courts to challenge the validity of a VER; second, the procedure provided for under the Trade Barriers Regulation (TBR); and third, a possible complaint under EU competition law.

1 Reliance on the Agreement on Safeguards before the Courts

Transposing the observations made in Chapter II to the situation where a VER is challenged before the European courts reveals that the success of such action would be dependent on whether both, the question on standing as well as on direct effect of the Agreement on Safeguards were answered in the affirmative. For the purposes of this dissertation, it is assumed that possible complainants, such as private undertakings not participating in the VER or consumers, would be "individually and

545 The limitation of the discussion to government-sponsored VERs is, as aforementioned, explained by the consideration that VERs of purely private nature most likely violate competition law (in terms of market-sharing and limitation of output), unless such VERs (as export cartels) benefit from a domestic exception from the application of competition law.

directly concerned" in the sense of Article 263(4) TFEU (*ex* Article 230(4) EC Treaty), or that, alternatively, the national courts do provide for remedies sufficient to ensure effective legal protection, thereby opening the door for a possible preliminary ruling under Article 267 TFEU (*ex* Article 234 EC Treaty).

Primarily, it shall be established whether the Agreement on Safeguards, and more particularly its Article 11, may be regarded as having direct effect in light of the ECJ's case-law. In order to do so, and for the sake of completeness, it will be discussed in general on how the Agreement on Safeguards has found entry into the EC legal order before turning to the evaluation of whether its provisions meet the criteria of the "implementation principle" established by the Court of Justice.

1.1 The Implementation of the Agreement on Safeguards in the EU Legal Order

The rationale of safeguards is that countries are entitled to take action in order to protect their industries from surges or other large volumes of imports. Therefore, it can only be used when an industry is threatened with serious injury from foreign competition, and where there is the reasonable prospect that a period of protection will enable the industry to recover and compete on equal terms. Unlike other trade policy instruments, such as anti-dumping or anti-subsidy, safeguards do not carry an accusation of unfair foreign competition. In its 18th Annual Report to the Parliament,[546] the Commission explains, however, that the 1999 report has been extended in scope in order to also offer an overview of certain other Community trade policy activities, in particular, the activities in relation to the safeguard measures adopted by third countries and actions under the dispute settlement understanding of the WTO. Rather mistakenly, the Commission contends that the reason for this extension is, *inter alia*, that anti-dumping, anti-subsidy

546 Report from the Commission – Eighteenth annual report from the Commission to the European Parliament on the Community's anti-dumping and anti-subsidy activities – Overview of the monitoring of third country safeguard cases and of the implementation of the Trade Barriers Regulation (1999), COM(2000) 440 final.

and the other trade policy activities – hence safeguard measures – covered by the report, all have the same goal which is to ensure fair competition [sic!], not only within the EC but also on the third country markets.[547]

After the completion of the GATT Uruguay Round and the Community's obligations deriving from it, the Council has approved[548] the Agreement on Safeguards and adopted Regulation 3285/94 on the common rules for imports[549] in order to transpose it. For the sake of completeness, it is noted that, besides the incorporation of the Agreement on Safeguards, Regulation 3285/94 represents the heritage of a series of regulations laying down the common import regime.[550] With the exception of textile products and products from certain third countries,[551] Article 1(2) of Regulation 3285/94 thus provides that imports into the Community of products originating in third countries shall

547 *Ibid.*, p. 11.

548 Uruguay Round of Multilateral Trade Negotiations (1986–1994) - Annex 1 - Annex 1A - Agreement on Safeguards (WTO-GATT 1994), OJ 1994 L 336/184.

549 Council Regulation (EC) No. 3285/94 of 22 December 1994 on the common rules for imports and repealing Regulation (EC) No 518/94 (OJ 1994 L 349/53, as modified by Regulation No. 139/96 (OJ 1996 L 21/7). The Regulation has been notified to the WTO/GATT Secretariat in accordance with Article 12:6 Agreement on Safeguards (cf. G/SG/N/1/EEC/1).

550 The last two ones being Council Regulation (EEC) No. 288/82 on common rules of import (OJ 1982 L 35/1) and Council Regulation (EC) No. 518/94 (OJ 1994 L 67/77). For the link between the evolution of the Common Commercial Policy and the Common Import Regime, cf. DIDIER, 254 *et seq.*

551 According to Article 1(1) of Regulation 3285/94, it applies to imports of products originating in third countries, with the exception of textile products covered by Council Regulation No. 517/94 on common rules for imports of textile products from certain third countries not covered by bilateral agreements, protocols or other arrangements, or by other specific Community import regimes, and of products originating in certain third countries listed in Council Regulation No. 519/94 (for example countries of the Commonwealth of Independent States (CIS) and China). Upon the accession of China to the WTO, the progressive removal of these quantitative restrictions by the year 2005 was agreed. Council Regulation (EC) No. 427/2003 (OJ L 65/1) and Commission Regulation (EC) No. 428/2003 (OJ L 65/12) implement this phase-out plan. This exemption remained unchanged in the regulation's successor, *i.e.* Council Regulation (EC) No. 260/2009 of 26 February 2009 (codified version) on the common rules for imports (OJ 2009 L 84/1).

take place freely, and accordingly, shall not be subject to any quantitative restrictions, without prejudice to the safeguard measures which may be taken under it. In respect of agricultural products, Regulation 3285/94 operates complementarily to instruments establishing the common organisation of agricultural markets, of Community or national administrative provisions derived there from or of the specific instruments applicable to goods resulting from the processing of agricultural products.[552] According to Recital 5 of Regulation 3285/94, ECSC products are also covered by the common rules for import, especially as regards safeguard measures.[553] Moreover, according to Article 26 of Regulation 3285/94,[554] residual national restrictions relating to products covered by the ECSC Treaty had to be progressively dismantled in accordance with the provisions of the WTO,[555] *i.e.* before 1999. Regulation 260/2009[556] has repealed Regulation 3285/94 but codified, by large and mostly *verbatim*, the substantial provisions thereof.

552 Article 25 of Regulation 3285/94 (now Article 25 of Regulation 260/2009). By means of Council Regulation 3290/94 on the adjustments and transitional arrangements required in the agriculture sector in order to implement the agreements concluded during the Uruguay Round of multilateral trade negotiations (OJ 1994 L 349/105), the safeguard clauses as incorporated in the market organisations were supplemented by a reference to the obligations flowing from international agreements, such as the Agreement on Safeguards; cf. Recital 7 of Regulation 3290/94.

553 Interestingly, the application of Regulation 3285/94 was without prejudice to any possible measures within an agreement specifically concerning ECSC products, which implies the EC's anticipation of future negotiations in this respect.

554 Allegedly, it may appear unexpected that Regulation 3285/94, based solely on Article 133 EC Treaty, is designed to also cover ECSC products. However, in *Opinion 1/94*, [1994] E.C.R. I-5267, the ECJ considered that the EC is competent by virtue of Article 133 EC Treaty (now Article 207 TFEU) to conclude external agreements of a general character, *i.e.* including all sorts of products – even ECSC products.

555 For details cf. Council Decision 95/251 on the progressive dismantling of certain quantitative restrictions on imports of certain ECSC products (OJ 1995 L 159/17).

556 Council Regulation (EC) No. 260/2009 of 26 February 2009 (codified version) on the common rules for imports (OJ 2009 L 84/1).

1.1.1 Relationship between the Agreement on Safeguards and GATT Article XIX

The objective of the Agreement on Safeguard is to clarify and reinforce the disciplines of GATT 1994, and specifically those of Article XIX (Emergency Action on Imports of Particular Products)[557], which is reiterated in Recital 4 of Regulation 3285/94 (now Regulation 260/2009). Recital 2 of Regulation 3285/94, on the other hand, merely recalls that due account was taken of the Community's international obligations "*when Regulation (EC) No. 518/94 was adopted*".[558] Regulation 260/2009 omits this reference and simply states that the common commercial policy should be based on uniform principles (Recital 2).

In this context, it may be recalled that the Court of Justice held, with regard to anti-dumping measures, that the provisions of the Anti-Dumping Code have the effect of binding the Community. Reiterating that the Anti-Dumping Code was adopted for the purpose of implementing GATT Article VI, and that the recitals in the preamble to the Anti-Dumping Code specify that it is designed to "*interpret the provisions of [...] the General Agreement*" and to "*elaborate rules for their application in order to provide greater uniformity and certainty in their implementation*", the ECJ referred to Recitals 2 and 3 of the EC basic Anti-Dumping Regulation, according to which it was adopted in accordance with existing international obligations, in particular those arising from GATT Article VI and from the Anti-Dumping Code. The ECJ thus concluded that the Anti-Dumping Regulation was adopted in order to comply with the international obligations of the Community, which is therefore under an obligation to ensure compliance with the GATT and its implementing measures.[559] In this context, it has to be noted, however, that there has been some indication that the Court, somewhat deviating from its consistent case-law, is ready to narrow the *Nakajima* exception in its scope when it held in the *Ikea*[560] case that the Anti-

557 Preamble to the Agreement on Safeguards, paragraph 2.

558 Regulation 3285/94 repealed Regulation 518/94 which means that, strictly speaking, the reference to the Community's international obligations is not explicit in relation to the adoption of Regulation 3285/94.

559 Case 69/89, *Nakajima,* [1991] E.C.R. I-2069, paragraphs 29–31.

560 Case C-351/04, *Ikea*, [2007] E.C.R. I-7723.

Dumping Regulation did not intend in any way to give effect to a "specific obligation" assumed in the context of WTO law.[561] Whilst this may imply that the WTO Anti-Dumping Agreement shall no longer be considered an "obligation",[562] it is not conceivable how such reasoning should void the Community from its duty to ensure compliance with WTO rules altogether.

It will therefore have to be elaborated whether, similarly to the stance taken towards the regulation of anti-dumping measures (prior to the inconclusive statement in *Ikea*), the Agreement on Safeguards, GATT Article XIX and Regulation 3285/94 (now Regulation 260/2009) form a comparable unity of rules that are apt to produce direct effect in the EC legal order although they do not provide explicitly for the elaboration of rules to enhance uniformity and certainty in the implementation of safeguard measures. This lack of clear reference has (partly) been rectified in Regulation 260/2009 which puts the codification in the interests of "clarity and rationality" (Recital 1).

The Agreement on Safeguards "*establishes rules for the application of safeguard measures which shall be understood to mean those measures provided for in Article XIX of the GATT*" (Article 1). Unlike the Anti-Dumping Code,[563] the Agreement on Safeguards does not provide a direct reference to the legal relationship between GATT Article XIX and the Agreement on Safeguards. The usage of the term "establishes rules"[564] suggests the existence of other rules despite the recognition in the Preamble to the Agreement on Safeguards to set up a "comprehensive agreement" applicable to all Members.[565]

561 *Ibid.*, paragraph 35.

562 ARCURI/POLI, 9 (with further annotations).

563 Article 1 of the Anti-Dumping Code provides that "an antidumping measure shall be applied only under the circumstances provided for in Article VI of GATT 1994 and pursuant to investigations initiated and conducted in accordance with the provisions of this Agreement. The following provisions govern the application of Article VI of GATT 1994 in so far as action is taken under antidumping legislation or regulation." This provision therefore defines the legal relationship between GATT Article VI and the Anti-Dumping Code.

564 The French version of Article 1 Agreement on Safeguards reads "établit *des* règles" (emphasis added).

565 Preamble to the Agreement on Safeguards, paragraph 4.

Admittedly, the term "comprehensiveness" does not equate to "uniformity" but this does not preclude, as such, the possible finding that the "implementation principle" established by the ECJ is applicable to Regulation 3285/94 (now Regulation 260/2009). In particular, one preliminary observation must be that the term "comprehensive agreement" surely reflects the compromise found between developing countries, which called for an application of the Agreement on Safeguards to all products, and developed countries, among others the EC, which preferred a system that provided more flexibility, particularly with regards to textiles, agricultural and steel products.[566]

The relationship between the Agreement on Safeguards and GATT Article XIX should therefore be inferred from other WTO provisions.[567] Article II:2 of the WTO Agreement provides that "*the agreements and associated legal instruments included in Annexes 1, 2 and 3 are integral parts of this Agreement, binding on all Members*". Both GATT Article XIX and the Agreement on Safeguards are included in Annex 1 which indicates that they both apply to safeguard measures to the extent that there is no conflict between the provisions of those rules.[568]

There has been considerable disagreement on whether both GATT Article XIX and the Agreement on Safeguards form an integral discipline on safeguards. In particular, it was maintained that there is a conflict between GATT Article XIX:1 and Article 2 Agreement on Safeguards. The wording of these Articles provides both a summary of the prerequisites that safeguard measures must fulfil and a useful starting point in analysing the mechanics of the actions taken under

566 For the major disagreements at the start of the Uruguay Round negotiations concerning safeguards, see the detailed description of STEWART/BRILLIANT, 1768 *et seq.*, and the report of GATT Director-General Dunkel as regards the product coverage of a safeguards agreement, *ibid.*, at 1795 *et seq.*

567 LEE, (2000) 34 JWT 132; LEE, (2001) 35 JWT 1237; MUELLER, (2003) 37 JWT 1124.

568 To the extent that the text of GATT Article XIX and the Agreement on Safeguards conflict, the rules in the Agreement on Safeguards prevail over the conflicting rules in GATT Article XIX (cf. General Interpretative Note to Annex 1A of the WTO Agreement).

the escape clause or the Agreement on Safeguards. GATT Article XIX:1(a) reads:

> If, [2] *as a result of unforeseen developments and of the effect of the obligations incurred by a contracting party under this Agreement, including tariff concessions*, [1] any product is being imported into the territory of that contracting party in such increased quantities and under such conditions as [3] to cause or threaten serious injury to [4] domestic producers in that territory of like or directly competitive products, the contracting party [5] shall be free, in respect of such product, and to the extent and for such time as may be necessary to prevent or remedy such injury, to suspend the obligation in whole or in part or to withdraw or modify the concession (brackets and emphasis added).

In comparison, Article 2:1 Agreement on Safeguards does not contain the "unforeseen developments" clause. The Article provides:

> A Member may apply a safeguard measure to a product only if that Member has determined, pursuant to the provisions set out below, that [1] such product is being imported into its territory in such increased quantities, absolute or relative to domestic production, and under such conditions as [3] to cause or threaten to cause serious injury to [4] the domestic industry that produces like or directly competitive products *(brackets added, original footnote omitted).*

Accordingly, the following three main features may be distinguished:

- It must be demonstrated that imports of a product are increasing [1], and that this increase is a causal result [2] of unforeseen developments and of the effect of WTO/GATT obligations.
- It must be shown that domestic producers of like or directly competitive products [4] are seriously injured or threatened with serious injury [3], and that this serious injury or the threat thereof is caused by the imports [1].
- Provided that the above conditions are met, an importing country is entitled to suspend, withdraw or modify the concessions to the extent and for such time as is necessary to prevent or remedy the injury [5].

It becomes apparent from the above that the wording of GATT Article XIX:1(a) corresponds to Article 2:1 Agreement on Safeguards inasmuch as both provide for the same legal prerequisites, with exception of the "unforeseen developments" clause. It has been highly controversial whether this clause creates an additional legal requirement for the application of safeguard measures, and whether an ongoing application of the "unforeseen developments" clause gives rise to a conflict between the two sets of rules. This controversy has been settled by a number of Panels and Appellate Body findings.

The Panel on *Argentina – Footwear* noted that, in its opinion, rules for the imposition of safeguard measures provided for in GATT Article XIX and the rules for the imposition of safeguard measures deriving from the Agreement on Safeguards have to be read in conjunction. It believed that they "*[h]ave become intrinsically linked, if not inseparable from one another since the entry into force of the WTO Agreement*".[569]

It continued by seeking inspiration from the Panel on *Brazil – Desiccated Coconut* which found that

> [t]he relationship between the GATT of 1994 and the other goods agreements in Annex 1A is complex and must be examined on a case-by-case basis. Although the provisions of the GATT of 1947 were incorporated into, and became part of the GATT 1994, they are *not the sum total of the rights and obligations of WTO Members concerning a particular matter (emphasis added).*[570]

This finding induced the Panel to conclude "*[t]hat [...] the Agreement on Safeguards as applying the disciplines of Article XIX of GATT, reflects the latest statement of WTO Members concerning their rights and obligations concerning safeguards. Thus the Agreement on Safeguards should be understood as defining, clarifying, and in some cases modifying the whole package of rights and obligations of Members with respect to safeguard measures as they currently exist.*"[571]

Nevertheless, the Panel reiterated that the Agreement on Safeguards does not supersede or replace Article XIX, which continues to remain in force as part of the GATT. It found that the original conditions contained in GATT Article XIX have to be read in the light of

569 Panel Report on *Argentina – Footwear*, WT/DS121/R, paragraph 8.56.
570 Panel Report on *Brazil – Desiccated Coconut*, WT/DS22/R, paragraph 227.
571 Panel Report on *Argentina – Footwear*, WT/DS121/R, paragraph 8.58.

the subsequently negotiated and much more specific provisions of the Agreement on Safeguards which place the original rule of GATT Article XIX within the entire package of the new WTO legal system and make it operational in practice. The Panel also considered that the express omission of the criterion of unforeseen developments in the Agreement on Safeguards must have meaning.

In light of these considerations, the Panel concluded that safeguard investigations conducted and safeguard measures imposed after the entry into force of the WTO agreements which meet the requirements of the new Agreement on Safeguards satisfy the requirements of GATT Article XIX.[572] This decision in fact recognised that the Agreement on Safeguards is the sole legal authority on safeguards, and that the "unforeseen developments" clause did not create any additional legal requirement for the application of safeguards.

The Appellate Body reversed, however, those Panel decisions. In its reports on *Argentina – Footwear*, on *Korea – Dairy* and on *US – Lamb*, the Appellate Body emphasised that there is nothing in the language of either Article 1 or Article 11:1(a) Agreement on Safeguards that suggests the subsumption of the requirements of GATT Article XIX under the Agreement on Safeguards, and hence to render the requirements of GATT Article XIX no longer applicable. To the contrary, it underlined that the purpose of the Agreement on Safeguards is to establish rules for the application of safeguard measures which, according to its Article 1, shall be understood to mean those measures provided for in GATT Article XIX. In the Appellate Body's view, this suggested that GATT Article XIX continues in full force, hence creating certain prerequisites for the imposition of safeguard measures. Read in conjunction with Article 11:1(a) Agreement on Safeguards which stipulates that any such action must conform with that Article applied in accordance with the Agreement on Safeguards, the Appellate Body concluded that any safeguard measure imposed after the entry into force of the WTO Agreement must comply with the provisions of both the Agreement on Safeguards and GATT Arti-

572 *Ibid.*, paragraph 8.69. A similar conclusion was reached by the Panel on *Korea – Dairy*, WT/DS98/R, paragraph 7.48.

cle XIX.[573] Put differently, the "unforeseen developments" clause remains a legal requirement[574] for the imposition of a safeguard measure.

This finding has since been confirmed on several occasions. For instance, the Panels on *Argentina – Preserved Peaches* and *US – Certain Steel Products* both clearly expressed the continuing applicability of GATT Article XIX.[575] In the latter case, the Panel specified that "unforeseen developments" should be demonstrated "*through a reasoned and adequate explanation*".[576] This standard of review has subsequently been challenged by the United States for being inappropriate.[577] The Appellate Body dismissed, however, this criticism by stating that the circumstances of unforeseen developments must be demonstrated as a matter of *fact* in the report of the competent authority and before a safeguard measure can be applied. It considered it impossible for a panel to objectively examine the consistency of a safeguard determination with GATT Article XIX if the competent authority had not set out an explanation supporting its conclusions on "unforeseen developments". The Appellate Body therefore concluded that there was no reason not to apply the same standard, *i.e.* the provision of a "reasoned and adequate explanation", generally to the obliga-

573 AB Reports on *Argentina – Footwear*, WT/DS121/AB/R, paragraph 83; on *Korea – Dairy*, WT/DS98/AB/R, paragraph 77; and on *US – Lamb*, WT/DS177/AB/R, WT/DS178/AB/R, paragraphs 69 and 70.

574 The Appellate Body reiterated in its report on *US – Lamb* that the existence of "unforeseen developments" is a "*pertinent issue of fact and law*" (WT/DS177/AB/R, WT/DS178/AB/R, paragraph 76).

575 Panel Report on *Argentina – Preserved Peaches*, WT/DS238/R, paragraph 7.12; and Panel Reports on *US – Certain Steel Products*, WT/DS248/R, WT/DS249/R, WT/DS251/R, WT/DS252/R, WT/DS253/R, WT/DS254/R, WT/DS258/R, WT/DS259/R, paragraph 10.36.

576 Panel Reports on *US – Certain Steel Products*, WT/DS248/R, WT/DS249/R, WT/DS251/R, WT/DS252/R, WT/DS253/R, WT/DS254/R, WT/DS258/R, WT/DS259/R, paragraph 10.38.

577 AB Report on *US – Certain Steel Products*, WT/DS248/AB/R, WT/DS249/AB/R, WT/DS251/AB/R, WT/DS252/AB/R, WT/DS253/AB/R, WT/DS254/AB/R, WT/DS258/AB/R, WT/DS259/AB/R, paragraph 274.

tions under the Agreement on Safeguards as well as to the obligations in GATT Article XIX.[578]

Various academics and scholars have voiced concern on whether the Appellate Body's opinion is convincing,[579] and it was pointed out that the necessity of demonstrating "unforeseen developments" represents a clause which is too ambiguous and equivocal to create objective legal criteria.[580] Admittedly, the standard of review set by a "reasoned and adequate explanation" does not provide much guidance,[581] but recent attempts to quantify and qualify other substantive legal requirements for safeguard measures, such as increased imports or serious injury, demonstrate that it is, in any event, extremely difficult to impose safeguard measures without having to face a nearly certain defeat if a case is brought against them.[582]

In light of the Appellate Body's findings, and considering that the EC has repeatedly argued before panels that both GATT Article XIX (and its "unforeseen developments" clause) and the Agreement on Sa-

578 AB Report on *US – Certain Steel Products*, WT/DS248/AB/R, WT/DS249/AB/R, WT/DS251/AB/R, WT/DS252/AB/R, WT/DS253/AB/R, WT/DS254/AB/R, WT/DS258/AB/R, WT/DS259/AB/R, paragraphs 276–279.

579 AHN, 16 *et seq.*; BRONCKERS (1995), 275; LEE, (2000) 34 JWT 131 *et seq.*; MUELLER, (2003) 37 JWT 1132 *et seq.*; in response to Mueller cf. LEE, (2003) 37 JWT 1153 *et seq.*; SYKES, 15 *et seq.*; TREBILCOCK/HOWSE, 228.

580 Lee, (2001) 35 JWT 1241.

581 For instance, the Appellate Body noted pragmatically in US – Certain Steel Products that *"[i]t is evident [...] that not just any development that is "unforeseen" will do. To trigger the right to apply a safeguard measure, the development must be such as to result in increased imports of the product"* (WT/DS248/AB/R, WT/DS249/AB/R, WT/DS251/AB/R, WT/DS252/AB/R, WT/DS253/AB/R, WT/DS254/AB/R, WT/DS258/AB/R, WT/DS259/AB/R, paragraph 316).

582 STEVENSON comes to the conclusion that most safeguard measures come short in demonstrating the standard of review of at least one of the legal requirements (STEVENSON, (2004) 38 JWT 307 *et seq.*), and SYKES, maintains that it is unrealistic to expect WTO members to produce a "reasoned and adequate explanation" as to how their safeguard measures are in compliance with the law as long as there are no coherent standards on their permissibility (SYKES, (2004) 7 JIEL 523 *et seq.*).

feguards are cumulatively applicable,[583] although Regulation 3285/94 does not provide explicitly for the "unforeseen developments" clause, it may be submitted that Regulation 3285/94 (now Regulation 260/2009) assumes the EC's international obligations to a degree comparable to the Anti-Dumping Regulation. In other words, the legal relationship between the Agreement on Safeguards and GATT Article XIX has been clarified reasonably enough so as not to preclude that Regulation 3285/94 (now Regulation 260/2009) satisfies, *prima facie*, the criteria of the "implementation principle" developed by the Court of Justice.

Before turning to the description of the other legal requirements of safeguard measures and how they have found entry into the EC legal order, the minimum standard set for the investigation to determine these legal requirements and their concepts shall be outlined. A detailed outline of the procedural matters or formal conditions for safeguard measures is, however, beyond the scope of this dissertation.[584]

1.1.2 The Regional Application of Safeguard Measures

Pursuant to Article 2:1 Agreement on Safeguards, a safeguard measure to a product may be applied only if the country has determined, in accordance with the provisions of that Agreement, that the product is being imported in its territory in such increased quantities, absolute or relative to domestic production, and under such conditions as to cause or threaten to cause serious injury to the domestic industry that produces like or directly competitive products. Whilst this rule has been reiterated in Recital 13 of Regulation 3285/94 (now Recitals 12 and 13 in Regulation 260/2009), unless international obligations permit derogation from it, it is noteworthy that the Regulation requires the Commission and the Council, when adopting a safeguard measure, to

583 See, for instance, Panel Report on *Argentina – Footwear*, WT/DS121/R, paragraphs 4.149–4.168, and Panel Report on *Korea – Dairy,* WT/DS98/R, paragraphs 4.412–4.446.

584 For a detailed description of the formal requirements concerning safeguard measures, such as the limitation of the measure to the elimination of the injury, adjustment measures, types of safeguard measures and the procedural requirements for notification, consultation and concession negotiations, see DIDIER, 285 *et seq*. Further formal requirements, for instance with regard to surveillance, have been codified in Regulation 260/2009.

consider the interests of the Community as a whole, encompassing the interest of Community producers, users and consumers.[585]

Footnote 1 to Article 2:1 Agreement on Safeguards specifies that a customs union, as for instance the EC, may apply a safeguard measure as a single unit or on behalf of a Member State. Whereas, in the first case, all the requirements for the determination of serious injury or threat thereof must be based on the conditions existing in the customs union as a whole, in the second case, they must be founded on the conditions existing in this Member State and be limited to this Member State.

The idea of regional safeguard measures is incorporated in Article 16(5)(a) of Regulation 3285/94 (now 16(5)(a) first subparagraph of Regulation 260/2009) which provides that they may be confined to one or more regions of the Community.[586] For this to happen, the Commission, after having examined alternative solutions, may exceptionally authorise the application of surveillance or safeguard measures limited to the region(s) concerned if it considers that such measures applied at that level are more appropriate than measures applied throughout the Community.[587] In addition, regional safeguard measures must be temporary and are required to disrupt the operation of the internal market as little as possible.

In order to ensure the efficacy of such measure, products under regional *surveillance* may be put into free circulation in the region concerned only on production of an import document.[588] The import

585 Recital 12 of Regulation 3285/94 (now Recital 11 of Regulation 260/2009).

586 The EC has communicated that the term "region" means any geographical entity which does not comprise the Community as a whole, *i.e.* a region may be part of a Member State, a Member State or more than one Member State. Cf. "Replies from the European Communities concerning questions posed by Canada concerning the notification of the European Communities laws and regulations", G/SG/W/35, at point 15, and "Replies from the European Communities concerning questions posed by Australia concerning the notification of the European Communities laws and regulations", G/SG/W/36, at point 2.

587 Article 18 of Regulation 3285/94 (now Regulation 260/2009, respectively).

588 Article 14(1) of Regulation 3285/94 (now Regulation 260/2009, respectively). This import document shall be endorsed by the competent authority designated by the Member State(s) concerned, free of charge, for any quantity requested and within a maximum of five working days of receipt by the national compe-

document thus accompanies the products when they transit the Community to the regional destination and may be used only as long as arrangements for imports remain liberalised in respect of the transactions concerned. Regional *safeguard* measures may, just like Community-wide safeguard measures, take either the form of import documents whose validity is limited in time[589] or the alteration of the import rules for the product by making its release for free circulation conditional on production of an import authorisation. It goes without saying that the survival of a provision allowing for regional application may cast doubts on the achievement of a veritable customs union, in particular, since the adoption of safeguard measures in the EC has usually been on a regional basis and rarely been preceded by regional surveillance measures.[590]

The problematic of safeguard measures applied by a region of a customs union is well illustrated in *Argentina – Footwear*. In its Report, the Panel noted that the "*essential question*" before it was:

> [...] whether Argentina was permitted under the Safeguards Agreement to take MERCOSUR imports into account in the analysis of injury factors and of a causal link between increased imports and the alleged (threat of) serious injury, and was at the same time permitted to exclude MERCOSUR countries from the application of the safeguard measure imposed.[591]

Examining the ordinary meaning of Footnote 1 to Article 2:1 Agreement on Safeguards, the Panel stated that in case of measures imposed by a customs union there are two options for imposing safeguard measures, *i.e.* (i) as a single unit, or (ii) on behalf of a Member State.[592] Under the assumption that it was dealing with a safeguard measure

tent authority of a declaration by any Community importer, regardless of his place of business in the Community. This declaration is deemed to have been received by the national competent authority no later than three working days after submission, unless it is proven otherwise.

589 Article 16(1)(a) and (b) in conjunction with Article 16(5)(a) of Regulation 3285/94 (now Regulation 260/2009, respectively). The granting of an import authorisation is governed by such provisions and subject to such limits as the Commission shall lay down.

590 See, for instance, the examples provided by DIDIER, 275 *et seq.*

591 Panel Report on *Argentina – Footwear*, WT/DS121/R, paragraph 8.75.

592 *Ibid.*, paragraph 8.78.

imposed by a customs union "on behalf of a Member State" within the meaning of Footnote 1, the Panel concluded that the Footnote does not concern to whom but rather by whom a safeguard measure may be applied.[593] In a next step, the Panel examined the context of Article 2:1 Agreement on Safeguards which can be found, in its view, in Article 2:2 Agreement on Safeguards. Article 2:2 provides that "*[s]afeguard measures shall be applied to a product being imported irrespective of its source*". According to the Panel, the ordinary meaning of Article 2:2 Agreement on Safeguards appears to imply that, as a result of a member-state-specific investigation, safeguard measures have to be imposed on a non-discriminatory basis against products from all sources of supply, regardless of whether they originate from within or from outside of the customs union.[594]

On the basis of this reasoning the Panel interpreted that the two options offered by Footnote 1 to Article 2:1, read in conjunction with Article 2:2 Agreement on Safeguards, imply a "parallelism" between the scope of a safeguard "investigation" and the scope of the "application" of safeguard measures. Thus, in the light of the context of Footnote 1 to Article 2:1, a member-state-specific investigation in which serious injury or threat thereof is found based on imports from all sources could only lead to the imposition of safeguard measures on a MFN-basis against all sources of intra-regional as well as extra-regional supply of a customs union.[595] Accordingly, the Panel concluded that a member-state-specific investigation that finds serious injury or threat thereof caused by imports from all sources cannot serve as a basis for imposing a safeguard measure on imports only from third-country sources of supply.[596]

In response to Argentina's argument that it was prevented from applying safeguard measures to other MERCOSUR countries by virtue of GATT Article XXIV:8 and by certain MERCOSUR regulations, the Panel stated that, after analysing the purpose of GATT Article XXIV:8, it disagreed with Argentina's interpretation.[597] The Panel

593 *Ibid.*, paragraph 8.83.
594 *Ibid.*, paragraph 8.84.
595 *Ibid.*, paragraph 8.87.
596 *Ibid.*, paragraph 8.91.
597 *Ibid.*, paragraph 8.101.

found that, in the light of Article 2 Agreement on Safeguards and GATT Article XXIV, in the case of a customs union, the imposition of a safeguard measure only on third-country sources of supply cannot be justified on the basis of a member-state-specific investigation that finds serious injury or threat thereof caused by imports from all sources of supply from within and outside a customs union.[598]

Upon appeal, Argentina claimed that the Panel misinterpreted Footnote 1 to Article 2:1 Agreement on Safeguards, thus imposing an obligation on a member of a customs union to apply any safeguard measure on other members of that customs union whenever imports from all sources are taken into account in a safeguards investigation.[599]

The Appellate Body started by questioning the Panel's implicit assumption that Footnote 1 to Article 2:1 Agreement on Safeguards applied to the case before it. It noted, in respect of the factual background, that Argentina imposed the safeguard measures after an investigation by the Argentine authorities of the effects of imports from all sources on the Argentine domestic industry. The Appellate Body stressed that, in its reading of Footnote 1, it only applies when a *customs union* applies a safeguard measure – whether as a single unit or on behalf of a member state. This is supported by the fact that Footnote 1 relates to the word "Member" in Article 2:1 Agreement on Safeguards which is commonly understood to mean a Member of the WTO.[600] In this respect, the Appellate Body noted that MERCOSUR did not apply the safeguard measures,[601] but rather, that they were introduced by Argentina. Accordingly, the Appellate Body considered that Argentina is to be regarded as a Member of the WTO for the purposes of Article 2 Agreement on Safeguards, and that it was Argentina

598 *Ibid.*, paragraph 8.102.

599 AB Report on *Argentina – Footwear*, WT/DS121/AB/R, paragraph 76.

600 *Ibid.*, paragraph 83.

601 According to the Appellate Body, this finding is not altered by the fact that Uruguay, as Pro Tempore President of MERCOSUR and on behalf of Argentina, notified the definitive safeguard measure imposed by Argentina since first, Argentina adopted all relevant resolutions alone, pursuant to Argentinean law, and second, Argentina itself transmitted a copy of the resolution implementing the safeguard measure to the WTO Committee on Safeguards the same day as Uruguay (*ibid.*, paragraph 84).

that applied the safeguard measures after conducting an investigation of products being imported into its territory and the effects of those imports on its domestic industry. For these reasons, the Appellate Body found that Footnote 1 to Article 2:1 did not apply to the safeguard measures imposed by Argentina in this case. As a result, the Panel was found to having erred in assuming that Footnote 1 applied, and the legal reasoning and findings of the Panel relating to Footnote 1 to Article 2:1 Agreement on Safeguards was reversed.[602]

The Appellate Body continued to examine whether an analysis of GATT Article XXIV was pertinent to the question of whether Argentina, after including imports from all sources in its investigation of "increased imports" of footwear products into its territory and the consequent effects of such imports on its domestic footwear industry, was justified in excluding other MERCOSUR Member States from the application of the safeguard measures. With reference to the Appellate Body Report on *Turkey – Textiles*,[603] the Appellate Body noted that, under certain conditions, GATT Article XXIV may justify a measure which is inconsistent with certain other GATT provisions.[604] This defence is, however, only available when the Member imposing the measure has demonstrated that "*[t]he measure at issue is introduced upon the formation of a customs union that fully meets the requirements of sub-paragraphs 8(a) and 5(a) of GATT Article XXIV*" and "*[t]hat the formation of that customs union would be prevented if it were not allowed to introduce the measure at issue*". Since Argentina did not rely on GATT Article XXIV to defend the finding of the safeguard measure to be in violation of GATT, the Appellate Body considered that the Panel erred in deciding that an examination of GATT Article XXIV:8 was relevant to its analysis of whether the safeguard measures were consistent with the provisions of Articles 2 and 4 Agreement on Safeguards.[605]

Finally, the Appellate Body turned to the examination of the Panel's interpretation that there is an implied "parallelism" between the

602 *Ibid.*, paragraph 85.
603 AB Report on *Turkey – Textiles,* WT/DS34/AB/R.
604 *Ibid.*, paragraph 58.
605 AB Report on *Argentina – Footwear*, WT/DS121/AB/R, paragraph 87.

scope of a safeguard "investigation" and the scope of the "application" of safeguard measures.[606] The Appellate Body considered that, read in conjunction, Articles 2:1 and 4:1(c) Agreement on Safeguards demonstrate that a Member of the WTO may only apply a safeguard measure after that Member has determined that a product is being imported "into its territory" in such increased quantities and under such conditions as to cause or threaten to cause serious injury to "its" domestic industry "within its territory". Consequently, all the relevant aspects of a safeguard investigation must be conducted by the Member that ultimately applies the safeguard measure, on the basis of increased imports entering its territory and causing or threatening to cause serious injury to the domestic industry within its territory. The Appellate Body thus found that Articles 2:1 and 4:1(c) Agreement on Safeguards set out the conditions for imposing a safeguard measure and the requirements for the scope of a safeguard "investigation", but do not concern the scope of "application" of a safeguard measure.[607]

Regarding such scope of application, Article 2:2 Agreement on Safeguards provides that "*[s]afeguard measures shall be applied to a product being imported irrespective of its source.*" Since Argentina's investigation evaluated whether serious injury or the threat thereof was caused by imports from "all" sources, the Appellate Body concluded that safeguard measures must be imposed on imports from "all" sources, including MERCOSUR countries. Therefore, such an investigation cannot serve as a basis for excluding imports from other members of the customs union from the application of the safeguard measure.[608] The Appellate Body thus agreed with the Panel on *Argentina – Footwear* as to the existence of parallelism between the scope of a safeguard investigation and the scope of the application of safeguard measures.

The Appellate Body stressed, however, that in this case it was not ruling on "*[w]hether, as a general principle, a member of a customs*

606 Panel Report on *Argentina – Footwear*, WT/DS121/R, paragraph 8.87.

607 AB Report on *Argentina – Footwear*, WT/DS121/AB/R, paragraphs 88 and 89.

608 *Ibid.*, paragraphs 89–91.

union can exclude other members of that customs union from the application of a safeguard measure."[609]

On later occasions, the Appellate Body confirmed its line of reasoning on the existence of parallelism between a safeguard investigation and the application of a safeguard measure, for instance in *US – Wheat Gluten*:

> [...] this provision [Article 2.1], as elaborated in Article 4 of the Agreement on Safeguards, sets forth the conditions for imposing a safeguard measure. Article 2.2 of the Agreement on Safeguards, which provides that a safeguard measure 'shall be applied to a product being imported irrespective of its source', sets forth the rules on the application of a safeguard measure.[610]

The Appellate Body found the United States to have acted inconsistently with Articles 2:1 and 4:2 Agreement on Safeguards when, after including imports from all sources in their investigation of increased imports of wheat gluten into the U.S. and the consequent effects of such imports on the domestic industry, the U.S. investigating authorities excluded imports from Canada from the application of the safeguard measure. This exclusion was based on an additional investigation conducted by the USITC focusing specifically on imports from Canada. The Appellate Body explained:

> The same phrase – 'product … being imported' – appears in both these paragraphs of Article 2. In view of the identity of the language in the two provisions, and in the absence of any contrary indication in the context, we believe that it is appropriate to ascribe the same meaning to this phrase in both Articles 2.1 and 2.2. To include imports from all sources in the determination that increased imports are causing serious injury, and then to exclude imports from one source from the application of the measure, would be to give the phrase 'product being imported' a different meaning […]. This would be incongruous and unwarranted.[611]

Likewise, in *US – Lamb* and *US – Certain Steel Products*, the United States was found to contravene the Agreement on Safeguards by excluding Mexico and Canada from the application of the safeguard

609 *Ibid.*, paragraph 114.
610 AB Report on *US – Wheat Gluten*, WT/DS166/AB/R, paragraph 95.
611 *Ibid.*, paragraphs 96 and 98.

measure on the ground that the injury determination on which the safeguard was imposed also included the imports from those two countries. Although the Appellate Body offered an avenue for justifying the discrepancy between the imports covered by the investigation and the imports covered by the safeguard measure, namely if the competent authority manages to "establish explicitly" that the imports from countries covered by the measure (third-country imports) cause or threaten to cause serious injury, the U.S. failed to do so.[612]

The cases discussed reveal that there is not only a "parallelism" between a safeguard investigation and the application of a safeguard measure but also the firm conviction that a "differential method" in the investigation of the products being imported does not stand up to the standard of review when invoking the legality of a safeguard measure. It may be questioned, however, why "parallelism" has been developed to an additional requirement. Considering that those cases centered around the problem that the injury determination covered all imports whereas the safeguard measure imposed merely covered third-country imports, it would have been conceivable to simply state a violation of Article 2:2 Agreement on Safeguards (non-discrimination). One explanation may be that the panels and the Appellate Body, so far, tried to avoid the question whether GATT Article XXIV on regional free-trade arrangements or customs unions can justify a discriminatory safeguard measure contravening Article 2:2 Agreement on Safeguards.[613]

With regard to the EC, and in particular Article 16(5)(a) of Regulation 3285/94 (now Article 16(5)(a) first subparagraph of Regulation

612 The Appellate Body, in *US – Lamb*, considered that the justification by "establishing explicitly" can be achieved, again, through a "reasoned and adequate explanation" on how the facts support the determination of the safeguard measure by the competent authority (WT/DS177/AB/R, WT/DS178/AB/R, paragraph 103), and in *US – Certain Steel Products*, it added that "one single joint determination" is required to demonstrate that imports from third countries cause or threaten to cause serious injury (WT/DS248/AB/R, WT/DS249/AB/R, WT/DS251/AB/R, WT/DS252/AB/R, WT/DS253/AB/R, WT/DS254/AB/R, WT/DS258/AB/R, WT/DS259/AB/R, paragraph 468).

613 PAUWELYN suggests that this question should be answered in the affirmative, and moreover, that GATT Article XXIV should also be able to provide a justification for a violation of "parallelism" (PAUWELYN, (2004) 7 JIEL 122 *et seq.*).

260/2009) providing for the possibility of a safeguard measure confined to one (or more) regions of the Community, it is difficult to see how a possible safeguard measure could satisfy these requirements and be congruent to a possible investigation undertaken.

1.1.3 The Conduct of an Investigation

Article 2:1 Agreement on Safeguards stipulates that the application of a safeguard measure is subject to its "determination in accordance with the provisions of the Agreement" of serious injury or threat thereof to the domestic industry caused by increased imports. Prior to the application of a safeguard measure, the Agreement on Safeguards thus requires the competent authorities to conduct an investigation pursuant to previously established procedures that have been made public in consonance with GATT Article X.[614] Regulation 3285/94 (now Regulation 260/2009) repeats this requirement by stating that an investigation must precede the application of any safeguard measure, subject to the reservation that the Commission be allowed in urgent cases to apply provisional measures.[615]

Article 3:1 Agreement on Safeguards further specifies that this investigation shall include reasonable public notice to all interested parties, public hearings or other appropriate means in which importers, exporters and other interested parties are able to present evidence and their views, including the opportunity to respond to the presentations of other parties. Thereby, particular reference is made to the expression of the view whether the application of a safeguard measure would be in the public interest.

Consequently, Article 5(1) of Regulation 3285/94 (now Regulation 260/2009, respectively) provides that the Community investigation procedure shall be implemented before any safeguard measure is applied, without prejudice to surveillance measures or provisional safeguard measures.[616] To this end, the Commission is assigned to

614 Article 3:1 Agreement on Safeguards.

615 Recital 15 of Regulation 3285/94 (now Recital 14 of Regulation 260/2009).

616 Article 8 of Regulation 3285/94 (now Regulation 260/2009, respectively) provides that the use of surveillance measures and provisional safeguard measures shall not be precluded at any time. Specifically, provisional safeguard measures

determine whether imports of the product in question are causing or threatening to cause serious injury to the Community producers concerned.[617] Whereas Article 3:1 Agreement on Safeguards states that interested parties shall be given the opportunity to express their views concerning the public interest of a safeguard measure, Regulation 3285/94 (now Regulation 260/2009) provides additionally that the introduction of such safeguard measure is subject to the existence of a "Community interest".[618]

According to Article 6(1)(a) of Regulation 3285/94 (now Article 6(1) first subparagraph, introductory sentence and points (a), (b) and (c) of Regulation 260/2009), the investigation by the Commission has to be initiated within one month of receipt of information from a Member State and be published in form of a notice in the Official Journal of the EC. The notice must give a summary of the information received, containing all evidence available regarding the evolution of the imports, their conditions and the serious injury to the domestic industry or threat thereof.[619] Whilst the initiation of an investigation implies that consultations are held with the Member States,[620] it is not subject to

shall be applied in critical circumstances where delay would cause damage which it would be difficult to repair, making immediate action necessary, and where a preliminary determination provides clear evidence that increased imports have caused or are threatening to cause serious injury. Whilst the duration of such measures is limited to 200 days and should take the form of an increase in the existing level of customs duty, the Commission is still required to immediately conduct whatever investigation measures are still necessary.

617 Article 5(2) in conjunction with Article 6(1)(a) of Regulation 3285/94 (now Regulation 260/2009, respectively).

618 Articles 16(1) and 17 of Regulation 3285/94 (now Regulation 260/2009, respectively). In this respect, it is noteworthy that the investigation pursuant to Article 5(2) of Regulation 3285/94 (now Regulation 260/2009, respectively) is only directed to the determination of injury and not to Community interest. Since the Commission is entrusted with the collection of all information it deems necessary (Article 6(3) of Regulation 3285/94, now Regulation 260/2009, respectively), this provision should, however, not be understood as being too restrictive.

619 Article 2 of Regulation 3285/94 (now Regulation 260/2009, respectively).

620 Article 4(1) of Regulation 3285/94 (now Regulation 260/2009, respectively). Already prior to the initiation of the investigation, the Commission is called upon to immediately pass on the information received to all the Member States (Article 2 of Regulation 3285/94, now Regulation 260/2009, respectively).

their authorisation. The same applies in case the Commission decides that there is insufficient evidence to justify an investigation.[621]

Only Member States are admitted to submit evidence justifying the initiation of an investigation. Private parties are excluded from invoking the need of a safeguard measure,[622] which makes the triggering of a safeguard investigation dependent on the success of lobbying activities with the competent authorities. Once an investigation has been initiated, however, private parties may assume a more important role as they are invited by notice (published in the Official Journal) to make known their views in writing, to submit information and to apply for being heard orally by the Commission.[623]

In order to appraise the situation, the Commission is to seek all information it deems necessary.[624] Therefore, where it considers it appropriate, the Commission checks the information with importers, traders, agents, producers, trade associations and organisations. Upon written request, interested parties, including representatives of the exporting country, may inspect all information made available to the Commission in connection with the investigation, with the exception of internal documents and provided that the information is not confi-

621 The Member States must be informed about the negative decision of the Commission within one month of receipt of the information (Article 6(6) of Regulation 3285/94, now Article 6(7) of Regulation 260/2009), and they must have been consulted previously (Article 3 of Regulation 3285/94, now Regulation 260/2009, respectively).

622 This is also reflected in Article 16(1) of Regulation 3285/94 (now Regulation 260/2009, respectively) which stipulates that the Commission, in order to safeguard the interests of the Community, may act at the request of a Member State or on its own initiative.

623 According to Article 6(4) of Regulation 3285/94 (now Article 6(5) of Regulation 260/2009), it is in the discretion of the Commission to hear the interested parties. The Commission's discretion is, however, limited to the extent that the Commission must hear the interested parties which have made a written application within the period laid down in the notice published in the OJ, showing that they are actually likely to be affected by the outcome of the investigation and that there are special reasons for them to be heard orally.

624 The Member States are thus required to supply the Commission, at its request, with the information at their disposal on developments in the market of the product being investigated (Article 6(3) of Regulation 3285/94, now Regulation 260/2009, respectively).

dential.[625] Although interested parties may communicate their views on the information in question, the Commission may only take them into consideration where they are backed by sufficient evidence.[626]

Article 3:1 Agreement on Safeguards finally obliges the competent authorities to publish a report setting forth their findings and reasoned conclusions reached on all pertinent issues of fact and law[627] at the end of the investigation. This obligation is not to be confused with Article 7(1) of Regulation 3285/94 (now Regulation 260/2009, respectively) which requires the Commission to submit a report, at the end of the investigation, to the Advisory Committee[628]. The publication envisaged by the Agreement on Safeguards is taken account of by the publication of the decision of the Commission[629] in the Official Journal.[630]

In case the Commission considers that no Community surveillance or safeguard measures are necessary within nine months of the initiation of the investigation, the Member States have to be consulted and the investigation is to be terminated by a decision stating the main conclusions of the investigation. The decision to terminate the investigation has to be taken within a month following the consultations and has to be published in the Official Journal.[631] If the Commission decides that Community surveillance or safeguard measures are to be

625 The confidentiality clause is contained in Article 9 of Regulation 3285/94 (now Regulation 260/2009, respectively). It reflects the requirement of Article 3:2 Agreement on Safeguards which provides that any information which is by nature confidential or which is provided on a confidential basis shall be treated as such by the competent authorities.

626 Article 6(2) of Regulation 3285/94 (now Article 6(4) of Regulation 260/2009).

627 In the words of the panels and Appellate Body, such report must contain "reasoned and adequate explanation" for the imposition of the safeguard measure.

628 The Advisory Committee is made up of representatives of each Member State with a representative of the Commission as chairman (Article 4(1) of Regulation 3285/94, now Regulation 260/2009, respectively).

629 For the sake of completeness it should be noted that any such decision may also be referred to the Council under the conditions of Article 16(7) and (8) or Article 17 of Regulation 3285/94 (now Article 16(6) and (7) or Article 17 of Regulation 260/2009).

630 Such "decision" takes the form of a "Commission Regulation".

631 Article 7(2) of Regulation 3285/94 (now Regulation 260/2009, respectively).

applied, it takes the necessary decisions no later than nine months from the initiation of the investigation.[632]

The investigation procedure set out by Regulation 3285/94 (now Regulation 260/2009) merits two important observations for the purposes of this dissertation:

- The procedural aspects of the investigation resemble remarkably the procedure of an anti-dumping investigation, with exception of the time periods that are comparably shorter in a safeguard investigation.[633]
- The affirmation of a "Community interest" as requirement for the imposition of a safeguard measure does not get in the way of the "implementation principle" established by the Court of Justice.

The above observation regarding "Community interest" is based on the following considerations. Already prior to the entry into force of Regulation 3285/94, the Commission usually required the application of a safeguard measure to be conditional on Community interest – also when a safeguard measure is applied only in respect of a Member State. For instance, in *Certain Quartz Watches With Digital Display*,[634] the Commission after having established that digital quartz watches are being imported into Germany and France in such greatly increased quantities and on such terms as to cause serious injury to the German and French industries producing assembled watches inquired whether regional protective measures for each of the two Member States are necessary to safeguard Community interests.[635] On the basis of various economic observations concerning the two industries, such

632 Article 7(3) of Regulation 3285/94 (now Regulation 260/2009, respectively). In exceptional circumstances, the time limit of nine months can be extended by a further maximum period of two months. In such a case, the Commission is required to publish a notice in the Official Journal setting forth the duration of the extension and a summary of the reasons for such extension.

633 BOURGEOIS, [2000] RDUE 107.

634 Commission Regulation No. 1087/84 introducing protective measures in respect of certain electronic piezo-electric quartz watches with digital display (OJ 1984 L 106/31).

635 *Ibid.*, Recital 39.

as the type of watch making, market structure and employment patterns,[636] the Commission concluded that the German watch-producing industry has already itself mitigated the substantial injury caused to it by imports of digital quartz watches, *inter alia*, due to the fact that restructuring in that industry was virtually complete. Accordingly, immediate regional protective measures for watchmakers in Germany were not considered necessary to safeguard Community interests whilst, in contrast, the serious injury suffered by the French industry producing assembled watches was found to make immediate regional protective measures for the French market indispensable in the interest of the Community.[637]

Moreover, the basic Anti-Dumping Regulation, as it currently stands,[638] as well as its predecessor that was examined by the ECJ in *Nakajima*,[639] provide for the "Community interest"-test. According to the Commission, this test is a public interest clause and states that measures can only be taken if they are not contrary to the overall interest of the Community. This requires an analysis of all the economic interests involved, including those of the Community industry, users, consumers and traders of the product concerned. The "Community interest"-test therefore goes beyond WTO obligations.[640] Although some legal scholars have initially argued that the inclusion of the "Community interest"-test is but one example for the indication that the "Community legislator" shares the conception which underlies the ECJ's long-standing case-law on the denial of direct effect to the rules of GATT 1947,[641] the Court of Justice has implicitly set aside this

636 *Ibid.*, Recital 40.

637 *Ibid.*, Recital 41.

638 Council Regulation (EC) No. 1225/2009 of 30 November 2009 (codified version) on protection against dumped imports from countries not members of the European Community (OJ 2009 L 343/51), repealing Council Regulation (EC) No. 384/96 of 22 December 1995 (OJ 1996 L 56/1 as amended by Council Regulation (EC) No. 461/2004 (OJ 2004 L 77/12)).

639 Case 69/89, *Nakajima*, [1991] E.C.R. I-2069.

640 Annex to the 22nd Annual Report from the Commission to the European Parliament on the Community's Anti-dumping, Anti-subsidy and Safeguard Activities (COM(2004) 828 final), entitled "Commission Staff Document" (SEC(2004) 1707), 7 *et seq.*

641 BOURGEOIS, 65 *et seq.* (with further annotations).

earlier argument by allowing for the "implementation exception" articulated in *Nakajima*. In other words, if it can be demonstrated that a particular obligation entered into within the framework of the WTO/GATT has been *implemented* (transposed into the EC legal order), the additional requirement of "Community interest" does not preclude that private parties may rely on such WTO/GATT rules before the European courts.

1.1.4 The Legal Prerequisites of Safeguard Measures

Besides the legal requirement of "unforeseen developments" which – as has been discussed above – continues to be applicable, the substantive criteria that have to be met for the imposition of a safeguard measure are an increase of import quantities (absolute or relative to domestic production), a serious injury or threat thereof to the domestic industry which produces like or directly competitive products, and causality between all these elements.

a) Increased Quantities and Conditions of Import

The product must be imported in such increased quantities and under such conditions as to cause or threaten to cause serious injury. Similar to GATT Article XIX, the Agreement on Safeguards thus requires that both criteria be cumulatively fulfilled.

Whilst some parameters to determine the existence of "serious injury" are provided for by the Agreement on Safeguards,[642] the Agreement is silent in respect of the *intensity* of the imports ("such increased" quantities and under "such" conditions). It merely indicates that the increase of imports may be measured in absolute or relative terms to domestic production.[643]

Article 16(1) of Regulation 3285/94 (now Regulation 260/2009, respectively) reiterates the conditions defined by the Agreement on Safeguards:

642 According to Article 4:1(a) Agreement on Safeguards, "serious injury" is defined as a significant overall impairment in the position of a domestic industry.

643 Article 2:1 Agreement on Safeguards.

> Where a product is imported into the Community in such greatly increased quantities and/or on such terms or conditions as to cause, or threaten to cause, serious injury to Community producers, the Commission, in order to safeguard the interests of the Community, may, acting at the request of a Member State or on its own initiative [...].

The examination of the trend in imported quantities is specified in Article 10(1)(a) of Regulation 3285/94 (now Regulation 260/2009, respectively) which states that it shall be measured by volume in absolute terms or relative to production, or – albeit not provided for by the Agreement on Safeguards – in relation to consumption in the Community. The terms or conditions in which imports take place refer primarily to the price of imports.[644] There are, however, other factors linked to sales that may have a bearing on the volume and the price of the product in question, such as delivery conditions or technical assistance and after sale services.

The double prerequisite of increased import volume and import conditions (*i.e.* price) is only applied in respect of WTO Members.[645] This implies that the application of a safeguard measure to a product originating in a country not Member to the WTO may be envisaged provided that one of the two conditions is met.[646]

Both the Agreement on Safeguards and Regulation 3285/94 (now Regulation 260/2009) are silent on the level that an increase in im-

644 According to Article 10(1)(b) of Regulation 3285/94 (now Regulation 260/2009, respectively), the main factor to examine the terms under which the imports take place is the *price* of imports, in particular where there has been a significant price undercutting as compared with the price of a *like* [but not directly competitive] product in the Community (emphasis added).

645 Article 16(2) of Regulation 3285/94 (now Regulation 260/2009, respectively).

646 According to the communication of the EC, the words "and/or" in Article 16(1) of Regulation 3285/94 (now Regulation 260/2009, respectively) should be interpreted in the light of paragraph 2 of the same Article. The provisions of paragraph 1 and 2 together thus mean that, in the case of a WTO Member, the EC will apply safeguard measures only when both conditions required by Article 2:1 Agreement on Safeguards are met. On the other hand, safeguard measures could be adopted when either of these conditions is met for countries not Members of the WTO; cf. "Replies from the European Communities concerning questions posed by Canada concerning the notification of the European Communities laws and regulations", G/SG/W/35, at point 11.

ports must reach so as to cause or threaten to cause serious injury. The Appellate Body has filled this *lacuna* by ruling that the increase in imports must have been "*recent enough, sudden enough, sharp enough, and significant enough*" (so-called RSSS test), both quantitatively and qualitatively, to cause or threaten to cause serious injury.[647] This finding bears important implications for the authorities conducting an investigation to establish an increase in imports under the provisions of the Agreement on Safeguards. Reliance on increased import volume may therefore only be consistent with the Agreement on Safeguards if the increase is recent and the trends of imports also support the argument of there being serious injury or threat thereof.

b) The Determination of "Serious Injury" or Threat thereof

According to Article 4:1(a) Agreement on Safeguards, "serious injury" is defined as significant overall impairment in the position of a domestic industry. "Threat of serious injury" is considered as serious injury that is clearly imminent (Article 4:1(b) Agreement on Safeguards). These definitions are reproduced *verbatim* in Articles 5(3)(a) and (b) of Regulation 3285/94 (now Regulation 260/2009), respectively.

In the investigation to determine whether increased imports cause or threaten to cause serious injury to a domestic industry, all relevant factors of an objective and quantifiable nature having a bearing on the situation of that industry have to be evaluated, particularly the [1] rate and amount of the increase in imports in absolute and relative terms, [2] the market share of the domestic market taken by the imported products, changes in the level of [3] sales, [4] production, [5] productivity, [6] capacity utilisation, [7] profits and losses, and [8] employment (Article 4:2 Agreement on Safeguards).

Article 10(1)(c) of Regulation 3285/94 (now Regulation 260/2009, respectively) repeats the factors enumerated in the Agreement on Safeguards, albeit specifying them and adding as factor the price of imports,[648] including the hindrance of price increases that

647 AB Report on *Argentina – Footwear*, WT/DS121/AB/R, paragraph 131.

648 The inclusion of the price and, more particularly, the "margin of price-undercutting" as factor in the determination of serious injury was criticised for lacking economic foundation. In general, it is alleged that the Commission should

normally would have occurred. In order to expand on the requirement contained in the Agreement on Safeguards that serious injury must amount to a significant overall impairment in the position of a domestic industry, the impact on Community producers is evaluated by means of trends in certain economic factors, such as production, capacity utilisation, stocks, sales, market share, prices (*i.e.* depression of prices or prevention of price increases which would normally have occurred), profits, return on capital employed, cash flow and employment.[649] Where a threat of serious injury is alleged, the Commission further examines whether it is clearly foreseeable that a particular situation is likely to develop into actual injury.[650]

It has been controversial whether the consideration of all the eight factors enumerated in Article 4:2 Agreement on Safeguards is mandatory. This issue was discussed for the first time by the Panel in *Korea—Dairy*[651] which found that the wording of Article 4:2 Agreement on Safeguards suggests that the investigating authorities shall evaluate all relevant factors, meaning that the consideration of the factors listed is always relevant and therefore required, even though the authority may later dismiss some of them as not having a bearing on the situation of that industry.[652] Whereas the Panel acknowledged that not all the eight factors would be needed to assess injury to the domestic industry, it nevertheless required the competent authority to consider every single factor listed under Article 4:2(a) before it could evaluate

enhance formal economic analysis in the context of serious injury determination; VERMULST/PERNAUTE/LUCENTI, (2004) 38 JWT 963 (with further annotations).

649 The list in Article 10(1)(c) of Regulation 3285/94 (now Regulation 260/2009) is not exhaustive as Article 10(1)(d) provides that factors other than trends in imports which are causing or may have caused injury to the Community producers may also be considered. For an analysis of the Commission's approach of determining injury, see VERMULST/PERNAUTE/LUCENTI, (2004) 38 JWT 961 *et seq.*

650 Article 10(2) of Regulation 3285/94 (now Regulation 260/2009, respectively). In this respect account may be taken of factors like the rate of increase of the exports to the Community and export capacity in the country of origin or export, as it stands or is likely to be in the foreseeable future, and the likelihood that that capacity will be used to export to the Community.

651 Panel Report on *Korea – Dairy*, WT/DS98/R.

652 *Ibid.*, paragraph 7.55.

its relevance. This position has been affirmed by other panels and the Appellate Body.[653]

For the purposes of this dissertation, it is important to note that Regulation 3285/94 (and now equally Regulation 260/2009) has not only restated all the eight factors of Article 4:2 Agreement on Safeguards, but added a few more factors that the Commission is to consider in a safeguard investigation (such as the assessment of the import volume relative to the consumption in the Community, or depression of prices). This clearly indicates that the requirements laid down by the Agreement on Safeguards have been fully transposed into the EC legal order, hence implying that the Community is willing to accept its international obligations with regard to safeguard measures. It may therefore be submitted that Regulation 3285/94, and equally its successor Regulation 260/2009, also satisfies the standard of the "implementation principle" in this respect.

A final remark – especially in view of this finding – shall be made regarding the usage of safeguard measures by the EC. As of mid-2005, the Commission has merely imposed definitive safeguard measures in three cases on the basis of Regulation 3285/94, namely against imports of citrus fruits, farmed salmon and certain steel products.[654] In addition, it has initiated an investigation concerning frozen strawber-

653 For instance, Panel Report on *Argentina – Footwear*, WT/DS121/R, paragraph 8.206, and AB Report on *Argentina – Footwear*, WT/DS121/AB/R, paragraph 136.

654 Commission Regulation (EC) No. 421/2005 of 14 March 2005 on the issue of licences for the import of certain prepared or preserved citrus fruits (namely mandarins, etc.) in the period from 11 April 2005 to 10 April 2006 (OJ 2005 L 68/3), in fact extending Commission Regulation (EC) No. 1055/2004 (OJ 2004 L 192/18); Commission Regulation (EC) No. 658/2004 of 7 April 2004 imposing definitive safeguard measures against imports of certain prepared or preserved citrus fruits (namely mandarins, etc.) (OJ 2004 L 104/67); Commission Regulation (EC) No. 206/2005 of 4 February 2005 imposing definitive safeguard measures against imports of farmed salmon (OJ 2005 L 33/8) as amended by Commission Regulation (EC) No. 580/2005 of 14 April 2005, and revoked by Commission Regulation (EC) No. 627/2005 of 22 April 2005; Commission Regulation (EC) No. 1694/2002 imposing definitive safeguard measures in relation to certain steel products (OJ 2002 L 261/1), and terminated by Commission Regulation (EC) No. 2142/2003 of 5 December 2003 (OJ 2003 L 321/11).

ries,[655] and set up a surveillance measure regarding footwear from China.[656] In the period from 2006 – 2008, no new safeguard measures were put in place. The last safeguard measure was imposed in 2004, on an *erga omnes* basis on citrus fruit, and lapsed in 2007. Prior to the entry into force of the Agreement on Safeguards, the Community's use of safeguard measures was equally rare.[657] The small number of safeguard measures that have been aspired to by the EC suggests that they are considered to be less attractive in terms of relief than, for example, anti-dumping duties.[658] Moreover, it appears that the EC considers that, as a matter of principle, safeguard measures should only be used as an *exceptional tool* in emergency situations.[659] This position is generally shared by the Appellate Body which noted expressly that:

655 Notice of initiation of a safeguard investigation under Council Regulations (EC) No. 3285/94 and (EC) No. 519/94 concerning imports of frozen strawberries (OJ 2005 C 165/2).

656 Commission Regulation (EC) No. 117/2005 of 26 January 2005 introducing Community surveillance of imports of certain footwear products originating in certain third countries (OJ 2005 L 24/8).

657 For an overview see INAMA/VERMULST, 22, and for an evaluation of the factors employed by the Commission to determine the seriousness of the injury, see DIDIER, 279 *et seq.*

658 Such interpretation appears justified considering that the EC has initiated a total of 152 review investigations concerning anti-dumping measures in the period from 1995 to 1999 (18th Annual Report, COM(2000) 440 final, at 7.1.), and in the period from 1999–2003 another 187 review investigations were initiated (Annex to the 22nd Annual Report (COM(2004) 828 final), Staff Working Document (SEC(2004) 1707, at 6.2).

659 Annex to the 22nd Annual Report (COM(2004) 828 final), Staff Working Document (SEC(2004) 1707, at 1.2.1).

> it is essential to keep in mind that a safeguard action is a 'fair' trade remedy,[660]

> safeguard measures were intended [...] to be matters out of the ordinary, to be matters of urgency, to be, in short, 'emergency actions',[661] and

> import restrictions that are imposed on products of exporting Members when a safeguard action is taken must be seen as extraordinary.[662]

c) The Causal Link between Imports and Injury

The determination of whether increased imports have caused or are threatening to cause serious injury must demonstrate the existence of a causal link between the increased imports and the serious injury or threat thereof on the basis of objective evidence. In cases where other factors than increased imports are causing injury to the domestic industry, the injury must not be attributed to increased imports.[663]

Whilst GATT Article XIX requires a causal link between the effect of WTO/GATT obligations, *i.e.* the concession, and the injury, the Agreement on Safeguards has transformed this obligation in causality between increased imports and the serious injury or threat thereof. This permits Members of the WTO to react against increases in imports irrespective of their cause and whether they are due or not to the concession.[664] In respect of the prohibition to attribute the injury to other factors than increased imports, it is unlikely that, in itself, the prohibition is capable of preventing other factors to be taken into account. This is to say that, in effect, every loss of competitiveness is

660 AB Report on *Argentina – Footwear,* WT/DS121/AB/R, paragraph 94. In its report on *Korea – Dairy,* the Appellate Body recalled that taking safeguard action results in restrictions on imports arising from "fair" trade, and that the application of a safeguard measure does not depend upon "unfair" trade actions, as is the case with anti-dumping or countervailing measures (WT/DS98/AB/R, paragraph 84).

661 AB Reports on *Argentina – Footwear,* WT/DS121/AB/R, paragraph 93, and on *Korea – Dairy,* WT/DS98/AB/R, paragraph 86.

662 AB Reports on *Argentina – Footwear,* WT/DS121/AB/R, paragraph 94, and on *Korea – Dairy,* WT/DS98/AB/R, paragraph 86.

663 Article 4:2(b) Agreement on Safeguards.

664 The increased import must have a "genuine and substantial relationship" with serious domestic injury, see AHN, p. 18.

accompanied by an increase in imports causing injury, without distinction being made between "normal" causes, such as currency fluctuations, and other causes. Inversely, it could be argued that an increase in imports attributable to a loss in competitiveness is the consequence of that latter, and not the cause of the injury. This line of reasoning is, however, unlikely to succeed.

Article 10 of Regulation 3285/94 (now Regulation 260/2009, respectively) does not explicitly require a causal link between the increased imports and the injury. It simply states that the examination of the trend of imports, of the conditions in which they take place and of serious injury or threat thereof to Community producers resulting from such imports also covers "*factors other than trends in imports which are causing or may have caused injury to the Community producers concerned*".[665]

It appears that the Commission's approach prior to the entry into force of the Agreement on Safeguards was to merely demonstrate the preponderant influence of imports on the injury, without revealing their assessment of other (secondary) factors. For instance, in *Certain Quartz Watches With Digital Display*, the Commission considered that, taken in isolation, imports of digital quartz watches are responsible for the substantial (now 'serious') injury suffered by the French and German industries producing assembled watches, at a time when adaptation of their industries is in full swing, by reason of the decline in overall production and sales levels and the resultant deterioration in financial results. The other factors that, individually or in combination, might affect these industries – be they imports of analogue quartz watches, imports of mechanical watches or even structural changes in demand – have played only a minor part in the substantial injury caused to the two industries in question.[666] Similarly, in *Unwrought Aluminium*, the Commission acknowledged that other factors may have contributed to the decline in the Community industry's position but concluded nevertheless that "*[i]t is clear that the goods in question and*

665 Article 10(1)(d) of Regulation 3285/94 (now Regulation 260/2009, respectively).

666 *Certain Quartz Watches With Digital Display,* Commission Regulation No. 1087/84 (OJ 1984 L 106/31), Recital 38.

the circumstances under which they were imported were the only cause *of serious injury to Community producers*"[667] (emphasis added).

A review of the few safeguard measures imposed under Regulation 3285/94 suggests, however, that the Commission has fundamentally changed this attitude. In order to examine the existence of a causal link between increased imports and the serious injury, and in order to ensure that injury caused by other factors is not attributed to increased imports, the Commission now follows a three-step procedure:[668] (i) the injurious effects of factors considered to be causing injury are distinguished from each other, (ii) these injurious effects are attributed to the factors which are causing them, and (iii) after having attributed injury to all causal factors present, it is determined whether increased imports are a "genuine and substantial" cause of serious injury.[669]

It is conceivable that the Commission's approach is influenced by the standard of review that is being applied by panels and the Appellate Body. For instance, regarding the requirements of causation laid down in Article 4:2(b) Agreement on Safeguards, the Panel in *Argentina – Footwear* considered that the analysis of causation undertaken by Argentina must meet three criteria: First, whether an upward trend in imports coincides with downward trends in the injury factors, and if not, whether a reasoned explanation is provided as to why nevertheless the data show causation; second, whether the conditions of competition in the Argentinean footwear market between imported and

667 *Unwrought Aluminium*, Commission Regulation No. 2227/93 (OJ 1993 L 198/21), Recital 'Conclusion'.

668 The Commission's approach has, however, been criticised for being "unsophisticated". It was argued that, in order to meet the criteria of Article 4:2 Agreement on Safeguards, the Commission must decompose injury into the underlying causes and statutorily defined factors, whereas the Commission effectively starts with the assumption that imports are causing the decline in domestic production, and then, by conducting a trends analysis of the other factors, determines whether these factors are significant; VERMULST/PERNAUTE/LUCENTI, (2004) 38 JWT 962.

669 For instance, Commission Regulation (EC) No. 658/2004 of 7 April 2004 imposing definitive safeguard measures against imports of certain prepared or preserved citrus fruits (namely mandarins, etc.) (OJ 2004 L 104/67), paragraph 64 *et seq.*; or Commission Regulation (EC) No. 206/2005 of 4 February 2005 imposing definitive safeguard measures against imports of farmed salmon (OJ 2005 L 33/8), paragraph 74 *et seq.*

domestic footwear as analysed demonstrate, on the basis of objective evidence, a causal link of the imports to any injury; and third, whether other relevant factors have been analysed and whether it is established that injury caused by factors other than imports has not been attributed to imports.[670]

The Panel continued to evaluate causation by stating that the "trends" – in both the injury factors and the imports – matter as much as their absolute levels. It further believed that Article 4:2(b) Agreement on Safeguards means that it is the *relationship* between the movements in imports (volume and market share) and the movements in injury factors that must be central to a causation analysis and determination. The Panel thus concluded that, if causation is present, an increase in imports normally should coincide with a decline in the relevant injury factors. Acknowledging that such a coincidence by itself cannot *prove* causation (because, *inter alia*, Article 3 Agreement on Safeguards requires an explanation – *i.e.*, "findings and reasoned conclusions"), the Panel held that "*[i]ts absence would create serious doubts as to the existence of a causal link, and would require a very compelling analysis of why causation still is present.*"[671]

On appeal, the Appellate Body fully upheld the Panel's interpretation of causation in the meaning of Article 4:2(b) Agreement on Safeguards and maintained the establishment of the three criteria for the analysis of causation.[672] These Reports demonstrate that the standards for an investigation are set at a high level and that they must comply with various criteria in order to provide a *legal* basis for the imposition of definitive safeguard measures. This position appears to be fully reflected in the Commission's approach when analysing causation.

d) The Notion of "Like or Directly Competitive Products"

In line with Article 2:1 Agreement on Safeguards, Article 16(1) of Regulation 3285/94 (now Regulation 260/2009, respectively) reiterates that the serious injury or the threat thereof must occur to the domestic industry, *i.e.* the Community producers. In determining serious injury

670 Panel Report on *Argentina – Footwear,* WT/DS121/R, paragraph 8.229.

671 *Ibid.*, paragraphs 8.237 and 8.238.

672 AB Report *on Argentina – Footwear,* WT/DS121/AB/R, paragraphs 143–145.

or threat thereof, a 'domestic industry' is understood to mean the producers as a whole of the like or directly competitive products operating within the territory of a WTO Member, or those whose collective output of the like or directly competitive products constitutes a major proportion of the domestic production of those products.[673] Accordingly, Article 5(3)(c) of Regulation 3285/94 (now Regulation 260/2009, respectively) defines "Community producers" as "*[t]he producers as a whole of the like or directly competing products operating within the territory of the Community, or those whose collective output of the like or directly competing products constitutes a major proportion of the total Community production of those products*".

Both the Agreement on Safeguards and Regulation 3285/94 (now Regulation 260/2009 likewise) are silent in respect of a definition of the terms "like products" or "directly competitive products". These notions – appearing several times in the GATT[674] – were, however, the object of an abundant 'case-law' of Panel and Appellate Body Reports, of which the "*Alcoholic Beverage Cases*" have come to particular prominence[675] and shall therefore serve as starting point for the discussion of the notion of "like or directly competitive products" in the context of safeguard measures.

At the heart of these cases was the taxation of alcoholic beverages and its alleged violation of GATT Article III. The underlying intention of GATT Article III is to ensure that imported products, which have cleared customs and entered domestic markets, are not given disadvantageous treatment in relation to like domestic products. This is the concept of "national treatment" which, in conjunction with the principle of

673 Article 4:1(c) Agreement on Safeguards.

674 For instance in GATT Articles III:2 and III:4. The term "like product" or "like domestic product" is used in several other GATT provisions as well, such as Articles I:1, II:2(a), VI:1(a), VI:1(b), IX:1, XI:2(c), XIII:1 and XVI:4. Other terms such as "like commodity" (GATT Article VI:7), "like merchandise" (GATT Article VII:2), and "like or competitive products" (GATT Article XIX:1) also occur. For the differences in meaning of "like product" in GATT Articles I and III, see HUDEC, 101 *et seq.*

675 The "*Alcoholic Beverage Cases*" have triggered an abundance of literature. To name but a few whose contributions are authoritative in the field of "like product" determination, cf. HUDEC, (1998) 32 International Lawyer 619 *et seq.*; REGAN, (2002) 36 JWT 443 *et seq.*; ROESSLER, (2003) 37 JWT 771 *et seq.*

most-favoured-nation treatment expressed in GATT Article I, forms the WTO/GATT doctrine of non-discrimination. In addition, GATT Article III:2 states that Contracting Parties must not use internal taxes or other internal charges to discriminate between imported goods and "like" domestic goods, or between imported goods and a "directly competitive (or substitutable)" product. As panels have noted on several occasions, the GATT makes a clear distinction between "like" products and "directly competitive and substitutable" products.[676]

aa) The "Two-Step Approach" versus the "Aim and Effects Test" in the Differentiation of Products

The traditional method used to interpret GATT Article III is the "*two-step approach*".[677] In the case of GATT Article III:2, this involves objectively verifying whether the products are "like" by considering such factors as their physical properties, the purposes for which they are used, and the tastes of consumers (step one), and if they are found to be "like", then determining if the taxes levied against imports are in excess of the taxes on domestic products (step two).[678]

676 For instance, *EEC – Measures on Animal Feed Proteins*, L/4599, paragraph 4.3; or 1950 Working Party Report on *The Australian Subsidy on Ammonium Sulphate* (GATT/CP.4/39, adopted on 3 April 1950, paragraph 8), GATT Analytical Index, p. 36.

677 The 1970 Working Party Report on *Border Tax Adjustments* noted that difficulties arising from the interpretation of the term "like or similar products" should be assessed on a case-by-case basis, but continued nevertheless suggesting certain criteria, such as the end-use of the product in a given market, consumer's habits and the product's properties, qualities and nature (L/5863, paragraph 51).

678 In *Japan – Customs Duties, Taxes and Labelling Practices on Imported Wines and Alcoholic Beverages*, the Panel considered that subsequent GATT practice in the application of Article III shows that past GATT panel reports adopted by the Contracting Parties have examined Article III:2 and 4 by determining, firstly, whether the imported and domestic products concerned were "like" or "directly competitive or substitutable" and, secondly, whether the internal taxation or other regulation is discriminatory (first sentence) or protective (second sentence of Article III:2). The Panel further noted that past GATT practice has clearly established that 'like' products in terms of Article III:2 are not confined to identical products but cover also other products, for instance if they serve substantially identical end-uses (L/6216, paragraph 5.5).

One could criticise this method as being too mechanical since such an approach fails to appreciate broader political concepts, which are, for example, recognised in GATT Article XX.[679] This Article does, however, not provide a comprehensive list of all social policy objectives,[680] and there is hence the danger that the existence of exceptions would provide a wedge by which to argue for different interpretations.

Aware of these issues, GATT panels attempted to depart from the simple "*two-step approach*" in the early 1990s. In *United States – Measures Affecting Alcoholic and Malt Beverages*,[681] the Panel began its examination by considering whether low alcohol beer and high alcohol beer should be considered "like products". In regard to like product determinations, the Panel considered that, in the context of GATT Article III, it is essential that such determinations be made not only in the light of such criteria as the products' physical characteristics, but also in the light of the purpose of Article III, which is to ensure that internal taxes and regulations "not be applied to imported or domestic products so as to afford protection to domestic production" – without, however, aiming at the harmonisation of the internal taxes and regulations of contracting parties.[682] Recognising that the treatment of imported and domestic products as like products under GATT Article III may have significant implications for, *inter alia*, the regula-

679 This was explicitly recognised in *Japan – Customs Duties, Taxes and Labelling Practices on Imported Wines and Alcoholic Beverages*, where the Panel noted that "[...] the 'general exceptions' provided for in GATT Article XX might also justify internal tax differentiations among like or directly competitive products [...]. The Panel found, therefore, that the GATT reserved each contracting party a large degree of freedom to decide autonomously on the objectives, level, principles and methods of its internal taxation of goods" (ibid., paragraph 5.13).

680 To summarise, the 'General Exceptions' of GATT Article XX include, *inter alia*, policies designed to protect public morals and human, animal, and plant life or health; policies necessary to comply with laws and regulations not inconsistent with the GATT, such as customs, anti-trust and intellectual property laws. The pursuance of these policies, however, cannot be disguised restrictions to trade or an arbitrary or unjustifiable discrimination between countries where the same conditions prevail.

681 Panel Report on *United States – Measures Affecting Alcoholic and Malt Beverages* (DS23/R).

682 *Ibid.*, paragraph 5.71.

tory autonomy of contracting parties with respect to their internal tax laws and regulations, the Panel considered that "*[i]t is imperative that the like product determination in the context of GATT Article III be made in such a way that it not unnecessarily infringes upon the regulatory authority and domestic policy options of contracting parties.*"[683]

After finding that on the basis of their physical characteristics low alcohol beer and high alcohol beer are similar, the Panel nevertheless noted that there is at the same time evidence for a certain degree of market differentiation and specialisation. Despite a certain overlap of the markets for the two types of beer, this differentiation is, for example, evident in the fact that beer manufacturers target different market segments in their advertising and marketing.[684] Considering the policy goals and legislative background of the laws regulating the alcohol content of beer, the Panel then found that the setting of different tax rates according to the alcoholic content of beer was not in violation of the GATT since the differentiation of beer into low alcohol and high alcohol beer did not have the "aim or effect" of protecting domestic production.[685]

The idea first propounded in *United States – Measures Affecting Alcoholic and Malt Beverages* was further refined into the "*aim and effects test*" in the Panel Report on *United States – Taxes on Automobiles.*[686] In this case, the Panel clearly departed from the "*two-step approach*". Using the wording "so as to afford protection" in GATT Article III:1, the Panel argued that the rationale underlying the finding of "like products" should be based on an analysis of the aim and effects of the measure in question. The Panel stated that notions of like-

683 *Ibid.*, paragraph 5.72. The Panel also stated that the purpose of GATT Article III is not to prevent contracting parties from differentiating between different product categories for policy purposes unrelated to the protection of domestic production (paragraph 5.25).

684 *Ibid.*, paragraph 5.73.

685 *Ibid.*, paragraph 5.74. Thus, for the purposes of its examination under GATT Article III, the Panel considered that low alcohol content beer and high alcohol content beer need not be considered as like products in terms of GATT Article III:4. Thereby, the Panel emphasised, however, that this determination is limited to this particular case and is not to be extended to other GATT Articles or other legislative contexts (paragraph 5.75).

686 DS31/R, dated 11 October 1994, unadopted.

ness and direct competition cannot be separated from the objectives of the regulatory scheme that draws a line between two otherwise similar products.[687]

Therefore, at the time the Panel on *Japan – Alcoholic Beverages II*[688] was called upon to state its view on the product differentiation for the purposes of GATT Article III:2, the case was closely watched to see, whether the "*aim and effects test*" was developed further to establish it as a 'precedent' in the new automated procedures of the WTO dispute settlement system or would return to the traditional "*two-step approach*".

In *Japan – Alcoholic Beverages II*, the European Community, the United States and Canada requested the Dispute Settlement Body (DSB) to form a panel to assess whether the Japanese system of internal taxation for liquors protected *shochu*, a predominantly domestic product, and discriminated against other, almost exclusively imported liquors. The complainants argued that the higher tax levied on liquors other than *shochu* decreased the competitive opportunities of these products in violation of Japan's obligations regarding national treatment on internal taxation and regulation under GATT Article III:2.

With respect to the determination of "like products" in the meaning of GATT Article III:2, first sentence, the EC essentially argued in favour of a "*two-step approach*" whereby the Panel should establish first whether *shochu* and other distilled alcoholic beverages are like and, if so, then proceed to examine whether the different taxes imposed on foreign products are in excess of those imposed on *shochu*.[689] Thereby the EC pointed out that the physical characteristics of the products concerned, their end-uses, as well as consumer preferences could provide relevant criteria for the Panel to judge whether the products concerned were like.[690] Unlike the EC, the United States

687 *Ibid.*, paragraphs 5.5 and 5.10.

688 Panel Report on *Japan – Alcoholic Beverages II,* WT/DS8/R, WT/DS10/R, WT/DS11/R.

689 *Ibid.*, paragraphs 3.1 and 4.12 *et seq.* As an alternative argument, the EC also claimed that *shochu* and other distilled alcoholic beverages were directly competitive and that the different tax rates were contrary to the second sentence of GATT Article III:2.

690 *Ibid.*, paragraph 6.14.

argued from the "*aim and effects*" position, claiming that the Japanese Liquor Tax Law had both the aim and the effect of protecting the domestic industry and that it essentially changed the competitive conditions between *shochu* and other alcoholic beverages, which constituted a violation of GATT Article III:2. Essentially, the U.S. called upon the Panel, when determining whether two products that were taxed differently under a Member's origin-neutral tax measure were nonetheless "like products" for the purposes of GATT Article III:2, to not only examine the similarity in physical characteristics and end-uses, consumer tastes and preferences, and tariff classifications for each product, but also to evaluate whether the tax distinction in question was *"applied [...] so as to afford protection to domestic production"*. In other words, the U.S. maintained that for the product differentiation it has to be considered whether the aim and effect of that distinction, considered as a whole, was to afford protection to domestic production.[691] According to this view, if the tax distinction in question is not being applied so as to afford protection to domestic production, the products between which the distinction is drawn are not to be deemed "like products" for the purpose of GATT Article III:2.

In defending the case, Japan also took the "*aim and effects*" position, claiming, however, in contrast to the view of the U.S., that the Liquor Tax Law had neither the aim nor the effect of protecting the domestic industry. It maintained that *shochu* and other distilled alcoholic beverages were neither "like products" nor "directly competitive" products, and that the Japanese tax laws were therefore not in violation of GATT Article III:2.[692] According to Japan's view, in case the aim and effect of the contested legislation does not operate so as to afford protection to domestic production, no inconsistency with GATT Article III:2 can be established.

The Panel on *Japan – Alcoholic Beverages II* reached the following conclusions: First, that *shochu* and vodka were "like products"[693] and, that Japan, by taxing the latter in excess of the former was in violation of its obligation under the first sentence of GATT

691 *Ibid.*, paragraphs 3.3 and 4.16 *et seq.*
692 *Ibid.*, paragraphs 3.4 and 4.19.
693 *Ibid.*, paragraph 6.23.

Article III:2. Second, as *shochu*, whisky, brandy, rum, gin, genever, and liquors were considered "directly competitive or substitutable products"[694], the Panel concluded that Japan, by not taxing them similarly, was in violation of its obligations under the second sentence of GATT Article III:2.

In the process of arriving at these conclusions, it is important to note that the Panel explicitly rejected the "*aim and effects test*" and elected instead for a theoretical construct based on the "*two-step approach*". The Panel stated that it did not find the "*aim and effects test*" appropriate for the following reasons: First, it held that the "*aim and effects test*" not only departed from the wording of GATT Article III,[695] but was also inconsistent with the general interpretative principles of international law established in Article 31 of the 1969 Vienna Convention on the Law of Treaties.[696] Second, the list of exceptions contained in GATT Article XX could become redundant or useless because the "*aim and effects test*" does not contain a definitive list of grounds justifying the departure from the obligations that are otherwise incorporated in GATT Article III.[697]

bb) The Determination of "Like Products"

Having decided not to apply the "*aim and effects test*", the Panel proceeded to interpret the notion of "like products", and noted preliminarily that it did not necessarily follow from the appearance of the term "like products" in various GATT provisions that it had to be interpreted in a uniform way. Accordingly, the Panel stressed that its conclusions reached in the present dispute are only relevant for the inter-

694 *Ibid.*, paragraph 6.32.

695 *Ibid.*, paragraph 6.16.

696 Article 31(1) of the Vienna Convention provides that "[a] treaty shall be interpreted in good faith in accordance with the ordinary meaning to be given to the terms of the treaty in their context and in the light of its object and purpose". Thereby, the Panel stressed that, according to Article 32 of the Vienna Convention, supplementary means of treaty interpretation (such as preparatory work) are required only as an exception in specific circumstances (*ibid.*, footnote to paragraph 6.16).

697 *Ibid.*, paragraph 6.17.

pretation of "like products" in the sense of GATT Article III:2.[698] With reference to previous panel and working party reports,[699] the Panel further noted that the term "like product" should be interpreted on a case-by-case basis, thus leaving it open to panels to use different criteria – such as the product's properties, nature and quality, its end-uses, consumers' tastes and habits, which change from country to country, and the product's classification in tariff nomenclatures – in order to establish likeness.[700]

After emphasising that a distinction must be drawn between, on the one hand, "like", and, on the other, "directly competitive (or substitutable)" products, the Panel considered that like products should be viewed as a *subset* of directly competitive or substitutable products.[701] According to the Panel, this conclusion is confirmed by the textual interpretation of the term "like products", in the sense, that all like products are, by definition, directly competitive or substitutable products, whereas all directly competitive or substitutable products are not necessarily like products. Moreover, the wording makes it clear that the appropriate test to define whether two products are "like" or "directly competitive or substitutable" is the *marketplace*, obviously the only place where competition exists. The Panel concluded that the definition of a precise cut-off point, distinguishing between like and directly

698 *Ibid.*, paragraph 6.20. In a similar sense, Panel Report on *United States – Measures Affecting Alcoholic and Malt Beverages,* DS23/R, paragraph 5.75.

699 1970 Working Party Report on *Border Tax Adjustment* (L/5863) as well as Panel Report on *Japan – Customs Duties, Taxes and Labelling Practices on Imported Wines and Alcoholic Beverages*, L/6216, paragraph 5.6; or Panel Report on *EEC – Measures on Animal Feed Proteins*, L/4599, paragraph 4.3.

700 Panel Report on *Japan – Alcoholic Beverages II*, WT/DS8/R, WT/DS10/R, WT/DS11/R, paragraph 6.21.

701 In other words, the concept of "directly competitive products" is of broader scope than "like products". The Panel also considered that although "like products" need not be identical in all respects, the term "like product" should be construed narrowly in the case of GATT Article III:2, first sentence. In the Panel's view, this approach is dictated, *inter alia*, because Article III:2 distinguishes between like and directly competitive or substitutable products, "*[t]he latter obviously being a much larger category of products than the former*" (*ibid.*, paragraph 6.20).

competitive (or substitutable) products, thus requires an *arbitrary* decision.[702]

Although the Panel opted for the use of *descriptive criteria* to determine whether two products are “like” or “directly competitive”, it nevertheless tried to compensate for the arbitrariness of its test by advocating a flexible line between “like” and “directly competitive” products: Flexibility emerges during the case-by-case analysis of product distinctions.[703] However, such flexibility only acknowledges that a panel’s delineation between the definitions is problematic for those products that could fall in either category. Moreover, flexibility in itself is an arbitrary concept because there is no indication of how much flexibility is permissible.

This is well illustrated by the Panel’s own approach to descriptive criteria: For instance, the Panel considered that descriptions used in the context of tariff classifications and bindings *can be used* in considering the content of “like” products, albeit holding that, by themselves, they *do not provide decisive guidance on likeness*. At the same time, the Panel found that the wording of “directly competitive” products does not suggest *at all* that physical resemblance is required in order to establish whether two products fall under this category. In contrast, in the Panel’s view, the decisive criterion in order to determine whether two products are *directly competitive or substitutable* is whether they have *common end-uses*, *inter alia*, as shown by elasticity of substitution. On the other hand, it considered that the wording of the term “like products” suggests that the commonality of end-uses is a necessary but *not a sufficient criterion to define likeness*. The Panel then deduced from the term “like” product that for two products to fall under this category they must share, apart from commonality of end-uses, essentially the *same physical characteristics*.[704]

Accordingly, the Panel found that *shochu* and vodka shared most physical characteristics,[705] with the exception of filtration. In addition, it held that a difference in the physical characteristic of alcoholic

702 *Ibid.*, paragraph 6.22.
703 *Ibid.*, paragraph 6.22.
704 *Ibid.*, paragraph 6.22.
705 They are both white/clean spirits and are made of similar raw materials.

strength of two products did not preclude a finding of likeness especially since alcoholic beverages are often drunk in diluted form. In support of this finding, the Panel further considered that the end-uses of *shochu* and vodka were virtually identical, and that both beverages were at the time classified in the same heading in the Japanese tariffs and were covered by the same Japanese tariff binding at the time of its negotiation.[706]

After having found that the tax imposed on vodka is in excess of the tax imposed on *shochu*,[707] the Panel addressed the argument put forward by Japan that its Liquor Tax Law, by keeping the tax/price ratio 'roughly constant', is trade neutral and that, consequently, the Liquor Tax Law has no protective aim and effect. In this context, most surprisingly, the Panel stated that "*[n]owhere in the contested legislation was it mentioned that* its purpose *was to maintain a 'roughly constant' tax/price ratio*" (emphasis added).[708] Although the Panel claimed that it would rely only on descriptive criteria, by holding that the existence or non-existence of a protective aim and effect is not relevant in an analysis under GATT Article III:2, first sentence,[709] it appears that the Panel's reasoning nevertheless included an analysis of the aim of the measure.

In its subsequent appeal, Japan maintained that the Panel erred in disregarding the need to determine whether the Liquor Tax Law has the aim of affording protection to domestic production. The Appellate Body, however, substantively upheld the structure of the panel report in this respect and rejected the "*aim and effects test*".[710] The Appellate Body also agreed that panels can only apply their "*best judgement*" in determining whether in fact products are "like" on the basis of descriptive criteria, such as a product's end-uses in a given market, consumers' tastes and habits, which change from country to country, the product's properties, nature and quality, and on the basis of other criteria that may also be relevant in certain cases. Acknowledging that

706 *Ibid.*, paragraph 6.23.
707 *Ibid.*, paragraph 6.24.
708 *Ibid.*, paragraph 6.25(iii).
709 *Ibid.*, paragraph 6.25.
710 AB Report on *Japan – Alcoholic Beverages II,* WT/DS8/AB/R, WT/DS10/AB/R, WT/DS11/AB/R, p. 18.

such evaluation will always involve an "*unavoidable element of individual, discretionary judgement*", the Appellate Body stressed, however, its disagreement with the Panel's observation that distinguishing between "like products" and "directly competitive or substitutable" products under GATT Article III:2 is "*an arbitrary decision*".[711]

In this context, the Appellate Body thus reiterated that no one approach to exercising judgement will be appropriate for all cases and that, accordingly, there can be no one precise and absolute definition of what is "like". It further made clear that:

> The concept of 'likeness' is a relative one that evokes the image of an accordion. The accordion of 'likeness' stretches and squeezes in different places as different provisions of the *WTO Agreement* are applied. The width of the accordion in any one of those places must be determined by the particular provision in which the term 'like' is encountered as well as by the context and the circumstances that prevail in any given case to which that provision may apply. [712]

In light of this statement it comes as no surprise that, shortly thereafter, the "*aim and effects test*" was equally rejected as an incorrect application of the "like product" test under GATT Article III:4.[713] Irrespective of whether the maintenance of the "*aim and effects test*" would have been a more sensitive test to distinguish between prohibition of discrimination and non-protectionist domestic regulation, as some have argued,[714] it should be noted that the "*two-step approach*" adopted by both the Panel and the Appellate Body does not necessarily provide predictable conclusions as it allows the deciding panel to exercise wide discretion. In addition, the decisions show little sign that the interpretation of "like product" focuses conceptually on the competitive relationship between the products – which it should do.

711 *Ibid.*, pp. 19 and 20.

712 *Ibid.*, p. 20.

713 AB Report on *European Community — Regime for the Importation, Sale and Distribution of Bananas*, WT/DS27/AB/R, paragraphs 215 and 216.

714 PORGES/TRACHTMAN, (2003) 37 JWT 783 *et seq.*; HUDEC, (1998) 32 International Lawyer 619 *et seq.*; WILLE, (1998) 9 EJIL 182 *et seq.*

cc) The Determination of "Directly Competitive" Products

Due to some noticeable differences in physical characteristics between the other alcoholic beverages at dispute, other than vodka, and *shochu* that would disqualify them from being regarded as like products,[715] the Panel turned to examine whether those beverages could qualify as directly competitive or substitutable products to *shochu* for the purposes of GATT Article III:2, second sentence.

Recalling that the term "directly competitive or substitutable" product should be interpreted more broadly than the term "like" product, the Panel stated that, independently of similarities with regard to physical characteristics or classification in tariff nomenclatures, greater emphasis should be placed on the elasticity of substitution. In this context, it was considered that factors like marketing strategies might equally constitute relevant criteria in order to determine the responsiveness of consumers to the products offered in the market.[716]

In the process of arriving at the conclusion that whisky, brandy, rum, gin, genever, liquors and *shochu* were "directly competitive or substitutable" products, the Panel relied first and foremost[717] on the findings of the Panel on *Japan – Customs Duties, Taxes and Labelling*

715 More specifically, the use of additives was considered to disqualify liqueurs, gin and genever; the use of ingredients disqualified rum; and the appearance (arising from manufacturing processes) disqualified whisky and brandy to be products "like" *shochu* (Panel Report on *Japan – Alcoholic Beverages II*, WT/DS8/R, WT/DS10/R, WT/DS11/R, paragraph 6.23).

716 *Ibid.*, paragraph 6.28. Aware of the implications of tax systems that discriminate against imports and thereby artificially create preferences for domestic goods, the Panel stressed, however, that the responsiveness of consumers, varying from country to country, should not be influenced by internal taxation. Accordingly, consumer surveys in such countries have to be weighed carefully. Not surprisingly, the Panel did thus not accept a consumer survey submitted by Japan on the grounds that Japan, in conducting this survey, failed to take into account price distortions caused by internal taxation (paragraph 6.31).

717 The Panel explicitly stated that, in its view, the conclusions of the Panel on *Japan – Customs Duties, Taxes and Labelling Practices on Imported Wines and Alcoholic Beverages* were sufficient to conclude that *shochu* and the other distilled beverages are directly competitive or substitutable, albeit buttressed by other evidence, such as market studies (*ibid.*, paragraph 6.32).

Practices on Imported Wines and Alcoholic Beverages[718] which based its conclusion essentially on the *substitutability* among the products *as a result of their respective prices*, their *availability through trade* and their *other competitive inter-relationships*.[719] In addition, the Panel considered a study put forward by the complainants demonstrating that there is significant elasticity of substitution among the products in dispute,[720] and the evidence submitted by the complainants concerning the Japanese tax reform which showed that whisky and *shochu* are essentially competing for the same market.[721] The Appellate Body affirmed the Panel's legal analysis regarding the direct competitiveness and substitutability of the products.[722]

From the above, it is difficult to see how panels will not find themselves in an awkward position when differentiating products. The implicit motive analysis suggested by the Appellate Body does not necessarily support the argument of using supposedly objective, *i.e.* descriptive, criteria. On the other hand, it has to be acknowledged that, by giving preference to the "*two-step approach*" and relying on the panels' "best judgement", the Appellate Body has contributed to the credibility of the WTO dispute settlement mechanism and the practice derived there from. As far as the principle of legitimate expectation is concerned, it remains to be seen whether the "best judgement", applied on a case-by-case basis, does not lead to arbitrary distinctions between products, and whether it is capable of providing clear guidance as to what constitutes likeness or direct competitiveness.

718 Panel Report on Japan – Customs Duties, Taxes and Labelling Practices on Imported Wines and Alcoholic Beverages, L/6216, paragraph 5.7.

719 Panel Report on *Japan – Alcoholic Beverages II*, WT/DS8/R, WT/DS10/R, WT/DS11/R, paragraph 6.29.

720 The market study submitted by the complainants concludes that there is a high degree of price-elasticity between *shochu*, on the one hand, and five brown spirits (Scotch whisky, Japanese whisky, Japanese brandy, cognac, North American whisky) and three white spirits (gin, vodka and rum), on the other (*ibid.*, paragraph 6.29).

721 *Ibid.*, paragraph 6.30. In the Panel's view, the fact that *shochu* and foreign whisky were in fact capturing the market share lost by domestically produced whisky after the Japanese tax reform is evidence that they are competing products and that there is elasticity of substitution between them.

722 AB Report on *Japan – Alcoholic Beverages II*, WT/DS8/AB/R, WT/DS10/AB/R, WT/DS11/AB/R., p. 26.

No sooner had the Reports on *Japan – Alcoholic Beverages II* been issued than the WTO also saw complaints brought before panels on alcoholic beverage taxation in Korea[723] and Chile[724]. Reiterating the tests developed in *Japan – Alcoholic Beverages II*, both Panels relied on a number of criteria for the determination of direct competitiveness and substitutability, including tariff classifications,[725] common end-users in a given market,[726] taking into account channels of distribution and points of sale,[727] cross-price elasticity,[728] consumer tastes

723 Panel Report on *Korea – Alcoholic Beverages*, WT/DS75/R, WT/DS84/R.

724 Panel Report on *Chile – Alcoholic Beverages,* WT/DS87/R, WT/DS110/R.

725 Panel Report on *Chile – Alcoholic Beverages,* WT/DS87/R, WT/DS110/R, paragraphs 7.28 and 7.29. In its report on *Korea – Alcoholic Beverages*, the Appellate Body considered that the grouping of products can be a helpful device in determining whether they are directly competitive. Such determination is, however, limited to the extent that the analysis must take into account the components of those products to determine whether there is enough similarity to warrant their being grouped together, notwithstanding some variation in composition, quality, function or price (WT/DS75/AB/R, WT/DS84/AB/R, paragraphs 142 and 143).

726 Panel Report on *Korea – Alcoholic Beverages*, WT/DS75/R, WT/DS84/R, paragraph 10.78 and paragraph 10.95, where the usefulness of market strategies for the determination of substitutability is reiterated; and Panel Report on *Chile – Alcoholic Beverages,* WT/DS87/R, WT/DS110/R, paragraph 7.47.

727 The Panel on *Korea – Alcoholic Beverages* noted that "[c]onsiderable evidence of overlap in channels of distribution and points of sale [...] is supportive of a finding that the identified imported and domestic products are directly competitive or substitutable" (WT/DS75/R, WT/DS84/R, paragraph 10.86). The Panel on Chile – Alcoholic Beverages concurred (WT/DS87/R, WT/DS110/R, paragraph 7.57).

728 With respect to studies on cross-price elasticity, the Panel on *Chile – Alcoholic Beverages* emphasised that the concept of substitution in markets should not be confused or equated with a numerical measurement of the extent of substitution as found in the coefficient of cross-elasticity. It admitted, however, that a high coefficient of cross-price elasticity would lend more credence to a claim of direct competitiveness or substitutability, but considered at the same time that a low coefficient of cross-price elasticity is not necessarily fatal to a claim of direct competitiveness or substitutability (WT/DS87/R, WT/DS110/R, paragraphs 7.69 and 7.70).

and habits by means of *potential* competition,[729] and physical characteristics,[730] such as the products' properties, nature and quality.

With respect to the significance of physical characteristics in the differentiation of products, it was considered that they are more critical in determining whether two products are "like" than in the determination of whether two products are "directly competitive or substitutable". This is, however, without prejudice to an actual consideration of the products' physical similarities when determining whether products are directly competitive or substitutable.[731] It was also stressed in both cases that an assessment of whether there is a direct competitive relationship between two products or groups of products requires evidence that consumers consider (or could consider) the two products or groups of products as alternative ways of satisfying a particular need or taste. The Panels reasoned, furthermore, that the focus should not be exclusively on the quantitative extent of the competitive overlap, but on the methodological basis on which a panel should assess the competitive relationship.[732] Both Panels admitted that quantitative analysis, while helpful, should not be considered necessary.[733] Similarly, quantitative studies of cross-price elasticity are relevant, but not exclusive or even decisive in nature.[734] A determination of the precise extent of the competitive overlap can further be complicated by the

729 Panel Report on *Korea – Alcoholic Beverages*, WT/DS75/R, WT/DS84/R, paragraph 10.50, upheld in AB Report on *Korea – Alcoholic Beverages*, WT/DS75/AB/R, WT/DS84/AB/R, paragraphs 112 *et seq.*; and Panel Report on *Chile – Alcoholic Beverages,* WT/DS87/R, WT/DS110/R, paragraph 7.25.

730 The Panel on *Chile – Alcoholic Beverages* clearly stated that the closer the physical similarity the greater the likelihood of a directly competitive or substitutable relationship (WT/DS87/R, WT/DS110/R, paragraph 7.48).

731 *Ibid.*, paragraph 7.51.

732 Panel Report on *Korea – Alcoholic Beverages*, WT/DS75/R, WT/DS84/R, paragraph 10.39; reiterated by the Appellate Body on *Korea – Alcoholic Beverages*, WT/DS75/AB/R, WT/DS84/AB/R, paragraphs 120–123 and 134; Panel Report on *Chile – Alcoholic Beverages,* WT/DS87/R, WT/DS110/R, paragraph 7.87.

733 Panel Report on *Korea – Alcoholic Beverages*, WT/DS75/R, WT/DS84/R, paragraph 10.42.

734 Panel Reports on *Korea – Alcoholic Beverages*, WT/DS75/R, WT/DS84/R, paragraph 10.44; and on *Chile – Alcoholic Beverages,* WT/DS87/R, WT/DS110/R, paragraph 7.77 respectively.

fact that protectionist government policies can distort the competitive relationship between products, causing the quantitative extent of the competitive relationship to be understated.

In the case of Chile, it is interesting to note that the Panel also considered a recent assessment of an anti-trust case carried out by the Chilean Central Preventive Commission, in which *pisco* was judged to face major competition of other alcoholic beverages, such as wine, beer and whisky, due to the practice of also drinking *pisco* diluted with non-alcoholic beverages.[735] The Panel consequently shared the view of the former Panel on *Korea – Alcoholic Beverages* that competitive conditions, sufficient for defining an appropriate market with respect to anti-trust analysis, would *a fortiori* suffice for a GATT Article III analysis,[736] before concluding that *pisco* is "directly competitive and substitutable" with the main types of distilled spirits exported from the EC, such as whisky, vodka, brandy, gin and rum.

dd) Lessons for Safeguard Investigations

The test developed by various panels and the Appellate Body, namely legal reasoning based on "best judgment", illustrates the need for future panels to clearly discuss the criteria upon which product differentiation is made. This is particularly true in light of the recurring statement that the interpretation of the term "like or directly competitive product" does not necessarily entail uniformity as the term appears in various provisions of the WTO agreements. Since panels have repeatedly stressed that their conclusions reached in a particular dispute are only relevant for the interpretation of the term in the sense of the allegedly violated provision, it appears logical that any assessment of

735 Panel Report on *Chile – Alcoholic Beverages,* WT/DS87/R, WT/DS110/R, paragraph 7.86.

736 *Ibid.*, paragraph 7.86. In addition, the Panel in *Korea – Alcoholic Beverages* pointed out that the definition of a market in anti-trust is not the same as under GATT Article III. It further felt that because the two concepts (anti-trust and competitive opportunities under Article III) are designed to address different concerns their definitions of the market need not be the same. According to the Panel, since Article III is primarily concerned with competitive opportunities, it defines markets more broadly than anti-trust which is designed to protect the actual mechanisms of competition (WT/DS75/R, WT/DS84/R, paragraph 10.81).

product definition can and must only be made on a case-by-case basis – may it concern the same or different provisions. Accordingly, the crucial issue is to what extent the use of descriptive criteria may serve as guidance for the interpretation of "like or directly competitive" products in the context of the Agreement on Safeguards and of its implementing legislation in the EC, *i.e.* Regulation 3285/94 (now Regulation 260/2009).

Before discussing this issue, it is important to note that the determination of "like or directly competitive" products in connection with safeguard measures appears to have raised comparatively little disagreement, *i.e.* in the majority of disputes on safeguard measures, the complainants did not challenge the definition of "like or directly competitive products" as such,[737] and emphasis was rather put on the alleged violation of other legal requirements, such as the determination of injury with respect to the like or directly competitive products, which is well illustrated in the following cases.

In *Argentina – Footwear*,[738] Argentina defined *footwear* as comprising the "like or directly competitive" products for the application of the safeguard measure. For the purposes of its investigation, however, it had chosen to divide the footwear market into five product groups (performance sports footwear, non-performance sports footwear, exclusively women's footwear, town and/or casual footwear, and other footwear). The EC, the complainant, argued that having adopted this segmented approach, Argentina was obliged to follow it consistently through its injury analysis and to prove serious injury in all segments in which safeguards were to be imposed. Although the EC maintained that Argentina did not investigate factors relating to import trends for each market segment, thus not proving serious injury in any of the selected five segments, it did not challenge a single category of Argentina's definition of like or directly competitive prod-

737 For the implicit agreement of the EC with the product qualification, see, for example, Panel Report on *US – Wheat Gluten* (WT/DS166/R), and the explicit consent of the product definition in the Panel Reports on *Korea – Dairy* (WT/DS98/R, paragraphs 4.293 and 4.294) and on *Argentina – Footwear* (WT/DS121/R, paragraph 5.207).

738 Panel Report on *Argentina – Footwear*, WT/DS121/R.

ucts.[739] The Panel hence considered that, given the undisputed definition of the like or directly competitive product as all footwear, Argentina was not required to conduct its injury and causation analysis on a disaggregated basis.[740]

In *US – Lamb*,[741] the USITC defined the domestic industry to include growers and feeders of live lambs, as well as packers and breakers of lamb meat. According to the USITC, this definition was justified due to the "continuous line of production from the raw to the processed product", and because there was a "substantial coincidence of economic interests" between and among the growers and feeders of live lambs, and the packers and breakers of lamb meat. New Zealand and Australia, the complainants, argued that the USITC had improperly interpreted the term "domestic industry" by including in that industry growers and feeders of live lambs, even though they did not produce the product at issue, lamb meat. Considering the meaning of the term "domestic industry" in Article 4:1(c) Agreement on Safeguards, the Panel found that "*[t]he relevant industry consists of producers that themselves have "output" of the "like" or "directly competitive" products*".[742] The Panel further stated that the term "producers as a whole", which forms part of the definition in Article 4:1(c), offered no support for the broader approach adopted by the USITC,[743] and concluded that the USITC's inclusion of input producers (*i.e.*, growers and feeders of live lamb) in the lamb meat investigation as producers of the like product at issue (*i.e.* lamb meat) was inconsistent with the Agreement on Safeguards.[744]

On appeal, the U.S. claimed that the USITC's determination is correct, and that the Agreement on Safeguards allows Members some discretion when defining the term "producers of like or directly com-

739 *Ibid.*, paragraph 8.135.

740 *Ibid.*, paragraph 8.137. According to the Panel, Argentina was required at a minimum to consider each injury factor with regard to all footwear, whereby it was free to consider the data on a disaggregated basis as long as it explained how the analysis of such segment was pertinent to the entire industry.

741 Panel Report on *US – Lamb*, WT/DS177/R, WT/DS178/R.

742 *Ibid.*, paragraph 7.68.

743 *Ibid.*, paragraph 7.74.

744 *Ibid.*, paragraph 7.118.

petitive products" in the light of the facts and circumstances of each case.[745] In assessing this claim, the Appellate Body stressed that the term "domestic industry" focuses exclusively on the producers of a very specific group of products. Producers of products that are not "like or directly competitive" do not, according to the Appellate Body, form part of the domestic industry.[746] In determining the scope of the domestic industry, there are therefore two steps that have to be performed: first, the identification of the products which are "like or directly competitive" with the imported product; and second, the identification of the "producers" of those products.[747] Although all parties agreed that in this case the "like product" is *lamb meat*,[748] the USITC nevertheless considered that the "domestic industry" producing the "like product", lamb meat, includes the growers and feeders of live lambs. Like the Panel, the Appellate Body dismissed the U.S.' argument, and found that, in the absence of a "like or directly competitive" relationship, there is no justification for giving credence to any of the criteria put forward by the U.S. in defining a "domestic industry", such as the "continuous line of production" or the "substantial coincidence of economic interests".[749]

This case clearly illustrates not only the importance of defining the like or directly competitive products but also the boundaries of the use of criteria, other than descriptive criteria, in determining the domestic industry. Once the likeness or the direct competitiveness of a domestically produced product with the imported product is established, there is little (or no) room for including other producers than those of the previously identified product group. It further provides a welcome opportunity to draw a parallel to the definition of the "relevant market" from a competition law point of view.[750]

745 AB Report on *US – Lamb*, WT/DS177/AB/R, WT/DS178/AB/R, paragraph 81.

746 *Ibid.*, paragraph 84.

747 *Ibid.*, paragraph 87.

748 *Ibid.*, paragraph 88. The USITC did not find that there were any products that were to be considered "directly competitive products", and this term was therefore not at issue in the dispute.

749 *Ibid.*, paragraphs 89 and 90.

750 In this context it is noteworthy that the Appellate Body on *Japan – Alcoholic Beverages II* also considered that "[t]he GATT 1994 is a commercial agreement,

Considering that safeguard measures are designed to accord to the domestic industry a temporary relief from competition caused by an import surge, it is conceivable to determine the "like or directly competitive" products based on descriptive criteria coupled with the concepts for market definition under competition law. For the purpose of this dissertation, the concept of the relevant product market under EU competition law appears suited to discuss such possible parallelism.

The concept of the relevant product market and how it is applied by the Commission is set out in the Commission Notice on the definition of the relevant market for the purposes of Community competition law,[751] and is defined as follows:

> A relevant product market comprises all those products and/or services which are regarded as interchangeable or substitutable by the consumer, by reason of the products' characteristics, their prices and their intended use.[752]

In order to define the relevant product market, the Commission usually evaluates two competitive constraints to which firms are subject: demand substitutability and supply substitutability.[753] Whereas the assessment of demand substitution entails a determination of the range of products which are viewed as substitutes by the consumer, supply-side substitutability is taken into account when suppliers are able to switch production to the relevant products and market them in the short term without incurring significant additional costs or risks in response to small and permanent changes in relative prices.[754] Potential competition, the third competitive constraint identified by the Commission, is usually not taken into account when defining markets since the conditions under which potential competition will actually repre-

and the WTO is concerned, after all, with markets. It does not seem inappropriate to look *at competition in the relevant markets* as one among a number of means of identifying the broader category of products that might be described as 'directly competitive or substitutable'" (emphasis added); AB Report on *Japan – Alcoholic Beverages II*, WT/DS8/AB/R, WT/DS10/AB/R, WT/DS11/AB/R., p. 25.

751 OJ 1997 C 372/5.

752 *Ibid.*, paragraph 7.

753 *Ibid.*, paragraph 13.

754 *Ibid.*, paragraphs 15 and 20.

sent an effective competitive constraint depend on the analysis of specific factors and circumstances related to the conditions of entry.[755]

In addition to product characteristics and intended use, factors the Commission considers relevant for demand substitution include evidence of substitution in the recent past (such as shocks in the market or the launch of new products), quantitative tests of econometric or statistical nature (such as cross-price elasticity or price movement over time), views of customers and competitors (different categories of customers or price discrimination), consumer preferences (market studies), barriers and costs associated with switching demand to potential substitutes (such as specific capital investment, the location of customers or human capital investment).[756] The Commission does, however, not follow a rigid hierarchy of different sources of information or types of evidence.

Already under the old import regime, *i.e.* prior to the enactment of Regulation 3285/94, a review of the safeguard measures adopted by the EC suggests that product differentiation followed similar lines to the one propounded under EC competition law. By relying on descriptive criteria, such as common end-uses in a given market, channels of distribution, cross-price elasticity, consumer tastes and habits by means of competition, and physical characteristics, the Commission considered, for instance, in *Certain Quartz Watches With Digital Display*,[757] that "directly competing products" are products which can essentially be substituted one for the other, that is to say, which are suitable for the same purposes and accordingly, are basically interchangeable. It thus found that, "*[o]nce a consumer has bought a digital quartz watch which tells him the time in a satisfactory manner, in the current Community context of stagnating purchasing power he will very likely not be concerned with buying another watch regardless of its type of display or technology [...].*"[758] Conversely, albeit on the basis of similar criteria, the Commission concluded in *Certain*

755 *Ibid.*, paragraph 24.

756 *Ibid.*, paragraphs 36 *et seq.*

757 *Certain Quartz Watches With Digital Display,* Commission Regulation No. 1087/84 (OJ 1984 L 106/31).

758 *Ibid.*, Recital 10.

Slippers and Other Indoor Footwear[759] that slippers and beach slippers are not directly competitive "*[w]hether with regard to import trends, prices or the impact of imports on French industry, since slipper production and beach slipper production constitute two different industries.*"[760]

Under the auspices of Regulation 3285/94, the Commission relied on criteria of demand substitutability also in order to determine the "like product". In *Citrus Fruits*,[761] the Commission found that the imported product and the Community product share, in addition to their international classification for tariff purposes, the same or similar physical properties such as taste, size, shape and texture. The Commission's safeguard investigation further revealed that the imported product and the Community product were sold via similar or identical sales channels, that price information was readily available to buyers, and that the product concerned and the product of the Community producers competed mainly on price. Considering that the imported product and the Community product both served the same or similar end-uses, the Commission considered them to be alternative or substitute products and easily interchangeable. Accordingly; it submitted that the imported product and the Community product were both perceived by consumers as alternatives to satisfy a particular want or demand, and that they were hence "like products" despite the minor quality variations identified by certain exporters and importers.[762]

The approach taken by the Commission in this safeguard investigation fully corresponds with the definition of the "relevant product market" comprising all those products which are regarded as interchangeable or substitutable by the consumer, by reason of the prod-

759 *Certain Slippers and Other Indoor Footwear,* Commission Regulation No. 3667/84 of 21 December 1984 instituting a system for the authorization of imports in respect of imports into France of certain beach slippers, slippers and other indoor footwear (OJ 1984 L 340/30). Criteria that were examined included, for example, physical characteristics (Recital 11) or prices (Recitals 13 and 17).

760 *Ibid.,* Recital 10.

761 *Citrus Fruits*, Commission Regulation (EC) No. 658/2004 of 7 April 2004 imposing definitive safeguard measures against imports of certain prepared or preserved citrus fruits (namely mandarins, etc.), OJ 2004 L 104/67.

762 *Ibid.*, paragraph 20.

ucts' characteristics, their prices and their intended use, under competition law. While it is commonly assumed that, for anti-trust purposes, the definition of the relevant market is a preliminary step to enabling assessment of market related breaches of the domestic competition laws, the better view is that consideration of the issues of market power and competition cannot be separated from the process of delineation of the market. It is better to say that market definition is not an end in itself, but merely provides an analytical framework in which market power and the processes of competition can be assessed.[763] The same applies for safeguard measures. This is – not at last – reflected in the fact that the Commission in the above determination of "like product" considered the views of competitors (exporters and importers). The fact that the Commission opted, in the end, to disregard those views does not alter this finding but merely reflects that the Commission is prepared to provide a "reasoned and adequate explanation" for its choice.[764]

1.2 Evaluation under the "Implementation Principle"

Private parties (as well as Member States) may only rely on WTO provisions in order to challenge the validity of Community acts under the "implementation principle", *i.e.* if the Community legislation concerned either expressly refers to them (the "clear reference exception", also called the *Fediol* doctrine), or if the EC intended to implement an obligation entered into under WTO/GATT (the "implementation exception", also called the *Nakajima* doctrine).

763 In the Comission's view, the objective of defining a market is to identify those actual competitors of the undertakings involved that are capable of constraining those undertakings' behaviour and of preventing them from behaving independently of effective competitive pressure (Commission Notice on the definition of the relevant market for the purposes of Community competition law, OJ 1997 C 372/5, paragraph 2).

764 *Citrus Fruits*, Commission Regulation (EC) No. 658/2004 of 7 April 2004 imposing definitive safeguard measures against imports of certain prepared or preserved citrus fruits (namely mandarins, etc.), OJ 2004 L 104/67, paragraph 20(d) read in conjunction with paragraphs 16 and 19.

1.2.1 Clear Reference to the Agreement on Safeguards?

In *Fediol IV*,[765] the Court of Justice established that reliance on a GATT provision before the Community courts is permissible if a Community act requires the EC to comply with its international obligations. This exception was *in casu* admissible because the EC's New Commercial Policy Instrument Regulation[766] stipulated, *inter alia*, in Article 2:

> 1. For the purposes of this Regulation, illicit commercial practices shall be any international trade practices attributable to third countries which are incompatible with international law or with the generally accepted rules.
>
> 2. For the purposes of this Regulation, *the Community's rights shall be those international trade rights of which it may avail itself either under international law* or under generally accepted rules *(emphasis added).*

In addition, Recital 2 of the preamble to the New Commercial Policy Instrument Regulation considered that the legitimate interests of the Community were to be defended in the appropriate bodies, in particular GATT, which lead the ECJ to conclude that, in the case before it, GATT Article III could be used to interpret the meaning of "illicit commercial practices" under the Regulation, and that "*[t]he GATT provisions have an independent meaning, which for the purposes of their application in specific cases, is to be determined by way of interpretation*".[767] In the following it shall therefore be assessed whether Regulation 3285/94 (now Regulation 260/2009) satisfies the standard for the "clear reference exception" set by the ECJ in *Fediol IV*.

Regulation 3285/94 (now Regulation 260/2009, respectively) merely refers to the Agreement on Safeguards in its Recitals, and most prominently in Recital 4:

> Whereas the Agreement on Safeguard meets the need to clarify and reinforce the disciplines of GATT 1994, and specifically those of Article XIX; whereas that

765 Case 70/87, *Fediol IV*, [1989] E.C.R. 1781.

766 Council Regulation (EEC) No. 2641/84 of 17 September 1984 on the strengthening of the common commercial policy with regard in particular to protection against illicit commercial practices (OJ 1984 L 252/1).

767 Case 70/87, *Fediol IV*, [1989] E.C.R. 1831.

> Agreement requires the elimination of safeguard measures which escape those rules, such as voluntary export restraints, orderly marketing arrangements and any other similar import or export arrangements.

Arguably, Recital 4 contains the prohibition of VERs stipulated in Article 11:1(b) Agreement on Safeguards which provides, *inter alia*, that

> [...] a Member shall not seek, take or maintain any voluntary export restraints, orderly marketing arrangements or any other similar measure on the export or the import side. [...] *(original footnote omitted).*

As far as a reference to the Community's international obligations is concerned, Recital 2 to Regulation 3285/94 reads:

> Whereas due account was taken *when Regulation (EC) No 518/94 was adopted* from the Community's international obligations, particularly those deriving from Article XIX of the General Agreement on Tariffs and Trade (GATT) *(emphasis added).*

Although the Community's international obligations are not referred to explicitly in relation to the adoption of Regulation 3285/94, and considering that Regulation 518/94 was repealed by Regulation 3285/94, the lecture of Recital 3 in conjunction with Recital 6 of the preamble to Regulation 3285/94 makes clear that the EC is prepared to accept its international obligations[768]:

> Whereas the completion of the Uruguay Round has led to the foundation of the World Trade Organization (WTO); whereas Annex 1A to the Agreement establishing the WTO contains inter alia the General Agreement on Tariffs and Trade 1994 (GATT 1994) and an Agreement on Safeguards;
>
> Whereas in the light of these new multilateral rules the common rules for imports should be made clearer and if necessary amended, particularly where the application of safeguard measures is concerned.

The textual review of Regulation 3285/94 (and now Regulation 260/2009) under the *Fediol* doctrine suggests, however, that it lacks a

768 The same applies to Regulation 260/2009 which has repealed Regulation 3285/94, and which states that in its Recital 3 that the Community has concluded the Agreement establishing the WTO and its Annex 1A.

"clear reference". Neither the international obligations nor the provisions of the Agreement on Safeguards have found explicit entry into the provisions of Regulation 3285/94 (now Regulation 260/2009) but are merely mentioned in its Recitals. Regarding VERs, for instance, it is also nowhere stated that WTO Members shall not encourage or support the adoption or maintenance by public and private enterprises of non-governmental measures equivalent to VERs as it is provided for by Article 11:3 Agreement on Safeguards.

Whereas it has thus to be concluded that Regulation 3285/94 (now Regulation 260/2009) is unlikely to satisfy the standard for the "clear reference exception", the above observations are significant for a review under the *Nakajima* doctrine.

1.2.2 Intention to Implement the Agreement on Safeguards?

In *Nakajima*,[769] the Court of Justice accepted that the GATT Anti-Dumping Code could be used as ground for reviewing the legality of an action taken under the EC's basic Anti-Dumping Regulation[770] because the regulation intended to implement the obligations deriving from GATT Article VI and the Anti-Dumping Code.[771] This exception was, according to the ECJ, justified in view of the second and third Recital of the preamble to the basic Anti-Dumping Regulation,[772] which read:

> Whereas *these* rules [the rules of Regulation 3017/79 and not those of the basic Anti-Dumping Regulation] were *adopted in accordance with existing international obligations*, in particular those arising from Article VI of the General Agreement on Tariffs and Trade (hereinafter referred to as "GATT"), from the Agreement on Implementation of Article VI of the GATT (1979 Anti-Dumping Code) [...]; *(emphasis added)*

769 Case 69/89, *Nakajima*, [1991] E.C.R. I-2069.

770 *In casu*, Council Regulation 2176/84/EEC on Protection Against Dumped or Subsidised Imports from Countries not Members of the European Economic Community (OJ 1984 L 201/1) as substituted by Council Regulation 2423/88 (OJ 1988 L 209/1).

771 Case 69/89, *Nakajima*, [1991] E.C.R. I-2069, paragraph 30.

772 *Ibid.*, paragraphs 29 to 32.

> Whereas in applying these rules it is essential, in order to maintain the balance of rights and obligations which these Agreements sought to establish, that the Community take account of their interpretation by the Community's major trading partners, as reflected in legislation or established practice.

The parallel to the textual construction of Regulation 3285/94 (now Regulation 260/2009) becomes apparent if one considers that Regulation 3017/79 was repealed by the basic Anti-Dumping Regulation, just like Regulation 518/94 was repealed by Regulation 3285/94, the "basic Safeguard Regulation". In other words, in both cases it was acknowledged that due account of the Community's international obligations has already been taken when the predecessors to the regulations in question were enacted. Considering that the Court of Justice accepted that the basic Anti-Dumping Regulation was adopted in accordance with the Community's existing international obligations, it is submitted that Regulation 3285/94 (and now Regulation 260/2009) equally satisfies the standard of the "implementation exception" as it is established in *Nakajima*.

This finding is further supported by a number of observations regarding the transposition of the obligations deriving from the Agreement on Safeguards into the EC legal order, in terms of both legal and practical implementation.

The Commission itself considers that Regulation 3285/94 was "*[i]mplementing the WTO Safeguards Agreement*".[773] No different must thus be the case for its successor Regulation 260/2009.

Although Regulation 3285/94 (now Regulation 260/2009) does not provide explicitly for the legal requirement of "unforeseen developments" as it is stated in GATT Article XIX, reference to this Article in Recital 2 of the preamble to Regulation 3285/94 appears to be compelling enough for the EC to accept the continuing application of the "unforeseen developments" clause. This is well illustrated in the following facts:

773 Annex to the 22nd Annual Report from the Commission to the European Parliament on the Community's Anti-dumping, Anti-subsidy and Safeguard Activities (COM(2004) 828 final), entitled "Commission Staff Document" (SEC(2004) 1707), 18.

- The EC has repeatedly argued before panels that both GATT Article XIX and the Agreement on Safeguards are cumulatively applicable.[774]
- The Commission acknowledges that the "unforeseen developments" requirement is the only principle that is not reflected in the relevant Community regulations, but that is has been "*[c]onfirmed as a self-standing condition by WTO jurisprudence*".[775] Accordingly, the Commission considers "unforeseen developments" in its safeguard investigations under Regulation 3285/94.[776] Since Regulation 260/2009 is identical with its predecessor in this respect, the same must apply.

Definitions and legal requirements other than "unforeseen developments" provided for by the Agreement on Safeguards (and GATT Article XIX respectively) are transposed *verbatim* and in their entirety in Regulation 3285/94 (now Regulation 260/2009, respectively). Examples include:

- Article 16(1) in conjunction with Article 10(1)(a) of the Regulation take on the legal requirements for a safeguard measure defined by Article 2:1 Agreement on Safeguards.
- Articles 5(3)(a) and (b) of the Regulation reiterate the definitions of "serious injury" and "threat of serious injury" of Articles 4:1(a) and (b) Agreement on Safeguards.

774 See, for instance, Panel Report on *Argentina – Footwear*, WT/DS121/R, paragraphs 4.149–4.168, and Panel Report on *Korea – Dairy,* WT/DS98/R, paragraphs 4.412–4.446.

775 Annex to the 22nd Annual Report from the Commission to the European Parliament on the Community's Anti-dumping, Anti-subsidy and Safeguard Activities (COM(2004) 828 final), entitled "Commission Staff Document" (SEC(2004) 1707), 10.

776 *Citrus Fruits*, Commission Regulation (EC) No. 658/2004 of 7 April 2004 imposing definitive safeguard measures against imports of certain prepared or preserved citrus fruits (namely mandarins, etc.) (OJ 2004 L 104/67), paragraph 31 *et seq.*; or *Farmed Salmon*, Commission Regulation (EC) No. 206/2005 of 4 February 2005 imposing definitive safeguard measures against imports of farmed salmon (OJ 2005 L 33/8), paragraph 35 *et seq.*

- Article 10(1)(c) of the Regulation includes all of the eight factors of Article 4:2 Agreement on Safeguards for the determination of the effect on the "domestic industry", *i.e.* the producers of like or directly competitive products.

The investigation procedure provided for by Regulation 3285/94 resembles largely[777] the procedure of an anti-dumping investigation, and both regimes require the existence of a "Community interest" in order to impose a measure. Although the "Community interest test" goes beyond WTO obligations,[778] the fact that the Community intended to implement the obligations entered into within the framework of the Agreement on Safeguards does not alter the assessment of Regulation 3285/94 (now Regulation 260/2009) under the "implementation exception".

1.3 Preliminary Conclusion

A review, both textual and conceptual, of Regulation 3285/94, which was adopted shortly after the conclusion of the WTO Agreement and its Annexes, and later codified – in substance – in Regulation 260/2009, under the "implementation principle" and in particular under the *Nakajima* doctrine suggests that the reliance on a provision of the Agreement on Safeguards before a Community court should be admissible. Put differently, the provisions of the Agreement on Safeguards may be used as ground for reviewing the legality of an action taken under Regulation 260/2009 because the Regulation intends to implement the obligations deriving from GATT Article XIX and the Agreement on Safeguards into the EC legal order.

With regard to VERs, Regulation 260/2009 recognises in its Recital 4 that safeguard measures which escape the rules of the Agreement on Safeguards and GATT Article XIX, such as voluntary export

777 Except the time periods that are comparably shorter in a safeguard investigation.

778 Annex to the 22nd Annual Report from the Commission to the European Parliament on the Community's Anti-dumping, Anti-subsidy and Safeguard Activities (COM(2004) 828 final), entitled "Commission Staff Document" (SEC(2004) 1707), 7 *et seq.*

restraints, orderly marketing arrangements and any other similar import or export arrangements, must be eliminated.

Arguably, the recognition of the elimination of VERs extends to all types of arrangements that are considered to be similar, whether they are taken by a single WTO Member or entered into by two or more WTO Members (Article 11:1(b) Agreement on Safeguards), or whether they are of non-governmental nature but encouraged or supported by a WTO Member (Article 11:3 Agreement on Safeguards).

Based on the observations made so far, it may therefore be summarised that possible complainants of VERs, such as private undertakings not participating in the VER or consumers, may – provided that they are "individually and directly concerned" in the sense of Article 263(4) TFEU (*ex* Article 230(4) EC Treaty), or that, alternatively, the national courts of the Community's Member States provide for remedies sufficient to ensure effective legal protection, thereby opening the door for a possible preliminary ruling under Article 267 TFEU (*ex* Article 234 EC Treaty) – successfully challenge the validity of a VER before Community courts by relying on Article 11 Agreement on Safeguards due to an application of the "implementation exception" to Regulation 260/2009.

2 Challenging Practices Inconsistent with the Agreement on Safeguards under the Trade Barriers Regulation (TBR)

Private parties have no direct access to any of the WTO bodies to complain about government practices that infringe the Agreement on Safeguards, such as government-sponsored VERs. Moreover, as has been discussed, possible complainants may face considerable practical and political constraints when bringing an action under the procedure of Articles 263(4) or 267 TFEU (*ex* Articles 230(4) or 234 EC Treaty respectively). This sounds discouraging. Nevertheless, it has to be noted that some improvements have been made in the Community to obtain enforcement of international trade rules for private litigants by means of the so-called Trade Barriers Regulation (TBR).[779]

The TBR is a legal instrument conferring Community enterprises and industries the right to lodge a complaint which obliges the Commission to investigate and evaluate whether there is sufficient evidence for the violation of international trade rules by third countries causing injury or otherwise adverse trade effects. The Council adopted the TBR in order to ensure the exercise of the Community's rights under international trade rules, in particular those established under the auspices of the WTO. This shall be achieved by procedures that lead to international dispute settlement, in particular WTO dispute settlement, whereby it is understood that the EC institutions remain, of course, bound to observe international law in any action they take under the TBR.

Put differently, although the WTO regime creates an institutional forum for international trade matters limited to states (*i.e.* only WTO Members are recognised as subjects of rights and obligations in international trade law), the Community has sought – albeit through its mediation – to consider private parties' interests in the enforcement of trade rules within the WTO despite settlement system by adopting the TBR.

The TBR replaced the so-called New Commercial Policy Instrument[780] under which private individuals, representing at least a major proportion of Community production or of Community consumption of the like product, could lodge a complaint with the Commission if they considered themselves injured or threatened by "illicit commercial practices" with respect to (international) trade in a given product.

779 Council Regulation (EC) No. 3286/94 laying down Community procedures in the field of the common commercial policy in order to ensure the exercise of the Community's rights under international trade rules, in particular those established under the auspices of the World Trade Organization (WTO) (OJ 1994 L 349/71), as amended by Council Regulation (EC) No. 356/95 of 20 February 1995 (OJ 1995 L 41/3) and by Council Regulation (EC) No. 125/2008 of 12 February 2008 (OJ 2008 L40/1).

780 Council Regulation (EEC) No. 2641/84 of 17 September 1984 on the strengthening of the common commercial policy with regard in particular to protection against illicit commercial practices (OJ 1984 L 252/1). An overview on the functioning of the New Commercial Policy Instrument is given by BOURGEOIS/LAURENT, [1985] RTDE 41 *et seq.*

The right to complain was, however, limited by standing requirements[781] as well as the fact that there was no clear-cut right to have measures taken or to have an investigation opened.[782]

While the TBR brought about some substantial changes,[783] it maintained the general structure of the procedures established under the New Commercial Policy Instrument, such as time-limits, decision-making process and the competences for judicial review.

The procedure under the TBR comprises four phases: the admissibility review, the internal investigation, the international dispute settlement procedure, and the review of retaliation.

- In the *admissibility review*, the Commission determines whether a complaint or a referral contains "sufficient evidence" to justify further examination, and whether such examination is "necessary in the interest of the Community". The internal investigation shall be opened within 45 days after the complaint or referral was lodged with the Commission (Articles 5(4) and 6(5) TBR respectively).
- In the *examination procedure*, the Commission's focus lies on the gathering of information from various sources which shall take between five and seven months (internal investigation). At the end of the examination, the Commission is to submit a report of its findings to the Advisory Committee, a body comprising representatives of each Member State, with a representative of the Commission as chairman (Article 8 in conjunction with Article 7(1) TBR). The deliberations of the Commission and the Member States (consultation procedure) are not subject to any time-limit. The silence of the TBR in this respect was interpreted by the Court of First Instance to provide the Commission with certain discretion as regards the date on

781 For a discussion of the difference between the standing of private applicants and Member States under the New Commercial Policy Instrument, see DENTON, (1988) 13 ELRev. 8 *et seq.*

782 For the few cases brought under the New Commercial Policy Instrument by a Community industry, see RYDELSKI/ZONNEKEYN, (1997) 31 JWT 150 *et seq.*, and SUNDBERG/VERMULST, (2001) 35 JWT 993 *et seq.*

783 BEEKMANN, (1995) 19 W. Comp. 63; BRONCKERS/MCNELIS, (2001) 35 JWT 431 *et seq.*

which a decision terminating an examination procedure needs to be adopted. At the same time, it pointed out that the recognition of such discretion does not mean that the Commission may delay the adoption of a decision taken under Article 11(1) TBR "beyond a reasonable time".[784]

- Provided that the Commission resorts to WTO dispute settlement (*international dispute settlement procedure*),[785] the time-limits of the DSU apply. Accordingly, a dispute (including an appeal to the Appellate Body) should generally not last longer than 18 months, and a WTO Member that has found to be in contravention of WTO rules is normally not accorded more than 15 months to comply with such a finding (Article 21:3 DSU).
- In case of a WTO Member's failure to comply with the Appellate Body's decision and to amend its legislation within the prescribed period, the counterparty to the dispute is entitled to take retaliatory measures (Article 22 DSU). Whereas the Commission is not subject to any time-limits for the *review of retaliation* (and hence to submit a proposal to the Council), the Council is required to take a decision, once it has the received the proposal, within 30 working days (Article 13(3) TBR).

As far as decision-making is concerned, the Commission continues to play the most important role from a practical point of view since it can essentially take most procedural decisions independently.[786] Whereas

784 *In casu*, the CFI considered that two months and twenty-four days is not unreasonable, having regard in particular to the obligation imposed on the Commission to undertake internal consultation with its various services on the draft decision, the duty to consult with Member States, and the duty to allow sufficient time for the decision to be translated into all the official languages of the Community; Case T-317/02, *FICF et al. v. Commission*, [2004] E.C.R. II-04325, paragraphs 198 *et seq.*

785 Instead of resorting to dispute settlement, the examination procedure may also result in the conclusion that no action is required which would lead to the termination of the procedure. Alternatively, the procedure may be suspended if a satisfactory solution to the complaint is offered by the country concerned.

786 Decision to initiate TBR proceedings, TBR decision to initiate WTO dispute settlement proceedings, the initiation of WTO proceedings, the request to the

any such decision may be appealed to the Council by a Member State,[787] decisions to open an investigation as well as other administrative actions which contain interpretations of substantive requirements can be challenged by private parties before the Court of First Instance.[788] As aforementioned, the competence to take an actual decision on retaliatory measures lies, however, with the Council alone.

For the purpose of this dissertation, the position of private complainants[789] in these procedures shall be analysed briefly before turning to a discussion of the first – and so far only – case brought before a Community court on the TBR by a private complainant.[790] The case review is decisive for the assessment of whether private parties' interests under the TBR are sufficiently considered in view of the Commission's large margin of discretion in the examination of a complaint.

2.1 The Position of Private Parties under the Trade Barriers Regulation

Under the Trade Barriers Regulation, complaints must be based on violations of "generally accepted rules" and refer to a "right of action" which the Community can derive from international trade rules (Article 2(1) TBR). Despite the direct link to the WTO framework, the wording of Article 2(2) TBR makes clear that it goes beyond the latter by referring to "rules applicable to trade between the Community and third countries". The ambiguity of this definition allows the interpretation to include not only violations of provisions contained in international

WTO for authorisation to retaliate, and the suspension or termination of the investigation; cf. Articles 13 and 14 TBR.

787 The annulation of such Commission decision would require the qualified majority of the Member States; see BRONCKERS/MCNELIS, (2001) 35 JWT 443.

788 Council Decision 93/350/ECSC, EEC, Euratom of 8 June 1993 amending Council Decision 88/591/ECSC, EEC, Euratom establishing a Court of First Instance of the European Communities, OJ 1993 L 144/21.

789 Any Member State may, of course, also ask the Commission to initiate either of the two procedures of Article 1 TBR (under the referral procedure of Article 6 TBR).

790 Case T-317/02, *FICF et al. v. Commission*, [2004] E.C.R. II-04325.

agreements but also practices which negate their intended effect, such as a "non-violation" complaint under GATT Article XXIII:1.

This may lead to a further implementation of the principle of public international law which states that treaty obligations have to be performed in good faith, as explicitly stated in Article 26 of the 1969 Vienna Convention on the Law of Treaties. This principle could also be of particular interest for private parties in order to challenge obstacles to trade on the basis of legal instruments other than the WTO/GATT. The context of the definition seems, however, to exclude the application of non-binding rules and principles (*e.g.* soft law) since it refers exclusively to "agreements". The 1969 Vienna Convention of the Law of Treaties can be seen as such an agreement although it contains rules applicable to the governance of international trade such as the *clausula rebus sic stantibus* (being a principle of law).

According to Article 2(1) TBR, complaints have to target practices of governmental, not private, measures, *i.e.* practices that are "maintained or adopted by a third country". Whereas this clearly excludes a possible complaint about VERs of non-governmental nature, there appears to be sufficient room to attack government-sponsored VERs, *i.e.* VERs of private nature that are encouraged or supported by a WTO Member. Arguably, complaints about government-sponsored VERs must be possible for two reasons: first, Article 11:3 Agreement on Safeguards explicitly outlaws the encouragement or support of non-governmental measures equivalent to VERs and Article 2(1) TBR states that "*[a] right of action exists when international trade rules [...] prohibit a practice outright*"; and second, the TBR clearly allows complaints about "non-violation" practices which can, after all, be directed against "any situation" that nullifies or impairs, directly or indirectly, the attainment of any objective of a WTO agreement (GATT Article XXIII:1(c)).

The right of private parties to lodge a complaint with the Commission is split in two different tracks:

- The first track tackles *trade barriers with an effect on export markets*, and is open for complaints by one or more "Community enterprises", or an association acting on their behalf which has suffered "adverse trade effects" as a result of these obstacles to trade, provided that that the complaint is based on a multilateral or plurilateral agreement (Article 4(1) TBR).[791] Since the definition of "Community enterprise" contained in Article 2(6) TBR is equivalent to the one in Article 54(1) TFEU (*ex* Article 48(1) EC Treaty), this remedy should also be available to subsidiaries of foreign companies.

- The second track is concerned with *trade barriers with an effect on the Community market*, and is open to complaints by a "Community industry" or professional association acting on its behalf which has suffered "material injury" from these obstacles to trade (Article 3(1) TBR). Article 2(5) TBR defines the term "Community industry" which includes, *inter alia*, not only all those *producers* that account for a major proportion of total Community production of identical, similar or directly competing goods and who have been affected by the trade barrier, but also "*consumers [...] of the product [...] which is the subject of an obstacle to trade*" (emphasis added).

The Community enterprise has to demonstrate that it has suffered an "adverse trade effect" in a third country market which is a somewhat lighter version of the "material injury" test that the Community industry is required to prove for a successful complaint. Pursuant to Article 10(1) TBR, the determination of "material injury"[792] may be based on the volume of Community imports or exports concerned, either in absolute terms or relative to production or consumption on the market in question, prices of the Community industry's competitors, trends in certain economic factors, such as production, utilisation of capacity, stocks, sales, market share, profits, return on capital, investment, and employment.[793]

791 As a result, complaints by private companies about obstacles to trade that have an effect on the market of a third country cannot be based on bilateral agreements, and trade barriers maintained by a country which is not a member of the WTO cannot be challenged by private companies; BRONCKERS, (1996) 33 CMLRev. 309.

792 For the examination of threat of injury, see Article 10(2) TBR.

793 The wording of Article 10(1) TBR ("*[...]shall involve* where applicable *the following factors*", (emphasis added) suggests that, unlike Article 4:2 Agreement on Safeguards, *not all* the factors have to be taken into account.

According to Article 2(4) TBR, trade barriers have an "adverse trade effect" if they have a material impact on the economy of the Community or of a region of the Community, or on a sector of economic activity therein.[794] Adverse trade effects may occur, *inter alia*, when trade flows concerning a product are prevented, impeded or diverted as a result of any obstacle to trade, or if trade barriers have materially affected the supply to Community enterprises (Article 10(4) TBR). In addition, Article 2(4) TBR stipulates that the fact that a complainant suffers from such adverse effects is not considered sufficient to justify, on its own, that the Community institutions proceed with any action. In other words, a Community enterprise must, beyond the losses it suffers individually, indicate a broader interest for the EC to pursue the matter which should usually be accomplished by demonstrating that an investigation is in the "Community interests" (as any complainant is required to do under Article 8(1) TBR). Allegedly, it should be sufficient to stress that other industries or market participants might also benefit from the complaint brought by the Community enterprise which is reflected in the language of the Commission:

> The European Community has repeatedly shown its commitment to abide by WTO rules and it expects its trading partners to equally do so: it is of utmost importance for the Community to ensure that WTO partners fully comply with their international obligations.[795]

> The principle of national treatment provided for by Article III of the GATT 1994 is one of the most important and basic WTO obligations. If practices like the Colombian one went unchallenged they would constitute an extremely negative precedent for the respect of WTO provisions.[796]

794 The examination of the impact of such adverse effects on the economy shall be based on the same factors that are used for the "injury" test; Article 10(4) TBR, *ab initio*.

795 Notice of initiation of an examination procedure concerning an obstacle to trade, within the meaning of Council Regulation (EC) No. 3286/94, consisting of trade practices maintained by Argentina in relation to the imports of textile and clothing products, OJ 1999 C 340/70, sec. 6.

796 Notice of initiation of an examination procedure concerning an obstacle to trade, within the meaning of Council Regulation (EC) No. 3286/94, consisting of trade practices maintained by Colombia in relation to the imports of motor vehicles, OJ 2000 C236/4, sec. 6.

> The Commission considers it essential to ensure a level playing field in third-country markets for our export industries, particularly with regard to internal taxes. Tariff protection should not be replaced with other protectionist barriers in breach of international commitments. [...][797]

It becomes apparent from this legal framework that challenging government-sponsored VERs through the TBR may be a valuable alternative to direct actions before the Community courts. This applies to all possible complainants of VERs that have been previously identified. For instance, private undertakings not participating in the VER, as "Community enterprise" may avail themselves of the first track by demonstrating "adverse trade effects". To consumers (or consumer associations) as "Community industry", the second track is open if they have sufficient evidence for supporting that they have suffered "material injury".

Before a complaint about a VER is brought to WTO dispute settlement, other practical constraints may, however, have to be overcome.[798] Since the Commission is in charge of essentially all procedural decisions, it is uncertain to what extent the interest of the Community enterprise or the Community industry will be taken into account. This is strengthened by the fact that the Commission must decide on whether the opening of an investigation is in the interests of the Community.[799]

If the Commission refuses to open an investigation because it disagrees, for example, with the interpretation that the private parties have given to the allegedly violated international trade law, the Community Courts (*in casu* the Court of First Instance) may well review the Commission's interpretation.[800] In trade policy proceedings, the

797 Notice of initiation of an examination procedure concerning obstacles to trade within the meaning of Council Regulation (EC) No. 3286/94, consisting of measures imposed and practices followed by the Eastern Republic of Uruguay affecting trade in Scotch whisky, OJ 2004 C 261/3, sec. 6.

798 And there may be further hurdles in the WTO dispute which will be discussed in Chapter IV.

799 Article 8(1) TBR.

800 There is no reason to assume that the Community courts would not test the Commission's interpretations of WTO rules. The judgments discussed in Chapter II, in which the Court refused to review the legality of Community acts under

Court has, however, previously limited the judicial review of Community interests to the verification of three factors: (i) whether the relevant procedures have been followed, (ii) the facts on which the decision has been based were sufficiently demonstrated, and (iii) whether a manifest error or misuse of powers has taken place.[801] In order to obtain an impression on how efficiently private parties' interests are protected, it will therefore be decisive to evaluate how the Court of First Instance has dealt with these matters in the first (and so far only) case brought before it under the TBR.

2.2 The Court of First Instance Ruling on the Trade Barriers Regulation in FICF et al. v. Commission

In this first – and as of mid-2005 only – case on the TBR, the Court of First Instance confirmed the Commission's decision not to open an examination procedure regarding the retaliatory measures imposed by the United States on a number of products originating in the Community. From the position of private complainants, this ruling has considerable implications for the assessment of how efficiently private parties' interests are protected under the TBR, and ultimately, for the purpose of this dissertation, of how successful the procedure laid down in the TBR is to challenge government-sponsored VERs.

The history of the *FICF* case[802] goes back more than twenty years and concerns the well-known dispute on hormones between the EC and the U.S. Between 1981 and 1996, the adoption by the Council of several directives banning the use of certain substances having a hormonal action in animal foodstuffs led the U.S. to lodge a complaint before the WTO. In January 1998, the Appellate Body declared the respective

WTO rules at the request of private litigants or even a Member State, have no (or little) bearing in this context.

801 Case C-179/87, *Sharp Corporation v. Council*, [1992] E.C.R. I-1635, paragraph 58; Case C-174/87, *Ricoh*, [1992] E.C.R. I-1335, paragraph 68; or Case T-2/95, *Industrie des poudres sphériques v. Council*, [1998] E.C.R. II-3939, paragraph 292.

802 Case T-317/02, *FICF et al. v. Commission*, [2004] E.C.R. II-04325.

Community legislation to be inconsistent with the WTO rules and requested the EC to bring it into conformity with these rules.[803]

In view of the EC's failure to comply with the Appellate Body's decision and to amend its legislation within the prescribed period, the DSB authorised the U.S. to suspend tariff concessions up to USD 116.8 million per year and to impose additional customs duties of 100% on a number of products originating in the EC, including prepared mustard. The U.S. decided, however, not to apply these suspension measures to products coming from the United Kingdom.[804]

In June 2001, the *FICF*, a trade organisation representing the principal French producers of prepared mustard, lodged a complaint with the Commission under Article 4 TBR, requesting the initiation of a procedure regarding the selective nature of the U.S. retaliatory measures to exports of prepared mustard and the adverse trade effects caused by these measures to the members of the *FICF*. The evidence produced by the *FICF* led the Commission to initiate an examination procedure under Article 8 TBR, and to invite other interested parties to make themselves known if they considered that the scope of the examination should also cover other products. Following such indications of interest,[805] the Commission decided to extend the procedure to foie gras, Roquefort and shallots.[806]

Upon completion of its examination, the Commission considered that the procedure was to be terminated without opening an investigation[807] and adopted Decision 2002/604/EC[808] which was subsequently

803 AB Report on *EC – Meat (Hormones)*, WT/DS26/AB/R, WT/DS48/AB/R.

804 Case T-317/02, *FICF et al. v. Commission*, [2004] E.C.R. II-04325, paragraphs 16 and 17.

805 Namely by the *Confédération générale des producteurs de lait de brebis et des industriels de Roquefort, the Comité national interprofessionnel des palmipèdes à foie gras and the Comité économique agricole régional fruits et légumes de la région Bretagne.*

806 Case T-317/02, *FICF et al. v. Commission*, [2004] E.C.R. II-04325, paragraphs 18 *et seq.*

807 *Ibid.*, paragraphs 19 and 30.

808 Decision 2002/604/EC terminating the examination procedures concerning obstacles to trade, within the meaning of Council Regulation No. 3286/94, consisting of trade practices maintained by the United States of America in relation to imports of prepared mustard (OJ 2002 L 195/72).

challenged by the *FICF* (and other interested parties) before the Court of First Instance. *FICF* essentially argued in support of its application for annulment of the decision that the Commission (i) misconstructed the definition of "obstacle to trade" under Article 2(1) of TBR, (ii) wrongly interpreted what constituted an "adverse trade effect" in the sense of Article 2(4) TBR, and (iii) confused the Community interests with those of the private complainants. In terms of procedural arguments, *FICF* mainly maintained that its right to a fair hearing has been violated, and that the Commission has failed to observe the time-limit laid down by Article 8(8) TBR.

2.2.1 Findings on Substantive Matters

a) The Definition of "Obstacle to Trade"

As a preliminary point, the Court of First Instance held that under the TBR, the minimum of three cumulative conditions under which the Community has a right of action pursuant to international trade rules against obstacles to trade created by a third country and having an effect on the market of that country are (i) the existence of an obstacle to trade, (ii) the presence of adverse trade effects which result from that obstacle, and (iii) the need to take action in the interests of the Community.[809]

The CFI then turned to an analysis of the concept of an "obstacle to trade", and found that, for there to be an obstacle to trade which may be relied upon for the purposes of the application of the TBR, there must be a right of action under international trade rules. A different interpretation would mean that any trade practice adopted or maintained by a third country could be considered to be an obstacle to trade, even where no right of action existed under international trade rules,[810] which contravenes the purpose of the TBR.

Whereas *FICF* accepted that the obstacle to trade at issue did not consist in the suspension of the concessions by the U.S. following the

809 This is to say that the Commission is entitled to decide that an action should not be proceeded with if the examination procedure reveals that one of these three conditions is not satisfied; Case T-317/02, *FICF et al. v. Commission*, [2004] E.C.R. II-04325, paragraph 48.

810 *Ibid.*, paragraph 53.

Hormones case, but in the way in which this suspension had been enforced, *i.e.* the selective application of the retaliatory measures, it took the view that there was a breach of WTO rules in that the U.S. could not lawfully choose to apply retaliatory measures to certain members of the EC and not to others as this would fail to reflect the predictability which the dispute settlement system requires.[811] The *FICF* did, however, not put before the CFI whether this view was correct which led the Court to simply note that the initiation of a procedure in relation to the U.S. measures suspending tariff concessions which had been authorised by the WTO would not have been possible, in that, as a matter of principle, no Community right of action under international trade rules existed in relation to those measures.[812]

Only in the context of *FICF's* argument that the Commission failed to state reasons regarding the legal analysis of the obstacle to trade, the CFI saw itself compelled to state that, *in casu*, there was no need for the Commission to assess the legality of the obstacle to trade under WTO law because there was no causality between the obstacle and the adverse trade effects (as will be discussed *infra*).[813] Naturally, in view of the absence of a legal obligation of the Commission to deal with the compatibility of the trade barrier, the standard applied to the requirement of the statement of reasons[814] is accordingly low. Dra-

811 *Ibid.*, paragraph 54. *FICF* maintained that conclusions and recommendations of the Panel and the Appellate Body referred to the EC (and not the individual Member States), and that the U.S. were accordingly obliged to apply their measures to the EC, *i.e.* all Member States since it was also all the Member States that had applied Community measures found to be in contravention of WTO rules.

812 *Ibid.*, paragraphs 55 *et seq.*

813 *Ibid.*, paragraph 133.

814 According to settled case-law, the statement of reasons required by Article 296(2) TFEU (*ex* Article 253(2) EC Treaty) must disclose in a clear and unequivocal fashion the reasoning followed by the Community institution which adopted the measure in question in such a way as to enable the persons concerned to ascertain the reasons for the measure and thus enable them to defend their rights and to enable the Community Court to exercise its power of review. Furthermore, the requirements to be satisfied by the statement of reasons depend on the circumstances of each case, in particular the content of the measure, the nature of the reasons given and the interest which the addressees of the measure, or other parties to whom it is of direct and individual concern, may have in ob-

wing on Article 11(1) TBR, the CFI found that, in this particular context, the statement of reasons in a decision terminating an examination procedure may be restricted to a note of the principal findings set out in the examination report, referring to that report, and that it would be pointless to require a specific statement of reasons for each of the factual and legal elements contained in that report.[815]

b) The Interpretation of "Adverse Trade Effects"

As regards adverse trade effects, *FICF* argued that the narrow view taken by the Commission with respect to the definition of an obstacle to trade led to a wrong analysis of the adverse trade effects, considering that the Commission should have analysed the consequences of both the suspension of the tariff concessions and the imposition of an additional 100% customs duties, instead of only focusing on the consequences of the selective application of these measures.[816]

The CFI did not follow this argument and considered that the definition of "adverse trade effects" contained in Article 2(4) TBR, read in conjunction with the seventh recital in its preamble,[817] shows that the TBR requires a *causal link* between the actual or potential adverse trade effects and the obstacle to trade. Considering that it had previously found the obstacle to trade to be the selective imposition of the retaliatory measures by the U.S., the CFI consequently held that the Commission was only required to take account of the consequences of the selective imposition of the retaliatory measures by the U.S. due to the causality requirement.[818] It further found that the Commission was right to consider that the selective measures did not cause any adverse

taining explanations; Case C-76/00 P, *Petrotub and Republica v. Council*, [2003] E.C.R. I-79, paragraph 81.

815 Case T-317/02, *FICF et al. v. Commission*, [2004] E.C.R. II-04325, paragraph 132 in conjunction with paragraph 129.

816 *Ibid.*, paragraph 59.

817 The seventh Recital of the preamble to the TBR states, *inter alia*, that the mechanism established by the regulation aims to allow Community institutions to react to obstacles to trade adopted or maintained by third countries which *cause* adverse trade effects (emphasis added).

818 Case T-317/02, *FICF et al. v. Commission*, [2004] E.C.R. II-04325, paragraph 65 *et seq.*

trade effect within the meaning of Article 2(4) TBR, inasmuch as the quantitative evidence analysed in the investigation did not support a finding that the imposition of the retaliatory measures to prepared mustard originating in the United Kingdom would have resulted in greater export opportunities to the U.S. market for *FICF*.[819]

In this respect it should further be noted that the CFI interpreted the meaning of Article 10(5) TBR[820] so as not to impose on the Commission a general obligation to assess the compatibility of the obstacle to trade complained of with WTO provisions. The CFI considered it thus admissible for the Commission not to take into account the WTO provisions which govern the right of action, in so far as one of the three cumulative conditions for such action is absent, as was, *in casu*, the causal link between the obstacle and the adverse trade effects.[821] *E contrario*, and not surprising, this finding only places upon the Commission the obligation to assess the legality of the obstacle to trade under rules of the WTO agreements when all three conditions, *i.e.* (i) the existence of an obstacle to trade, (ii) the presence of adverse trade effects which result from that obstacle, and (iii) the need to take action in the interests of the Community, are answered in the affirmative.

c) The Requirement of "Community Interests"

On the assessment of Community interests, *FICF* essentially submitted that the Commission's decision confused the interests of the Community, referred to in Article 11(1) TBR, with the interests of *FICF*,

819 *Ibid.*, paragraphs 71 *et seq.* Statistics demonstrated that the increase in exports of prepared mustard to the U.S. from the United Kingdom during the time of the selective application of the retaliatory measures was extremely small in size and proportion in comparison with exports from other Member States which led the Commission (and the CFI) to conclude that, even if exporters from Member States other than the United Kingdom could have benefited from that increase, it would have been to little to qualify as "greater export opportunities".

820 Article 10(5) TBR reads: "The Commission shall also, in examining evidence of adverse trade effects, have regard to the provisions, principles or practice which govern the right of action under relevant international rules referred to in Article 2(1)" (emphasis added).

821 Case T-317/02, *FICF et al. v. Commission*, [2004] E.C.R. II-04325, paragraphs 81 *et seq.*

and that such an approach contravened that provision.[822] In assessing this allegation, the Court of First Instance first pointed out that the TBR neither provides a definition of the "interests of the Community", nor does it state the rules governing the examination of those interests. Noting, however, that there are a number of provisions of the TBR which refer to the notion of "Community interest", the CFI found that these provisions must all be read in the light of the fifteenth Recital in its preamble which states:

> [I]t is incumbent on the Commission […] to act in respect of obstacles to trade adopted or maintained by third countries, within the framework of the Community's international rights and obligations, only when the interests of the Community call for intervention, and […] when assessing such interests, the Commission […] should give due consideration to the views [of] all interested parties in the proceedings.[823]

In view of the complex economic situations that are involved in the appraisal of the Community interests, the CFI recalled its traditional approach that the judicial review of such an appraisal must be limited to (i) verifying that the relevant procedural rules have been complied with, (ii) that the facts on which the choice is based have been accurately stated, and (iii) that there has not been a manifest error of assessment of those facts or a misuse of powers. In addition, it found, however, that where proceedings are brought before it for the annulment of a Commission decision terminating an examination procedure relating to obstacles to trade for reasons relating to the absence of a Community interest under the TBR, the scope of judicial review includes verifying the absence of errors of law.[824]

The CFI explained this finding by way of analogy to judicial review it has performed regarding the examination of anti-dumping measures,[825] where it had found that with respect to the criteria of the

822 *Ibid.*, paragraph 84.

823 *Ibid.*, paragraphs 89 *et seq.*

824 *Ibid.*, paragraph 94.

825 It has also been suggested in legal literature that, in view of the lack of previous cases under Regulation 3286/94, the standard of legal protection and judicial review developed in anti-dumping matters could be used for the purposes of the Trade Barriers Regulation; NOWAK, (2000) 11 EuZW 456.

"Community interest" the different aspects of economic policy interests and their evaluation need to be disclosed in the Commission's reasoning. On this basis, the Commission then must undertake a transparent balancing of interest by justifying its conclusions as to each of the interests involved. Only on the basis of the documentation of this balancing process, the CFI was willing to restrict its review of the Commission's discretion to the absence of errors of law or of manifest errors in the assessment of fact in economic policy matters in anti-dumping matters.[826]

In the opinion of the CFI it was justified to *a fortiori* apply this restriction of judicial review in the present case because the proceedings under the TBR are of a much wider scope and may, depending on the circumstances, result in an international complaint being brought. In the light of these considerations, the CFI assessed whether the Commission had assimilated the "Community interests" to the individual interest in two distinct phases of the procedure:

- The assessment of the Community interests carried out when the examination procedure is *initiated*, is, by definition, of a preparatory nature. The CFI therefore found that it cannot be compared with the assessment which must be carried out subsequently, that is to say on termination of the examination procedure, when deciding whether action is necessary in the Community interests. In the Court's view, any other interpretation would deprive the Commission of its power of discretion in the examination procedure.[827]
- At the stage of the *examination procedure*, the assessment of the Community interests requires an evaluation of the interests of the various interested parties and of the general interest. This is also supported by the reading of Article 11(1) TBR, interpreted in the light of the fifteenth Recital of its preamble. The CFI therefore considered that the interest of a complainant should first be established before a Community interest may

826 Case T-132/01, *Euroalliages and Others v. Commission*, [2003] E.C.R. II-2359, paragraphs 47 *et seq.*

827 Case T-317/02, *FICF et al. v. Commission*, [2004] E.C.R. II-04325, paragraphs 97 *et seq.*

> itself exist. The mere fact that the Commission's decision did not refer to the interests of certain parties does hence not constitute a breach of Article 11(1) TBR if it can be deduced from the decision that the Commission has taken these interests into account when determining the Community interests.[828]

In addition, the CFI deduced from the wording of Article 12(1) TBR, in order to urge the Commission to take action in defence of the general Community interest, a complainant must have itself suffered from the adverse trade effects to a larger extent than that legitimately foreseen by the retaliatory measures, which was not the case here. The CFI thus concluded that the Commission rightfully terminated the procedure in the absence of a specific Community interest. In this respect, it further explained that the fact that the Commission considered it to be relevant, for the sake of completeness, not to exclude the possibility of a long-term Community interest in taking action in the future if the U.S. were to practice "selective sanctioning" in order to undermine the EC internal cohesion, cannot be used against the Commission in order to show that it infringed Article 11(1) TBR but merely reflected compliance with the principle of sound administration.[829]

2.2.2 Findings on Procedural Matters

a) The Right to a Fair Hearing

From a procedural point of view, *FICF* mainly complained that the Commission had failed to allow it to state its position in relation to the factual and legal matters of the examination report prior to the adoption of the decision.[830] Recalling that the respect of the right to a fair hearing is a recognised fundamental principle of Community law, the Court of First Instance first pointed out that the general scheme of the TBR is directed towards taking an action in the Community interests against a non-Member State, *i.e.* a third country, which has adopted or maintained a trade barrier. Accordingly, the right to a fair hearing may

828 *Ibid.*, paragraphs 104 *et seq.*
829 *Ibid.*, paragraphs 119 *et seq.*
830 *Ibid.*, paragraph 165.

only be relied upon by private parties which are complainants under the TBR under the conditions set out in the regulation, unless those conditions are themselves considered to be contrary to this principle of Community law.[831]

In the light of this consideration, the CFI examined Articles 8(4)(a) and (b) TBR and considered that complainants and the exporters and importers concerned, as well as the representatives of the country or countries concerned are provided with a right to information, subject to the conditions laid down in those provisions, and they could accordingly may ask to be kept informed of the principal facts and considerations resulting from the examination procedure.[832] In this context, the CFI pointed out, however, that no provision of the TBR required the Commission to inform those persons on its own initiative, but that they rather have to request to be informed as it is explicitly stated in Article 8(4) TBR. The Court concluded its observations by noting that the right to be informed of the principal facts and considerations resulting from the examination procedure is not impeded by the fact that it is subject to the (sole) condition that complainants submit such a request to the Commission. Only if the Commission had failed to react, or unduly refused to provide information upon receipt of a request, the right to a fair hearing would have been infringed.[833]

b) The Non-Binding Nature of Time-Limits

FICF noted that, under Article 8(8) of TBR, the Commission is normally to submit the examination report to the Advisory Committee within five months of the notice of initiation of the procedure, unless the complexity of the examination is such that the Commission extends the period to seven months. Whereas *FICF* acknowledged that the examination was complex, it argued, however, that the seven months period cannot be extended. Considering that the examination report was only submitted to the Advisory Committee after almost eight months had elapsed since the initiation of the procedure, it there-

831 *Ibid.*, paragraphs 170 *et seq.*
832 *Ibid.*, paragraphs 172 *et seq.*
833 *Ibid.*, paragraphs 175 *et seq.*

fore alleged that the Commission contravened Article 8(8) TBR.[834] The Court of First Instance had hence to assess whether the Commission's failure to comply with the seven months period can result in the annulment of the decision.

In this respect, the CFI pointed out that, whilst the excess of a mandatory time-limit will result in the nullity of every act adopted after the expiry of the time-limit, the failure to comply with a time-limit that is purely indicative does not, as a matter of principle, mean that an act adopted after its expiry falls to be annulled.[835] As regards the nature of the period referred to in Article 8(8) TBR, the CFI held that the period of five months allowed for the submission of the examination report is indicative which is reflected in the term "normally". In addition, it found that the possibility to extend the "straightforward or normal" examination in the presence of complex circumstances to seven months should not be treated any differently, and that this time-limit is therefore equally of indicative nature.[836]

That point made, the CFI stressed, however, that the Commission ought not to delay the submission of the examination report beyond a period which is reasonable. Without specifying what constituted such a "reasonable period", the Court concluded that the Commission's failure to comply with the indicative time-limit of seven months may not be qualified as unreasonable in view of the fact that it was exceeded by less than one month.[837]

2.3 Preliminary Conclusion

The mechanism provided for by the TBR presents itself as a valuable avenue for private parties, such as undertakings not participating in the VER or consumers, to challenge government-sponsored VERs. Strictly speaking, the TBR is, however, not a remedy provided for in the EC legal order, like a direct action under Article 263(4) TFEU (*ex*

834 *Ibid.*, paragraph 182.
835 *Ibid.*, paragraph 187 (with further annotations).
836 *Ibid.*, paragraphs 188 *et seq.*
837 *Ibid.*, paragraphs 190 *et seq.*

Article 230(4) EC Treaty) or the procedure for a preliminary ruling under Article 267 TFEU (*ex* Article 234 EC Treaty). Instead, it may allow private parties affected by a VER to urge the Commission to bring the case to WTO dispute settlement.

Whereas the TBR undoubtedly improves enforcement of international trade rules for private litigants, there are still considerable hurdles. As regards the (minimum of) three conditions that have to be fulfilled before the Community considers bringing a case to WTO dispute settlement, *i.e.* (i) the existence of an obstacle to trade, (ii) the presence of adverse trade effects which result from that obstacle, and (iii) the need to take action in the interests of the Community, private parties may surely play a decisive role – at least in respect to the first two conditions – by supplying the Commission with unambiguous and convincing evidence. The threat of an unsatisfactory outcome remains, however, in view of the large discretion accorded to the Commission in the determination of Community interests.

Although it is has become apparent from the Court of First Instance ruling in *FICF* that the Commission is required to undertake a transparent balancing of interests by justifying its conclusions as to each of the interests involved when it comes to determine Community interests, the judicial review of the Commission's discretion is clearly limited. Provided that the process of balancing of interests is documented in the above sense, the review is restricted to the absence of errors of law or of manifest errors in the assessment of fact in economic policy matters. In any event it may be noted that, due to a plurality of interests, the difficulty lies in the fact that different interests will in any normal case be opposed to each other, especially in large markets like the Community.[838] In this respect, it will be hard to challenge the Commission's discretion.

838 For instance, whereas consumers may be adversely affected by a VER, the Community producers of the product concerned may benefit from diverted market effects.

3 Applicability of EU Competition Law to VERs

As has been discussed at the outset of this dissertation, a domestic industry's attempt to remove the immediate threat of international competition by negotiating export restraints with foreign firms amounts, strictly speaking, to some sort of market-sharing agreement. Consequently, VERs are likely to restrict competition, as the supplying firms are required to form an export cartel. Possible complainants of VERs, such as private undertakings not participating in the VER or consumers, may therefore consider attacking VERs for infringing competition law as an alternative to a direct action under Article 263(4) TFEU (*ex* Article 230(4) EC Treaty), the procedure for a preliminary ruling under Article 267 TFEU (*ex* Article 234 EC Treaty) on the grounds of a violation of Article 11 Agreement on Safeguards, or the avenue provided for by the Trade Barriers Regulation.

Challenging VERs under competition law may, however, not be as easy as it seems: Most countries (i) do not apply their competition laws to (domestic) export cartels, unless these agreements produce effects on the domestic market, and/or (ii) allow for the "state compulsion defence" under which undertakings are not liable where the State by measures of public authority requires them to engage in anti-competitive behaviour.

Whereas the emphasis in the following discussion will be put on the legality of government-sponsored VERs under EU competition law, it is nevertheless considered to be useful to briefly address VERs of purely private nature.

3.1 The Commission's Approach to Privately Negotiated VERs and Other Restrictions on Trade

As early as 1972 the Commission issued a general warning to private enterprises engaged in trade with Japanese enterprises that arrangements under which imports of Japanese products into the Community are limited may be caught under Article 81 [*ex* Article 85 EEC] EC Treaty (now Article 101 TFEU) and recommended that they be notified to the Commission.[839] Soon after, in 1974, the Commission was called upon to state its view as regards the compatibility of VERs with EC competition law concerning an agreement between French and Japanese ball-bearing manufacturers. In this agreement, the French ball-bearings manufacturers sought to convince their Japanese counterparts to first, increase the prices of the Japanese ball-bearings imported into France; second, maintain a maximum price difference of 5% in the future; and third, establish an effective system for controlling (and reducing) imports of Japanese ball-bearings into France.[840] After defining the relevant market as the "French market in ball-bearings of standard type, excluding other categories of bearing, such as needle bearings, roller bearings or special-type bearings for which there is no substitute because of their technical characteristics",[841] the Commission turned to the examination of the agreement under Article 81 EC Treaty (now Article 101 TFEU).[842] According to the Commission, four types of measures, constituting a VER, could be distinguished, of which each is subject to a different assessment:

- Measures taken in pursuance of trade agreements between the Community and Japan, which are to be considered as acts of external commercial policy and which are, as such, outside the scope of Article 81 EC Treaty (now Article 101 TFEU);[843]

839 Commission communication concerning imports of Japanese products to which the Treaty of Rome is applicable, OJ 1972 C 111/13.

840 Commission Decision 74/634 of 29 November 1974 relating to proceedings under Article 85 of the Treaty establishing the EEC (IV/27.095 – *Franco-Japanese ball-bearings agreement*), OJ 1974 L 343/19, point I.1.

841 *Ibid.*, point I.2(a).

842 Article 101(1) TFEU (*ex* Article 81(1) EC Treaty) prohibits as incompatible with the common market all agreements between undertakings, decisions by associations of undertakings and concerted practices which may affect trade between Member States and which have as their object or effect the prevention, restriction or distortion of competition within the common market.

843 Commission Decision 74/634 of 29 November 1974 relating to proceedings under Article 85 of the Treaty establishing the EEC (IV/27.095 – *Franco-Japanese ball-bearings agreement*), OJ 1974 L 343/19, point II.1(a).

- Measures imposed on Japanese undertakings by the Japanese authorities, which are also outside the scope of Article 81 EC Treaty (now Article 101 TFEU);[844]
- Measures resulting from agreements or concerted practices between undertakings which are merely authorised by the Japanese authorities under Japanese law, whereby such authorisation does not necessarily mean that Article 81 EC Treaty (now Article 101 TFEU) could not apply, since it would in no way alter the fact that the enterprises concerned were free to refrain from entering into an agreement or engaging in concerted practices;[845]
- Measures resulting solely from agreements, concerted practices, or decisions by associations of undertakings entered into or engaged in either unilaterally by Japanese undertakings or in concert with the appropriate European undertakings, which are of private nature and may also come within the provisions of Article 81 EC Treaty (now Article 101 TFEU).[846]

With regard to the facts, the Commission considered that the VER between the French and Japanese ball-bearings manufacturers constituted a bilateral measure of private nature, which has not been the subject of any government intervention from either the French or the Japanese side, and consequently comes under the terms of Article 81 EC Treaty (now Article 101 TFEU). It further specified that for the said provision to apply, it is not essential that such an agreement take the form of a contract in the sense of civil law. According to the Commission, it is sufficient that one of the parties "*voluntarily undertakes to limit its freedom of action with regard to the other*".[847]

Similarly, in a decision concerning *Preserved Mushrooms*, the Commission declared an export limitation agreement between French and Taiwanese producers of canned mushrooms to be contrary to Ar-

844 *Ibid.*, point II.1(b).
845 *Ibid.*, point II.1(c).
846 *Ibid.*, point II.1(d).
847 *Ibid.*, point II.2.

ticle 81 EC Treaty (now Article 101 TFEU).[848] The agreement between the French and Taiwanese producers provided, *inter alia*, for the programming of the production of canned mushrooms and of sales in Germany, so as to enable the parties to fix their selling prices. In addition, the parties agreed to inform each other in advance of sales forecast for the German market and to share the market accordingly.[849]

In its assessment under Article 81 EC Treaty (now Article 101 TFEU), the Commission made clear that the obligation entered into by the French and Taiwanese producers is indeed likely to eliminate all effective competition between the parties once competition in prices is excluded while at the same time each party is obliged to refrain from new deliveries on the relevant market when it has exhausted its annual quota. It also noted that such obligation is likely to deprive purchasers of all freedom of choice or discussion.[850] The object of the agreement being the allocation of outlets within the common market, and in particular Germany, the Commission found that the agreement is likely to affect trade perceptibly between Member States by exerting a direct influence on trade flowing between these States.[851] Most interestingly, however, the Commission was of the opinion that even if the French producers of preserved mushrooms had reason to fear serious market disturbances caused by an unrestrained increase of imports from Taiwan, it was not permissible for them, in order to alleviate this situation, to take the initiative and negotiate export restraints with their Taiwanese counterparts, thereby infringing the Treaty or participating in an infringement thereof.[852]

Following a similar line of reasoning, the Commission also condemned an international cartel agreement between Eastern- and Western-European traders and producers of *Aluminium* which provided for the increase of prices of aluminium exported from Eastern Europe

848 Commission Decision 75/77 of 8 January 1975 relating to a proceeding under Article 85 of the EEC Treaty (IV/27.039 – *Preserved Mushrooms*), OJ 1975 L 29/26, point II.5.

849 *Ibid.*, points I.4.a) and b).

850 *Ibid.*, point II.2.a).

851 *Ibid.*, point II.3.

852 *Ibid.*, point IV.2.

through, *inter alia*, market sharing arrangements.[853] In their defence, the western producers of aluminium contended that the governments of all EC Member States, and those of all western European countries outside the EC, would have introduced measures having the same or more restrictive effects than those resulting form their agreements. In addition, they maintained that governmental measures, such as anti-dumping duties, would have been ineffective to protect the producers of aluminium in Western Europe against low-price aluminium imports from Eastern Europe.

The Commission simply rejected these contentions, and found that enterprises "*[a]re not entitled to make restrictive agreements which damage the interests of competitors and consumers merely because they consider that the existing legislation is not adequate or practical for their own purposes.*" It further stressed that, "*[i]f governments of States, whether within or outside the Community, decide to adopt legislation which requires a certain procedure to be followed and certain criteria to be fulfilled before a public authority will intervene to regulate trade, this decision in no sense justifies what is said to be remedial action, in the form of restrictive agreements, by the industries concerned […].*" Finally, the Commission flatly held that "*[t]he alleged impracticability of* (trade) *legislation is a matter for legislative correction and does not justify the making of restrictive agreements by undertakings*" (emphasis added).[854]

This decision comes as no surprise since, merely four months earlier, the Commission likewise deemed an international cartel agreement between *Zinc* producers concerning the fixing of prices and export restrictions for certain countries to be incompatible with Article 81 EC Treaty (now Article 101 TFEU).[855] One of the arguments used by participants to defend the cartel was that the zinc producers faced difficult market conditions and that their agreement helped to prevent

853 Commission Decision 85/206 of 19 December 1984 relating to a proceeding under Article 85 of the EEC Treaty (IV/26.870 – *Aluminium Imports from Eastern Europe*), OJ 1985 L 92/1.

854 *Ibid.*, point 12.2.

855 Commission Decision 84/405 of 6 August 1984 relating to a proceeding under Article 85 of the EEC Treaty (IV/30.350 – *Zinc Producer Group*), OJ 1984 L 220/27.

dumping by centrally planned economies. The Commission was not impressed by this line of reasoning and made the point that, "*[i]n attempting to cope with difficult market conditions or extreme falls in demand, firms must use only means which are consistent with competition*", and "*[t]he prevention of alleged dumping practices does not justify attempts to regulate [...] markets through private agreements.*"[856]

The interesting detail in the *Zinc* decision is, however, that the zinc producers additionally submitted that government agencies in the Member States were aware of the agreements and that some Member State authorities had expressly approved them. In reply to this argument, the Commission considered bluntly that the fact that Member State authorities had knowledge of, participated in or approved the agreements does not protect the concerned enterprises from the application of EC competition law.[857]

The finding of the Commission that, in regard to Member State authorities, neither their knowledge of, their participation in nor their approval of privately arranged restrictions on trade can remove them from the applicability of competition law is worth revisiting: Whilst the Commission is apparently not ready to accept immunity from the application of EC competition law of anti-competitive and trade restricting agreements due to the toleration or approval of either Member State governments or governments of third countries, as clearly stated in its *Ball-bearings* decision, the Court of Justice, in intra-Community relations, appears to be more sympathetically inclined towards private enterprises when government authorities intervene in private actions in ways that restrict competition.

856 *Ibid.*, point 73.

857 *Ibid.*, point 74. This is, however, without prejudice to the provisions of Article 106 TFEU (*ex* Article 86 EC Treaty) which, *inter alia*, confers upon Member States the right to grant to public or private companies certain special or exclusive rights as long as Member States do not enact or maintain in force any measure that contradicts the Treaties, and in particular the competition rules of the TFEU (Article 106(1) TFEU).

3.2 The Approach of the European Courts Regarding Immunity from Competition Liability due to Government Involvement

In its *Suiker Unie* judgment,[858] the European Court of Justice declared null and void the part of a Commission decision[859] which described the selling and purchasing practices of a number of French, Belgian, German and Italian sugar buyers as conduct agreed between them contrary to Article 101 TFEU (*ex* Article 81 EC Treaty). In essence, the ECJ based the partial annulment on two considerations: First, it regarded that the Italian rules, which were partly designed to implement the common market on the organisation of sugar, left very little opportunity for competition,[860] and that consequently, the arrangement between the industries could not appreciably impede competition.[861] Second, the Court considered that the Italian rules and their manner of implementation[862] had a "determinative effect" on the conduct of the industries concerned, so that it had not been for these regulations, the challenged arrangement would not have taken place or would have assumed a different form.[863] Presumably, what the Court of Justice meant to say, is that it is prepared to recognise an appeal for immunity under Article 101 TFEU (*ex* Article 81 EC Treaty) provided that the enterprises concerned can prove that if a government had not intervened, their conduct would have been different.[864]

858 Joined cases 40–48, 50, 54–56, 111, 113 and 114/73, *Suiker Unie et al.*, [1975] E.C.R. 1663.

859 Commission Decision 72/1600 of 2 January 1973 relating to proceedings under Articles 85 and 86 of the EEC Treaty (IV/26.918 – *European Sugar Industry*), OJ 1973 L 140/17.

860 *Ibid.*, paragraphs 67–69.

861 *Ibid.*, paragraph 72.

862 In this respect, the ECJ particularly noted (*ibid.*, paragraph 54) that "[t]he Italian government never concealed the fact that it always 'wanted and requested' Italian producers 'to take part in and proceed […] to import the requisite quantities of sugar to make good the amount by which national production falls short of demand' and to do so 'in a rationalised way' that is to say by *concerted action* […]" (emphasis added).

863 *Ibid.*, paragraph 65.

864 In the United States, enterprises may avail themselves with the defence of "foreign sovereign compulsion". This limited immunity from antitrust enforcement

After the Commission had condemned *Fedetab*, a trade association containing almost all Belgian and Luxembourg tobacco manufacturers, for various violations of Article 101 TFEU (*ex* Article 81 EC Treaty),[865] *Fedetab* brought an action for annulment, *inter alia*, on the ground that the Belgian rules and their application had as their effect to exclude the opportunity for Belgian tobacco manufacturers and importers to compete significantly in relation to the margins allowed to the trade or to cast serious doubt on the existence of such opportunity. With respect to this defence, the Court of Justice considered that, in both cases, it would be led to find that the contested Commission decision did not correctly or insufficiently take account of the effect of the Belgian rules and their application by the Belgian authorities on the opportunities for competition by those industries.[866] Acknowledging that in the manufactured tobacco sector certain Belgian rules, such as price controls, and their application pursuant to the revenue policy of the state have the effect of making it practically impossible for manufacturers and importers to compete in such a way that there would be an effect upon the amount of the retail selling price, the Court nevertheless concluded that the Belgian government's involvement was insufficient to immunise the conduct of *Fedetab* with respect to wholesale margins from antitrust liability.[867]

actions must, according to the DoJ and the FTC, satisfy certain criteria: First, the foreign government must have compelled the anti-competitive conduct in circumstances in which a refusal to comply with the foreign government's command would give rise to the imposition of penal or other severe sanctions. Second, the defence normally applies only when the foreign government compels conduct which can be accomplished entirely within its own territory cf. *Antitrust Enforcement Guidelines for International Operations*, issued by the U.S. Department of Justice (DoJ) and the Federal Trade Commission (FTC), April 1995, sec. 3.32 (available at: http://www.usdoj.gov/atr/public/guidelines/guidelin.htm).

865 Commission Decision 78/670 of 20 July 1978 relating to a proceeding under Article 85 of the EEC Treaty (IV/28.852 – *GB-Inno-BM v. Fedetab*; IV/29.127 – *Mestdagh-Huyghebaert v. Fedetab* and IV/29.149 – *Fedetab Recommendation*), OJ 1978 L 224/29.

866 Joined cases 209–215 and 218/78, *van Landewyck et al. v. Commission (Fedetab)*, [1980] E.C.R. 3125, paragraph 126.

867 *Ibid.*, paragraphs 130–132.

In a subsequent judgment, again concerning the tobacco industry, the ECJ appears, however, to have slightly altered its approach. In the *SSI* case,[868] tobacco industries – participating in price arrangements which were found to be contrary to Article 101 TFEU (*ex* Article 81 EC Treaty) by the Commission[869] – argued extensively that the Dutch government had played a decisive role in bringing about these arrangements.[870] In contrast to the approach taken in *Suiker Unie* and *Fedetab*, the Court of Justice simply refrained from considering to what extent pressure or encouragement on the part of the Dutch authorities may have the effect of removing agreements entered into by undertakings from the ambit of Article 101 TFEU (*ex* Article 81 EC Treaty). It dismissed the defence of *SSI* for lack of factual proof that the Dutch authorities, admittedly in discussing the objectives they wished to see achieved, had indicated that those objectives were to be attained by arrangements restrictive of competition.[871]

The summary fashion in which the Court of Justice reviewed and dismissed the defence of the tobacco industries is not altogether satisfying. Whilst it may be welcomed that the Court does not accept *every* excuse based on government inducement or involvement for engaging in anti-competitive practices, it is hard to see what standards of evidence must be submitted in order to qualify for immunity. It may also be argued that the Court, and to an even greater extent, the Commission ignore certain realities: in practice, governments seek to influence industries in their market behaviour and, certain industries will find it difficult to resist such informal pressures. Moreover, in situations of market disruptions, authorities may encourage industries to conclude arrangements with their foreign counterparts rather than address the matter with the foreign or, in the case of a Member State, with the EC authorities over commercial policy.

In this context, it has to be retained, however, that a measure introduced by a Member State, which contributes towards export restrai-

868 Joined cases 240–242, 261, 262, 268 and 269/82, *SSI*, [1985] E.C.R. 3831.

869 Commission Decision 82/506 of 15 July 1982 relating to a proceeding under Article 85 of the EEC Treaty (IV/29.525 and IV/30.000–*SSI*), OJ 1982 L 232/1.

870 Joined cases 240–242, 261, 262, 268 and 269/82, *SSI*, [1985] E.C.R. 3831, paragraph 38.

871 *Ibid.*, paragraph 40.

ning arrangements between national and foreign undertakings, could itself prove contrary to EC competition law. Drawing upon its *Inno/Atab* judgment,[872] the Court of Justice has consistently ruled that whilst it is true that the competition rules of the EC Treaty are concerned with the conduct of undertakings and not with national legislation or regulation, Member States were none the less obliged under Article 10(2) EC Treaty[873] not to detract, by means of such national rules, from the full and uniform application of competition law or from the effectiveness of its implementing measures. Moreover, the Treaty imposes on Member States the duty not to adopt or maintain in force measures, even of legislative nature, which may render ineffective the competition rules applicable to undertakings.[874] In other words, Member States are not to compromise the "effet utile" of the EC competition rules.[875] The Court of Justice's assessment peaked when it held that "*[s]uch would be the case, in particular, if a Member State were* to require or favour *the adoption of agreements, decisions or concerted practices contrary to Article 81* or to reinforce the effects thereof" (emphasis added).[876]

Despite the Court's finding in the *Suiker Unie* case, it is clear from the *SSI* judgment that non-binding action such as mere persuasion or encouragement by a (Member State) government to enter into

872 Case 13/77, *Inno/Atab*, [1977] E.C.R. 2115. It is, however, not entirely clear whether the Court referred to Article 106 TFEU (*ex* Article 86 EC Treaty, *i.e.* Article 90 EEC Treaty), or the more general obligations deriving from Article 10 EC Treaty (cf. paragraphs 30–33).

873 Article 10(2) EC Treaty provided that Member States shall abstain from any measure which could jeopardise the attainment of the objectives of the Treaty, and, Article 3(1)(g) included into the activities of the Community 'a system ensuring that competition in the internal market is not distorted'. Article 10(2) EC Treaty is replaced, in substance, by Article 4(3) *in fine* TEU. Article 3(1)(g) EC Treaty has been repealed by the Treaty of Lisbon.

874 For instance, Case 229/83, *Au Blé Vert*, [1985] E.C.R. 1, paragraph 14, or, Joined cases 209–213/84, *Nouvelles Frontières*, [1986] E.C.R. 1425, paragraph 71.

875 Various contributions have been made regarding the application of EC competition law to national regulations governing the economic activity of enterprises; see, among many, GYSELEN, (1989) 26 CMLRev. 33 *et seq.*; WAELBROECK, 781 *et seq.*

876 *Nouvelles Frontières*, [1986] E.C.R. 1425, paragraph 72. Confirmed, for instance, in Case 311/85, *Vlaamse Reisbureaus*, [1987] E.C.R. 3801, paragraph 10, and Case 66/86, *Ahmed Saeed*, [1989] E.C.R. 803, paragraph 48.

anti-competitive agreements is no defence under the EC competition rules. Moreover, the Court of Justice, for instance, in *BNIC v. Clair* went even further and stated that the recommendation of minimum prices for cognac by a private trade association infringes Article 101 TFEU (*ex* Article 81 EC Treaty), although the trade association was set up by ministerial order and the minimum prices were approved by the French authorities. The Court also agreed with the Commission that the adoption of a measure by a public authority making an agreement binding on all traders on the market, even if they are not parties to that agreement, cannot remove the agreement from the scope of Article 101 TFEU (*ex* Article 81 EC Treaty).[877] Following a similar line of reasoning, the Court considered in *Ahmed Saeed* that the German government, by approving tariff agreements for certain scheduled flights contrary to Article 101 TFEU (*ex* Article 81 EC Treaty) and by requiring travel agents to abide by these approved fares, is in breach of Article 10 EC Treaty.[878]

With respect to state measures that reinforce the effects of anti-competitive agreements, the Court of Justice ruled in *BNIC v. Aubert*[879] that a French ministerial order imposing, *inter alia*, a production quota of *eaux de vie*, thereby making it binding upon all the traders, is itself subject to Articles 3(1)(g), 10 and 81 EC Treaty since such order reinforces the effects of agreements which are contrary to Article 81 EC Treaty (now Article 101 TFEU). Hence, the ministerial order was not of such nature as to be relied upon to prosecute a trader who exceeded the quota fixed by the agreement.[880] Similarly, in *Vlaamse Reisbureaus*[881] agreements among travel agents and between travel agents and tour operators to observe the prices set by the tour operators were considered to violate Article 81 EC Treaty (now

877 Case 123/83, *BNIC v. Clair*, [1985] E.C.R. 391, paragraphs 21–23.

878 Case 66/86, *Ahmed Saeed*, [1989] E.C.R. 803, paragraph 49. The Court also stressed that it followed from Article 10 that the aeronautical authorities must refrain from taking any measure which might be construed as encouraging airlines to conclude tariff agreements contrary to the Treaty.

879 Case 136/86, *BNIC v. Aubert*, [1987] E.C.R. 4789.

880 *Ibid.*, paragraphs 22–24.

881 Case 311/85, *Vlaamse Reisbureaus*, [1987] E.C.R. 3801.

Article 101 TFEU).[882] According to the Court, such assessment is not altered by the fact that this professional conduct was given legal effect by a Belgian decree which required the travel agents to observe the prices and tariffs set by the tour operators and thus prohibiting them to share the commission with their clients or to grant rebates. Quite the opposite, the royal decree was judged to be incompatible with the obligations of the Member States pursuant to Article 10, read in conjunctions with Articles 3(1)(g) and 81 EC Treaty since the object or effect of the Belgian legislation was to reinforce the effects of agreements contrary to Article 81 EC Treaty (now Article 101 TFEU).[883] The conclusion reached in *Vlaamse Reisbureaus* is less controversial in that the Belgian government had not encouraged and supervised the restrictive agreement, as was the case for the French government in *BNIC v. Aubert*, but merely reinforced the agreement that had been freely concluded.

The Court of Justice was not only concerned with national rules that require or favour agreements contrary to EC competition law or that reinforce the effects thereof. In *Au Blé Vert*,[884] the question arose as to whether national legislation rendering corporate behaviour prohibited by Article 101(1) TFEU (*ex* Article 81(1) EC Treaty) superfluous deprives the competition rules from their effectiveness and is therefore contrary to Article 10(2) EC Treaty (now Article 4(3) *in fine* TEU).[885] The case concerned the French *Loi Lang* which required all importers or publishers of books to fix minimum retail prices, and prohibited, as criminal offence, retail sales of books at a discount exceeding 5%. *Leclerc*, the operator of a supermarket chain, sold various books below the permitted level and was therefore sued by several competing booksellers. The French Court of Appeal concerned with this dispute stayed proceedings and referred to the ECJ for preliminary ruling whether the *Loi Lang* infringed EC competition law in light of Articles 3(1)(g) and 10 EC Treaty.[886] After reiterating the principle

882 *Ibid.*, paragraph 17.

883 *Ibid.*, paragraph 24.

884 Case 229/83, *Au Blé Vert*, [1985] E.C.R. 1.

885 *Ibid.*, paragraph 15.

886 For a discussion of the *Au Blé Vert* judgment and more generally book price fixing see, for example, CANDELA SORIANO, [1999] RMUE 373 *et seq.*

first established in *Inno/Atab*, and introducing the issue of national legislation which makes collusion unnecessary, the Court concluded, however, that, under the Community law as it stood, the obligations of Member States deriving from Articles 3(1)(g), 10 and 81 EC Treaty are not specific enough to preclude them from enacting legislation of the type at issue, *i.e.* a purely national system on book trade, provided that such legislation is consonant with other Treaty provisions, such as those on the free movement of goods.[887] Interestingly enough, whilst the argument that the government enabled traders to fix the prices at which others were allowed to trade was not accepted in *Vlaamse Reisbureaus*, resale price maintenance in the trade of books, as sponsored by the French *Loi Lang*, evaded this argument. In light of the reoccurring disputes over the past two decades on book price fixing by publishers in (and among) various Member States,[888] the judgment in *Au*

887 Case 229/83, *Au Blé Vert*, [1985] E.C.R. 1, paragraph 20. The legality of the *Loi Lang* has most recently been confirmed in Case C-9/99, *Echirolles Distribution SA v. Association du Dauphiné et al.*, [2000] E.C.R. I-8207, paragraph 26.

888 See, for instance, Joined cases 43 and 63/82, *VBBB–VBVB*, [1984] E.C.R. 19. The ongoing dispute concerning (trans-)national book price fixing is also reflected in the partly diverging positions of the EC institutions: Compare, on the one hand, the Resolution of the European Parliament on common book price-fixing across borders (OJ 1998 C 379/391) in which it calls for binding rules to be laid down which will enable not only national systems of fixed book prices *but also bilateral agreements* on fixed book prices within single linguistic areas to be declared legal and not in breach of the rules on competition (point 6, emphasis added). On the other hand, Council Resolution of 8 February 1999 on fixed book prices in homogeneous cross-border linguistic areas (OJ 1999 C 42/3) which calls on the Commission, whilst applying EC competition rules to agreements in cross-border linguistic areas, to take account of the provisions and implications of Article 151(4) EC Treaty (now Article 167(4) TFEU), of the special cultural role of the book market and of the specific value of the book as a cultural object, as well as of relevant national cultural policies. The Commission, like the ECJ, considers purely national book price fixing systems as compatible with the EC competition rules as long as the resale price maintenance does not apply to trans-national direct sales and parallel import is not undermined. Under these conditions, national book price fixing is considered not to appreciably affect trade between Member States (see, for example, Notice pursuant to Article 19(3) of Council Regulation No. 17 concerning an application for negative clearance or exemption under Article 81(3) of the EC Treaty (COMP/34.657 – *Sammelrevers* and COMP/35.245 to 35.251 – *Einzelreverse*), OJ 2000 C 162/25,

Blé Vert may well mantle a political compromise[889] by giving a rather vague indication what was considered to compromise the "effet utile" of the EC competition rules.

In *Van Eycke*,[890] the Court of Justice was once more asked to examine the legality of a Belgian state measure in a preliminary ruling under Article 267 TFEU (*ex* Article 234 EC Treaty). The case concerned a royal decree which provided that the holder of a savings deposit was only entitled for tax relief on the income if interest rates did not exceed 7%. *Van Eycke*, the complainant, alleged that the decree was merely a continuation, in legislative form, of the previously existing agreements or concerted practices among Belgian banks. In its assessment, the ECJ expanded its previous stance and added that the "effet utile" of the prohibition contained in Article 101(1) TFEU (*ex* Article 81(1) EC Treaty) also risks to be eliminated if a Member State were "*[...] to deprive its own legislation of its official character by delegating to private traders responsibility for taking decisions affecting the economic sphere.*"[891]

Noting that there were agreements between Belgian banks or concerted practices designed to restrict the yield on savings deposits prior to the adoption of the royal decree, it nevertheless considered that in light of the submissions before it the decree neither intended to require

paragraphs 11–14). For critical remarks, see MONTI, (2002) 39 CMLRev. 1084 *et seq.*

889 In this context, it is important to note that the various book price fixing systems were usually operated and agreed by private enterprises. Until recently, France was the only Member State in which the resale price maintenance of books was incorporated in national legislation. Subsequent to the abolition of the transnational book price fixing between, *inter alia*, the German and Austrian booksellers, as effective from 30 June 2000, the German government has, however, amended the German competition law (Gesetz gegen Wettbewerbsbeschränkungen, GWB) so as to exempt national book price fixing from the applicability of the competition rules (§ 15(1) GWB).

890 Case 267/86, *Van Eycke*, [1988] E.C.R. 4769.

891 *Ibid.*, paragraph 16. In this context, it was also pointed out that the requirement for Member States not to introduce or maintain in force measures, even of a legislative nature, which may render ineffective the competition rules applicable to undertakings under Article 81 EC Treaty derives from Article 10 EC Treaty (HINTON, (1999) 31 JILP 338).

or favour the adoption of new restrictive agreements nor the implementation of new practices. The Court continued that it is therefore necessary merely to ascertain, first, whether the decree may be regarded as intended to reinforce the effects of pre-existing agreements and, second, whether there are circumstances capable of depriving the decree of its official character.[892] Whilst pointing out that the decree may be qualified as intended to reinforce the effects of pre-existing agreements, decisions or concerted practices "*[...] only if it incorporates either wholly or in part the terms of agreements concluded between undertakings and requires or encourages compliance on the part of those undertakings*", the ECJ referred the enquiry into this point back to the national court. Considering the circumstances which could deprive the decree from its official character, the Court simply stressed that the Belgian authorities reserved to themselves the power to fix the maximum rates of interest on savings deposits and did not delegate that responsibility to any private trader. It thus concluded that the decree had an official character which cannot be called in question by the mere fact, as emphasised by *Van Eycke*, that according to the preamble to the decree its adoption followed consultations with the representatives of associations of credit establishments.[893]

With regard to the hypothesis whether the decree reinforced the effects of agreements contrary to Article 101 TFEU (*ex* Article 81 EC Treaty), it is regretful that the Court's judgment in *Van Eycke* was less clear-cut than in *Vlaamse Reisbureaus*. In addition, in a series of subsequent cases the Court of Justice failed to establish a test for the third hypothesis introduced in *Van Eycke*, *i.e.* that a Member State is in breach of its obligations under the EC Treaty in cases where it deprived its own legislation of its official character by delegating to private traders responsibility for taking decisions affecting the economic sphere.[894]

892 Case 267/86, *Van Eycke*, [1988] E.C.R. 4769, paragraph 17.

893 *Ibid.*, paragraphs 18 and 19. For a critical appraisal of the *Van Eycke* judgment see, for example, HOFFMANN, (1990) 11 ECLR 11 *et seq.*

894 For a critical review of the "delegation test" and how it may be filled with substance in the light of the ECJ's subsequent case-law, see SCHEPEL, (2002) 39 CMLRev. 31 *et seq.*

In two distinct references for a preliminary ruling, *Meng* and *Ohra*,[895] both concerning the insurance sector, the Court considered that national measures making it unnecessary for undertakings in that sector to agree, such as a national prohibition on an insurance company to share the commission with its customers,[896] do not infringe Article 10(2), read in conjunction with Articles 3(1)(g) and 81 EC Treaty. In both cases, the ECJ started with observing that the national rules neither require nor favour the conclusion of any unlawful agreement, decision or concerted practice by insurance agencies, since the prohibition they lay down is "self-contained".[897] Then turning to the determination whether the national rules have the effect of reinforcing an anti-competitive agreement, it simply held that it was common ground that these rules were not preceded by an agreement in the sectors to which they relate.[898] Finally, without further discussion, the Court concluded that the national rules themselves prohibit the grant of financial advantages to policyholders and do not delegate to private traders responsibility for taking decisions affecting the economic sphere.[899]

895 Case C-2/91, *Meng*, [1993] E.C.R. I-5751, and Case C-245/91, *Ohra*, [1993] E.C.R. I-5851.

896 In *Meng*, the Court had to consider the prohibition of transferring the commission as regards health insurance, indemnity insurance and legal expenses insurance under German law ([1993] E.C.R. I-5751, paragraphs 4 and 5). In *Ohra*, it was concerned with insurance companies operating in the Netherlands which are prohibited from granting rebates or other financially quantifiable advantages under the Dutch law on insurance agencies ([1993] E.C.R. I-5851, paragraph 4).

897 *Meng* (*ibid.*, paragraph 15), and in the parlance of *Ohra* "self-sufficient" (*ibid.*, paragraph 11).

898 *Meng* (*ibid.*, paragraphs 16 and 17), and *Ohra* (*ibid.*, paragraph 12). In the case of *Meng*, however, the Court provided an indication of its reasoning when it dismissed the Commission's argument that an agreement among agencies in the *life assurance* sector contained a similar prohibition and that, by rendering that agreement applicable to other insurance sectors, the German rules reinforced its scope. The ECJ found that, in order to reinforce the effects of such agreement, it should have existed previously in the *health insurance*, *indemnity insurance* and *legal expenses insurance* sector, and reproduce the elements of such agreement in whole or in part (emphasis added, cf. paragraphs 18 and 19).

899 *Meng* (*ibid.*, paragraph 20), and *Ohra* (*ibid.*, paragraph 13).

The omission of the Court of Justice to articulate its line of reasoning has clearly contributed to a further watering down of the third hypothesis established in *Van Eycke*. Instead of providing a clear test what constitutes a delegation of responsibility to private traders affecting their (and their trading partners') economic activities, the Court appears simply not prepared to touch upon Member State power. Whilst it has to be acknowledged that cutting back state power is a politically sensitive issue, the Court's approach is nevertheless hard to understand since a privately arranged horizontal agreement among insurance agencies, containing a similar prohibition as those at issue in *Meng* and *Ohra*, would most certainly be considered as restricting competition and affecting trade between Member States.

A similar criticism applies to yet another set of preliminary rulings rendered by the Court of Justice which all related to the mandatory approval of tariffs in certain sectors after consultation with representatives of these industries. Such tariffs had been fixed by virtue of national rules, for example, for road haulage in Germany[900] and in Italy[901], and for inland waterways in Germany.[902] The commonality of the two German cases, which shall serve here as illustration, is first, that the boards entrusted with the fixing of tariffs were composed by representatives of the industries;[903] second, that, once appointed, these members of the tariff boards were to discharge their duties in an hon-

900 Case C-185/91, *Reiff*, [1993] E.C.R. I-5801.

901 Case C-96/94, *Spediporto v. SMG*, [1995] E.C.R. I-2883. In this case, the Court entirely relied on its line of reasoning established in *Reiff* (*supra*) and *Germany v. Delta* (*infra*), and is therefore not discussed in detail.

902 Case C-153/93, *Germany v. Delta*, [1994] E.C.R. I-2517.

903 In *Reiff*, the Court examined the German law on the carriage of goods by road which provided that the tariff boards was to consist of "experts" in the long-distance haulage industry, chosen by the Federal Minister of Transport from a number of persons suggested to him by the undertakings or associations in the sector ([1993] E.C.R. I-5801, paragraph 4). The German law on inland waterways traffic, which was at issue in *Germany v. Delta*, laid down that the freight commissions, which were responsible for setting the tariffs, were to be made up of two numerically equal groups of representatives of shipping and shippers appointed by the supervisory authority acting on a proposal from the professional associations concerned ([1994] E.C.R. I-2517, paragraph 4).

orary capacity and were not to be bound by orders or instructions;[904] and finally, that the tariffs suggested by the boards required approval by the Minister of Transport or if it was in the public interest, were fixed by the Minister himself.[905]

In its assessment of the German rules in *Reiff*, the Court recalled the finding in *BNIC v. Clair*[906] that the fact that a public authority appoints as members of a body responsible for fixing prices persons proposed by trade organisations which are directly concerned does not exclude the existence of an agreement, decision or concerted practice within the meaning of Article 101 TFEU (*ex* Article 81 EC Treaty) if those persons have negotiated and concluded an agreement on prices as representatives of the organisations which proposed them. In a disappointingly cursory fashion, the Court concluded, however, that the mandatory approval of tariffs as laid down by the German law on the carriage of goods by road was not as such as to violate Articles 3(1)(g), 10(2) and 81 EC Treaty. In essence, it based its conclusion on two considerations: first, the members of the tariff boards, albeit chosen by the public authorities on a proposal from the relevant trade sectors, were considered *independent* experts called on to fix the tariffs on the basis of public interest considerations; and second, the public authorities were not found to have abandoned their prerogatives since the national rules reserved the right to substitute the decision of the boards, if considered necessary in the public interest.[907] Drawing upon its findings in *Reiff*, the Court of Justice came to the same conclusion as in *Germany v. Delta*.[908]

904 *Reiff* (*ibid.*, paragraph 4), and *Germany v. Delta* (*ibid.*, paragraph 6).

905 *Reiff* (In the case of tariffs for road haulage, the Minister of Transport is required to act in agreement with the Minister of Economic Affairs; *ibid.*, paragraph 6), and *Germany v. Delta* (*ibid.*, paragraph 7). In both cases, the approved tariffs are issued by the Minister in the form of orders and are binding on all undertakings.

906 Case 123/83, *BNIC v. Clair*, [1985] E.C.R. 391, paragraph 19.

907 Case C-185/91, *Reiff*, [1993] E.C.R. I-5801, paragraph 24.

908 Case C-153/93, *Germany v. Delta*, [1994] E.C.R. I-2517, paragraph 23. One of the differences between the two cases, as pointed out by the Court, was that the members of the freight commission were not to be regarded as "experts". This circumstance did, however, not alter the Court's assessment since the decisive criterion was their "independence" (paragraph 16).

With regard to these judgments, some concern must be felt at the risk that the interests of members of the industry may in practice predominate, so that the outcome may be remarkably similar to a price cartel for that industry. This concern appears justified notwithstanding the theoretical safeguards in the process leading up to the mandatory fixing of tariffs, namely the requirement that the appointed members are to be free of instructions emanating from the trade sectors they are coming from and the fact that the national authority did not entirely relinquish their right to substitute the suggested tariffs by the boards.

An important distinction was, however, drawn by the Court of First Instance in *Asia Motor France II*[909]: A number of French undertakings marketing vehicles of Japanese makes in France lodged a complaint with the Commission alleging that Article 101 TFEU (*ex* Article 81 EC Treaty) had been infringed. They claimed to be victims of an unlawful cartel between five importers of Japanese cars into France since those five importers had engaged with the French administration not to sell on the French domestic market any cars exceeding 3% of the motor vehicles registered in France during the preceding calendar year. In return for this voluntary limitation, it was argued *inter alia*, that the French administration had established a number of obstacles impeding the free movement of Japanese vehicles of makes other than those distributed by the five importers, such as a registration procedure differing from the normal system for parallel imports.

In the course of its investigation, the Commission addressed a request for information to the French authorities which replied by stating, in essence, that "*[...] the questions concerning the conduct of the undertakings (the five importers) are [...] irrelevant in this context in so far as that conduct is connected with regulatory rules laid down by the public authorities: those undertakings have no autonomy in operating the regulatory system.*"[910] Largely based upon this response, the Commission rejected the complaints arguing, *inter alia*, that the conduct of the five importers in question constituted an integral part of the import policy followed by the French public authorities with regard to

909 Case T-7/92, *Asia Motor France II*, [1993] E.C.R. II-669.
910 *Ibid.*, paragraph 6.

imports of Japanese cars into France. It considered that in the framework of such national import policy, it is on the French public authorities not only to set the total quantities of vehicles allowed into France each year, but also to determine the rules for the allocation of those quantities, thus leaving the five importers in question with "no freedom of action" in this respect.[911]

The complainants subsequently brought an action for annulment against the Commission's decision arguing, in particular, that the Commission did not carry out the measures of inquiry necessary but confined itself to the statements of the French authorities. This was considered the more inaccurate since the regulatory system introduced by the French authorities was not based on any binding legislation or regulation, but appeared to be merely an administrative practice.

At the outset, the Court of First Instance recalled the Community courts' consistent case-law that the Commission is not obliged to adopt a position on all the arguments relied on by the parties concerned, but that it is sufficient to set out the facts and legal considerations having decisive importance in the context of a decision.[912] In addition, it pointed out that the judicial review of Commission measures involving an appraisal of complex economic matters must be limited to verifying, *inter alia*, whether the facts have been accurately stated and whether there has been any manifest error of appraisal or a misuse of powers.[913] Where the Commission has a power of appraisal, the rights guaranteed by the Community legal order in administrative procedures include, in particular, the duty of the competent institution to examine carefully and impartially all the relevant aspects of a case, the right of the person concerned to make his views known and to have an adequately reasoned decision.[914]

911 *Ibid.*, paragraph 13.

912 Case T-44/90, *La Cinq v. Commission*, [1992] E.C.R. II-1, paragraph 41 (with further references); *Asia Motor France II*, [1993] E.C.R. II-669, paragraph 31.

913 Joined Cases 142/84 and 156/84, *BAT and Reynolds*, [1987] E.C.R. 4487; Case C-225/91, *Matra v. Commission*, [1993] E.C.R. I-3203, paragraphs 23 and 25; *Asia Motor France II*, [1993] E.C.R. II-669, paragraph 33.

914 Case C-269/90, *Technische Universität München v. Hauptzollamt München-Mitte,* [1991] E.C.R. I-5469, paragraph 14; *Asia Motor France II*, [1993] E.C.R. II-669, paragraph 34.

The CFI then found the documentary evidence to be sufficiently clear to set aside the French authorities' argument that the traders in question had no autonomy or "freedom of action", and that the Commission consequently erred in finding Article 101 TFEU (*ex* Article 81 EC Treaty) not to be applicable.[915]

The *Asia Motor France* case reveals that the Commission is prepared to accept the approach taken by the ECJ in the *Suiker Unie* case where it considered that the rules of a Member State and their manner of implementation were determinative for the conduct of the undertakings concerned, recognising an appeal for immunity under Article 101 TFEU (*ex* Article 81 EC Treaty) provided that the undertakings concerned can prove that if a government had not intervened, their conduct would have been different, *i.e.* competitive. At the same time, the CFI made it clear that if there remains the slightest "freedom of action", the undertakings fall under in the ambit of Article 101 TFEU (*ex* Article 81 EC Treaty).

After recalling that, in accordance with settled case-law, the fact that anti-competitive conduct was fostered or encouraged by the authorities of a Member State has in itself no bearing on the applicability of Article 101 TFEU (*ex* Article 81 EC Treaty), the CFI advanced its previous findings by holding:

> It follows that the cessation of the alleged anti-competitive practice at the behest of the Commission would, if proved, certainly have been capable of altering the conditions governing the complainant undertakings' access to the motor vehicle distribution market in France, irrespective of the question of their authorization by the French public authorities.[916]

The Commission was consequently considered to be wrong when it held that there is no link between the complainants' interest and the application of Article 101(1) TFEU (*ex* Article 81(1) EC Treaty) to a practice whose purpose or effect is to limit access to the motor vehicle distribution market for Japanese makes to five specific makes. The same line of reasoning was subsequently followed in *Asia Motor*

915 Case T-7/92, *Asia Motor France II*, [1993] E.C.R. II-669, paragraphs 54 *et seq.*
916 *Ibid.*, paragraphs 71 and 72.

France III,[917], still concerning the importation and marketing of certain Japanese vehicles into metropolitan France.[918]

Building upon the extensive case-law discussed, the Community courts appear to have found to a more straight-forward approach regarding state compulsion as a defence by simply holding that undertakings are not liable under Article 101 TFEU (*ex* Article 81 EC Treaty) where a state by measures of public authority requires them to engage in anti-competitive conduct.[919] In such a situation, they cannot be held accountable for the infringement of Article 101 TFEU (*ex* Article 81 EC Treaty).[920] This "state compulsion defence" operates, however, only where the state requires a certain behaviour.[921] Consequently, if a national law merely allows, encourages or makes it easier for undertakings to engage in autonomous anti-competitive conduct, the state compulsion defence is not accepted.[922]

Moreover, even where the state requires the undertakings to engage in anti-competitive conduct, if the undertakings remain at least partially capable to autonomously restrict competition – for example because they enjoy a margin of discretion in the implementation of the national legislation[923] – both the undertakings and the state can be held liable. Indeed, state legislation which requires economic operators to

917 Case T-387/94, *Asia Motor France III*, [1996] E.C.R. II-00961, paragraphs 60 *et seq.*

918 Another follow-up of the "*Asia Motor France* cases" was Case C-401/96, *Somaco v. Commission*, in which it was alleged that the CFI was not entitled to hold, on the one hand, that there was an agreement within the meaning of Article 81 EC Treaty (now Article 101 TFEU) between authorised importers relating to the territory of metropolitan France, while holding, on the other, that irresistible pressure was exerted by the state on the dealers in Martinique who were dependent on those importers. The ECJ rejected, however, this plea based on the fact that the distinct findings were not down to different standards of legal assessment but due the absence of evidence pointing to the existence of such pressure in the case of metropolitan France ([1998] E.C.R. I-02587, paragraphs 56 *et seq.*).

919 This simple statement is, however, not new and was already made in the 1970s; Case 13/77, *Inno/Atab*, [1977] E.C.R. I-02115.

920 Case C-198/01, *CIF*, [2003] E.C.R. I-08055, paragraph 51.

921 C-359/95 P and C-379/95 P, *Ladbroke*, [1997] E.C.R. I-6265, paragraphs 33 and 34; Case T-228/97, *Irish Sugar v. Commission*, [1999] E.C.R. II-2969, paragraph 130.

922 Joined cases T-191/98, T-212/98 to T-214/98, *Atlantic Container Line v. Commission*, [2003] E.C.R. II-3275.

923 Case T-513/93, *CNSD*, [2001] E.C.R. II -1807, paragraphs 71 and 72.

engage in anti-competitive conduct may itself infringe the EC Treaty, namely Articles 3(1)(g), 10(2) and Articles 81 or 82. More recently, in the *CIF* judgment,[924] the Court of Justice provided an additional interpretation of the principle according to which undertakings are not liable of infringing competition law where an anti-competitive conduct is required by national legislation. Asked to clarify whether a national competition authority could or should disapply anti-competitive national legislation, the Court pointed out that a national authority has the duty to disapply internal rules which, by requiring or facilitating the adoption of anti-competitive conduct by undertakings, clash with Articles 3(1)g, 10(2) and 81 or 82 EC Treaty. Once the authority's decision to disapply the national legislation becomes definitive, the state compulsion defence principle is no longer available[925] to the previously shielded undertakings as regards the conduct they maintain after the disapplication of the anti-competitive national measures.[926]

3.3 Preliminary Conclusion

The review of the case-law reveals that the Community courts have come a long way before they consistently held that the competition provisions of the EC Treaty (now TFEU) are infringed when a Member State requires or favours the adoption of anti-competitive agreements, decisions or concerted practices, or reinforces their effects, or where it divests its own rules of the character of legislation by delegating to private economic operators responsibility for taking decisions affecting the economic sphere. In this way competition law has been able to prevent harmful anti-competitive practices (such as market-sharing or price fixing) even in cases where these were approved by state law. In the recent *CFI* judgement, the Court of Justice has increased the effectiveness of this prohibition further by deciding that

924 Case C-198/01, *CIF*, [2003] E.C.R. I-08055.
925 *Ibid.*, paragraph 55.
926 *Ibid.*, paragraph 54.

national competition authorities have the duty not to apply such measures.

Judging by the Commissions' earlier decisions where it was not ready to accept immunity from the application of EC competition law of anti-competitive and trade restricting agreements due to the toleration or approval of either Member State governments or governments of third countries, the Commission appears to have now fully embraced the Community courts' approach. For instance, in a recent decision it pointed out that

> [a]ccording to settled case law, if anti-competitive conduct is required of undertakings by national legislation or if the latter creates a legal framework which itself eliminates any possibility of competitive activity on their part, Article 81 of the [EC] Treaty does not apply since, at that time, the restriction of competition is not attributable, as that provision implicitly requires, to the autonomous conduct of the undertakings. By contrast, Article 81 of the [EC] Treaty does apply «if it is found that the national legislation does not preclude undertakings from engaging in autonomous conduct which prevents, restricts or distorts competition»,[927]

and that

> if a national law merely encourages or makes it easier for undertakings to engage in autonomous anti-competitive conduct, those undertakings remain subject to Articles 81 EC and 82 EC and may incur penalties [...].[928]

The difficulty of applying this case-law by way of analogy to (as a hypothesis) government-sponsored VERs lies in the fact that the Community courts have usually dealt with practices of Member States. Considering that Articles 101 and 102 TFEU are directed to undertakings, not to Member States, the courts have sought to fill gaps in the effectiveness of EC competition law by relying on Article 10(2) EC Treaty (now Article 4(3) *in fine* TEU) which mandates a negative obligation for Member States to refrain from undermining Community objectives. A similar line of reasoning is clearly not possible in respect

927 Commission Decision of 20 October 2004 relating to a proceeding under Article 81(1) of the EC Treaty (Case COMP/C.38.238/B.2 – *Raw Tobacco Spain*), not yet published in the OJ, paragraph 349 (with further annotations).

928 *Ibid.*, paragraph 355 (with a further annotation).

of foreign governments. Accordingly, measures imposed on foreign undertakings to restrict their exports by the foreign government fall outside the scope of Article 101 TFEU. Measures resulting from agreements or concerted practices between undertakings which are, however, merely favoured by the foreign government or whose effect is only reinforced by practices of the foreign government may still be caught under EU competition law. This is the case if the exporters accepting the VER still have certain autonomy in choosing their line of conduct, *i.e.* if the undertakings concerned are ultimately free to refrain from entering into an agreement or engaging in concerted practices – even if the non-acceptance of the VER is against their economic interest.

CHAPTER IV

The Boundaries of Challenging Voluntary Export Restraints within the WTO Dispute Settlement System

The WTO dispute settlement system envisages different situations under which a complaint can be brought: "violation" complaints, in the case of a failure of a WTO Member to carry out its obligations under one of the existing agreements (GATT Article XXIII:1(a)), and "non-violation" complaints, where the claim concerns the application by another WTO Member of any measure that, even if not found in violation of any specific legal obligation, nevertheless has the effect of nullifying or impairing the market access benefits that a Member has expected arising from the commitments made in a trade agreement (GATT Article XXIII:1(b)).[929]

According to Article 14 Agreement on Safeguards, the provisions of, *inter alia*, GATT Article XXIII as elaborated and applied by the Dispute Settlement Understanding apply to consultations and the settlement of disputes arising under the Agreement on Safeguards.

As far as challenging VERs is concerned, a complainant would have to demonstrate, in the case of a violation complaint, that

- due to the VER, its benefit under the Agreement on Safeguards is nullified or impaired, or that that the attainment of any objective of the Agreement on Safeguards is being impeded, and
- that the VER is inconsistent with or violates the Agreement on Safeguards.

929 The other "non-violation" complaint, usually named "situation complaint", allows Members to bring a complaint under the dispute settlement procedures when benefits are nullified or impaired as a result of the existence of "any other situation" (GATT Article XXIII:1(c)). "Situation complaints" are highly exceptional and are therefore not discussed further.

Whereas Article 11:1(b) Agreement on Safeguards prohibits Members to "seek, take or maintain" VERs, Article 11:3 Agreement on Safeguards further obliges Members not to "encourage or support" the adoption or maintenance by public and private enterprises of non-governmental VERs. It becomes apparent from the wording of these provisions that VERs of purely private nature escape, *prima facie*, the application of GATT Article XXIII:1(a) as there must be at least a minimum of government involvement, namely either encouragement or support.

Nullification or impairment of a benefit is "presumed" to exist whenever an infringement or a violation is established.[930] The successfulness of attacking government-sponsored VERs by means of a violation complaint will therefore mainly be dependent on whether the complainant manages to demonstrate a violation of either Article 11:1(b) or Article 11:3 Agreement on Safeguards which is inseparably linked to a demonstration of some sort of government involvement.

Considering that government involvement plays, as will be discussed below, a comparably important role in "non-violation" complaints pursuant to GATT Article XXIII:1(b), it shall therefore first be reviewed what may constitute government involvement, and second, what standard may be used to qualify such government involvement as amounting to "encouragement" or "support" in order to establish a contravention of the Agreement on Safeguards.

930 With regard to GATT 1947, the Panel Report on Uruguayan Recourse to Article XXIII stipulated, *inter alia*, that "[i]n cases where there is a clear infringement of the provisions of the General Agreement, or in other words, where measures are applied in conflict with the provisions of GATT [...], the action would, *prima facie*, constitute a case of nullification or impairment and would *ipso facto* require consideration of whether the circumstances are serious enough to justify the authorization of suspension of concessions or obligations" (L/1923, paragraph 15). This presumption has since been codified, and Article 3:8 DSU provides: "In cases where there is an infringement of the obligations assumed under a covered agreement, the action is considered prima facie to constitute a case of nullification or impairment. This means that there is normally a presumption that a breach of the rules has an adverse impact on other Members parties to that covered agreement, and in such cases, it shall be up to the Member against whom the complaint has been brought to rebut the charge".

1 Government Involvement

"Government involvement" is not a legal term used in Article 11:1(b) or Article 11:3 Agreement on Safeguards. Accordingly, its meaning may not be directly inferred from the Agreement, but must be assessed with reference to other terms used in WTO language.

A first observation must be that the *nature* of government involvement under Article 11:1(b) Agreement on Safeguards appears to be irrelevant in as much as the government involvement is capable of "seeking, taking or maintaining" a VER. It is therefore of no importance whether the VER is codified (*e.g.* in laws, regulations) or established in an informal manner. The same appears to apply regarding Article 11:3 Agreement on Safeguards, with the difference that the *degree* of government involvement is restricted to "encouragement or support".

In the light of this observation, it is suggested that government involvement in Articles 11:1(b) and 11:3 Agreement on Safeguards is probably best compared with – what is termed in other WTO provisions – as "measures", in particular "governmental" measures.

1.1 The Concept of "Governmental" Measure

The concept of "governmental" measure has been examined on a number of occasions in respect of different articles of the GATT. For instance, the Panel on *Japan – Restrictions on Imports of Certain Agricultural Products*[931] found that the informal administrative guidance used by the Japanese Government to restrict the production of certain agricultural products could be considered a governmental measure within the meaning of GATT Article XI:2 because it emanated from the government and was effective in the Japanese context where ad-

931 Panel Report on *Japan – Restrictions on Imports of Certain Agricultural Products*, L/6253.

ministrative guidance is a traditional tool of government policy based on consensus and peer pressure.[932]

Likewise, the Panel on *Japan – Trade in Semi-Conductors*[933] considered that legally non-mandatory measures could constitute restrictions within the meaning of GATT Article XI:1 if "*[s]ufficient incentives or disincentives existed for non-mandatory measures to take effect*", and that the operation of the measures is essentially dependent on government action or intervention because the measures would be operating in a manner equivalent to mandatory requirements such that the difference between the measure and mandatory requirements is only one of form and not of substance.[934]

Yet another Panel had to examine whether the EC's marketing system of dessert apples, mainly carried out through market withdrawals by producer groups, was to be considered as "governmental" measure. Taking note of the EC's argument that this system could not be considered a "governmental" measure in terms of GATT Article XI:2(c) because of the voluntary basis of the organisation and the non-obligatory method of its operation, the Panel observed that the internal marketing system was of a "hybrid" nature, combining elements of public and private responsibility. From a legal point of view, the system allowed for two possibilities, either direct buying-in of apples by Member State authorities or market withdrawals by producer groups. Under the latter option, the Panel found that the operational involvement of public authorities was (only) "indirect". Considering, however, that the structure of the entire marketing regime, including the disposal of the withdrawn apples by producer groups, was established by Community regulations, the Panel concluded that the withdrawal system was to be qualified as "governmental" measure.[935]

In the light of the fact that panels have focused on the functionality of "governmental" measures (rather than form), it is proposed that "government involvement" under Articles 11:1(b) and 11:3 Agreement on Safeguards is, *de facto*, no different from the concept of

932 *Ibid.*, paragraph 5.4.1.4.

933 Panel Report on *Japan – Trade in Semi-Conductors*, L/6309.

934 *Ibid.*, paragraph 111 *et seq.* See also Chapters II.1.1.1 and II.1.1.2, *supra*, to that end.

935 Panel Report on *EEC – Restrictions on Imports of Dessert Apples – Complaint by Chile*, L/6491, paragraphs 12.8 and 12.9.

"governmental measures". This appears justified also in view of the following findings of the Panel on *US – Exports Restraints*[936]:

> [F]or the purposes of this case [...], [we consider it unnecessary] to define *what* "measures" are susceptible to review under WTO dispute settlement. [A] measure may be *any act* of a Member, *or an omission or a failure to act* on the part of a Member, [and] could consist of both binding and non-binding acts, including non-binding administrative guidance by a government. We agree, and in *particular find no reason or basis to rule in the abstract that a given type of instrument or action cannot be the subject of claims* in WTO dispute settlement *(emphasis added).*[937]

This does not mean, however, that all measures are capable by themselves of giving rise to violations of WTO obligations, but an analogous line of reasoning must clearly be possible if government involvement is such as to "seek, take or maintain", or "encourage or support" VERs. It is thus this latter question which is crucial in determining the successfulness of a violation complaint. In view of the absence of cases on the (il)legality of VERs under the Agreement on Safeguards, the discussion of this question is obviously limited as it cannot be made in the abstract. Nevertheless, it shall be evaluated what degree of government involvement may be required to establish "encouragement or support" in the sense of Article 11:3 Agreement on Safeguards.

1.2 The Degree of Government Involvement Required for there to be "Encouragement" or "Support" under Article 11:3 Agreement on Safeguards

Article 11:3 Agreement on Safeguards provides that "*[M]embers shall not encourage or support the adoption or maintenance by public and private enterprises of non-governmental measures equivalent to [VERs].*" Seemingly, the prohibition to encourage or support VERs of private nature reflects the concern that government-sponsored VERs may be replaced by private industry-to-industry arrangements. It ap-

936 Panel Report on *US – Export Restraints*, WT/DS194/R.
937 *Ibid.*, paragraph 8.80.

pears to be accepted that where private restrictive practices are fostered (*i.e.* encouraged or supported) they can act to block the entry into market of imported goods, notwithstanding the prohibition for WTO Members to engage in VERs and similar import or export arrangements. If domestic enterprises enter into (international) cartel arrangements to protect local markets from foreign suppliers, thereby depriving domestic consumers of cheaper or alternative goods,[938] the stimulus from international competition is lost. It is not conceivable that this is intended by Articles 11:1(b) and 11:3 Agreement on Safeguards.

Provided that it is accepted that, where VERs are essentially private, they closely resemble international (export) cartels, distort competition[939] and are generally subject to competition laws prohibiting cartels or other forms of collusive behaviour,[940] the prohibition to encourage or support VERs of private nature constitutes a gangway between the application of the Agreement on Safeguards and competition law. This is supported by the following observation made by the WTO Working Group on the Interaction between Trade and Competition Policy:

> The argument was made that the WTO rules on safeguard measures also needed to be reviewed from a competition perspective. For example, Article 11 of the Agreement on Safeguards did not address purely private business practices, which raised the question of whether measures such as voluntary restraints initiated by private firms were prohibited under this Article. *The reason why Article 11 banned grey-area measures such as voluntary export restraints and ordinary market arrangements was that such measures adversely affected competition.* Therefore, whether or not certain grey-area measures were prohibited under Article 11 *should be decided on the basis of the effects these measures had on competition rather than on the basis of whether the government was involved* in the establishment of such measures. This interpretation appeared to be *consistent with the letter and the spirit of the Preamble to the Agreement on Safeguards,*

938 1994 Competition Policy Workshop: Background Paper of the OECD Secretariat, p. 6.

939 As a result of trade protection, it was even argued that grey-area measures, such as VERs, are the most competition-distortive; VERMULST, (1993) 27 JWT 57.

940 *Competition and Trade Policies – Their Interaction*, OECD, 1984, paragraph 115. Conversely, certain export cartels have been approved by their governments in response to requests from the importing country to limit their exports, thus amounting to VERs (*ibid.*, paragraph 9).

> which emphasized the need to enhance rather than limit competition in international markets *(emphasis added)*.[941]

Put differently, the effectiveness of the obligation not to engage in or foster VERs envisaged by the Agreement on Safeguards is not limited to the observance of the legal requirement but extends to the expectations and interests of the other WTO Members to do so. It could therefore be argued that a WTO Member's mere toleration of private VERs may be considered as a violation of the "good faith" requirement in treaty observation[942] and remove the substance of the Agreement on Safeguards,[943] if it can be demonstrated that the private VERs have an (appreciable) effect on competition (hereinafter called the "effects on competition"-test).

Accepting such "effects on competition"-test would not only facilitate bringing private VERs to WTO dispute settlement, but also reflect a true commitment towards the effectiveness of the Agreement on Safeguards.

941 WTO Report (1999) of the Working Group on the Interaction between Trade and Competition Policy to the General Council, WT/WGTCP/3, paragraph 68.

942 The observance and effectiveness of international obligations undertaken by states is determined by expectations and interests as it is by the legal requirement to do so (*pacta sunt servanda*): Article 26 of the 1969 Vienna Convention on the Law of Treaties provides that a treaty is binding upon the parties and must be performed in good faith. Although the EC is not a signatory to the Vienna Convention on the Law of Treaties, the Court has applied the provisions of this Convention as a matter of customary international law, as for example in its *Opinion 1/91*, EEA, [1991] E.C.R. I-6079, paragraph 14. For a detailed description of this issue, see KUIJPER, (1998) 25 LIEI 8.

943 In this sense, DIDIER, 305 et seq. The OECD also noted that "*[i]ncreasing globalisation of business may reflect the success of trade policy but also creates new challenges [...] certain business practices may frustrate trade liberalisation [...]*" (Trade and Competition Policies, Joint Report by the Committee on Competition Law and Policy and the Trade Committee, OECD/GD(94)36, 1994, paragraph 1).

1.3 The Application of Domestic Competition Laws versus "Effects on Competition"-Test

The traditional approach in finding a violation of Article 11:3 Agreement on Safeguards in respect of private VERs would mean that there is "government involvement" amounting to "encouragement or support". Looking at a dictionary, "to encourage" means, *inter alia*, "to help or stimulate the development of".[944] Accordingly, "encouragement" is something that encourages which is a synonym for inspiration, motivation or stimulation.[945] "To support" in legal terms is defined as "to promote the interests or cause of", "to uphold or defend as valid or right" or "to argue or vote for".[946] Though not much, at least it may be deduced from the nuances in terminology that "to encourage" is a somewhat lighter version of "to support".

Under the *proviso* that private VERs restrict competition, the most obvious way to challenge them would be under competition law. For argument's sake, transposing this hypothesis to the wording of Article 11:3 Agreement on Safeguards in terms of "government involvement" could be understood as follows:

- The WTO Member concerned does not have a domestic competition law. The failure to enact a competition law "encourages or supports" private VERs; or
- the WTO Member concerned has a domestic competition law but does not enforce it, thereby "encouraging" private VERs; or
- the WTO Member concerned has a domestic competition law which exempts VERs (as export cartels) from its application, thereby "supporting" private VERs.

It appears, however, unrealistic to pretend that WTO panels and the Appellate Body would effectively embrace (all of) these arguments. In legal literature, the application of a violation complaint pursuant to GATT Article XXIII:1(a) for the lack of enactment or enforcement of competition law has simply been rejected on the ground that there are

944 See Compact Oxford English Dictionary, http://www.askoxford.com.

945 The American Heritage® Dictionary of the English Language, Fourth Edition, 2000.

946 Merriam-Webster's Dictionary of Law, 1996.

no WTO provisions obliging WTO Members to enact or enforce domestic competition law.[947] Clearly, nothing in the Agreement on Safeguards may be construed so as to oblige WTO Members to *enact* a domestic competition law for the sake of prohibiting private VERs. It may, however, be discussed whether the Agreement on Safeguards has an impact on the *enforcement* of existing competition laws.

Whereas it is true that (i) WTO/GATT does not impose common competition law disciplines on its Members, and that (ii) Members are therefore free to adopt any competition law they see fit, domestic competition law is not entirely free from considerations under WTO/GATT disciplines.

It becomes apparent from *Japan – Film*[948] that domestic competition laws are covered by the national treatment obligation of GATT Article III. Kodak had lobbied the U.S. government (first the Bush (George H.W.) and then the Clinton Administration) over years, alleging that Japan's structure of the film market was such as to prevent Kodak from competing with Fuji film. Although Kodak was effectively making an antitrust claim, the Clinton Administration decided to take Kodak's claim to the WTO dispute resolution system,[949] where the Panel explicitly subjected Japanese competition law to the national treatment obligation,[950] and implicitly accepted that the term "affecting" extends to domestic competition laws. National competition law is therefore covered by national treatment insofar as its *enforcement* is a "requirement affecting" trade.[951] Admittedly, the significance of this observation is limited in respect of VERs since an instrumentalisation of GATT Article III is barely helpful considering that national treatment is directed at (imported) "like" foreign products which are treated less favourably (GATT Article III:4).[952] There appears thus to

947 SPITZER, 106 (with further annotations).

948 Panel Report on *Japan – Film*, WT/DS44/R.

949 BREWSTER, (2006) 92 Virginia Law Review 277.

950 Panel Report on *Japan – Film*, WT/DS44/R, paragraphs 10.376 *et seq.*

951 HOEKMAN/MAVROIDIS (2002), 17.

952 For instance, it is established that the standard of effective equality of competitive conditions on the internal market (of a WTO Member) is the standard of national treatment (AB Report on *Japan – Alcoholic Beverages II*, WT/DS8/AB/R, WT/DS10/AB/R, WT/DS11/AB/R, p. 16), and that this standard is equated with

be no room for an application of this Article to export restrictions (VERs in the form of export cartels).[953]

More interestingly, the Panel on *Mexico – Telecoms*[954] found that Mexico has failed to maintain appropriate measures to prevent anti-competitive practices in its market that impede the entry of foreign competitors.[955] The dispute relates to provisions in Mexico's domestic laws and regulations on telecommunications which govern the supply of telecommunication services. In particular, it was alleged that the practices mandated by domestic law constituted unlawful practices under WTO law, more specifically under the "Telecoms Reference Paper"[956] which stipulates that it is a Member's duty to ensure interconnection with a major supplier at any technically feasible point in the network under non-discriminatory, reasonable, and cost-oriented terms and conditions. To this end, Mexico had, *inter alia*, undertaken to maintain *"appropriate measures [...] for the purpose of preventing suppliers who, alone or together, are a major supplier from engaging in or continuing anti-competitive practices."*[957] Whilst Mexico contended that it had put in place "appropriate measures" to prevent anti-competitive practices under its general competition laws,[958] the Panel noted that there is no definition of anti-competitive practices in the Telecoms Reference Paper and subsequently drew upon open-ended

the standard of "upsetting the competitive relationship" under GATT Article XXIII:1(b) (Panel Report on *Japan – Film*, WT/DS44/R, paragraph 10.380). The Panel on *Japan – Film* did not see a significant distinction between the two standards apart from the fact that the GATT Article III:4 standard calls for no less favourable treatment for imported products in general, whereas the GATT Article XXIII:1(b) standard calls for a comparison of the competitive relationship between foreign and domestic products at two specific points in time, *i.e.* when the concession was granted and at the time of the measure complained of (*ibid.*).

953 KOOPMANN, 13.

954 Panel Report on *Mexico – Telecoms*, WT/DS204/R.

955 For critical appraisals of this case, see, *e.g.*, FOX, (2006) 9 JIEL 271 *et seq.*, NEVEN/MAVROIDIS, (2006) 5 World Trade Review 271 *et seq.*, MARSDEN, (2004) May, Competition Law Insight 3 *et seq.*

956 Mexico: Schedule of specific Commitments, Supplement 2 ("Mexico Reference Paper"), GATS/SC/56/Suppl.2.

957 *Ibid.*, Section 1.1 of the Mexico Reference Paper.

958 *Mexico – Telecoms*, WT/DS204/R, paragraph 7.223.

language (definitions from the Merriam-Webster and Shorter Oxford Dictionaries) to state:

> The word "practices" thus indicates "actions" in general, or can mean actions that are "usual" or "customary." [...] the word "anticompetitive" has been defined as "tending to reduce or discourage competition." On its own, therefore, the term "anticompetitive practices" is broad in scope, suggesting actions that lessen rivalry or competition in the market.[959]

The Panel continued to observe that the list of anti-competitive practices in Section 1.2 of the Telecoms Reference Paper was not exhaustive, and expanded that the meaning of "anti-competitive practices" is also informed by the use of this term in Members' own competition legislation. Whilst it acknowledged the pluralism among Members, *i.e.* that the range of anti-competitive practices that are prohibited varied between Members, it simply found, by relying on a note of the WTO Secretariat[960], that they included cartels or collusive horizontal agreements between firms, such as agreements to fix prices or share markets, thereby ultimately expanding the scope of the commitments undertaken within the WTO framework.[961]

Albeit stressing that, pursuant to doctrines applicable under the competition laws of some Members, a firm complying with a specific legislative requirement of such a Member may be immunised from breaching domestic competition law, the Panel in *Mexico – Telecoms* emphasised Article 27 of the Vienna Convention on the Law of Treaties which provides that *"a party may not invoke the provisions of its internal law as justification for its failure to perform a treaty"*. It concluded that acts required by governments could constitute prohibited anti-competitive practices.[962]

In view of the findings in *Japan – Film* and *Mexico – Telecoms*, it is suggested that domestic competition laws may, at least to a certain

959 *Ibid.*, paragraph 7.230.

960 "Overview of Members' National Competition Legislation", Note by the Secretariat, WT/WGTCP/W/128/Rev.2, 4 July 2001.

961 *Ibid.*, paragraphs 7.235 and 7.237. This finding was criticised since the WTO Members in signing the Telecoms Reference Paper did not agree that a cartel ban is a WTO commitment, see MARSDEN, (2004) May, Competition Law Insight 3.

962 *Mexico – Telecoms*, WT/DS204/R, paragraph 7.244.

extent, be disciplined by WTO provisions, more specifically in the case of VERs by the Agreement on Safeguards. For instance, it was argued that, if there is a legal export cartel in a foreign country, acceptance of the goods that are higher priced (due to the export cartel) by the importing country constitutes discrimination in favour of the foreign producers (exporters), who are permitted to cartelise, over the domestic producers of like or directly competitive products who are prohibited from horizontal price arrangements under the domestic competition law. Thus, where the anti-competitive behaviour of the foreign exporters reduces competition in the supply to the domestic market, the national competition law of the importing country may address the VERs pursuant to the national treatment principle.[963] On a more general note, it has further been suggested that the responsibility to review export cartels rests with the competition authorities of the importing country since it is the consumers in the importing country that are being wronged.[964]

1.3.1 The Nature and Effect of Export Cartels

Pursuant to a definition of the OECD, an export cartel is an agreement or arrangement between firms to charge a specified export price and/or to divide export markets.[965] This definition appears to be insufficient inasmuch as the agreement or arrangement between exporters may amount to act collusively in respect of any aspect of their export activity, ranging from joint production, joint marketing to market allocation.[966]

963 IACOBUCCI, (1997) 21 W. Comp. 31.

964 BHATTACHARJEA, (2004) 38 JWT 340 *et seq.* Whereas BHATTACHARJEA suggested that governments of exporting countries could play a more active role in regulating the export cartels (for instance in exchange for market access), MAGNUS observed that there is no basis for an extension of national domestic laws, under which governments would assume responsibility for policing the offshore market behaviour of their exporters (MAGNUS, (2005) 39 JWT 182). For further details of the debate, see also BHATTACHARJEA, (2005) 39 JWT 185 *et seq.*

965 Glossary of Industrial Organisation Economics and Competition Law, compiled by R. S. Khemani and D. M. Shapiro, commissioned by the Directorate for Financial, Fiscal and Enterprise Affairs, OECD, 1993.

966 SWEENEY, (2007) 10 JIEL 86.

Within the WTO Working Group on the Interaction between Trade and Competition Policy export cartels were discussed as practices which (potentially) had a differential impact on the affected countries, thereby stating that the extent of such cartels and their deleterious effects on international trade might be greater than is widely known.[967] At the same time, there appears to be little consensus among the WTO Members on the significance or on how or whether to regulate export cartels.[968] Among commentators – whether economists or lawyers – the views are equally divided.[969] Nevertheless, common ground may be found in the allegation that the participants of an export cartel achieve monopoly gains that have to be borne by the consumers in the importing country by paying prices above the competitive level. There seems thus to be agreement that export cartels "impose severe costs on importing countries",[970] which does, however, not preclude that they also produce domestic effects. If, for instance, an export cartel covers a substantial share of domestic production, there is the likelihood of a spill over-effect which influences domestic supplies and prices. In addition, the operation of the cartel is likely to require an exchange of information that may amount to a parallelism (*i.e.* parallel conduct) in the domestic market. Therefore, it is conceivable that export cartels will have some effect on the local market.[971]

Comparable effects are evidenced in the event of VERs: In addition to the total size of the market being restricted, the level of imports

967 Report (1998) of the Working Group on the Interaction between Trade and Competition Policy to the General Council, WT/WGTCP/2, paragraph 89.

968 Report (1999) of the Working Group on the Interaction between Trade and Competition Policy to the General Council, WT/WGTCP/3, paragraph 26; Report (2000) of the Working Group on the Interaction between Trade and Competition Policy to the General Council, WT/WGTCP/4, paragraph 25; Report (2002) of the Working Group on the Interaction between Trade and Competition Policy to the General Council, WT/WGTCP/6, paragraphs 27, 36 and 57; Report (2002) of the Working Group on the Interaction between Trade and Competition Policy to the General Council, WT/WGTCP/7, paragraphs 50 *et seq.*

969 BECKER, (2007) 3 J. Competition L. & Econ. 115 *et seq.* (with further annotations); BHATTACHARJEA, (2004) 38 JWT 339 *et seq.*; SOKOL, (2008) 4 J. Competition L. & Econ. 968 *et seq.*

970 TREBILCOCK/HOWSE, 602.

971 IMMENGA, (1995) 1 Pacific Rim Law & Policy Journal, 125 *et seq.*

is restrained and consumers experience higher prices than they would in the absence of a VER. The market structure is likely to be static as the relative market shares of the participants in the VER remain unchanged as of the introduction of the VER and collusive behaviour is likely to be fostered.[972]

Under the assumption that (i) VERs produce comparable effects to export cartels, (ii) WTO Members may not invoke the provisions of its internal law as justification for its failure to perform its commitments under the WTO, and (iii) the *enforcement* of competition law is a "requirement affecting" trade, then the *dispensation* of export cartels from the application of (domestic) competition law could *arguendo* be "encouragement or support" of private VERs under Article 11:3 Agreement on Safeguards.

1.3.2 The Limitations of Positive Comity

Based on the foregoing observations, the extent to which domestic competition laws may be disciplined by WTO provisions, particularly the Agreement on Safeguards, appears to center around the question whether the *enforcement* of such domestic competition laws is mandated or even required by Article 11:3 Agreement on Safeguards. In other words, "encouragement or support" could be interpreted so as to introduce the concept of *positive comity* into the Agreement on Safeguards. Considering that positive comity is a recognised device to promote international co-operation in the enforcement of competition laws,[973] it may represent a decisive tool in giving effect to Article 11:3 Agreement on Safeguards regarding private VERs.

Positive comity[974] means that a party to an agreement invokes, upon request of another party, its domestic competition law to remove anti-competitive practices that occur within its jurisdiction and that adversely affect the other party. This would be a way to control anti-

972 See Chapter I, 2.1.5.

973 OECD CLP Report on Positive Comity, DAFFE/CLP(99)19.

974 The term "positive comity" has never been formally defined but it appears justified to define it as request that another country open or expand an enforcement action (as opposed to a request for assistance in the requesting country's enforcement action, also termed investigatory assistance); *ibid.*, paragraphs 6 and 8.

competitive activities, such as VERs, that adversely affect a WTO Member without resorting to an extraterritorial application of its competition law that may result in a conflict of jurisdiction. Whilst promising at the outset, the effectiveness of the concept of positive comity is limited in several ways, of which at least two bear significance in the context of Article 11:3 Agreement on Safeguards, namely (i) the illegality of the anti-competitive practice in the country concerned and (ii) the voluntary nature of positive comity.

Firstly, positive comity can only be effective when the anti-competitive effects of a VER affect not only the jurisdiction of the requesting country but also that of the requested country. In other words, since the concept relates to possible enforcement action by the requested country, it applies only to conduct that is illegal in that country.[975] If the conduct affects only the requesting country, the requested country has no reason to intervene to prohibit the conduct which it actually may permit and encourage within its jurisdiction.[976] The relevance of this limitation of the effectiveness of positive comity is well illustrated in the case of VERs.[977]

The application of competition policy to export trade arrangements, such as VERs, contains the basic problem that most of the countries do not apply their competition laws to domestic export agreements,[978] unless these agreements produce effects on the domes-

975 *Ibid.*, paragraph 50.

976 MATSUSHITA, (2002) 1 Washington University Global Studies Law Review 470.

977 *Antitrust and Market Access: The Scope and Coverage of Competition Laws and Implications for Trade*, OECD, 1996, p. 33. One suggestion made in an OECD study is that export cartels should demonstrate that they do not adversely affect competition in the home market and that they serve to overcome barriers to competition in importing countries (*Obstacles to Trade and Competition*, OECD, 1993, p. 92). Whilst this suggestion takes into account the view that export cartels can gain efficiencies through pooling skills and resources, thus enabling firms to trade where they might not otherwise be able to, it appears inappropriate for situations where an export cartel takes the form of a VER.

978 For an overview of competition laws that explicitly or implicitly exclude export cartels, see BHATTACHARJEA, (2004) 38 JWT 337.

tic market.[979] Hence, there is a potential conflict between the trade policy of one country and the competition law of its trading partner.

For example, in the United States,[980] the Webb-Pomerene Act of 1918 (15 U.S.C. § 61 *et seq.*) provides a limited antitrust exemption for the formation and operation of associations of otherwise competing enterprises that deal in "goods, wares or merchandise" to engage in collective export sales. Whilst such export cartels must file their agreement and annual reports with the Federal Trade Commission (15 U.S.C. § 65), their immunity from antitrust application does not extend to conduct that restrains "*the export trade of any domestic competitor*" or "*artificially or intentionally enhances or depresses prices within the United States, [...] substantially lessens competition in the United States or otherwise restrains trade therein*" (15 U.S.C. § 62). Similarly, cartels among EC exporters are normally outside the scope of Article 101(1) TFEU, unless they appreciably restrict competition within the Community and affect trade between the Member States. In Japan, under the Export and Import Transaction Act[981] export cartels on price, quantity, quality, design and other terms for the exportation of particular goods and the establishment of exporters' associations were allowed for the purposes of, *inter alia*, establishing and maintaining orderly marketing in exporting goods to foreign countries until 1997.[982]

In addition to the predicament where external trade activities of private enterprises are exempted from the application of domestic competition law,[983] the challenge of VERs with governmental involve-

979 For an overview, see LEVENSTEIN/SUSLOW, (2005) 20 Am. U. Int'l L. Rev. 785 *et seq.*

980 The other exemption from the antitrust laws is made under Title III of the Export Trading Company Act of 1982, under which applicants may receive an Export Certificate of Review from the Department of Commerce (15 U.S.C. 4012 *et seq.*).

981 *Yushutsunyu torihiki ho* [Export and Import Transactions Law], Law No. 299 of 1952, as amended, Article 33.

982 The exemption of export cartels from antitrust liability under the Export and Import Transaction Act was, however, abolished in 1997. Cf. YAMADA, Appendix III.

983 HOEKMAN/SAGGI claim that the legal status of export cartels in developed countries is an example of a national competition law whose sole purpose is to benefit local firms at the expense of consumers in importing countries, and that developed countries should therefore be required to alter their legislation to ban exports cartels and practices with similar effects (HOEKMAN/SAGGI, 27 *et seq.*).

ment may prove as unsuccessful under competition law as under the Agreement on Safeguards. The application of competition laws to VERs represents as much an unsettled issue as it is controversial. In this respect, the OECD noted that:

> There is probably a general consensus that competition laws do not apply to intergovernmental agreements. Inasmuch as many [...] of these agreements involve significant governmental involvement [...], it is not surprising that actual competition law enforcement appears modest.[984]

For instance, in the U.S., antitrust laws do not apply to intergovernmental agreements as such. On the other hand, it does not follow there from that antitrust laws fail to apply to private anti-competitive conduct merely because the conduct is contemplated by an intergovernmental agreement. On the contrary, in the absence of a treaty or a statutory exemption or in cases where a doctrine such as the foreign sovereign compulsion defence does not apply, U.S. antitrust laws would ordinarily apply.[985] Similarly, in the EC, VERs between foreign and domestic enterprises are usually covered by EC competition law, unless they merely implement a trade agreement entered into by the Community. Foreign exporters do, however, not violate EC competition law where their actions are compelled by non-EC governments.

Nonetheless, arrangements between private or public enterprises that achieve or facilitate inter-firm collusion are viewed with scepticism under competition policy. Competition laws therefore widely prohibit collusion among firms to restrain competition through such practices as joint horizontal price fixing, output control or market division. Consequently, attempts by private or public enterprises – whether at national or international level – to fix prices, restrict out-

984 Antitrust and Market Access: The Scope and Coverage of Competition Laws and Implications for Trade, OECD, 1996, p. 35.

985 Then again, within the U.S., State regulation is also not considered a violation of federal antitrust laws if (i) the challenged restraint is clearly articulated and affirmatively expressed as state policy, and (ii) the state policy is actively supervised by the State itself. The U.S. "state action doctrine" thus accords antitrust immunity while the EC's "state compulsion defence" appears to define criteria to expand the application of competition law. For a comparison between the two doctrines, see EHLE, (1998) 19 ECLR 380 *et seq.*

put, divide or share (world) markets are usually in direct violation of the competition laws of the markets affected,[986] subject to the territorial scope of a particular country's competition law.

In the EC, the case-law of the Court of Justice suggests that agreements between undertakings within the EC and their counterparts, situated in third countries, come within the scope of Article 101 TFEU. Most explicitly in *EMI/CBS*,[987] the ECJ considered that a "*[r]estrictive agreement between traders within the common market and competitors in third countries that would bring about an isolation of the common market as a whole, which in the territory of the Community, would reduce the supply of products originating in third countries [...] might be of such a nature as to affect adversely the conditions of competition within the common market.*"[988] It can be inferred from this finding that a VER that is instituted in response to pressure from an EC industry, *e.g.* by threatening that otherwise an anti-dumping complaint will be brought, may be considered contrary to EC competition law (for aspects of market-sharing or limitation of output).

Nevertheless, it becomes apparent from the above discussion that the concept of positive comity will be difficult to apply in the context of VERs, and accordingly problematic to interpret "encouragement or support" in Article 11:3 Agreement on Safeguards so as to incorporate positive comity in a multilateral sense. This negative finding is further supported by the second limit that is placed on the effectiveness of positive comity, *i.e.* its voluntary nature.

It appears to be common understanding that positive comity is of voluntary nature,[989] and that accordingly, a requested country cannot be compelled to investigate and remedy conduct that it either believes is "not occurring or regards as beneficial, benign, or unimportant".[990] Whereas the non-binding nature is to the detriment in the present dis-

986 *Hard Core Cartels*, OECD, 2000, p. 6.
987 Cases 51/75, 86/75, 96/75, *EMI/CBS*, [1976] E.C.R. 811.
988 *Ibid.*, paragraph 28.
989 OECD CLP Report on Positive Comity, DAFFE/CLP(99)19, paragraph 54. MATSUSHITA, for instance, points out that all current agreements that explicitly provide for positive comity are non-binding "soft" laws (MATSUSHITA, (2002) 1 Washington University Global Studies Law Review 468).
990 OECD CLP Report on Positive Comity, DAFFE/CLP(99)19, paragraph 55.

cussion, its voluntary nature appears to be deemed beneficial in some instances: The EC considered that the voluntary nature of the positive comity principle contained in the EC/U.S. Co-operation Agreement in competition law matters[991] assures that there is "*[n]o risk that a [requested country] would be obliged to investigate a case where it was not in its interests to do so.*"[992]

Recalling moreover that positive comity is a means of international co-operation in the enforcement of competition laws, it cannot be neglected that the WTO Working Group on the Interaction between Trade and Competition Policy noted that

> [...] since one third of WTO Members [does] not have a competition regime in place, there was no point in discussing the prospects for *cooperation* in the Organization *(emphasis added).*[993]

In addition, there appears to be a consensus that co-operation in competition law matters is, at least at present, in general merely achievable on a voluntary basis.[994] For instance, it has been stated by the Secretariat that, in discussions of the WTO Working Group on the Interaction

991 Agreement between the Government of the United States of America and the Commission of the European Communities regarding the application of their competition laws, OJ 1995 L 95/47; and Agreement between the European Communities and the Government of the United States of America on the application of positive comity principles in the enforcement of their competition laws, OJ 1998 L 173/28.

992 OECD CLP Report on Positive Comity, DAFFE/CLP(99)19, paragraph 54 (with further annotations).

993 WTO Report (2001) of the Working Group on the Interaction between Trade and Competition Policy to the General Council, WT/WGTCP/5, paragraph 101.

994 "Modalities for Voluntary Cooperation", Background Note by the Secretariat, WT/WGTCP/W/192. Even with respect to co-operation in enforcement against hard-core cartels, governments in the framework of the OECD have used the *caveat "a Member country may decline to comply with a request for assistance, or limit or condition its co-operation on the ground that it considers compliance with the request to be not in accordance with its laws or regulations or to be inconsistent with its important interests or on any other grounds, including its competition authority's resource constraints or the absence of a mutual interest in the investigation or proceeding in question*" (OECD Council, *Recommendation concerning Effective Action against Hard Core Cartels*, 25 March 1998, C(98)35/FINAL, Article I.B(2)(c)).

between Trade and Competition Policy, the modalities for voluntary co-operation, as reflected in recent contributions by WTO Members, contain two main elements: (i) provisions to facilitate case-specific co-operation on anti-competitive practices having an impact on international trade, and (ii) provisions relating to general exchanges of information and experiences and joint analysis of global trade-related competition issues.[995] Quite clearly, either element does not extend to a concept that is comparable to binding positive comity.[996]

1.3.3 Advocating an "Effects on Competition"-Test under the Agreement on Safeguards

In view of the absence of binding positive comity, it has to be concluded that a mandated *application* of national competition law is not covered by Article 11:3 Agreement on Safeguards insofar as its requirement of "encouragement or support" cannot be construed so as to amount to "government involvement" – whether it be by a WTO Member exempting export cartels from the scope of its domestic competition law or abstaining from testing their foreign effects (such as the reduction of welfare in the importing country, and possibly global welfare). In sum, it must therefore be found that nothing in the Agreement on Safeguards suggests that WTO Members are obliged to either enact or enforce domestic competition laws in order to prevent private VERs.

This finding is, however, substantially different to the suggestion that a WTO Member's toleration of private VERs may be considered as a violation of the "good faith" requirement in treaty observation which removes the substance of the Agreement on Safeguards, and merely illustrates that the traditional approach in trying to subsume a government's inaction under the "encouragement or support" requirement of Article 11:3 Agreement on Safeguards is virtually impossible.

995 *Ibid.*, paragraph 5.

996 In fact, "positive comity" is merely mentioned in the context of bilateral co-operation agreements, and there appears little room to presently include such an approach on a multilateral level; *ibid.*, paragraph 12.

Instead, it should be focussed on the demonstration that private VERs have an adverse effect on competition in the sense that their toleration amounts to a "failure of another [Member] to carry out its obligations" under the Agreement on Safeguards, *i.e.* that the government's inaction is involved as part of the original competition claim. It is suggested that such argumentation should be allowed regarding private VERs since the "impediment of the attainment of any objective of the Agreement", *i.e.* the prohibition of grey-area measures such as VERs, can never be invoked if the toleration of the same measure cannot be found to constitute a "failure to carry out obligations" under the Agreement on Safeguards. In the event of private VERs, the requirements of a successful violation complaint under GATT Article XXIII:1(a) are therefore intrinsically linked with and cannot be separated from each other.

If such is accepted, an *"effects on competition"-test* would solve this dilemma and appears plausible in view of the following considerations. Although there seems to be a common perception that countries have no incentives to ban export cartels because they allegedly lack immediate effects on the domestic market, economic analysis demonstrates that they have undoubtedly adverse effects on consumers (domestic and foreign). The lack of enforcement action against export cartels is therefore clearly difficult to reconcile with a coherent competition policy since export cartels are, like any other cartel behaviour, among the most obvious competition law infringements if account is taken of *all* effects.[997] It has therefore been suggested that, from a legal perspective, the defence and maintenance of export cartels would become much more difficult if a standard of global welfare was applied.[998] If this suggestion was transposed to the situation of private VERs challenged under Article 11:3 Agreement on Safeguards, an introduction of an "effects on competition"-test would provide a viable solution.

997 For example, it has been suggested that the effects of foreign export cartelisation on consumers, producers and tariff revenues in the importing country should be evaluated; BHATTACHARJEA, (2004) 38 JWT 349.

998 DURAND/FONT GALARZA/MEHTA, (2004) 27 W. Comp. 6.

Such an outcome would further be supported by the fact that economic operators are relevant in the context of WTO dispute settlement. The *Panel on US – Section 301*[999] observed, for instance, that

> [i]t would be entirely wrong to consider that the position of individuals is of no relevance to the GATT/WTO legal matrix. Many of the benefits to Members which are meant to flow as a result of the acceptance of various disciplines under the GATT/WTO depend on the activity of individual economic operators in the national and global market places,[1000]

and that

> [t]he multilateral trading system is, per force, composed not only of States but also, indeed mostly, of individual economic operators.[1001]

Considering that the Panel further held that the needs of such operators should be a factor in determining whether a particular WTO provision is being violated by a government,[1002] and that exposing an individual operator to the risk of WTO inconsistent action by a government can itself constitute a WTO violation because of the "chilling effect" and loss of "confidence" by such operators,[1003] it could be argued that panels may consider not just the interests of the sovereign WTO Members, but also the interests of private market participants. In that sense, it could be maintained that consumers, as private economic operators, are part of the world trading system, and that therefore, an "effects on competition"-test may be justified when reviewing private VERs under the "encouragement or support" requirement of Article 11:3 Agreement on Safeguards.

The impact of private VERs on consumers could then, for instance, be measured in the same dimensions as the "serious injury"-test which is applied to determine the effect that import competition has on the industry that is seeking protection.[1004] "Serious injury" is

999 Panel Report on *US – Section 301*, WT/DS152/R.

1000 *Ibid.*, paragraph 7.73.

1001 *Ibid.*, paragraph 7.76.

1002 *Ibid.*, paragraphs 7.90, 7.94, and 7.167.

1003 *Ibid.*, paragraphs 7.91 and 7.93 *et seq.*

1004 For instance, such approach was also suggested when it comes to decide on an import restriction; FINGER/ZLATE, 10. After all, import restrictions (as safe-

defined as significant overall impairment in the position of a domestic industry (Article 4:1(a) Agreement on Safeguards), and shall be determined by *all* relevant factors of an objective and quantifiable nature having a bearing on the situation of the industry in question. In particular, the rate and amount of the increase in imports in absolute and relative terms, the market share of the domestic market taken by the imported products, changes in the level of sales, production, productivity, capacity utilisation, profits and losses, and employment shall be considered (Article 4:2 Agreement on Safeguards). The EC goes beyond this and stipulates in Regulation 260/2009 to further consider the price of imports, including the hindrance of price increases that normally would have occurred.[1005]

A comparable approach could be taken in respect of an "effects on competition"-test, requiring the evaluation of *all* relevant factors having a bearing on the competitive situation of the markets that are related to a private VER – whether domestic or foreign. If such overall assessment were to reveal that the private VER in question has a detrimental effect on competition, it would have to be considered in breach of Article 11:3 Agreement on Safeguards, irrespective of whether the relevant domestic competition laws allow for the immunity or the simple toleration of the export cartel-like VER due to alleged lack of effect on the domestic market where the VER was instigated. Certainly, the overall evaluation of the anti-competitive effects would have to be "appreciable" (rather than "serious").

As correlative, this approach would boil down to asking whether the VERs in question are the least trade-restrictive means available in relation to other available trade protection instruments, such as the imposition of a safeguard measure in accordance with the Agreement on Safeguards. Prohibiting private VERs that have a net anti-competitive effect would under these considerations be reasonable from both a trade and a competition policy perspective.

guard measures) afford the domestic industry protection from import surges just like VERs do.

1005 Article 10(1)(c) of Regulation 260/2009.

2 The Application of "Non-violation" Complaints to Competition Law Matters

In this context, it may further be interesting to elaborate whether further inspiration may be drawn from the approach taken towards the application of "non-violation" complaints[1006] under GATT Article XXIII:1(b) to competition law matters.

In view of the absence of general competition law disciplines in the WTO/GATT,[1007] some authors have argued that, given the broad

1006 The other "non-violation" complaint, usually named "situation complaint", allows Members to bring a complaint under the dispute settlement procedures when benefits are nullified or impaired as a result of the existence of "any other situation" (GATT Article XXIII:1(c)). Although the term "situation" suggests an adverse circumstance for which governments could not be responsible for, and would therefore, *prima facie*, be suitable for comprising anti-competitive practices arising from private parties, it is important to note "situation" complaints were initially meant to address situations affected by macro-economics factors, such as general economic depression, high unemployment and other similar emergency situations (SPITZER, 107). It becomes apparent that "situation" complaints are highly exceptional which is also reflected in the fact that virtually no panel has ruled on such complaints since 1947 (in 1983, the EC requested consultations with Japan alleging the "present situation" of "continuing imperviousness of the Japanese market" constitutes nullification or impairment by Japan, but ultimately did not pursue the complaint; L/5479, p. 3 in connection with p. 1).The exceptional character of "situation" complaints makes their application unlikely to be suited for competition law matters, and are therefore not further discussed in this book.

1007 Abundant literature, both legal and economic, has been dedicated to the issue whether there is a need for co-operation in the field of international competition policy (in order not to impede international trade), and whether general principles of competition law should be included in the WTO framework. See, for instance, AMATO, (2001) 24 W. Comp. 451 *et seq.*; BOSCHECK, (2001) 24 W. Comp. 48 *et seq.*; CADOT/GRETHER/DE MELO, (2000) 34 JWT 1 *et seq.*; DE LEÓN, (1997) 18 ECLR 162 *et seq.* and (1997) 21 W.Comp. 35 *et seq.*; EVENETT/LEVENSTEIN/SUSLOW, 1 *et seq.*; FIKENTSCHER/HEINEMANN, (1994) 44 WuW 97 *et seq.*; IMMENGA, 107 *et seq.*; JUNG, (2000) 34 JWT 89 *et seq.*; KOJIMA, 1 *et seq.*; MARSDEN, (1997) 21 W. Comp. 91 *et seq.*; PAPAKRIVOPOULOS, (1999) 22 W. Comp. 45 *et seq.*; PETERSMANN, (1993) 27 JWT 35 *et seq.*; VERMULST, (1993) 27 JWT 63 *et seq.* Largely in response to some of the research

wording of the provision contained in GATT Article XXIII:1(b), competition-related measures can be brought before the WTO dispute settlement procedure if they nullify or impair benefits or frustrate the "effet utile" of the agreement concerned.[1008] Although these complaints are based on the legal principles of effectiveness of the concessions, reciprocity and good faith in the protection of the legitimate expectations[1009] for better market access,[1010] it has been pointed out that a number of requirements are nevertheless needed for private anti-competitive behaviours to be challenged: (i) the behaviour of private undertakings that shall be challenged is not illegal under the agreement concerned and denotes some sort of government involvement (application of a "measure"), (ii) this measure has an adverse effect on previously negotiated competitive conditions which is reflected in the reduction of the value of concessions by this measure, and (iii) the

findings, international organisations such as the OECD have also sponsored research into the area of international competition policy: *Consistencies and Inconsistencies between Trade and Competition Policies*, COM/TD/DAFFE/CLP (98) 25/FINAL, OECD, 1998; *Complementarities between Trade and Competition Policies*, COM/TD/DAFFE/CLP(98) 98/FINAL, OECD, 1998; *Competition Elements in International Trade Agreements: a Post-Uruguay Round Overview of WTO Agreements*, COM/TD/DAFFE/CLP (98) 26/FINAL, OECD, 1998.

1008 CHO, 10 *et seq.*; HOEKMAN/MAVROIDIS (1993), 21 *et seq.*; KOOPMANN, 16; SPITZER, 107.

1009 "Legitimate expectation" is understood as what could reasonably have been expected as a consequence of the agreements, and the Panel on *Japan – Film* found that "*[f]or expectations to be legitimate, they must take into account all measures of the party making the concession that could have been reasonably anticipated at the time of the concession*" (WT/DS44/R, paragraph 10.61). The concept of "legitimate (or reasobale) expectations" the result of GATT jurisprudence, and is meant to protect three interests: first, the validity of assumptions on which governments act; second the value of the concessions made during the negotiations; and third, the protection of the mutuality of the obligations, according to a more general principle of reciprocity in international law; CHUA, (1998) 32 JWT 31.

1010 The intention is hence to protect the competitive conditions created by the agreement which resembles the national treatment provision of GATT Article III; see GARCÍA-CASTRILLÓN, (2001) 35 JWT 116.

measure could not have been reasonably anticipated when the concession was bound.[1011]

2.1 "Measure" as a Practice Tolerated or Required by Domestic Regulations

The interesting aspect to consider in this context is that legal academics have discussed whether the term "measure" in GATT Article XXIII:1(b) can also comprise a mere government tolerance of an existing restrictive business practice;[1012] specifically, whether it provides sufficient grounds to challenge a government for having failed to use its legal powers to stop or prevent the reiteration of the practice. Whereas some authors have argued that if the rationale of GATT Article XXIII is to provide a remedy for nullification and impairment of the benefits arising (directly or indirectly) from the agreement concerned, then "measures" should be interpreted in a flexible manner,[1013] other authors have maintained that the wording "application of a measure" in GATT Article XXIII:1(b) entails some sort of positive action by the government,[1014] thus arguing that "inaction" is not a measure.

As much as it is unclear what constitutes a "measure" for the purposes of "non-violation" complaints, and acknowledging that, on a general note, the present dispute settlement system does not generally allow for challenging anti-competitive private practices without establishing a serious finding of governmental responsibility,[1015] it must be stressed

1011 HOEKMAN/MAVROIDIS, (1996) 30 JWT 42 *et seq.*; KOOPMANN, 16.

1012 FURSE, (1999) 20 ECLR 12.

1013 GARCÍA-CASTRILLÓN, (2001) 35 JWT 118.

1014 HOEKMAN/MAVROIDIS (2002), 16; KOMURO, (1998) 35 JWT 183; SPITZER, 112 (with further annotations).

1015 ROESSLER, (1999) 2 JIEL 413 *et seq.* It has also been observed that, instead of using GATT Article XXIII:1(b) to challenge other countries' competition policy practices, the "linkage" of trade and competition policy has been accepted by nearly all WTO Members, and that its underlying rationale may be described as: "*Opening markets will lead to increased trade, but this increase can be frustrated by public and private business practices that proximately nullify the effects of the enhanced openness; as a result, we* may negotiate mu-

that there is no reason to come to the same conclusion in respect of challenging VERs in the context of the Agreement on Safeguards.

The Panel on *Japan – Film* believed, for instance, that it "*[s]hould be open to a broad definition of the term measure for the purposes of Article XXIII:1(b) which considers whether or not a non-government binding action has an effect similar to a binding one*",[1016] and further admitted that "*[i]t is difficult to establish bright-line rules in this regard and it will need to be examined on a case-by-case basis*".[1017]

Whereas it is clear that the fact that an action is taken by private parties does not rule out the possibility that it is deemed governmental if there is sufficient government involvement with it,[1018] the Panel on *Argentina – Hides and Leather*[1019] illustrated how difficult it is to demonstrate that private practices are attributable to government authorities. In *Argentina – Hides and Leather*, the EC claimed that an Argentine resolution authorising the presence of representatives of the domestic tanning industry during customs clearance of exports of bovine hides operated as a *de facto* export restriction in violation of GATT Article XI:1. In the EC's view, the presence of the tanning industry allowed it to access the exporters' confidential business information which was subsequently used, in the framework of the Argentine tanners cartel, to exercise pressure on the Argentine slaughterhouses not to export their hides (hence allowing for the creation of a captive market).[1020] Although the Panel stressed that it agreed with the approach taken by the panel in *Japan – Film*, it found that it follows neither from that panel's statement nor from the text or context of GATT Article XI:1 that Members are "*[u]nder an obligation to exclude any possibility that governmental measures may enable private parties, directly or indirectly, to restrict trade, where those measures themselves are not trade-restrictive*".[1021]

tually acceptable rules *(under the rubric of "competition policy") in regard thereto at the WTO*" (emphasis added); cf. BHAGWATI, (2002) 96 AJIL 130.

1016 Panel Report on *Japan – Film*, WT/DS44/R, paragraph 10.49.

1017 *Ibid.*, paragraph 10.56.

1018 *Ibid.*

1019 Panel Report on *Argentina – Hides and Leather*, WT/DS155/R.

1020 *Ibid.*, paragraphs 4.65 *et seq.*

1021 *Ibid.*, paragraph 11.19.

Ultimately, the EC's arguments were, however, rejected on the basis of a lack of evidence. The Panel noted in this context:

> [I]t is possible that a government could implement a measure which operated to restrict exports because of its interaction with a private cartel. *Other points would need to be argued and proved* (such as *whether there was or needed to be knowledge of the cartel practices on the part of the government*) or [...] it would need to be established that the actions are properly attributed to the Argentinean government under the rules of state responsibility. [...] It may be the case that it will be difficult for one Member to prove that there is a cartel operating within the jurisdiction of another Member. Nonetheless, we cannot ignore the need for sufficient proof of a party's allegations simply because obtaining such proof is difficult *(emphasis added).*[1022]

A further issue which deserves commenting was addressed by the Panel on *Mexico – Telecoms*[1023], namely whether practices that are required (and tolerated) under domestic law can be sanctioned by the relevant WTO provisions. In particular, it was scrutinized whether the obligation to *"[maintain] appropriate measures [...] for the purpose of preventing suppliers who, alone or together, are a major supplier from engaging in or continuing anti-competitive practices"* under Section 1 of Mexico's Telecoms Reference Paper was violated in that sense. Like Mexico, the European Communities (as third party) argued that the said provision imposes an *obligation of means*, not of result; contending that if a WTO Member chooses not to allow competition in a certain area, there is no scope for anti-competitive practices in such area. The European Communities stressed in that context that competition cannot be restricted where competition is not allowed.[1024] The US, as complainant, naturally disagreed with this argument and submitted that the Telecoms Reference Paper is deprived of meaning if Mexico was free to introduce legislation which induces firms to engage in anti-competitive practices. The issue put before the Panel was thus whether the Telecoms Reference Paper (i) acts as a constraint on domestic regulation, or (ii) curtails domestic measures (for instance competition policy) that may be taken.

1022 *Ibid.*, paragraph 11.51.

1023 Panel Report on *Mexico – Telecoms*, WT/DS204/R.

1024 *Ibid.*, paragraph 5.61.

The Panel on *Mexico – Telecoms* answered this question with little regard to possible political and legislative diversities of the WTO Members[1025] and declared that:

> [i]nternational commitments made under the GATS "for the purpose of preventing suppliers ... from engaging in or continuing anti-competitive practices" are [...] *designed to limit the regulatory powers of WTO Members.* Reference Paper commitments undertaken by a Member are international obligations *owed to all other Members* of the WTO *in all areas of the relevant GATS commitments.* In accordance with the principle established in Article 27 of the Vienna Convention, a requirement imposed by a Member under its internal law on a major supplier cannot unilaterally erode its international commitments made in its schedule to other WTO Members to prevent major suppliers from "continuing anti-competitive practices". The pro-competitive obligations in Section 1 of the Reference Paper *do not reserve any such unilateral right of WTO Members to maintain anti-competitive measures* [emphasis added].[1026]

Inspired by these findings, it could be argued that the obligation of the WTO Member under Article 11:3 Agreement on Safeguards, not to encourage or support the adoption or maintenance of, *inter alia*, VERs is a general *"international commitment made under GATT for the purpose of preventing private (and public) enterprises from engaging in or continuing practices (such as VERs) and is designed to limit the regulatory powers of WTO Members."* Ultimately, this would mean that a domestic competition legislation, which were to allow for the presence of VERs (as export cartel-like practice) as consequence of its unilateral legislative power, was to be considered in breach with the Agreement on Safeguards.

Put differently and summing up, the mere existence of a domestic competition law is a measure which itself is not trade-restrictive. If, however, it can be inferred from the text or context of Article 11:3 Agreement on Safeguards that Members are under an obligation to

1025 The Panel merely noted that some Members pursue competition law doctrines under which a firm complying with a specific legislative requirement of such a Member is considered not be in violation of the domestic competition law, and added that the reason for these doctrines is that, in most jurisdictions, domestic legislatures have the legislative power to limit the scope of its competition law. *Ibid.*, paragraph 7.244.

1026 *Ibid.*, paragraph 7.244.

exclude the possibility that this "measure" (*i.e.* the competition law) enables private parties, directly or indirectly, to restrict trade, it could further be argued that there is sufficient government involvement to generate a "legitimate (or reasonable) expectation" of protection from private restrictive business practices, such as private VERs, if the competition law in question immunises export cartels (and comparable practices, such as VERs).

The complaining government would then have to show that it expected the defendant government to enforce competition laws in its territory as a guarantee of the effectiveness of the concessions agreed through previous negotiations. Though, in order to make such complaint effective, the claimant would have to prove its ignorance of the practice at the moment of the negotiations and, simultaneously establish the defendant government's foreknowledge of the existence of the practice.[1027] Clearly, this is very difficult,[1028] as the majority of WTO Member that have a competition law that – albeit often implicitly – exempt export cartels1029, thereby excluding them from scrutiny under a rule of reason (case-by-case) approach (mostly) already at the time of negotiation.

1027 In this context, it was pointed out that two additional requirements are necessary in "non-violation" complaints based on the principle of "reasonable expectation": the measure must not have been reasonably foreseeable by the complainant at the time the expectation arose, and the measure must, as such, frustrate the complainant's reasonable expectation of better market access arising as a result of the negotiations. The first requirement is said to ensure the good faith of the complainant, while the second is directed at the good faith of the respondent; CHUA, (1998) 32 JWT 41.

1028 Inversely, in the context of market access, it has also been pointed out by legal commentators that if the country where market foreclosures take place lacks a domestic competition law, or when possessing, it is enforced in a rather discriminatory or ineffective fashion, there is presently no remedy available for foreign firms seeking market access; AMATO, (2001) 24 W. Comp. 454.

1029 LEVENSTEIN/SUSLOW, (2005) 20 Am. U. Int'l L. Rev. 819 *et seq.*

2.2 Different Terms – Similar Meanings

Drawing upon the aspects discussed above, the following parallels may be drawn to a possible violation complaint under GATT XXIII:1(a) with regard to Article 11:3 Agreement on Safeguards:

- It has been established that Article 11:3 Agreement on Safeguards requires a minimum of "government involvement" for there to be encouragement or support of the prohibited practice (*e.g.* a VER) which is, *prima facie*, similar to what constitutes a "measure" under GATT Article XXIII:1(b).
- For the purposes of GATT Article XXIII:1(b), such "measure" is broadly interpreted and will have to be examined on a case-by-case basis. There is no reason to conclude otherwise for "government involvement" under Article 11:3 Agreement on Safeguards, and accordingly, to find a violation in the sense of GATT Article XXIII:1(a).
- If it is said that competition-related measures can be brought to WTO dispute settlement under GATT Article XXIII:1(b), provided that they nullify or impair the benefits or frustrate the "effet utile" of the agreement concerned, the same should be possible in the case of private VERs since the "effet utile" of the Agreement on Safeguards would be frustrated if private VERs go unchecked.

Ultimately, these considerations suggest, however, that there is no room for non-violation complaints regarding private VERs as the requirements under GATT Article XXIII:1(a) are *de facto*, and in large, identical to the ones established under GATT Article XXIII:1(b) when it comes to challenging private VERs. Either way, it would have to be demonstrated that there is sufficient "government involvement". Considering, moreover, that nullification and impairment is presumed to exist in case of a violation of a WTO provision, choosing the avenue of a non-violation complaint to attack private VERs would make little sense in terms of burden of proof that is placed on the complainant.

3 Preliminary Conclusion

Under the current WTO dispute settlement system, effectively challenging private VERs would require to allow for an "effects on competition"-test under Article 11:3 Agreement on Safeguards which were to take into account *all* relevant factors that are pertinent to the competitive situation of the markets that are related to a private VER – whether domestic or foreign. If, thereby, an *overall* detrimental effect on competition, including the effect in the market of the importing country, is demonstrated, Article 11:3 Agreement on Safeguards would be violated, irrespective of whether the domestic competition law of the exporting country allows for the immunity or the simple toleration of the export cartel-like VER due to alleged lack of effect on its domestic market.

In the absence of such constructive expansion, the use of a violation complaint (GATT Article XXIII:1(a)) in this respect essentially boils down to the demonstration of the same criteria, as far as sufficient "government involvement" is concerned, as the ones required under a non-violation complaint pursuant to GATT Article XXXIII:1(b).

Likewise, the use of a non-violation complaint is deemed to be ineffective in challenging private VERs since a claimant would have to demonstrate its ignorance of the practice – here: (domestic) regulatory environment touching upon the handling of VERs, such as competition laws – at the moment of the negotiations and, simultaneously establish the defendant government's foreknowledge of the existence of the practice. In view of the predominance of national competitions laws being not applicable to or immunising export cartels and like behaviour, this requirement is unlikely to be met by the complainant.

In this context, it is further noteworthy that knowledgeable sources have pointed out that the use of non-violation complaints is, in any event, difficult to resolve with the binding nature of the WTO dispute settlement system:

> The negotiators of the GATT […] regarded the concept of non-violation nullification or impairment as a benchmark guiding consultations, negotiations and

> multilateral decision-making. They did not envisage the application of the concept in binding third-party adjudication procedure. [...] The open-ended nature of the concept of nullification and impairment therefore *did not entail a threat to the sovereignty of the contracting parties*. Under the WTO Agreement, however, the decisions determining the benefits that might accrue under a provision in addition to the benefit of its observation would be determined by the Appellate Body, whose decisions must be unconditionally accepted *(emphasis added)*.[1030]

Whereas the suggestion that there is, practically speaking, no room for non-violation complaints regarding private VERs may be welcome in the light of the argument that the WTO system has largely removed the traditional justification of non-violation complaints, economists support that the prospect of non-violation complaints may still be beneficial in the sense that it may restrict national sovereignty over domestic policy choices in a positive way.[1031] Such has been supported to a certain extent by the finding in the *Mexico – Telecoms* case which established that certain international commitments under the WTO regime are designed to limit the regulatory powers of WTO Members, thereby ultimately restricting, in effect, their sovereignty.

Coupled with the observation that the needs of private economic operators, including consumers, should be a factor in determining whether a particular WTO provision is being violated by a government, such benefits could, as suggested at the outset, effectively be reaped by allowing for an "effects on competition"-test when reviewing private VERs under the "encouragement or support" requirement of Article 11:3 Agreement on Safeguards. In treating all affected interests as equal, and in placing a private VER's effect into context with all the market conditions, the application of a "global welfare standard" would support a true commitment towards the prohibition and abolition of grey-area measures. Admittedly, such an approach is at the cost of sovereignty, but it appears justified in the limited scope of tackling private VERs.

1030 ROESSLER, (1999) 2 JIEL 418.

1031 This is the case if governments aim at implementing their domestic policy through tariff negotiations alone provided that the standards (or policies) set by each government encourages market access relative to the standard policy pursued; BAGWELL/STAIGER, 34.

CHAPTER V

Summing Up the "Non-Complaint" Situation of Voluntary Export Restraints

The prohibitions of VERs, as contained in Articles 11:1(b) and 11:3 Agreement on Safeguards, are an illustrative example of the interrelationship between trade and competition policy:

- a Member shall not seek, take or maintain any voluntary export restraints; and
- Members shall not encourage or support the adoption or maintenance by public and private enterprises of non-governmental measures equivalent to voluntary export restraints.

Given that VERs, for the purposes of the review undertaken in this book, encompass any restriction on exports administered unilaterally by the exporters or their government, but is induced (directly through negotiation or indirectly by means of alternative pressure and intimidation) by the importers or their government, one would suspect that the above prohibitions leave no room for manoeuvre. From a legal perspective, the only decisive criterion would be whether, at any stage of giving effect to the VER, it was to be qualified as governmental or non-governmental in nature for it to fall within the scope of either of the above prohibitions.

Trade policy and competition policy *can* be mutually reinforcing policy tools. This is implicitly acknowledged by the above prohibitions. In the absence of effective competition policy, private restraints of trade can, however, nullify the benefits of negotiated trade liberalisation. Likewise, governments can act affirmatively to distort the operation of private markets, for instance by government authorised exemptions to national competition laws or trade policy measures that directly affect cross-border sales, such as voluntary export restraints. Alternatively, government practices can affect competition through acts of omission, by tolerating anti-competitive arrangements or failing to enforce competition laws (if such are in place).

However, trade policy and competition policy are designed to address economic distortions from different sources. Whereas trade policy focuses on governmental restraints of trade that restrict foreign access to markets and discriminate against foreign market participants, competition laws principally address private restraints of trade that restrict the operation of domestic markets. The effect of these two types of distortions is, at least in the case of VERs, the same: less competition and higher costs for consumers.

Nevertheless, the very concept and nature of VERs seem to create a "non-complaint" situation, a sort of safe-harbour in which they flourish despite their illegality. This seems to be particularly true for non-governmental VERs, *i.e.* VERs implemented by private parties, as they remain largely outside the reach of international trade rules (due to the lack of government involvement) or competition rules (due to the alleged lack of effect of an export cartel on the domestic market). Successfully targeting the "non-complaint" situation would therefore require the introduction of a standard of global welfare, such as an "effects on competition"-test.

1 VERs: Flexible Enough to Bend (not Break) the Law?

The main features of VERs that appeal to their promoters may be summarised as follows:

- at the surface, VERs originate on the export side;
- they are non-transparent;
- they are temporary;
- the promoters, whether public or private, of VERs reap large enough (political and/or economic) benefits from the VERs to overlook their negative consequences;
- the VERs result in a rent transfer to the restricted exporters; and

- appear, *prima facie*, as trade instruments that are not geared towards protectionism and do, therefore, not induce retaliation.

Put differently, VERs benefit from such flexibility that it affords them a "no-fault" insurance protection.

1.1 The "No-Fault" Insurance Protection

As elaborated in Chapter I, the popularity of VERs among governments and industries (importing and exporting competitors) resides mainly in the fact that they represent a convenient tool to "resolve" trade problems without being subjected to the scrutiny of domestic or international proceedings. This includes the political advantage that the promoters of VERs do not have to define their objectives in any but the vaguest of terms, thereby pre-empting the risk of later being accused of failure.

This lack of "publicity" further removes the incentive for industries to embrace the challenges of the market. To the contrary, both the exporters and the protected industry have an incentive to maintain the protection, and neither is under pressure to adjust to competitive market conditions for the following reasons:

- The export-competing producers benefit from the quantitative limitation the VER places on the output, or rather from the administration and allocation thereof. The VER is likely to promote the formation of an export cartel, in which the collusive nature of VERs may be extended into the structure of world markets, thereby providing the possibility to share markets and to build up barriers to market entry.
- The import-competing producers are allocated a minimum level of projected domestic demand. This leaves the exporting producers with a market share that is subject to future demand fluctuations (as their relative market shares are essentially frozen at the time of the implementation of the VER). In order to compensate the risk of such fluctuations, they may all choose to influence their market position by price increases, trade di-

version and surreptitious redistributive effects, such as protection rents.

- Effectively, the VER leads both the higher-cost domestic producers and the low-cost exporting producers to raise their prices above the level that would otherwise prevail due to the total size of the market being restricted and the level of imports into the domestic market being restrained. Nevertheless, most economists agree that a VER does not necessarily accrue benefits to the exporters concerned in absolute terms, but merely helps to avoid a harsher unilateral trade measure imposed by the importing country. This means, ultimately, that the only winners from a VER are producers in third countries.

The flexibility of the VER thus creates a "no-fault" insurance protection for the promoters of the VER, whether they are governmental or private, at a cost to domestic consumers. In this sense, VERs benefit from a "non-complaint" situation as they elude effective legal disciplines and judicial control – unless the consumers (as ultimate losers under a VER) act as complainants.

1.2 Security and Predictability for All Economic Operators

Considering that the multilateral trading system and hence the national and global markets are composed not only of states but, indeed mostly, of individual economic operators, including consumers, the position of individuals must be of relevance to the WTO legal matrix. Transposed to VERs, whether they are government-sponsored or private in nature, the most pertinent impact is, as outlined in Chapter I, on consumers:

- The domestic industry is protected by the VER at a high cost to domestic consumers. They are adversely affected by carrying the burden of higher domestic prices (both of the imported and the domestically produced good) and by missing out on potential tariff revenues. The welfare reduction of consumers therefore not only derives from paying the net social cost of a

- VER, but also the fact that the change in relative prices brought about by the VER is not truly market-driven but the consequence of a policy measure. Whatever the distribution of the associated rents of a VER, they are associated with dead-weight losses on the consumption and on the production side.
- In addition to the economically adverse effects, a VER bears significant information costs because of its non-transparency. The deliberate circumvention of "due process guarantees" available under other trade measures that occurs under a VER may even amount to a violation of individual freedoms and property rights of the adversely affected consumers.
- However, a VER's lack of transparency furthers the unlikelihood of a reaction on the part of consumers.

Since consumers are those most affected by VERs, it is important to find a way to somehow accommodate their interests within the multilateral trading system. This can, however, only be achieved if the legal system provides security and predictability. Having these central elements in mind, what legal remedies are available to private economic operators which are faced with the adverse effects of VERs?

2 The (In)Availability of Legal Remedies to Private Economic Operators

Irrespective of whether VERs are implemented secretly, they arguably bypass international trade law as well as domestic competition laws. This is particularly true for VERs that are private, *i.e.* not government-sponsored. Based on the analysis undertaken in Chapters II, III and IV it is contended that the legal instruments currently in place within the EC legal order and the WTO dispute settlement system are insufficient to tackle this problem. The following summary substantiates these points.

2.1 No Direct Access of Private Parties to the WTO Dispute Settlement System

Private parties have no direct access to any of the WTO bodies to complain about VERs that infringe the Agreement on Safeguards, irrespective of whether they are government-sponsored or private. Accordingly, challenging VERs is dependent on the success of lobbying activities whereby the domestic relevant political decision-makers are actively convinced to take action.

In the case of the European Community, there is, however, an additional – formalised – possibility: the Trade Barriers Regulation (TBR) envisages private complaints about unfair trade practices of third countries. Although the TBR allows private parties affected by a VER to urge the Commission to bring the case to WTO dispute settlement, complainants would have to overcome considerable hurdles by demonstrating (i) the existence of an obstacle to trade, (ii) the presence of adverse trade effects which result from that obstacle, and (iii) the need to take action in the interests of the Community. Whilst private parties may play a decisive role by presenting to the Commission unambiguous and convincing evidence, the Commission is accorded extensive discretion in the determination of Community interests. Should the Commission find against the existence of Community interests, the complainants against VERs are severely limited in their appeal against such finding because the judicial review is restricted to the absence of errors of law or of manifest errors in the assessment of fact in economic policy matters. Put differently, if the Commission cannot be motivated to initiate proceedings under the WTO dispute settlement system based on the allegations and evidence presented by the private parties, then the chances of practically "forcing" the Commission to act by means of a court decision overruling the Commission's assessment are extremely limited.

The mechanism provided for by the TBR represents a valuable recognition of private parties as being part of the multilateral trading system, but – due to the discretionary uncertainties – complainants against VERs may prefer to bring a test a remedy provided by the EC legal system, such as a direct action according to Article 263(4) TFEU (*ex* Article 230(4) EC Treaty) or the procedure for a preliminary ruling under Article 267 TFEU (*ex* Article 234 EC Treaty).

2.2 Incomplete Access of Private Parties to Domestic and/or Community Courts

The analysis of remedies provided by the EC legal system in the context of challenging VERs by private parties, possibly consumers, is equally unsatisfactory.

Article 263(4) TFEU (*ex* Article 230(4) EC Treaty) allows non-privileged applicants, *i.e.* every natural or legal person, to challenge directly any allegedly illegal Community act as a result of the direct effect of Community law. Theoretically, VERs sponsored by EC institutions may therefore be subject to an action of annulment provided that the Agreement on Safeguards (notably its Article 11) produces direct effect within the domestic legal order.

In reality such possibility is, however, limited due to the very strict requirements concerning the *locus standi* conditions (private parties can only bring an action if they are concerned both "directly and individually"):

- For a private party to be "directly concerned" by a Community measure of general application, the latter must directly affect the legal situation of the individual and leave no discretion to the addressees of the measures, which are entrusted with the task of implementing it. Thus, it must be substantially certain that the VER would affect the applicant at the time it was adopted.
- For private party to be regarded as "individually concerned" by a measure not addressed to them, the measure must affect their position by reason of certain attributes peculiar to them, or by reason of a factual situation which differentiates them from all other persons and distinguishes them individually in the same way as the addressee.

These restrictions imposed by the EC Treaty (now the TFEU) and the narrow interpretation of the Court of Justice represent an important hindrance to access by private parties to the European courts.

Alternatively, private parties may always choose to demonstrate that the national courts of the EC's Member States provide for remedies sufficient to ensure effective legal protection, thereby opening the door for a possible preliminary ruling under Article 267 TFEU (*ex* Article 234 EC Treaty). The advantage of this procedure is that the conditions for standing are less strict then in annulment proceedings, and preliminary references from national courts have allowed individuals and undertakings to obtain a ruling on the validity of EC measures that they would have otherwise been prevented from due to their lack of *locus standi.* Often, the challenged measures had infringed general principles of law or Treaty provisions, or concerned situations where the Community institutions had exceeded their powers. Whilst this may sound promising with a view to complain about VERs, the following considerations may end up in private parties being deprived from any remedy:

- There is no guarantee that the national court finds it necessary to refer the question to the Court of Justice, and the private parties are not instrumented to compel the national court to make that reference.
- There must be a national measure implementing the Community measure for the private parties to be able to bring proceedings before the national court. In cases of VERs that do not entail any intervention by the Member States, there is thus no proceeding before the national courts available to the private parties and the possibility of a reference to the Court of Justice is ruled out.
- Finally, a national court cannot declare an EC measure (here: a VER) invalid. At the most, an interim order suspending the application of the VER in question may be issued, pending the ruling of the Court of Justice.

Summing up, the Community courts' stance towards giving private parties a right to effective remedy is hampered by the high standard placed on standing. Individuals may challenge VERs that they cannot contest directly in the Community courts, theoretically, by a dual system of protection. Where a Community institution were to be responsible for the administrative implementation of the VER, private parties may bring a direct action before the ECJ against implementing measures addressed to them and plead the illegality of the VER under Articles 263 and 277 TFEU (*ex* Articles 230 and 241 EC Treaty respectively). Where implementation were to be a matter for national authorities, the private parties can plead the invalidity of the VER before the national court and encourage the latter to request the Court of Justice for a preliminary ruling.

In practice, either way is additionally hindered by the reluctance of the Community courts to give direct effect to WTO provisions and DSB reports.

2.2.1 Limited Invocability of WTO Provisions and DSB Reports

The reasons that led the Community courts to deny individuals the possibility to challenge Community measures on the basis of WTO law may briefly be summarised as follows:

- Since the Community's main trading partners do not recognise the direct effect of WTO law in their legal systems, the Community should not do so either because the WTO/GATT "is based on principles of negotiations undertaken on the basis of reciprocal and mutually advantageous arrangements".
- The WTO/GATT system is "characterised by the great flexibility of its provisions, in particular those conferring the possibility of derogation, the measures to be taken when confronted with exceptional difficulties, and the settlement of conflicts". Accordingly, they are not such as to be invoked by individuals.
- If a Community measure were to be declared null and void due to a violation of WTO provisions or of DSB reports, the Community institutions would be deprived from finding an alternative solution by means of negotiation, even temporarily, to bring about conformity with the Community's WTO obligations.

Whilst the above general arguments against direct effect of WTO law reflect the Court of Justice's dedication not to endanger the autonomy of the EC, it has nevertheless allowed private parties to rely on *specific* WTO provisions to challenge the legality of Community measures in exceptional circumstances:

- Under the "implementation principle" WTO/GATT provisions are exceptionally accorded direct effect (either under the "implementation exception" as developed under the *Nakajima* or the "clear reference exception" under the *Fediol* doctrines) because the EC has explicitly indicated its intention to implement WTO/GATT law in the relevant EC legislation.
- In the rare instances where direct effect is granted to a specific WTO provision, it is to be expected that the Court of Justice will adhere to the following two principles: (i) It is likely to revert to relevant DSB rulings concerning such a provision (irrespective of the expiry of a time-limit accorded to the Community to comply with the DSB's decision) because, according to the ECJ, there is no distinction to be drawn between the direct effect of a (substantive) WTO provision and the direct effect of a DSB decision; and (ii) a private party may not rely in proceedings before a court of a Member State on the fact that Community legislation is incompatible with a given WTO provision even where the DSB has declared that legislation to be incompatible with such provision. Exceptions to this principle are only accepted if the Community measure was intended to ensure the enforcement within the Community legal order of a particular obligation assumed in the context of the WTO, or if it expressly refers to specific provisions of the WTO agreements.

In Chapter III, Regulation 3285/94 (as later codified in Regulation 260/2009) was reviewed textually and conceptually with a view to contest VERs before the Community courts. Thereupon, it is contended that private parties may (theoretically) rely on provisions of the Agreement on Safeguards before a Community court in light of the "implementation principle" and, in particular, under the *Nakajima* doctrine because the Regulation intends to implement into the EC legal order the obligations deriving from GATT Article XIX and the Agreement on Safeguards.

In addition, it may be noted that the Community courts are willing to apply the principle of treaty-consistent interpretation to the WTO Agreements as long as private litigants do not challenge the legality of EC (or national) measures on the basis of WTO law or DSB rulings, and therefore seek to avoid inconsistencies. In that sense, WTO rules may still be referred to (but not relied upon) by private parties in order to substantiate general principles of law. Conceivably, such interpretative value may be enhanced in the context of liability claims as opposed to actions for annulment of the contested measure.

2.2.2 Denial of Compensation for Damages

Considering that all economic operators affected by non-compliance with WTO provisions and DSB rulings should be entitled to seek protection, some advancement regarding private parties' rights may result from liability claims. Not at least with reference to the principle of effective judicial protection, an action for damages against the EC institutions is particularly conceivable when a DSB ruling is not implemented. Whilst a possible non-implementation may be justified by the public interest, it may also provoke retaliatory restrictions that have to be borne by specific private parties (especially those that are "unrelated" to the measure – for instance, consumers in the case of a VER). Private parties directly affected by the WTO violation or by the sanctions imposed as a result of the non-compliance should be allowed to claim damages before the Community courts.

In this context it should be recalled that, according to the Community courts' consistent interpretation of Article 340(2) TFEU (*ex* Article 288(2) EC Treaty), a claimant asserting non-contractual liability of the Community must demonstrate the unlawfulness of the institutions' alleged conduct, actual damages and a causal link between that conduct and the damage. When establishing "unlawful conduct", the discussion on whether some WTO rules or DSB rulings should have direct effect within the EC legal order ought to be slightly different to the question as to whether some WTO rules or DSB rulings are intended to confer rights on individuals. However, as far as a WTO provision (or the relevant DSB ruling) is concerned, the analysis in Chapter II.3.3.3 demonstrates that EC institutions are not considered to act unlawfully if they fail to bring EC legislation into conformity with WTO law by the deadline established under the WTO dispute settlement procedure because a DSB ruling cannot be fundamentally distinguished from the substantive WTO provision that conveys obligations on the WTO member. This means that the ECJ refused (i) to accept direct responsibility for ensuring that EC law complies with WTO law as this would effectively deprive the EC's legislative or executive organs of the scope of manoeuvre enjoyed the WTO dispute settlement, and (ii) to admit a possible claim for damages for lawful conduct in the absence of direct effect.

There is thus no basis for liability in the absence of unlawful conduct, at least in respect of legislative activity. The motivation behind this is twofold: (i) where the legality of a measure is subject to judicial review, the prospect of actions for damages must not impair legislative action whenever the general interest of the Community requires legislative measures to be adopted which may adversely affect individual interests; and (ii) the EC cannot incur liability in a legislative context characterised by the exercise of a wide discretion, unless the institution concerned has manifestly and gravely exceeded its powers.

Uncertainty remains, however, as to whether the remedy for non-contractual liability for lawful conduct is not available altogether or whether it may (still) be available to private parties in the event of a directly effective provision. This uncertainty is heightened by the possibility that a Community legislative measure whose application leads to restrictions of the right to property or the freedom to pursue a trade or profession could give rise to non-contractual liability on the part of the Community, where these restrictions "impair the very substance of these rights in a disproportionate and intolerable manner, perhaps precisely because no provision has been made for compensation calculated to avoid or remedy that impairment".[1032] In cases where lawful

1032 Joined Cases C-120/06P and C-121/06P, *FIAMM & Fedon*, [2008] E.C.R. I-6513, paragraph 184.

measures of the EC institutions impose disproportionate burdens on some private parties situated in the Common market for the benefit of the public good as a whole (*i.e.* in the Community interest), there could therefore well be a founded claim for damages. Nonetheless, it remains to be seen whether liability claims that refer to DSB recommendations and rulings in a "principled" way (as opposed to alleging them having direct effect) are capable of increasing the Community's commitment to be(come) compliant with such recommendations and rulings, and therefore, the Community's assumption of liability.

2.2.3 Insufficient Reach of EU Competition Law

In view of the incomplete access of private parties to domestic and/or Community courts, or rather the lack of security and predictability of their rights to judicial control in the context of VERs under the EC regime, another avenue to test the illegality or the alleviation of the negative effects of VERs on consumers may be found in the application of competition law, as discussed in Chapter III.3 regarding EU competition law.

The motivation for such review lies in the fact that effects comparable to those of export cartels are evidenced in VERs: The total size of the market is restricted, the level of imports is restrained and consumers experience higher prices than they would in the absence of a VER. The market structure is likely to be static as the relative market shares of the participants in the VER remain unchanged as of the introduction of the VER and collusive behaviour is likely to be fostered (as reiterated in Chapter IV.1.3.1).

However, challenging VERs under EU competition law proves to be equally unsuccessful and burdensome:

- Private VERs towards the Community market are difficult to catch under Article 101(1) TFEU (*ex* Article 81(1) EC Treaty) due to the limits placed by the extraterritorial application of EU competition law. Similarly, VERs instigated among EC exporters (amounting to an export cartel) are normally outside the scope of Article 101(1) TFEU (*ex* Article 81(1) EC Treaty), unless they appreciably restrict competition within the Community and affect trade between the Member States.

- Regarding government-sponsored VERs, the discussion of the case-law of the Community courts in Chapter III.3 suggests that the competition provisions of the EC Treaty (now TFEU) are infringed when a Member State requires or favours the adoption of anti-competitive agreements, decisions or concerted practices, or reinforces their effects, or where it divests its own rules of the character of legislation by delegating to private economic operators responsibility for taking decisions affecting the economic sphere. This consistent finding derives from the Community courts' reliance on Article 10(2) EC Treaty (now Article 4(3) *in fine* TEU) which mandates a negative obligation for Member States to refrain from undermining Community objectives. Whilst VERs that are sponsored by Member States may therefore be caught under EU competition law, a comparable line of reasoning is clearly not possible in respect of VERs that are sponsored by foreign governments. Accordingly, measures imposed on foreign undertakings to restrict their exports by the foreign government fall outside the scope of Article 101 TFEU. Measures resulting from agreements or concerted practices between undertakings which are, however, merely favoured by the foreign government or whose effect is only reinforced by practices of the foreign government may still be caught under EU competition law, for instance if the exporters accepting the VER have a certain autonomy in choosing their line of conduct.

The summary of the variety of hurdles placed by the law (and its application) illustrates why VERs benefit from a "non-complaint" situation. Certainly, there is a documented absence of cases on VERs altogether, and the limited potential of the legal remedies discussed in Chapters III and IV does not encourage cases on VERs to put to a test. Nevertheless, it may be hoped that possible complainants of VERs, such as consumers, will chose to either lobby their government to take the necessary steps to prevent VERs or to directly pursue action against such grey-area measures.

Reform would therefore depend on the entrepreneurship of lobbyists and lawyers to organise the consumers into an effective political force, thereby allowing them (indirect) access to the WTO dispute settlement system voiced through their government. If such could be achieved, there may be an avenue to advocate an "effects on competition"-test for the purposes of Article 11 Agreement on Safeguards, measuring the impact of VERs on consumers under a global welfare standard.

3 Targeting the "Non-Complaint" Situation by Introducing an "Effects on Competition"-Test

The analysis of the "non-complaint" situation of VERs calls for a new approach if the provisions in Article 11 Agreement on Safeguards are to be truly effective. Giving effect to the obligation not to engage in or foster VERs must be viewed in the light of the expectations and interests of the other WTO Members to do so. This is particularly the case in the event of private VERs that are tolerated by the government and thereby contravene the "good faith" requirement in treaty observation and remove the substance of the Agreement on Safeguards.

In practice, litigation of disputes in the WTO/GATT focussing on private business practices restricting access to markets that are encouraged, supported or tolerated by governments has been rare and difficult. In *Japan – Trade in Semi-Conductors Semiconductors*, it was found that even non-binding administrative guidance by the Japanese could constitute a "government measure" if certain criteria were met, namely (i) that reasonable grounds exist for believing that the government measures created sufficient incentives to persuade private parties to conform their conduct to the non-mandatory measures, and (ii) that the effectiveness of the private conduct was "essentially dependent" on the non-mandatory actions taken by the government. Building upon these findings, in order to be considered actionable government measures, it was held in *Japan – Film* that they must "proceed in a manner that is sensitive to the context in which these governmental actions are taken and the effect they have on private actors".

The record shows that the legal possibility of claims around such mix of private and governmental practices under WTO/GATT rules is inseparably linked to the demonstration of sufficient "government involvement". Whilst the GATT's non-violation provision (GATT Article XXIII:1(b)) provides some scope for a complaint of competitive foreclosure of a market if, for example, non-application of national competition laws were adjudged to be a "government measure", there remain at least two other conditions that have to be met: (i) the measure would need to have altered the competitive conditions established by other WTO/GATT undertakings, and (ii) the government measure taken would have to be one that could not reasonably have been anticipated at the time that the tariff or other concession was made. Ultimately, this means that there is no room for non-violation complaints regarding private VERs since a complainant WTO Member cannot conceivably argue that it expected the defendant government to enforce its competition laws against a private VER although such law, most likely, exempts export cartels from its scope.

The application of a violation complaint pursuant to GATT Article XXIII:1(a) for the lack of enactment or enforcement of competition law appears equally unsuccessful since WTO/GATT does not impose common competition law disciplines on its Members, and nothing in the Agreement on Safeguards may be construed so as to oblige WTO Members to enact or enforce a domestic competition law for the sake of prohibiting private VERs.

This finding is, however, substantially different to the suggestion that a WTO Member's toleration of private VERs may frustrate the substance of the Agreement on Safeguards. It merely illustrates that the traditional approach in trying to subsume a government's inaction under the "encouragement or support" requirement of Article 11:3 Agreement on Safeguards is virtually impossible. Instead, it should be focussed on the demonstration that private VERs have an adverse effect on competition in the sense that their toleration amounts to a "failure of another Member to carry out its obligations" under the Agreement on Safeguards, *i.e.* that the government's inaction is involved as part of the original competition claim, and amounts to an impediment of the attainment of an objective of the Agreement.

The crucial question that would reflect a true commitment towards the effectiveness of the Agreement on Safeguards is thus: Is there an adverse effect on competition deriving from private VERs?

Whereas there seems to be a common perception that countries have no incentives to ban private VERs that take the form of export cartels because they allegedly lack immediate effects on the domestic market, economic analysis demonstrates that they have undoubtedly adverse effects on consumers (domestic and foreign). The lack of enforcement action against export cartels is therefore clearly difficult to reconcile with a coherent competition policy since export cartels are, like any other cartel behaviour, hard-core infringements if *all* effects, domestic and foreign, would be taken into consideration. Ultimately, this would allow testing private VERs against a standard of global welfare under an "effects on competition"-test.

The impact of private VERs on consumers could then, for instance, be measured in the same dimensions as the "serious injury" test which is applied to determine the effect import competition has on the industry that is seeking protection. When determining serious injury, all relevant factors of an objective and quantifiable nature having a bearing on the situation of that industry have to be evaluated. A comparable approach could apply to the "effects on competition"-test, for instance:

- the rate and amount of product regulated by the VER in absolute and relative terms,
- the market share of the domestic market taken by the product regulated by the VER,
- changes in the level of sales (*ante* and *post* the implementation of the VER),
- production, productivity and capacity utilisation,
- quantitative tests of elasticities, and
- profits and losses.

Moreover, this would take due account of the general principle of proportionality because the VERs in question would have to be assessed as to whether they are the least trade-restrictive means available in relation to other available trade protection instruments, such as the imposition of a safeguard measure in accordance with the Agreement on Safeguards. In that sense, the practices that affect the competitive structure of the market are evaluated and weighed against each other.

Prohibiting private VERs that have an *appreciable net anti-competitive effect* would under these considerations be reasonable from both a trade and a competition policy perspective, as all affected interests, *i.e.* interests of all economic operators, including consumers, would have to be treated as equal.

Studies in Global Economic Law
Studien zum globalen Wirtschaftsrecht
Études en droit économique mondial

Present and future economic, technological and societal changes and evolutions fundamentally affect traditional legal structures of the territorial state system. They increasingly call for global approaches and solutions, transgressing the tools of classical public international law. This trilingual series publishes monographs, studies and collected papers dedicated to these challenges. The contributions examine existing instruments, in particular within the framework of the international trading system. They explore new approaches and search for innovative solutions within the global process of legal integration. Research efforts are dedicated to different walks of life and areas of regulation, and to the quest for adequate constitutional structures of transnational and democratic processes.

Wirtschaftliche, technologische und gesellschaftliche Entwicklungen der Gegenwart und Zukunft bewirken tiefgreifende Änderungen traditioneller Strukturen des Rechts des Territorialstaats und rufen zunehmend nach globalen Vorgehensweisen und Lösungen, die oftmals über das Instrumentarium des klassischen Völkerrechts hinaus weisen. Die dreisprachige Reihe publiziert Monographien, Studien und Tagungsbände, die sich vertieft mit diesen Herausforderungen auseinandersetzen. Die Beiträge untersuchen das bestehende Instrumentarium namentlich im Rahmen des Welthandelssystems und forschen nach neuen Ansätzen und Lösungen im Rahmen des globalen Integrationsprozesses. Dazu gehören Studien zu den Regelungen einzelner Sach- und Lebensbereiche wie auch zu Fragen adäquater transnationaler demokratischer Verfassungs- und Entscheidungsstrukturen.

Les évolutions actuelles et futures sur le plan technique, économique et social ne cesseront d'influencer profondément les structures traditionnelles du droit de l'état territorial. Par conséquent, des approches et des solutions dépassant les instruments du droit international public classique deviennent de plus en plus nécessaires. Cette collection trilingue publie des monographies, études et actes de colloques qui analysent et font face à ces défis. Les contributions examinent les instruments existants, notamment dans la domaine du système commercial mondiale. Elles cherchent à développer des approches nouvelles et des solutions innovatrices dans le contexte du processus d'intégration globale en incluant des études de droit touchant aux différents secteurs et domaines de vie. De plus, les travaux de recherche seront également destinés à trouver les procédures consti-tutionnelles et décisionnelles les plus adéquates et démocratiques au niveau transnational.

Studies in Global Economic Law
Studien zum globalen Wirtschaftsrecht
Études en droit économique mondial

edited by THOMAS COTTIER

Vol. 1 MARTIN A. GIRSBERGER – Biodiversity and the Concept of Farmers' Rights in International Law. Factual Background and Legal Analysis, 1999

Vol. 2 DAVID WYSS – Bankdienstleistungen im Allgemeinen Dienstleistungsabkommen der WTO. Auswirkungen auf das schweizerische Bankenrecht, 1999

Vol. 3 BENOÎT MERKT – Harmonisation internationale et entraide administrative internationale en droit de la concurrence. Droit du GATT/OMC, droit européen, accords bilatéraux et perspectives pour le droit suisse, 2000

Vol. 4 INGO MEITINGER – Der Schutz von Geschäftsgeheimnissen im globalen und regionalen Wirtschaftsrecht. Stand und mögliche Entwicklungen der internationalen und regionalen Rechtsharmonisierung, 2001

Vol. 5 JOËLLE DE SÉPIBUS – Die Umweltschutzsubvention im Gemeinschaftsrecht. Eine umweltrechtliche Kritik der europäischen Beihilfekontrolle, 2003

Vol. 6 BOBJOSEPH MATHEW – The WTO Agreements on Telecommunications, 2003

Vol. 7 LUKAS ENGELBERGER – Die unmittelbare Anwendbarkeit des WTO-Rechts in der Schweiz. Grundlagen und Perspektiven im Kontext internationaler Rechtsentwicklungen, 2004

Vol. 8 THOMAS M. FISCHER – Die Entbündelung der letzten Meile in der Schweiz im Lichte des GATS, 2004

Vol. 9 DAE-WON KIM – Non-Violation Complaints in WTO Law. Theory and Practice, 2006

Vol. 10 QI ZHANG – Consultation within WTO Dispute Settlement. A Chinese Perspective, 2007

Vol. 11 Felix Bloch – Technologietransfer zum internationalen Umweltschutz. Eine völkerrechtliche Untersuchung unter besonderer Berücksichtigung des Schutzes der Ozonschicht und des Weltklimas, 2007

Vol. 12 Bettina Beck – Die Regelung von Slots (Zeitnischen) im Luftverkehrsrecht. Vergabe, Übertragung und Anfechtung in der Schweiz und der EG unter rechtsvergleichender Berücksichtigung US-amerikanischer Normen, 2008

Vol. 13 Sabina Nüesch – Voluntary Export Restraints in WTO and EU Law. Consumers, Trade Regulation and Competition Policy, 2010

Vol. 14 Chuyang Liu – Maritime Transport Services in the Law of the Sea and the World Trade Organization, 2009

FSC
www.fsc.org
MIX
Papier | Fördert
gute Waldnutzung
FSC® C083411

Kolibri 360 GmbH
Ferdinand-Jühlke-Straße 7
99095 Erfurt, Deutschland
produktsicherheit@kolibri360.de